The Econometrics of Disequilibrium

Richard E. Quandt

Basil Blackwell

Copyright © Richard E. Quandt 1988

First published 1988

Basil Blackwell Inc.
432 Park Avenue South, Suite 1503
New York, NY 10016, USA

Basil Blackwell Ltd
108 Cowley Road, Oxford, OX4 1JF, UK

British Library Cataloguing in Publication Data

Quandt, Richard E. (Richard Emeric), 1930−
 The econometrics of disequilibrium.
 1. Economics. Disequilibria. Econometric
  models
 I. Title
330′.0724

ISBN 0-631-14402-1

Library of Congress Cataloging-in-Publication Data

Quandt, Richard E.
  The econometrics of disequilibrium.

  Bibliography: p.
  Includes index.
   1. Equilibrium (Economics)−−Econometric models.
 I. Title.
HB145.Q36 1988   339.5   88-9549
ISBN 0-631-14402-1

Typeset in 10 on 12pt Times
by Colset Private Limited, Singapore
Printed in the United States of America

Contents

Preface

This volume is the outgrowth of many years' concern with the formulation and estimation of econometric models of disequilibrium phenomena. As has often been noted, the term "disequilibrium" is a misnomer. We refer by it to the whole class of models in which some degree of rationing occurs or in which markets do not clear, or, in any event, to models in which some agents are failing to realize their desires. Presumably the term came into vogue because in the simple perfectly competitive model only the intersection of the demand and supply curves is characterized as an equilibrium, yet in these models trading may occur at different points as well. However, disequilibrium models in the present context may perfectly well be equilibria in the sense that no forces exist that will alter the solution values for the endogenous variables. For the sake of simplicity and in conformity with much current usage, we stick with the term "disequilibrium."

The volume contains a detailed, if not complete, treatment of the problems of model formulation, estimation, and testing in the disequilibrium context. Since disequilibrium econometrics deals in an essential way with latent or qualitative dependent variables, our subject matter falls within that broader subject. Although we relate disequilibrium models, wherever relevant, to other qualitative variable models such as probit, tobit, and switching regression models, the present volume is not a substitute for a broader approach such as is contained in G. S. Maddala's excellent *Limited-Dependent and Qualitative Variables in Econometrics* (Cambridge University Press, 1983), but rather complements it.

A particular distinguishing feature of the present work is that we are mindful of some of the computational difficulties encountered by researchers. In order to alleviate some of these difficulties, we provide in appendices selections of appropriate FORTRAN computer programs, particularly for the evaluation of particular likelihood functions and for numerical integration in up to three dimensions. In addition, exercises are provided at the end of each chapter.

I am very grateful for helpful comments from John Bomhoff, Gregory

Chow, Stephen Goldfeld, Mark Plant, Harvey Rosen, and Glenn Rudebusch, and for support from the National Science Foundation. Of course, all responsibility for errors is my own.

Richard E. Quandt
Princeton University

1

Introduction to Latent Variables

1.1 General Introduction

Our discussion of disequilibrium models alternates among analyses of (a) model specification, (b) model estimation, (c) testing, and (d) computation. As will become clear in the subsequent chapters, the most useful methods of estimation tend to be methods of maximum likelihood and of least squares. In the present context, the maximization of the likelihood function and the minimization of the sum of squares of (some appropriately defined) residuals invariably involves one in a numerical maximization (minimization) problem. The state of the art in this area is now sufficiently well developed that only the most fainthearted should shy away from attempting these procedures. But in order to ease the reader's burdens in doing so, we provide numerous computer programs that solve specific tasks. Thus, for example, appendices 2.A, 2.B, and 4.A provide FORTRAN subroutines that evaluate particular likelihood functions.[1] Appendix 4.B provides a simple algorithm to solve numerically a nonlinear equation in a single variable. Appendices 6.A, 6.B, and 6.C provide subroutines for numerical integration in up to three dimensions; this type of problem is typically encountered in more complicated latent variable models.

The remainder of this chapter outlines some elementary latent variable models, i.e. models in which some endogenous variable is not, or is not completely, observed. A more detailed introduction to simple disequilibrium models is undertaken in chapter 2. Several submodels are considered and the principal estimating methods are described, including maximum likelihood estimation, minimum distance estimation and the EM algorithm. Chapter 3 is principally devoted to models which can exhibit both "equilibrium regimes" and "disequilibrium regimes." The appropriate likelihood functions are derived and questions of testing are investigated. The ordinary tests

---

[1] Such subroutines are essential ingredients for all numerical optimization programs. The present ones are written to be in a general format compatible with GQOPT, a general purpose numerical optimization package available from the author.

of hypotheses concerning individual coefficient values do not present problems of great novelty. However, somewhat novel questions are (a) how one can tell whether an equilibrium model or a disequilibrium model is more appropriate, and (b) how one can reasonably conclude that a particular disequilibrium model is compatible with all observations corresponding to excess demand (supply). Chapter 4 deals with a variety of alternative specifications, including a modification of the so-called min condition, the formulations we obtain in the presence of aggregation problems, and the case of serially correlated errors.

While chapters 2–4 deal exclusively with single-market models, chapters 5 and 6 consider multimarket models – models in which two or more markets may simultaneously be in disequilibrium. Chapter 5 deals with the internal consistency (coherency) of these models, while chapter 6 is devoted to problems of estimation. Finally, chapter 7 reviews a number of empirical applications, selected not to provide a comprehensive coverage of applications but only to illustrate a few of the principal approaches that have been employed.

1.2   An Elementary Latent Variable Model

The specification of econometric models customarily includes observable variables, unknown parameters, and intrinsically unobservable error terms. Thus, the ordinary regression model may be written for the tth observation on the data as

$$y_t = \beta' x_t + u_t \tag{1.2.1}$$

where y_t is the tth observation on the dependent variable, x_t is the $k \times 1$ vector of the tth observation on the independent variables, β is a vector of unknown parameters, and u_t is an unobserved random variable. The econometrician makes assumptions about how u_t is generated (e.g. u_t is drawn from a distribution with zero mean, perhaps from one with variance that is constant, i.e. does not depend on t) but is unable to actually record measurements for it. If the parametric form of the distribution of u_t is assumed to be known, the joint density of the u_t usually allows the derivation of the joint density, i.e. the likelihood, of the y_t from which maximum likelihood estimates may be derived.[2] If the u_t $(t = 1, \ldots, T)$ are identically and independently normal, with density $[1/\sqrt{(2\pi)}\sigma] \exp\{-u_t^2/2\sigma^2\}$, the likelihood clearly is

$$L = \left[\frac{1}{\sqrt{(2\pi)}\sigma} \right]^T \exp\left\{ -\frac{1}{2\sigma^2} \sum_{t=1}^{T} (y_t - \beta' x_t)^2 \right\} \tag{1.2.2}$$

---

[2] See, for example, Chow (1983).

the maximization of which yields estimates for β that obviously coincide with the usual least squares estimates.

The fact that the u_t are unobservable creates no difficulty. Equation (1.2.1) provides a mapping $u_t \rightarrow y_t$ which allows the density of the unobservable u_t to be transformed into the density of the observable y_t.

Since y_t is an economic variable, it is normally observable for every $t = 1, \ldots, T$. However, it may happen that for reasons outside the investigator's control, some particular value of y_t, say y_τ, is missing. In the context of (1.2.1) and (1.2.2), no special problems arise. The term in (1.2.2) corresponding to τ is omitted and the rest of the analysis proceeds unchanged.

The situation changes noticeably and in an instructive manner for the analysis of latent variables if the regression model is autoregressive. Assume that the model is

$$y_t = \alpha y_{t-1} + u_t \qquad t = 1, \ldots, T \tag{1.2.3}$$

We first note that the precise form of the likelihood depends on what specific assumption we are willing to make about how the process "starts up." One alternative is to assume that there is a nonstochastic, fixed number y_0 that is the "seed" of the process in (1.2.3). The transformation $u_t \rightarrow y_t$ ($t = 1, \ldots, T$) can then be written as

$$Ay - b = u \tag{1.2.4}$$

where u and y are T-element vectors, and where

$$A = \begin{bmatrix} 1 & 0 & \cdots & & 0 \\ -\alpha & 1 & \cdots & & 0 \\ & \cdot & \cdot & & \cdot \\ & & \cdot & & \\ & & \cdot & & \\ 0 & 0 & \cdots & -\alpha & 1 \end{bmatrix} \qquad b = \begin{bmatrix} \alpha y_0 \\ 0 \\ 0 \\ \cdot \\ \cdot \\ 0 \end{bmatrix}$$

Transforming from u to y yields

$$L = \left[\frac{1}{\sqrt{(2\pi)}\sigma} \right]^T \exp\left\{ -\frac{1}{2\sigma^2} \sum_{t=1}^{T} (y_t - \alpha y_{t-1})^2 \right\} \tag{1.2.5}$$

An alternative assumption is that the process never "starts up," i.e. has gone on forever. For the process to be stationary, we must require $|\alpha| < 1$. We can then express y_1 as $\sum_{j=0}^{\infty} \alpha^j u_{1-j}$ (see exercise 1.1). The variance of y_1 then is $\sigma^2/(1-\alpha^2)$ and (1.2.5) is replaced by

$$L = \left[\frac{1}{\sqrt{(2\pi)}\sigma} \right]^T (1-\alpha^2)^{1/2} \exp\left\{ -\frac{1}{2\sigma^2} \sum_{t=2}^{T} (y_t - \alpha y_{t-1})^2 - \frac{1-\alpha^2}{2\sigma^2} y_1^2 \right\} \tag{1.2.6}$$

Now consider the situation in which a particular value of y_t, say y_τ, is unavailable to the investigator. We can rewrite (1.2.6) as

$$L = \left[\frac{1}{\sqrt{(2\pi)}\sigma}\right]^T (1-\alpha^2)^{1/2} \exp\left\{-\frac{1}{2\sigma^2} \sum_{\substack{t \neq 1, \\ \tau, \tau+1}} (y_t - \alpha y_{t-1})^2 - \frac{1-\alpha^2}{2\sigma^2} y_1^2\right\}$$

$$\times \exp\left\{-\frac{1}{2\sigma^2} [(y_{\tau+1} - \alpha y_\tau)^2 + (y_\tau - \alpha y_{\tau-1})^2]\right\}$$

(1.2.7)

We now concentrate on the second $\exp\{\ \}$ term in (1.2.7). Since this term involves y_τ, it includes an unobservable and hence (1.2.7) is not practical. From the joint density of all the ys given in (1.2.7) we must obtain the marginal p.d.f. of $y_1, \ldots, y_{\tau-1}, y_{\tau+1}, \ldots, y_T$ which is obtained by integrating out y_τ. Completing the square on y_τ in the second $\exp\{\ \}$ yields

$$\exp\left\{-\frac{1+\alpha^2}{2\sigma^2}\left[\left(y_\tau - \frac{\alpha}{1+\alpha^2}(y_{\tau-1} + y_{\tau+1})\right)^2 + \frac{(y_{\tau+1} - \alpha^2 y_{\tau-1})^2}{(1+\alpha^2)^2}\right]\right\}$$

(1.2.8)

This allows us to rewrite (1.2.7) as

$$L = \left[\frac{1}{\sqrt{(2\pi)}\sigma}\right]^{T-2} (1-\alpha^2)^{1/2}$$

$$\times \exp\left\{-\frac{1}{2\sigma^2} \sum_{\substack{t \neq 1, \\ \tau, \tau+1}} (y_t - \alpha y_{t-1})^2 - \frac{1-\alpha^2}{2\sigma^2} y_1^2\right\}$$

$$\times \frac{1}{\sqrt{(2\pi)}\sigma\,(1+\alpha^2)^{1/2}} \exp\left\{-\frac{(y_{\tau+1} - \alpha^2 y_{\tau-1})^2}{2\sigma^2(1+\alpha^2)}\right\}$$

$$\times \frac{1}{\sqrt{(2\pi)}\sigma/(1+\alpha^2)^{1/2}} \exp\left\{-\frac{[y_\tau - (\alpha/(1+\alpha^2))(y_{\tau-1}+y_{\tau+1})]^2}{2\sigma^2/(1+\alpha^2)}\right\}$$

(1.2.9)

The joint density is the product of three terms. The first is the joint density of the terms not involving y_τ, $y_{\tau+1}$. The second is the density of $y_{\tau+1}$, conditional on $y_{\tau-1}$ (since $y_{\tau+1} = \alpha^2 y_{\tau-1} + \alpha u_\tau + u_{\tau+1}$, the term $y_{\tau+1} - \alpha^2 y_{\tau-1}$ has variance $\sigma^2(1+\alpha^2)$). The last term is the density of y_τ conditional on $y_{\tau+1}, y_{\tau-1}$ (see exercise 1.2). Integrating (1.2.9) with respect to y_τ from $-\infty$ to $+\infty$ yields unity for the last term, leaving the first two terms as the likelihood for the sample in which y_τ is not observed. It is trivial to note that this is the same likelihood as would be obtained by arguing that when y_τ is not observed, $y_{\tau+1}$ can be expressed as $y_{\tau+1} = \alpha^2 y_{\tau-1} + \alpha u_\tau + u_{\tau+1}$ and transforming from u to y in the usual manner.

The crucial feature of our procedure is to start out with the joint density of the error terms, to obtain from that the joint density of the economic variables, and finally to integrate out those that are not observable, which then yields the joint density of the observable variables. This is the procedure that will be followed in numerous cases discussed in this volume.

1.3   Other Latent Variable Models

In the present section we provide a brief introduction to some of the principal types of latent variable models – models in which some economic variable is not observed or not fully observed.[3] The models are also often referred to as "qualitative variable" models. They differ from the model of section 1.2 in which, one might argue, the unobservability feature is an accident, i.e. one particular datum happened to be unavailable. In the present models the unobservability feature tends to be an intrinsic aspect of the data generation process and frequently involves not an outright loss of an observation but the "compression" of the observation into a qualitative form, such as a "yes–no" form. Many of these models arise naturally in discrete choice situations in which consumers face choices among several discrete alternatives; choice of travel mode (train versus auto) is a classic illustration. One of the interesting dimensions along which the various models differ from one another is the amount of information that is missing from the model. We illustrate several types of models.

Probit Model

Imagine that we want to determine the factors that are responsible for the promotion to brigadier-general of army officers who have already reached the rank of colonel. We might have available a sample of such officers, some of whom have ended their army careers as colonels and some of whom were promoted to the rank of general. A person's suitability for promotion may well be modelled as a continuous function of a number of observable variables, such as objective measures of his past conduct in a variety of situations, etc. But promotion is clearly a discrete, yes–no type of event. It may therefore be reasonable to model the promotion process for the ith person as follows. We let y_i^* denote the suitability for promotion, $y_i (= 0,1)$ the qualitative variable indicating promotion, u_i a normally distributed error term, and x_i a vector of observable explanatory variables. The exogenous variables determine (with a disturbance term) a continuously varying indicator; promotion occurs if this indicator is positive and does not occur otherwise. Then

$$y_i^* = \beta' x_i + u_i$$

---

[3] Readers who need more detailed coverage of the full range of latent variables should consult Maddala (1983b), Daganzo (1979), Domencich and McFadden (1975), Train (1986), and others.

$$y_i = \begin{cases} 1 & \text{if } y_i^* > 0 \\ 0 & \text{if } y_i^* \leq 0 \end{cases} \tag{1.3.1}$$

If u_i is assumed to be normally distributed with mean zero and variance σ^2, the density function of y_i^* is obtained easily.[4] It is

$$f(y_i^*) = \frac{1}{\sqrt{(2\pi)}\sigma} \exp\{-(y_i^* - \beta'x_i)^2/2\sigma^2\} \tag{1.3.2}$$

But y_i^* is intrinsically unobservable; we merely observe whether the ith person has been promoted to brigadier-general or not. Hence we require for maximum likelihood estimation the distribution of y_i, not y_i^*. This will be fully specified if we can write down the probabilities of the two possible outcomes. By the straightforward rules of the probability calculus we have

$$\begin{aligned} \Pr\{y_i = 1\} = &\Pr\{y_i = 1 | y_i^* > 0\} \Pr\{y_i^* > 0\} \\ &+ \Pr\{y_i = 1 | y_i^* \leq 0\} \Pr\{y_i^* \leq 0\} \end{aligned} \tag{1.3.3}$$

$$\begin{aligned} \Pr\{y_i = 0\} = &\Pr\{y_i = 0 | y_i^* > 0\} \Pr\{y_i^* > 0\} \\ &+ \Pr\{y_i = 0 | y_i^* \leq 0\} \Pr\{y_i^* \leq 0\} \end{aligned} \tag{1.3.4}$$

But $\Pr\{y_i = 1 | y_i^* \leq 0\} = \Pr\{y_i = 0 | y_i^* > 0\} = 0$ by the posing of the problem in (1.3.1), and $\Pr\{y_i = 1 | y_i^* > 0\} = \Pr\{y_i = 0 | y_i^* \leq 0\} = 1$ by the same token. But $\Pr\{y_i^* > 0\}$ and $\Pr\{y_i^* \leq 0\}$ are immediate from the first equation of (1.3.1):

$$\begin{aligned} \Pr\{y_i^* > 0\} &= \Pr\{\beta'x_i + u_i > 0\} \\ &= \Pr\{u_i > -\beta'x_i\} = \Pr\left\{\frac{u_i}{\sigma} > -\frac{\beta'x_i}{\sigma}\right\} \\ &= 1 - \Phi\left(-\frac{\beta'x_i}{\sigma}\right) \end{aligned} \tag{1.3.5}$$

where $\Phi(\ )$ is the cumulative standard normal integral,

$$\Phi(x) = \int_{-\infty}^{x} \frac{1}{\sqrt{(2\pi)}} \exp(-z^2/2)dz$$

By the same reasoning,

$$\Pr\{y_i^* \leq 0\} = \Phi\left(-\frac{\beta'x_i}{\sigma}\right)$$

Hence, if in a sample I_1 is the set of indices for which colonels were promoted and I_2 the set for which they were not, the likelihood function is

---

[4] But note below the normalization $\sigma^2 = 1$.

$$L = \prod_{i \in I_1} \left[1 - \Phi\left(-\frac{\beta'x_i}{\sigma} \right) \right] \prod_{i \in I_2} \Phi\left(-\frac{\beta'x_i}{\sigma} \right) \qquad (1.3.6)$$

It is immediately evident that we cannot separately estimate the coefficient vector β and the variance σ^2 since the likelihood attains the same value under proportionate changes of β and σ. It is therefore customary to set $\sigma^2 = 1$.

The likelihood function given by (1.3.6) appears to be quite different from the likelihood function of the normal regression model and, in principle, leaves open the possibility that it is less well behaved, e.g. exhibits multiple maxima. Fortunately, it is not difficult to show that, as in the case of the normal regression model, the probit model has a strictly concave log-likelihood function from which it follows that the maximum likelihood estimator is unique. We can write from (1.3.6)

$$\log L = \sum_{i \in I_1} \log \Phi(w_i) + \sum_{i \in I_2} \log[1 - \Phi(w_i)]$$

where w_i denotes $\beta'x_i$. We have to show that $\partial^2 \log L / \partial\beta\partial\beta'$ is a negative definite matrix. We note that (a) the sum of concave functions is concave and (b) a concave function of a linear function is concave (exercise 1.3). It is therefore sufficient to show that $d^2 \log \Phi(w_i)/dw_i^2 < 0$ (and that $d^2 \log[1 - \Phi(w_i)]/dw_i^2 < 0$). But

$$\frac{d^2 \log \Phi(w_i)}{dw_i^2} = \frac{\phi'(w_i)\Phi(w_i) - \phi(w_i)^2}{\Phi(w_i)^2}$$

where $\phi(\ )$ is the standard normal density. Since $\phi'(w_i) = -w_i\phi(w_i)$, the numerator will be negative if $w_i\Phi(w_i) + \phi(w_i) > 0$. But this inequality follows from the fact that the mean of the standard normal variate w, conditional on $w < w_i$, is

$$\int_{-\infty}^{w_i} \frac{w\phi(w)}{\Phi(w_i)}\, dw = -\frac{\phi(w_i)}{\Phi(w_i)} < w_i$$

since the mean must be smaller than the truncation point w_i.

A slightly different model, called the *logit model*, is obtained if we make the assumption that u_i is logistically distributed, i.e. that the cumulative distribution function of u is

$$F(u) = \frac{1}{1 + e^{-u}}$$

Then (1.3.5) is replaced by

$$\Pr\{y_i^* > 0\} = 1 - \frac{1}{1 + e^{\beta'x_i}} = \frac{e^{\beta'x_i}}{1 + e^{\beta'x_i}}$$

and (1.3.6) is replaced by

$$L = \prod_{i \in I_1} \frac{e^{\beta'x_i}}{1 + e^{\beta'x_i}} \prod_{i \in I_2} \frac{1}{1 + e^{\beta'x_i}}$$

This can also be rewritten as

$$L = \prod_{i=1}^{n} \left(\frac{e^{\beta'x_i}}{1 + e^{\beta'x_i}}\right)^{y_i} \left(\frac{1}{1 + e^{\beta'x_i}}\right)^{1-y_i}$$

from which the log-likelihood is

$$\log L = \sum_{i=1}^{n} \beta'x_i y_i - \sum_{i=1}^{n} \log(1 + e^{\beta'x_i}) \tag{1.3.7}$$

Differentiating (1.3.7) we obtain first and second partial derivatives

$$\frac{\partial \log L}{\partial \beta} = \sum_{i=1}^{n} x_i y_i - \sum_{i=1}^{n} \left(\frac{e^{\beta'x_i}}{1 + e^{\beta'x_i}}\right) x_i$$

$$\frac{\partial^2 \log L}{\partial \beta \partial \beta'} = -\sum_{i=1}^{n} \left[\frac{e^{\beta'x_i}}{(1 + e^{\beta'x_i})^2}\right] x_i x_i'$$

We see immediately that the matrix of second partial derivatives is negative semidefinite and is negative definite if the number of linearly independent x_i vectors is at least equal to the number of parameters, since it can be written as $-\sum_{i=1}^{n} q_i q_i'$, where q_i is the vector $e^{\beta'x_i/2} x_i/(1 + e^{\beta'x_i})$ (see exercise 1.8). As in the probit model, the maximum likelihood estimator is unique.

Although the probit and logit models differ in some important respects (see section 6.1), the normal and logistic distributions are fairly similar. The logistic distribution has mean zero and variance $\pi^2/3$. Thus, replacing u by $u\pi/\sqrt{3}$ will give a rescaled distribution with unit variance. Table 1.1 gives the standard normal and logistic probabilities for selected u values and scale factors. The greatest similarity (in a sense) between the two is obtained for the scale factor 1.7009, which minimizes the sum of the squares of deviations between the normal and logistic probabilities over the u-values -4.0, -3.9, ..., -0.1. This shows that, loosely speaking, the logistics are very similar to the normal, particularly in the central ranges, although the proportionate discrepancy at points fairly far from the origin is sizeable.

Tobit Model

This model is obtained if y_i^* in the probit model is actually observed some of the time – specifically, if $y_i^* > 0$. In this context, $\beta'x_i + u_i$ might represent

Table 1.1   Comparison of normal and logistic distributions

u	Normal prob. $\{z \leq u\}$	Logistic prob. $\{z \leq u\}$ Scale factor $\pi/\sqrt{3}$	Logistic prob. $\{z \leq u\}$ Scale factor 1.7009
-4.0	0.00003	0.00071	0.00111
-3.0	0.00135	0.00431	0.00604
-2.0	0.02275	0.02589	0.03224
-1.5	0.06681	0.06176	0.07232
-1.0	0.15866	0.14018	0.15434
-0.8	0.21186	0.18984	0.20412
-0.6	0.27425	0.25194	0.26492
-0.4	0.34458	0.32618	0.33618
-0.2	0.42074	0.41029	0.41576

the desired purchase quantity of a durable good. If the desired amount is positive, the consumer purchases the desired amount and we observe it; otherwise we observe zero purchases. We say that the observed variable is the result of "censoring." The model then is

$$y_i^* = \beta'x_i + u_i$$

$$y_i = \begin{cases} y_i^* & \text{if } y_i^* > 0 \\ 0 & \text{otherwise} \end{cases} \tag{1.3.8}$$

This case differs from the previous one in that we now have some values of y_i over which a continuous density is defined as well as a value which is a mass point, i.e. a point which has a discrete probability. The density part is just $[1/\sqrt{(2\pi)}\sigma]\exp\{-(y_i-\beta'x_i)^2/2\sigma^2\}$ and the discrete probability part is $\Phi(-\beta'x_i/\sigma)$; the likelihood is

$$L = \prod_{i \epsilon I_1} \frac{1}{\sqrt{(2\pi)}\sigma} \exp\{-(y_i - \beta'x_i)^2/2\sigma^2\} \prod_{i \epsilon I_2} \Phi(-\beta'x_i/\sigma) \tag{1.3.9}$$

where σ no longer has to be normalized to unity. It can be shown that the second partial derivative matrix of the log-likelihood function is negative definite (see Maddala 1983b, pp. 156-7). Maximum likelihood estimation is thus not hampered by the possibility of multiple local maxima.

As is sometimes the case, the computation of the maximum likelihood estimates in the tobit model does not necessarily require that a general purpose numerical optimization algorithm be available. A simple iterative algorithm due to Fair (1977) is available for computing the estimates.[5] The algorithm can be motivated as follows. Write the log-likelihood as

$$\log L = -\frac{1}{2}\sum_{i\epsilon I_1}\log(2\pi\sigma^2) - \frac{1}{2\sigma^2}\sum_{i\epsilon I_1}(y_i-\beta'x_i)^2 + \sum_{i\epsilon I_2}\log[1 - \Phi(\beta'x_i/\sigma)]$$

---

[5] See also the EM algorithm in section 2.7.

Differentiating with respect to β and σ^2 we obtain

$$\frac{\partial \log L}{\partial \beta} = \frac{1}{\sigma^2} \sum_{i \in I_1} (y_i - \beta' x_i) x_i - \sum_{i \in I_2} \frac{\phi(\beta' x_i / \sigma)(x_i / \sigma)}{1 - \Phi(\beta' x_i / \sigma)} = 0 \qquad (1.3.10)$$

$$\frac{\partial \log L}{\partial \sigma^2} = \frac{1}{2\sigma^4} \sum_{i \in I_1} (y_i - \beta' x_i)^2 + \frac{1}{2\sigma^3} \sum_{i \in I_2} \frac{\phi(\beta' x_i / \sigma)(\beta' x_i)}{1 - \Phi(\beta' x_i / \sigma)} - \frac{N_1}{2\sigma^2} = 0$$

$$(1.3.11)$$

where N_1 is the number of observations with positive y_i. Now multiply (1.3.10) by $\beta'/2\sigma^2$ and add the result to (1.3.11); this causes the summations over I_2 to cancel, yielding

$$\frac{\beta'}{2\sigma^4} \sum_{i \in I_1} (y_i - \beta' x_i) x_i - \frac{N_1}{2\sigma^2} + \frac{1}{2\sigma^4} \sum_{i \in I_1} (y_i - \beta' x_i)^2 = 0$$

or

$$\sigma^2 = \sum_{i \in I_1} (y_i - \beta' x_i) y_i / N_1 \qquad (1.3.12)$$

from which σ^2 can be determined if β is known. We now proceed by denoting $\phi(\beta' x_i / \sigma)/[1 - \Phi(\beta' x_i / \sigma)]$ by r_i. Then, multiplying (1.3.10) by σ, we can rewrite it as

$$\frac{1}{\sigma} \sum_{i \in I_1} (y_i - \beta' x_i) x_i - \sum_{i \in I_2} x_i r_i = 0 \qquad (1.3.13)$$

It is clear that if X_1, Y_1 represent the matrices of observations on x_i, y_i for $i \in I_1$ and X_2 represents the matrix of x_is for $i \in I_2$, if r is the vector of r_is and $\hat{\beta}$ is the OLS estimator based on X_1, Y_1, then (1.3.13) determines a $\hat{\hat{\beta}}$ given by

$$\hat{\hat{\beta}} = \hat{\beta} - \sigma(X_1' X_1)^{-1} X_2' r \qquad (1.3.14)$$

(see exercise 1.6). We can then establish an iteration between (1.3.12) and (1.3.13). Pick some initial values for β and compute σ^2 from (1.3.12) (if this should yield a negative σ^2, chose $\beta = 0$; this guarantees a positive σ^2). Use the definition of r_i and (1.3.13) to compute a new β. Return to (1.3.12) and continue iterating until convergence is obtained.

The uniqueness of the maximum likelihood estimator and the relative ease with which it can be computed make it (as well as some other, two-stage estimators) a particularly desirable method of estimation since the application of ordinary least squares to a tobit problem does not produce consistent estimates.

Truncated Regression Model

This type of model arises if certain individual observations are not included in the sample on the basis of the value of the dependent variable for those observations. A common illustration is the case of an earnings equation in which we attempt to find the relationship between earnings and exogenous variables such as education, but where we include in the sample only those individuals whose earnings do not exceed some cutoff C. We thus have

$$
\begin{aligned}
y_i &= \beta'x_i + u_i & &\text{if } y_i \leq C \\
&\text{no observations} & &\text{if } y_i > C
\end{aligned}
\tag{1.3.15}
$$

The density of y_i is then the density conditional on $y_i \leq C$ when y_i is observed, or

$$
f(y_i) = \left[\frac{1}{\sqrt{(2\pi)}\sigma} \exp\left\{ -\frac{(y_i - \beta'x_i)^2}{2\sigma^2} \right\} \right] \bigg/ \Phi\left(\frac{C - \beta'x_i}{\sigma} \right)
$$

and the log-likelihood is

$$
\log L = \sum_{i=1}^{n} \log\left[\frac{1}{\sqrt{(2\pi)}\sigma} \exp\left\{ -\frac{(y_i - \beta'x_i)^2}{2\sigma^2} \right\} \right] - \sum_{i=1}^{n} \log\Phi\left(\frac{C - \beta'x_i}{\sigma} \right)
$$

Again, as before, the matrix of second partial derivatives is negative definite and estimation by ordinary least squares produces inconsistent results.

The three models discussed so far already differ from one another in terms of the amount of information present or absent in them. Thus in the probit model, we only know whether y^* was positive or negative and, of course, we know the associated exogenous variable values. In the tobit model we know somewhat more: we actually observe y^* in some situations. The price that the probit model has to pay for the sparser information it contains is an inability to estimate the variance of u. In the truncated regression model we observe the dependent variable when it exceeds a threshold (as in the tobit model) but do not even observe the exogenous variables when it falls short of the threshold. It thus contains less information than the tobit model but is not directly comparable with probit because in one respect it has more information and in another respect less. We now consider some other models that show yet further patterns of information availability.

Switching Regression Model

Consider now a case in which data are generated from a regression model that is not constant over the observation period. Of course, there are several ways in which this type of data generation could be modelled. Here we examine the following simple form:

$$
\begin{aligned}
y_t &= \beta_1' x_{1t} + u_{1t} & &\text{with probability } \lambda \\
y_t &= \beta_2' x_{2t} + u_{2t} & &\text{with probability } 1 - \lambda
\end{aligned}
\tag{1.3.16}
$$

An example is provided by Lee and Porter (1984) who examine the transportation prices charged by the Joint Executive Committee railroad cartel from 1880 to 1886. Their price equation is

$$\log p_t = \beta_0 + \beta'x_t + \beta_2 I_t + u_t$$

where x represents a vector of various exogenous variables (such as whether the Great Lakes were open for navigation or not) and where I_t is a dummy variable representing whether the cartel was in cooperative mode ($I_t = 1$) or price-war mode ($I_t = 0$), and where β_2 is hypothesized to be positive. Since I_t is intrinsically unobservable, the price equation may be written as

$$\log p_t = \beta_{01} + \beta'x_t + u_t \qquad \text{with probability } \lambda = \Pr\{I_t = 1\}$$
$$\log p_t = \beta_{02} + \beta'x_t + u_t \qquad \text{with probability } 1 - \lambda = \Pr\{I_t = 0\}$$

The likelihood function for the model given by (1.3.16) is obtained from the unconditional density of the random variable y_t. Denote the two forms of the regression model as regime 1 (R1) and regime 2 (R2). Then the density of y_t is

$$h(y_t) = f(y_t|R1)\Pr\{R1\} + f(y_t|R2)\Pr\{R2\} \qquad (1.3.17)$$

If u_{1t}, u_{2t} in each regime are normally distributed with zero mean and variances σ_1^2, σ_2^2, (1.3.17) leads to the likelihood function

$$L = \prod_{t=1}^{T} \left[\frac{\lambda}{\sqrt{(2\pi)}\sigma_1} \exp\left\{ -\frac{(y_t - \beta_1'x_{1t})^2}{2\sigma_1^2} \right\} \right.$$
$$\left. + \frac{1-\lambda}{\sqrt{(2\pi)}\sigma_2} \exp\left\{ -\frac{(y_t - \beta_2'x_{2t})^2}{2\sigma_2^2} \right\} \right] \qquad (1.3.18)$$

A customary standard of comparison to the maximum likelihood estimator is the ordinary least squares estimator. Although not recommended in the tobit case, we can at least define what a "reasonable" OLS estimator would consist of: one would take all the observations for which the dependent variable has taken positive values and compute from those observations the OLS estimates. In the present case it is not entirely clear what one is to do, since here we do not observe which regime each observation corresponds to (in the tobit case the value of y reveals which regime we are observing). In the present case it would make no sense to pool all the observations and estimate a single regression. We might do better perhaps if we had a possibly noisy indicator variable J_t ($= 1,0$) that allowed us to sort the observations into two regimes., Thus let I_t ($= 1,0$) be the true regime indicator and J_t the observed one; for each true state of nature I_t there is some probability that the observed J_t is zero (or one). What happens now if we sort the data according to J_t and estimate separate regressions from the two subsamples?

Let T_1 be the number of observations for which $J_t = 1$ and assume that they are listed first. The OLS estimate $\hat{\beta}_1$ then is

$$\hat{\beta}_1 = \left(\sum_{t=1}^{T_1} x_{1t} x'_{1t} \right)^{-1} \sum_{t=1}^{T_1} x_{1t} y_t$$

$$= \left(\sum_{t=1}^{T} J_t x_{1t} x'_{1t} \right)^{-1} \sum_{t=1}^{T} J_t x_{1t} y_t$$

The dependent variable is, by definition,

$$y_t = I_t(\beta_1' x_{1t} + u_{1t}) + (1 - I_t)(\beta_2' x_{2t} + u_{2t})$$

and then $\hat{\beta}_1$ becomes

$$\hat{\beta}_1 = \left(\frac{1}{T} \sum_{t=1}^{T} J_t x_{1t} x'_{1t} \right)^{-1}$$

$$\times \left[\frac{1}{T} \sum_{t=1}^{T} J_t x_{1t} I_t(\beta_1' x_{1t} + u_{1t}) + \frac{1}{T} \sum_{t=1}^{T} J_t x_{1t}(1 - I_t)(\beta_2' x_{2t} + u_{2t}) \right]$$

$$(1.3.19)$$

where we have divided and multiplied by T on the right hand side. Under general conditions it is true that

$$\text{plim} \frac{1}{T} \sum_{t=1}^{T} J_t x_t I_t u_{1t} = \text{plim} \frac{1}{T} \sum_{t=1}^{T} J_t x_{1t}(1 - I_t) u_{2t} = 0$$

Now denote the limits to which $(1/T) \Sigma x_{1t} x'_{1t}$ and $(1/T) \Sigma x_{1t} x'_{2t}$ converge (or their probability limits if the xs are stochastic) as S_{11}, S_{12}, and let $p = \text{Pr}\{J_t = 1\}$, $p_{11} = \text{Pr}\{J_t = 1 | I_t = 1\}$, $p_{01} = \text{Pr}\{J_t = 0 | I_t = 1\}$. Then, taking the probability limit of (1.3.19),

$$\text{plim} \hat{\beta}_1 = (pS_{11})^{-1} [\lambda p_{11} S_{11} \beta_1 + (1 - \lambda) p_{01} S_{12} \beta_2]$$

where λ, as before, is $\text{Pr}\{I_t = 1\}$. Hence OLS gives inconsistent estimates, as is to be generally expected in latent variable models.[6]

Models of this type can be extremely flexible. As a first and simple generalization we may note that the probability λ may itself be a function of exogenous variables; in such a case λ in the likelihood function would have to be replaced by $\lambda(z_t)$. A second possibility is that the state indicator I_t is a Markov chain with transition probabilities q_{ij} denoting the probability that the system will move from state i at time $t - 1$ to state j at time t. Such models are considered by Goldfeld and Quandt (1973) and Cosslett and Lee (1985). If we denote by λ_t the vector of probabilities for the two states, λ_t obeys the recursion

---

[6] See Lee and Porter (1984) for further details, e.g. the probability limits of the estimates $\hat{\sigma}_1^2$ and $\hat{\sigma}_2^2$ from ordinary least squares.

$$\lambda'_t = \lambda'_{t-1} Q$$

where Q is the matrix of transition probabilities

$$Q = \begin{bmatrix} q_{00} & q_{01} \\ q_{10} & q_{11} \end{bmatrix}$$

Goldfeld and Quandt propose maximizing the function

$$\sum_{t=1}^{T} \log [f(y_t|R1) \Pr\{R1_t\} + f(y_t|R2) \Pr\{R2_t\}] \qquad (1.3.20)$$

where the probabilities of the regimes are the unconditional probabilities and are given by the vector $(\Pr\{R1_t\}, \Pr\{R2_t\}) = \lambda'_0 Q^t$. As Cosslett and Lee point out, this will yield consistent estimates but is not the correct likelihood, which must take into account the fact that the regime probabilities at time t are affected by the realized state at the previous time. There being 2^T mutually exclusive possibilities (or patterns of regimes), the proper log-likelihood is the logarithm of the sum of the probability weighted densities. Letting $f_1(y_t)$, $f_2(y_t)$ be shorthand for $f(y_t|R1), f(y_t|R2)$ and letting $k_t = 2 - I_t$, this is

$$\log L = \log \left\{ \sum_{I_T=0}^{1} \cdots \sum_{I_1=0}^{1} \left[\prod_{t=1}^{T} f_{k_t}(y_t) \prod_{t=2}^{T} \Pr\{I_t|I_{t-1}\} \Pr\{I_1\} \right] \right\}$$

where $\Pr\{I_t|I_{t-1}\}$ is one of the four transition probabilities and, for a stationary Markov process, $\Pr\{I_t\}$ is either $q_{10}/(q_{01}+q_{10})$ or $1 - q_{10}/(q_{01}+q_{10})$ (see exercise 1.7).

Disequilibrium Models

Disequilibrium models come in many varieties and we postpone detailed consideration to later chapters. Here we only introduce the simplest variety and motivate the terminology.

Consider a single market with a demand and a supply function given by

$$D_t = \beta'_1 x_{1t} + u_{1t}$$
$$S_t = \beta'_2 x_{2t} + u_{2t} \qquad (1.3.21)$$

where the price of the product is included among the variables that constitute the vectors x_{1t}, x_{2t}. In the ordinary competitive case markets are assumed to clear, i.e. the price adjusts so that $D_t = S_t$. Replacing D_t and S_t by the common symbol Q_t then yields the ordinary simultaneous equations model.

If prices are rigid (in the present case, completely rigid and thus set exogenously), D_t equals S_t with probability zero. The observing econometrician will indeed observe a certain quantity that is transacted in the marketplace, but if buyers cannot be forced to buy more than they want to buy and sellers cannot be forced to sell more than they want to sell, the econometrician will only be able to observe the lesser of the quantities demanded and supplied. The model of (1.3.21) is then completed by adding

$$Q_t = \min(D_t, S_t) \tag{1.3.22}$$

The resulting model is called a disequilibrium model because prices do not fulfill the usual market clearing function.[7]

Contrasting Several Models

Each of the models discussed in this section contains the important feature that something is unobservable in it. The models differ among each other in precisely what this unobservability consists of. In the probit model the endogenous variable y^* is entirely unobservable but the "regimes" are fully observable, i.e. we observe when y^* is positive and when it is not. In the tobit model y^* is observable some of the time (when it is positive) but the regime is always observable. In both of these cases, the exogenous variables are also always observable. In the truncated regression model, y^* and the exogenous variables are observable for only one of the regimes. In the switching regression model, all the variables are always observed, but we fail to observe the "regime." Finally, in the disequilibrium model we observe either D_t or S_t but not both; moreover we may or may not know which it is when we observe Q_t.[8]

The fact that all of these models are closely related can also be seen from a formalization as shown by Kiefer (1978b) and Poirier and Ruud (1981). Write the models as

$$\begin{aligned}
y_t &= \beta_1' x_{1t} + u_{1t} && \text{if } z_t > 0 \\
y_t &= \beta_2' x_{2t} + u_{2t} && \text{if } z_t \leq 0 \\
z_t &= \beta_3' x_{3t} + u_{3t}
\end{aligned} \tag{1.3.23}$$

This model can replicate several of the above. In the special case when $u_{1t} = u_{2t} = 0$, $\beta_1' x_{1t} = 1$ and $\beta_2' x_{2t} = 0$, the model is

$$y_t = \begin{cases} 1 & \text{if } \beta' x_{3t} + u_{3t} > 0 \\ 0 & \text{if } \beta' x_{3t} + u_{3t} \leq 0 \end{cases}$$

which is just the probit model if u_{3t} is distributed $N(0, 1)$. If we assume instead that $\beta_1' x_{1t} + u_{1t} = \beta_3' x_{3t} + u_{3t}$ and that $\beta_2' x_{2t} + u_{2t} = 0$, we reproduce the tobit

---

[7] "Disequilibrium" may well be a misnomer because the term suggests that forces exist that will restore an equilibrium. This interpretation is not intended since the excess demand (supply) that exists when the rigid price is too low (high) may well represent an equilibrium situation if demands and supplies by all agents in the market already represent their optimal behavior in the face of possible rationing.

[8] In general, we would not know whether $D_t < S_t$ or $D_t \geq S_t$. In some cases there may be *a priori* information which actually tells us which regime is at work in each time period.

model. If x_{3t} is a set of constants that does not change with t, $z_t > 0$ with a constant probability and we have the switching regression model. Finally, if $\beta_3' x_{3t} + u_{3t}$ is identically the same (i.e. is defined as) $\beta_2' x_{2t} - \beta_1' x_{1t} + u_{2t} - u_{1t}$, we have the disequilibrium model. Models in this general class also exhibit other similarities that will be discussed in subsequent chapters, such as the fact that in certain cases their likelihood functions can become unbounded in parameter space.

1.4   Some Examples

In this section we illustrate latent variable models with two "disequilibrium" examples which do not entirely conform to the standard, or canonical, model introduced in section 1.3. We cite these examples to provide a slightly richer view of the types of models that have been applied. For a more complete coverage of empirical models the reader should consult chapter 7.

Harvest Model

Suits (1955) introduced a model of watermelon cultivation, which was subsequently reformulated by Goldfeld and Quandt (1975) as an explicit disequilibrium model. Suits took as his point of departure the observation that if current wages and transport costs are high relative to produce prices, it may not pay farmers to harvest the entire crop of watermelons. This gives rise to a model of the following sort, which we present in abbreviated fashion. Define

q_t = crop of watermelons
p_t = price of watermelons
x_t = intended harvest of watermelons
y_t = quantity of watermelons harvested

and let z_{1t}, z_{2t}, z_{3t} represent vectors of exogenous variables. We first have a crop equation

$$q_t = \alpha_1 p_{t-1} + \beta_1' z_{1t} + u_{1t}$$

which specifies the crop as depending on the predetermined variable p_{t-1} and other, exogenous, variables such as the lagged prices of competing products and dummy variables representing government agricultural policy. Secondly, we have a conventional demand equation

$$p_t = \alpha_2 y_t + \beta_2' z_{2t} + u_{2t}$$

which expresses that price depends on the quantity brought to the market, as well as exogenous variables such as disposable income. Finally, we have an equation that describes farmers' intentions to harvest watermelons; this is given by

$$x_t = \alpha_3 p_t + \alpha_4 q_t + \beta_3' z_{3t} + u_{3t}$$

where z_{3t} certainly includes factors such as wages that affect the cost of harvesting. The equation specifies that, *ceteris paribus*, farmers desire to harvest more if the prices they can realize are higher and if the crop is greater.[9] It should be immediately clear that so far the model is compatible with an unrealistic state of affairs: farmers may wish to harvest an amount x_t that exceeds the actual crop q_t. In such a case, farmers' harvest desire is not observable by the econometrician. We must, in fact, complete the model by adding the relationship

$$y_t = \min(q_t, x_t)$$

There are then two regimes in this model: (1) $x_t < q_t$, in which case farmers harvest what they want to harvest, $x_t = y_t$, and the balance of the crop, $q_t - x_t$, is left on the field's to rot; (2) $q_t < x_t$, in which case farmers harvest the entire crop, $y_t = q_t$, and farmers have a "pent-up demand" for additional harvestable watermelons, which demand must remain unsatisfied. As in the case of the ordinary demand–supply model of section 1.3, some agents are "off their behavioral curves"; they are rationed and their desired (otherwise also called "notional" or "Walrasian") quantities are not observable.[10]

Model of Banking

Goldfeld, Jaffee and Quandt (1980) have considered a model of the relationship between the Federal Home Loan Bank Board (FHLBB) and the Savings and Loan Associations (SLAs). The latter make mortgage loans for residential construction and borrow from the FHLBB. The FHLBB provides loans (advances) to its member SLAs with a view toward stabilizing mortgage and housing markets. In doing so, it may alter the interest rate charged on advances to increase or reduce their flow to the desired level; it may also engage in nonprice rationing and simply deny advances to SLAs without raising the interest rate on them. Two basic equations in the model represent the demand for advances and the housing starts. The first of these is

$$A_t^d = \alpha_1 R_t + \beta_1' x_{1t} + u_{1t}$$

where R_t is the rate paid on advances and x_{1t} is a vector that includes numerous predetermined and exogenous variables such as the mortgage interest rate, deposit levels of SLAs, the level of mortgage commitments by SLAs, and so on. The second is

---

[9] The term $\alpha_4 q_t$ is included for the sake of historical accuracy; it may be argued that its inclusion represents a type of "crop illusion" that cannot be justified on rational grounds.

[10] The harvest model may contain an internal inconsistency in that it may apparently require the data to satisfy the conditions of both regimes. See chapter 5 for a discussion of this problem.

$$H_t = \alpha_2 A_t + \beta_2' x_{2t} + u_{2t}^{\cdot}$$

where A_t is the volume of advances and x_{2t} includes the real value of the stock of housing, the household sector's net worth, consumption expenditures, the cost of capital for housing investment, the inflow of deposits and mortgage repayments, and other variables. It may be noted that the actual volume of advances, A_t, need not equal the desired volume A_t^d.

The FHLBB is posited to minimize in each period a quadratic loss function, a simplified form of which is given by

$$W_t = (R_t - C_t)^2 + v_1(R_t - R_{t-1})^2 + v_2(H_t - H_t^*)^2 + v_3(A_t^d - A_t)^2$$

where C_t represents the FHLBB's own cost of funds and where H_t^* represents the desired volume of housing starts. Minimization is with respect to the FHLBB's choice variables, namely R_t and A_t. The first term represents the desideratum that the interest rate charged by the FHLBB not depart too radically from its own cost of capital. The second term expresses the objective of not allowing interest rate fluctuations that are too large. The third term attempts to steer actual housing starts as close as possible to the desired volume. The last term recognizes that a discrepancy between the SLA's demand for advances and the actual volume granted is, *ceteris paribus*, undesirable. Obviously, SLAs cannot be forced to accept more advances than they wish to have; the loss function is thus minimized subject to the constraint

$$A_t^d \geqq A_t$$

From this exercise one can also derive an interest rate equation which has the form

$$R_r = [(C_t - v_1 R_{t-1}) - v_2 \alpha_2 \alpha_1 (H_t - H_t^*)]/(1 + v_1)$$

and an advances equation which "switches":

$$A_t = \begin{cases} A_t^d & \text{if } R_t \leqq (C_t + v_1 R_{t-1})/(1 + v_1) \\ A_t^d - \dfrac{v_2 \alpha_2}{v_3}(H_t - H_t^*) & \text{otherwise} \end{cases}$$

As the previous model, this too has two regimes or modes of operation. A price-clearing regime is in operation if $H_t < H_t^*$. In this case housing needs to be stimulated and the rate R_t is set at a low level (below $(C_t + v_1 R_{t-1})/(1 + v_1)$). A rationing regime occurs if $H_t > H^*$; in this case R_t is set at a higher level and A_t is set to fall short of A_t^d. Once again, some agents end up off their behavioral curve in certain situations; in these, the desired level of the endogenous variable in question is not observable.

Exercises

1.1 On the assumption that the process given by (1.2.3) has gone on forever,
show that $y_1 = \sum_{j=0}^{\infty} \alpha^j u_{1-j}$ and derive the likelihood function (1.2.6).

1.2 Let x, y be jointly normal vectors with means μ_x, μ_y and covariance
matrix

$$\Sigma = \begin{bmatrix} \Sigma_{xx} & \Sigma_{xy} \\ \Sigma_{yx} & \Sigma_{yy} \end{bmatrix}$$

Use the fact that the conditional mean of x given y is $\mu_{x|y} = \mu_x + \Sigma_{xy}\Sigma_{yy}^{-1}(y - \mu_y)$ to prove that

$$\frac{\alpha}{1 + \alpha^2} (y_{\tau+1} + y_{\tau-1})$$

is the mean of y_τ conditional on $y_{\tau+1}$, $y_{\tau-1}$ (see (1.2.9)).

1.3 Prove that (a) the sum of concave functions is concave, (b) a concave
function of a linear function is concave.

1.4 Show that the tobit log-likelihood function has a negative definite matrix
of second partial derivatives.
Hint: It may be easiest to show this by reparameterizing the model
through division by σ. Letting $\alpha = 1/\sigma$, we then have

$$\begin{aligned} \alpha y_i &= \gamma x_i + v_i && \text{if } \gamma x_i + v_i > 0 \\ \alpha y_i &= 0 && \text{otherwise} \end{aligned}$$

where $\gamma = \beta/\sigma$ and $v_i \sim N(0, 1)$.

1.5 Show that the application of ordinary least squares to a tobit problem
does not yield consistent estimates.

1.6 Assume that convergence has occurred in the iterative computation of
the maximum likelihood estimator in the tobit model and $\hat{\beta}$ and $\hat{\hat{\beta}}$ in
(1.3.14) are nearly identical. What is the interpretation of this
phenomenon?

1.7 Show that if the event $I_t (= 0, 1)$ follows a stationary Markov process with
transition matrix Q,

$$Q = \begin{bmatrix} q_{00} & q_{01} \\ q_{10} & q_{11} \end{bmatrix}$$

then $\Pr\{I_t = 1\} = q_{01}/(q_{01} + q_{10})$.

1.8 Let q_i be a vector of m elements and let Q be the matrix $Q = \sum_{i=1}^{n} q_i q_i'$.
Show that Q is positive semidefinite. Show that Q is positive definite if
the number of linearly independent q_i vectors is at least m.

1.9 Consider the following two-limit tobit problem, where z_{i1} and z_{i2} are observable variables:

$$y_i^* = \beta' x_i + u_i$$

$$y_i = \begin{cases} z_{i1} & \text{if } y_i^* \leq z_{i1} \\ y_i^* & \text{if } z_{i1} < y_i^* < z_{i2} \\ z_{i2} & \text{if } z_{i2} \leq y_i^* \end{cases}$$

Formulate the likelihood function for this model.

2

Canonical Models

2.1 Introduction and Specification of Models

In this chapter we begin a systematic examination of different types of disequilibrium models. In the present section we classify some of the important types of models. In section 2.2 we discuss the price adjustment equation that is frequently part of disequilibrium models. Maximum likelihood estimation is the subject of section 2.3, while sections 2.4 and 2.5 are devoted to certain theoretical problems that may be encountered and that may lead to serious computational difficulties. Section 2.6 deals with minimum distance methods of estimation, and section 2.7 deals with the EM algorithm. Finally, in section 2.8 we take up the question of computing the probability of excess demand.

The classification of models that follows is restricted to the standard models of a single market in which a demand and a supply function are the indispensible economic relations. The models that follow are thus not intended to cover more wide-ranging applications such as those described in chapter 1 and elsewhere in this volume. For the purpose at hand, it is convenient to adopt the taxonomy employed by Maddala and Nelson (1974) who were concerned with four types of models.

Model A

The simplest model consists of a demand equation, a supply equation, and a transactions equation. Thus

$$D_t = \beta_1' x_{1t} + u_{1t} \tag{2.1.1}$$

$$S_t = \beta_2' x_{2t} + u_{2t} \tag{2.1.2}$$

$$Q_t = \min(D_t, S_t) \tag{2.1.3}$$

The vectors x_{1t}, x_{2t} contain exogenous variables and normally include the price of the commodity which is also exogenous in this model. The error terms u_{1t}, u_{2t} are distributed with mean 0 and covariance matrix Σ; ordinarily

u_{1t}, u_{2t} are assumed to be jointly normal and independent over time. D_t and S_t are not observed by the econometrician; only Q_t is observed. Equation (2.1.3) expresses the assumption of voluntary exchange: in the presence of excess demand, sellers cannot be forced to supply more than they wish to supply; and in the presence of excess supply, purchasers cannot be made to purchase more than they wish to purchase.

In all subsequent models in this section, the price is no longer construed to be fully rigid. Prices adjust, but not fully as in an equilibrium model. The subsequent models differ from one another in terms of the information available to the econometrician and in terms of the precise manner in which prices adjust.

Model B

A variant on model A is obtained if prior information is available that allows the econometrician to "sort" the observations, i.e. to assign them *a priori* to excess demand or excess supply regimes. Fair and Jaffee (1972) proposed in their "directional model" a further variety which consists of (2.1.1)–(2.1.3) plus the following:

$$p_t > p_{t-1} \qquad \text{if and only if } D_t > S_t$$

$$p_t = p_{t-1} \qquad \text{if and only if } D_t = S_t \qquad\qquad (2.1.4)$$

$$p_t < p_{t-1} \qquad \text{if and only if } D_t < S_t$$

Conditions (2.1.4) express the usual price dynamics of the Walrasian auctioneer, according to which price rises if excess demand is positive. However, as Maddala (1986) points out, this variant is not a useful model since price has to be endogenous in the model, yet there is no mechanism specified for determining it. We shall not consider it further.

Model C

The model again consists of (2.1.1)–(2.1.3), but it is now convenient to rewrite these equations to display the role of the price:

$$D_t = \alpha_1 p_t + \beta_1' x_{1t} + u_{1t} \qquad\qquad (2.1.5)$$

$$S_t = \alpha_2 p_t + \beta_2' x_{2t} + u_{2t} \qquad\qquad (2.1.6)$$

$$Q_t = \min(D_t, S_t) \qquad\qquad (2.1.7)$$

These equations are now supplemented by a price adjustment equation

$$p_t = p_{t-1} + \gamma(D_t - S_t) \qquad\qquad (2.1.8)$$

in which the price change is proportional to excess demand.

Model D

This model is identical with model C except that the price adjustment equation contains an error term as well:

$$p_t = p_{t-1} + \gamma(D_t - S_t) + u_{3t} \tag{2.1.9}$$

In this case, the three error terms u_{1t}, u_{2t}, u_{3t} are customarily assumed to be distributed as $N(0,\Sigma)$.

It is interesting to note that this model may also be reparameterized as suggested by Bowden (1978a, 1978b). Setting $D_t = S_t$ yields the equilibrium price

$$p_t^* = \frac{\beta_2' x_{2t} - \beta_1' x_{1t}}{\alpha_1 - \alpha_2} + \frac{u_{2t} - u_{1t}}{\alpha_1 - \alpha_2} \tag{2.1.10}$$

Substituting (2.1.5) and (2.1.6) into (2.1.9) yields

$$p_t = \mu p_{t-1} + (1 - \mu)p_t^* + v_t \tag{2.1.11}$$

where $\mu = 1/[(1 + \gamma(\alpha_2 - \alpha_1)]$ and is in the $(0,1)$ interval for economically meaningful coefficients. Equation (2.1.11) represents a (stochastic) partial adjustment to equilibrium. The case of $\mu = 0$ corresponds in fact to equilibrium, since $v_t = \mu u_{3t}$, $\lim_{\mu \to 0} \sigma_v^2 = \lim_{\mu \to 0} \mu^2 \sigma_3^2 = 0$, and thus in the limit $p_t = p_t^*$. As an alternative, one might wish to relax the assumption that $\lim_{\mu \to 0} \sigma_v^2 = 0$; in that case one has

$$Q_t = \alpha_1 p_t^* + \beta_1' x_{1t} + u_{1t}$$

$$Q_t = \alpha_2 p_t^* + \beta_2' x_{2t} + u_{2t}$$

$$p_t = p_t^* + v_t$$

in which case the actually observed price departs randomly from the equilibrium price.

Models C1, D1

Either model C or model D may incorporate the assumption that excess demand has an effect of different magnitude on the price, depending on whether it is positive or negative. Accordingly we could add to either model the following specification:

$$\begin{aligned} \gamma &= \gamma_1 \quad &\text{if } D_t > S_t \\ \gamma &= \gamma_2 \quad &\text{otherwise} \end{aligned} \tag{2.1.12}$$

Models C2, D2

Either model C or model D could be altered by changing the lag structure of the price adjustment equation. Thus the price adjustment for model D could be given by

$$p_t = p_{t-1} + \gamma(D_{t-1} - S_{t-1}) + u_{3t} \qquad (2.1.13)$$

Laffont and Garcia (1977) write the price adjustment equation as

$$p_{t+1} - p_t = \gamma(D_t - S_t) \qquad (2.1.14)$$

which expresses the hypothesis that *current* excess demand causes *future* price rises. A similar shift in timing occurs in a model of central planning by Portes, Quandt, Winter and Yeo (1984, 1987) where the central plan adjusts in response to excess demand, and the plan for period $t + 1$ depends on excess demand in period t. This change affects the date for which the price is endogenous; in (2.1.14) p_t is predetermined and p_{t+1} is endogenous. In addition, there is no reason why there might not be additional explanatory variables on the right hand side; thus we might rewrite (2.1.13) as

$$p_t = \gamma(D_{t-1} - S_{t-1}) + \beta_3' x_{3t} + u_{3t} \qquad (2.1.15)$$

Estimation of most of the models is discussed in section 2.3.

Model E

Rudebusch (1986) has formulated a class of models involving exact excess demand indicators by adjoining to (2.1.5), (2.1.6), and (2.1.7) the equation

$$D_t - S_t = \gamma(I_t - I_t^e) \qquad (2.1.16)$$

where I_t is an excess demand indicator and I_t^e is its equilibrium value. In general I_t is endogenous, and if the model refers to a labor market it might be represented by the inverse of the unemployment rate. In any event I_t is observed and, if I_t^e is observed or appropriately proxied, exact sample separation is obtained and econometrically the model resembles model C.

   The price adjustment equations generally express the sensible notion that prices tend to rise when there is excess demand. In settling on some particular specification it is important to keep in mind the length of the period and the question of *when* the price increase occurs. The longer is the duration of the unit period, the more sense it makes to write the price adjustment equation in the form of (2.1.7) or (2.1.8), in which case p_t is endogenous. For the shorter period it may be more sensible to model price adjustment (2.1.14), in which case p_t is exogenous.

2.2   Price Rigidity and Price Adjustment

All the basic models share the feature that prices do not fully adjust to the market clearing level. In specifying an econometric disequilibrium model one needs to have some justification for the assumption of rigidity. In some instances the assumption of price or wage rigidity is adequately justified by appeal to certain institutional factors; thus, in the planned economies of Eastern Europe, the assumption of rigidity appears to bc rcasonably well founded (Portes and Winter 1980; Portes, Quandt, Winter and Yeo 1984). The assumption of rigidity may be more difficult to justify in an economy with extensive free-market sectors. Nevertheless, several theoretical treatments of labor markets have suggested reasons for wage rigidity. Eaton and Quandt (1983) posit that firms and workers are characterized by a fundamental informational asymmetry, in that workers cannot observe the factors that impel the firm to want to hire specific numbers of workers. If hiring occurs on the basis of seniority and if attracting workers to the firm is costly (because a recruitment fee has to be paid), it may be profitable for the firm to set a fixed wage (at a relatively high level) and to let employment fluctuate. Under these circumstances we may obtain a model not unlike model A. In the theoretical work of Salop (1979) there also appears the possibility of unemployment. In his case this is due to the firm facing two labor markets. In the first of these, the firm attempts to replace workers who have quit. In the second, it attempts to hire new workers whose number cannot exceed the number of applicants. Both the quit rate and the size of the applicant pool depend on the wage offered by the firm (relative to general labor market conditions) and it may occur that the actual wage cannot equilibrate both markets. The existence of unemployment will then be compatible with optimizing behavior by all agents.

Finally, rigid wages and unemployment may arise from the efficiency wage model of Yellen (1984). In this model, output per worker depends on his effort, which in turn depends on the real wage. The firm chooses optimal values of both the amount of labor hired and the real wage (by setting the nominal wage). The optimal real wage may, however, exceed workers' reservation wage and thus unemployed workers would be willing to work for a lower wage. But the firm will not find it profitable to hire them even at a lower wage, since lowering the wage would reduce the effort of those already employed.

A related question is the source of price adjustment as specified in (2.1.4) or (2.1.8) or (2.1.9). It is generally admitted that the theoretical foundations of the price adjustment equation are not as strong as, say, those of the demand and supply functions themselves. The latter can be derived from utility and profit maximization respectively (with due account being taken of quantity constraints where relevant). The price adjustment equation expresses in discrete terms the usual dynamic assumption of the perfectly competitive model that $\dot{p} = k(D - S)$. Taking it to represent the behavior of the auctioneer raises the question of how trading at nonequilibrium prices may affect the underlying demand and supply relations. Several researchers have argued that a price adjustment equation can be derived by minimizing certain costs. If, for example, costs were incurred as a result of price changes (costs due to having to revise plans) and to the presence of disequilibrium (due to unfulfilled expectations), the cost function would be

$$C = (p_t - p_{t-1})^2 + \theta(D_t - S_t)^2 \tag{2.2.1}$$

Minimization with respect to p_t yields

$$p_t = p_{t-1} + \theta(D'_t - S'_t)(D_t - S_t) \tag{2.2.2}$$

Equation (2.2.2) looks somewhat like (2.1.8) and formally coincides with it if both demand and supply are linear. A more complicated adjustment equation results if it is assumed that a cost is incurred due to adjusting the supply as well. The cost function then is

$$C = (p_t - p_{t-1})^2 + \theta_1(D_t - S_t)^2 + \theta_2(S_t - S_{t-1})^2 \tag{2.2.3}$$

and minimization with respect to p_t yields

$$p_t = p_{t-1} - \theta_1(D'_t - S'_t)D_t + [\theta_1(D'_t - S'_t) - \theta_2 S'_t]S_t + \theta_2 S'_t S_{t-1} \tag{2.2.4}$$

Although cost minimization does provide a choice theoretic foundation for an adjustment equation, one must ask who the agent is who performs the minimization. In an economy with atomistic agents, this may not be evident. In other contexts, the agent responsible for cost minimization may be more easily identified. Thus Portes, Quandt, Winter and Yeo (1984, 1987) posit that the central planning agency in East European countries minimizes a cost function that takes into account the magnitude of disequilibrium, the costs of plan adjustment and the costs of plan nonfulfillment.

Let Q_t^* be the planned output for period t (decided by the authorities at the end of period $t-1$). The cost function is then posited to be

$$
\begin{aligned}
C = {}& \theta_1 [Q_{t+1}^* - (1+g)\{\rho Q_t + (1-\rho)Q_t^*\}]^2 \\
& + \theta_2 [(Q_t - Q_t^*)(Q_{t+1}^* - (1+g)\{\rho Q_t + (1-\rho)Q_t^*\})] \\
& + \theta_3 [D_{t+1} - S_{t+1}]^2 + \theta_4 [(D_{t+1} - S_{t+1})(D_t - S_t)]
\end{aligned} \tag{2.2.5}
$$

where $g > 0$ is a desired growth rate, $0 \le \rho \le 1$ and where $\theta_1, \theta_3, \theta_4 > 0$ and $\theta_2 < 0$. It might be argued that a steady growth objective may be calculated by taking a convex combination of the current plan Q_t^* and current reality Q_t, and then incrementing this by the desired growth rate. The first term then measures the costs of departure from the steady growth objective, the third the costs of disequilibrium. The second term allows upward (downward) departures from steady growth if recent plans have been over (under) fulfilled. Finally, the last term accounts for intertemporal disequilibrium costs. With a conventional demand equation and a supply equation that depends, among others, on planned output, the minimization of C with respect to Q_{t+1}^* yields the following adjustment equation for the centrally planned output:

$$Q_{t+1}^* = \rho Q_t + (1-\rho)Q_t^* - \frac{\theta_2}{\theta_1}(Q_t - Q_t^*) + \frac{\theta_3}{\theta_1}(D_{t+1} - S_{t+1})$$

$$+ \frac{\theta_4}{\theta_1}(D_t - S_t) \tag{2.2.6}$$

2.3   Estimation of Models by Maximum Likelihood

Ordinary Least Squares

Consider for the moment the simplest possible model, model A. Since observations on D_t, S_t are not available, there is no way of computing ordinary least squares estimates for (2.1.1) and (2.1.2). Let us therefore imagine the most favorable circumstances in which *a priori* information is available that allows "sorting" the sample with respect to excess demand; that is, we are assumed to know index sets T_1, T_2 such that

$$D_t < S_t \quad \text{for } t \in T_1$$
$$D_t \geq S_t \quad \text{for } t \in T_2$$

The following question may then be asked: since for $t \in T_1$, $Q_t = D_t$ and for $t \in T_2$, $Q_t = S_t$, why not calculate the least squares regressions

$$Q_t = \beta_1' x_{1t} + u_{1t} \quad \text{for } t \in T_1 \tag{2.3.1}$$

and

$$Q_t = \beta_2' x_{2t} + u_{2t} \quad \text{for } t \in T_2 ? \tag{2.3.2}$$

The problem is that the density function of u_{1t}, given that $t \in T_1$, is the density of u_{1t} *conditional* on the event $\beta_1' x_{1t} + u_{1t} < \beta_2' x_{2t} + u_{2t}$.

We introduce the following notation. We denote the univariate normal density of the variable u with mean μ and variance σ^2 by

$$\psi(u; \mu, \sigma^2) = \frac{1}{\sqrt{(2\pi)}\sigma} \exp\left\{-\frac{1}{2}\frac{(u-\mu)^2}{\sigma^2}\right\}$$

and the cumulative normal distribution function by

$$\Psi(v; \mu, \sigma^2) = \int_{-\infty}^{v} \psi(u; \mu, \sigma^2) du$$

We further denote the standard normal density ($\mu = 0$, $\sigma^2 = 1$) and distribution functions by $\phi(u)$, $\Phi(v)$ respectively. The conditional density of u_{1t} in (2.3.1) is

$$f(u_{1t} | \beta_1' x_{1t} + u_{1t} < \beta_2' x_{2t} + u_{2t}) = f\left(u_{1t} \left| \frac{u_{1t}}{\sigma_1} < v_t\right.\right) \tag{2.3.3}$$

where $v_t = (\beta_2' x_{2t} - \beta_1' x_{1t} + u_{2t})/\sigma_1$ and further equals $\psi(u_{1t}; 0, \sigma_1^2)/\Phi(v_t)$. Hence the expected value of u_{1t} is

$$E(u_{1t}|D_t < S_t) = \int_{-\infty}^{\sigma_1 v_t} u_{1t}\psi(u_{1t}; 0, \sigma_1^2)\mathrm{d}u_{1t}/\Phi(v_t)$$

$$= \frac{\sigma_1}{\Phi(v_t)} \int_{-\infty}^{v_t} z\phi(z)\mathrm{d}z = -\frac{\phi(v_t)\sigma_1}{\Phi(v_t)} \tag{2.3.4}$$

after making the substitution $u_{1t}/\sigma_1 = z$. It follows that the expected value of the error term is nonzero and is in fact negative. This is intuitively appealing because it says that, in periods in which supply exceeded demand, this must have come about because the average value of the demand function error was unusually small. Moreover, the conditional expectation of u_{1t} depends on x_{1t} and so the error term and the regressors are correlated. Ordinary least squares will thus produce inconsistent estimates and is not recommended (but see also section 2.6).

Maximum Likelihood Estimation: model A

We now return to assuming that no *a priori* knowledge is available. The likelihood function in this case was first derived by Maddala and Nelson (1974). Given the joint p.d.f. of the error terms u_{1t}, u_{2t}, it is straightforward to obtain the joint p.d.f. $g(D_t, S_t)$ of the unobservable random variables D_t, S_t. The p.d.f. of Q_t, $h(Q_t)$, can then be formally written as

$$h(Q_t) = f(Q_t|D_t < S_t)\mathrm{Pr}\{D_t < S_t\} + f(Q_t|D_t \geq S_t)\mathrm{Pr}\{D_t \geq S_t\} \tag{2.3.5}$$

The conditional density $f(Q_t|D_t < S_t)$ is

$$f(Q_t|D_t < S_t) = \int_{Q_t}^{\infty} g(Q_t, S_t|D_t < S_t)\mathrm{d}S_t$$

$$= \int_{Q_t}^{\infty} g(Q_t, S_t)\mathrm{d}S_t/\mathrm{Pr}\{D_t < S_t\} \tag{2.3.6}$$

and similarly for $f(Q_t|D_t \geq S_t)$. Substituting (2.3.6) and a corresponding expression for $f(Q_t|D_t \geq S_t)$ in (2.3.5) yields

$$h(Q_t) = \int_{Q_t}^{\infty} g(Q_t, S_t)\mathrm{d}S_t + \int_{Q_t}^{\infty} g(D_t, Q_t)\mathrm{d}D_t \tag{2.3.7}$$

The geometric interpretation of $h(Q_t)$ is given in figure 2.1, which shows a section of the density of (D_t, S_t). The density $h(Q_t)$ is the sum of the two hatched areas. The likelihood function then is

$$L = \prod_{t=1}^{T} h(Q_t) \tag{2.3.8}$$

A somewhat different approach, due to Kooiman, van Dijk and Thurik (1985), allows the same result to be obtained in extremely simple fashion. Let q_t be a random variable and let Q_t be a particular value, and consider the distribution function $H(Q_t)$ which is $\Pr\{q_t \leq Q_t\}$. The observed quantity q_t is either D_t and then $D_t \leq S_t$ or it is S_t and then $S_t < D$. Hence, the probability that q_t is less than or equal to some given number Q_t is

$$H(Q_t) = \Pr\{D_t \leq Q_t, D_t \leq S_t\} + \Pr\{S_t \leq Q_t, S_t < D_t\}$$

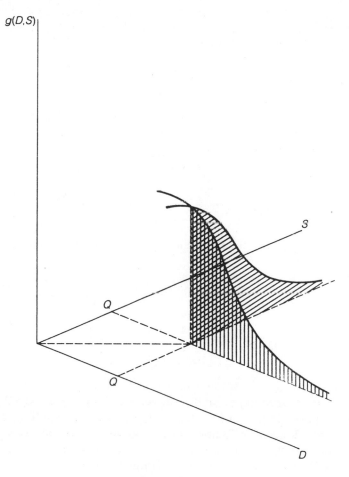

Figure 2.1

which, by the definition of the joint probabilities, can be written as

$$
\int_{-\infty}^{Q_t} \int_{D_t}^{\infty} g(D_t, S_t)\,dS_t\,dD_t + \int_{-\infty}^{Q_t} \int_{S_t}^{\infty} g(D_t, S_t)\,dD_t\,dS_t
$$

We obtain the density function by differentiating the above with respect to Q_t, which yields

$$
\int_{Q_t}^{\infty} g(Q_t, S_t)\,dS_t + \int_{Q_t}^{\infty} g(D_t, Q_t)\,dD_t
$$

as before.

The customary assumptions are that (u_{1t}, u_{2t}) are jointly normally distributed with mean zero, covariance matrix Σ, and that (u_{1t}, u_{2t}) are temporally uncorrelated. We can complete the square on D_t (S_t) in $g(D_t, S_t)$ and integrate it out, while replacing S_t (D_t) by Q_t. This leads to

$$
h(Q_t) = \frac{1}{\sqrt{(2\pi)}\,\sigma_1} \exp\left\{ -\frac{1}{2}\,\frac{(Q_t - \beta_1' x_{1t})^2}{\sigma_1^2} \right\}
$$

$$
\times \left[1 - \Phi\left(\frac{Q_t - \beta_2' x_{2t} - \rho(\sigma_2/\sigma_1)(Q_t - \beta_1' x_{1t})}{\sigma_2(1 - \rho^2)^{1/2}} \right) \right]
$$

$$
+ \frac{1}{\sqrt{(2\pi)}\,\sigma_2} \exp\left\{ -\frac{1}{2}\,\frac{(Q_t - \beta_2' x_{2t})^2}{\sigma_2^2} \right\}
$$

$$
\times \left[1 - \Phi\left(\frac{Q_t - \beta_1' x_1 - \rho(\sigma_1/\sigma_2)(Q_t - \beta_2' x_{2t})}{\sigma_1(1 - \rho^2)^{1/2}} \right) \right] \tag{2.3.9}
$$

where $\rho = \sigma_{12}/\sigma_1\sigma_2$. In the (frequently assumed) special case when $\sigma_{12} = 0$, (2.3.9) becomes

$$
h(Q_t) = \frac{1}{\sqrt{(2\pi)}\,\sigma_1} \exp\left\{ -\frac{1}{2}\,\frac{(Q_t - \beta_1' x_{1t})^2}{\sigma_1^2} \right\} \left[1 - \Phi\left(\frac{Q_t - \beta_2' x_{1t}}{\sigma_2} \right) \right]
$$

$$
+ \frac{1}{\sqrt{(2\pi)}\,\sigma_2} \exp\left\{ -\frac{1}{2}\,\frac{(Q_t - \beta_2' x_{2t})^2}{\sigma_2^2} \right\} \left[1 - \Phi\left(\frac{Q_t - \beta_1' x_{1t}}{\sigma_1} \right) \right]
$$

$$
\tag{2.3.10}
$$

FORTRAN subroutines for evaluating the log-likelihood based on (2.3.10) and its first and second partial derivatives are given in appendix 2.A.

This is probably the most frequently analyzed disequilibrium model. Hartley and Mallela (1977) have shown that under standard conditions an adaptation of Wald's (1943) proof demonstrates the strong consistency of the maximum likelihood estimate. The assumptions are:

1   The set of error terms $(u_{1t}, u_{2t}, t = 1, \ldots, T)$ is a random sample from a normal distribution with mean zero and nonsingular covariance matrix.

2   The right hand side variables p_t, x_{1t}, x_{2t} are uniformly bounded and their empirical distribution function converges to a nondegenerate distribution function.

3   The parameter vector is in the interior of a compact parameter space which does not include the region $\sigma_i^2 \leq 0$, $i = 1, 2$ and $|\rho| \geq 1$.

4   The parameters are functionally independent and each equation contains at least one right hand variable not contained in the other.

5   The limit of the moment matrix of the right hand side variables is positive definite.

Under these circumstances the maximum likelihood estimate is strongly consistent as well as asymptotically normal. An alternative proof of (weak) consistency is due to Amemiya and Sen (1977), who show that with limit probability of 1 the likelihood function attains a local maximum in an arbitrarily small ϵ-ball around the true parameter point.

Maximum Likelihood Estimation: model B

We now assume prior information about when excess demand and supply occurred and use T_1 and T_2 to denote the index sets corresponding to these two types of events. The likelihood then is

$$L = \prod_{T_1} \int_{Q_t}^{\infty} g(D_t, Q_t) \mathrm{d}D_t \times \prod_{T_2} \int_{Q_t}^{\infty} g(Q_t, S_t) \mathrm{d}S_t \qquad (2.3.11)$$

The actual formulas are immediate from the development of model A.

Maximum Likelihood Estimation: model C

Model C contains more information than model D, in which no sample separation information is available, and model B, in which we know only when excess demand is positive and when it is negative. This is due to the nature of the price adjustment equation (2.1.8). The magnitude of excess demand is given by $D_t - S_t = (p_t - p_{t-1})/\gamma$ and, on the reasonable economic assumption that $\gamma > 0$, we can rewrite the system in the following convenient fashion.

Let $p_t - p_{t-1}$ be denoted by Δp_t, and write the price adjustment equation as

$$Q_t = S_t + \Delta p_t/\gamma \qquad (2.3.12)$$

when $D_t < S_t$ (since then $D_t = Q_t$), and as

$$Q_t = D_t - \Delta p_t/\gamma \qquad\qquad (2.3.13)$$

when $D_t \geq S_t$. Hence, the system of equations determining the endogenous variables is

1   When $D_t < S_t$:

$$Q_t = \alpha_1 p_t + \beta_1' x_{1t} + u_{1t}$$
$$Q_t = \alpha_2 p_t + \beta_2' x_{2t} + \Delta p_t/\gamma + u_{2t} \qquad\qquad (2.3.14)$$

2   When $D_t \geq S_t$:

$$Q_t = \alpha_1 p_t + \beta_1' x_{1t} - \Delta p_t/\gamma + u_{1t}$$
$$Q_t = \alpha_2 p_t + \beta_2' x_{2t} + u_{2t} \qquad\qquad (2.3.15)$$

The two sets of equations (2.3.14) and (2.3.15) may be coalesced by defining the following artificial variables:

$$\Delta p_t^+ = \begin{cases} \Delta p_t & \text{if } \Delta p_t > 0 \\ 0 & \text{otherwise} \end{cases}$$

$$\Delta p_t^- = \begin{cases} -\Delta p_t & \text{if } \Delta p_t < 0 \\ 0 & \text{otherwise} \end{cases}$$

It follows that we can write the system as

$$Q_t = \alpha_1 p_t + \beta_1' x_{1t} - \Delta p_t^+/\gamma + u_{1t}$$
$$Q_t = \alpha_2 p_t + \beta_2' x_{2t} - \Delta p_t^-/\gamma + u_{2t} \qquad\qquad (2.3.16)$$

A similar development can be applied to model E.

As usual, we assume that $u_t' = (u_{1t}, u_{2t})$ is i.i.d. $N(0,\Sigma)$. The Jacobian of the transformation $u_t \rightarrow (Q_t, p_t)$ must be evaluated separately for $\Delta p_t > 0$ and $\Delta p_t < 0$. In either event, the absolute value of the Jacobian is $|\alpha_2 - \alpha_1 + 1/\gamma|$. Hence, (2.3.16) implies the standard simultaneous equations density for the endogenous variables, and the log-likelihood function is

$$L = T\log|\alpha_2 - \alpha_1 + 1/\gamma| - T\log 2\pi - \frac{T}{2}\log|\Sigma| - \frac{1}{2}\sum_t u_t'\Sigma^{-1}u_t$$

$$(2.3.17)$$

where

$$u_t' = (Q_t - \alpha_1 p_t - \beta_1' x_{1t} + \Delta p_t^+/\gamma, \quad Q_t - \alpha_2 p_t - \beta_2' x_{2t} + \Delta p_t^-/\gamma)$$

An alternative way of deriving this likelihood function (Amemiya 1974a) is to obtain the joint density of p_t, Q_t from (2.3.14) and (2.3.15), denoted by $f_1(Q_t, p_t)$ and $f_2(Q_t, p_t)$ respectively. The appropriate log-likelihood function then is

$$L = \sum_{\Delta p_t < 0} \log f_1(Q_t, p_t) + \sum_{\Delta p_t > 0} \log f_2(Q_t, p_t) \qquad\qquad (2.3.18)$$

which is the same as (2.3.17). Fair and Kelejian (1974) suggested maximizing the conditional (log) likelihood

$$L = \sum_{\Delta p_t < 0} \log[f_1(Q_t, p_t)/\Pr\{D_t < S_t\}] + \sum_{\Delta p_t > 0} \log[f_2(Q_t, p_t)/\Pr\{D_t > S_t\}]$$

The use of the latter is incorrect since it in effect fails to use the information on the observed sample separation (Maddala 1983b).

Maximum Likelihood Estimation: model D

In this model, as in model A, there is no *a priori* partition of the sample and the derivation of the likelihood function is analogous to the former case. We rewrite (2.1.5), (2.1.6), and (2.1.12) as

$$\begin{bmatrix} 1 & 0 & -\alpha_1 \\ 0 & 1 & -\alpha_2 \\ -\gamma & \gamma & 1 \end{bmatrix} \begin{bmatrix} D_t \\ S_t \\ p_t \end{bmatrix} = \begin{bmatrix} \beta_1' x_{1t} \\ \beta_2' x_{2t} \\ \beta_3' x_{3t} \end{bmatrix} + \begin{bmatrix} u_{1t} \\ u_{2t} \\ u_{3t} \end{bmatrix} \qquad (2.3.19)$$

From the joint p.d.f. on the u_ts it is easy to obtain the joint p.d.f. of (D_t, S_t, p_t), denoted by $g(D_t, S_t, p_t)$. Analogously to (2.3.5)–(2.3.7), we can write

$$h(Q_t, p_t) = f(Q_t, p_t | D_t < S_t)\Pr\{D_t < S_t\} + f(Q_t, p_t | D_t \geqq S_t)\Pr\{D_t \geqq S_t\}$$

$$= \int_{Q_t}^{\infty} g(Q_t, S_t, p_t) \, dS_t + \int_{Q_t}^{\infty} g(D_t, Q_t, p_t) \, dD_t \qquad (2.3.20)$$

If u_{1t}, u_{2t}, u_{3t} are distributed as the multivariate normal $N(0, \Sigma)$ with *diagonal* Σ, the joint density of D_t, S_t, p_t is

$$g(D_t, S_t, p_t) = \frac{|1 + \gamma(\alpha_2 - \alpha_1)|}{(2\pi)^{3/2} \sigma_1 \sigma_2 \sigma_3} \exp\left\{ -\frac{1}{2} \left[\frac{(D_t - \alpha_1 p_t - \beta_1' x_{1t})^2}{\sigma_1^2} \right. \right.$$

$$\left. \left. + \frac{(S_t - \alpha_2 p_t - \beta_2' x_{2t})^2}{\sigma_2^2} + \frac{(p_t - \gamma(D_t - S_t) - \beta_3' x_{3t})^2}{\sigma_3^2} \right] \right\}$$

$$(2.3.21)$$

where $|1 + \gamma(\alpha_2 - \alpha_1)|$ is the absolute value of the Jacobian of the transformation. Performing the integrations in (2.3.20), as well as in other similar cases, invariably involves completing the square on the latent endogenous variables. First, replace S_t by Q_t and rewrite the square bracket [ ] in the exponent as

$$\frac{(D_t - A_{1t})^2}{\sigma_1^2} + A_{2t} + \frac{(-\gamma D_t + A_{3t})^2}{\sigma_3^2} \qquad (2.3.22)$$

where

$$A_{1t} = \alpha_1 p_t + \beta_1' x_{1t}$$

$$A_{2t} = \frac{(Q_t - \alpha_2 p_t - \beta_2' x_{2t})^2}{\sigma_2^2}$$

$$A_{3t} = p_t + \gamma Q_t - \beta_3' x_{3t}$$

Then we can write (2.3.22) as

$$\frac{1}{\sigma_1^2 \sigma_3^2} [\sigma_3^2 (D_t - A_{1t})^2 + \sigma_1^2 (-\gamma D_t + A_{3t})^2] + A_{2t}$$

$$= \frac{1}{\sigma_1^2 \sigma_3^2} [(\sigma_3^2 + \gamma^2 \sigma_1^2) D_t^2 - 2D_t(A_{1t}\sigma_3^2 + \gamma A_{3t}\sigma_1^2)$$
$$+ \sigma_3^2 A_{1t}^2 + \sigma_1^2 A_{3t}^2] + A_{2t}$$

$$= \frac{\sigma_3^2 + \gamma^2 \sigma_1^2}{\sigma_1^2 \sigma_3^2} [D_t^2 - 2D_t B_{1t} + B_{2t}] + A_{2t}$$

where

$$B_{1t} = \frac{A_{1t}\sigma_3^2 + \gamma A_{3t}\sigma_1^2}{\sigma_3^2 + \gamma^2 \sigma_1^2}$$

$$B_{2t} = \frac{A_{1t}^2 \sigma_3^2 + A_{3t}^2 \sigma_1^2}{\sigma_3^2 + \gamma^2 \sigma_1^2}$$

We can finally write the exponent as

$$\frac{\sigma_3^2 + \gamma^2 \sigma_1^2}{\sigma_1^2 \sigma_3^2} [(D_t - B_{1t})^2 + B_{2t} - B_{1t}^2] + A_{2t}$$

The second term of (2.3.20) can therefore be written as

$$\frac{|1 + \gamma(\alpha_2 - \alpha_1)|}{2\pi\sigma_2(\sigma_3^2 + \gamma^2 \sigma_1^2)^{1/2}} \exp\left\{ -\frac{1}{2} \left[\frac{(B_{2t} - B_{1t}^2)}{\sigma_1^2 \sigma_3^2/(\sigma_3^2 + \gamma^2 \sigma_1^2)} + A_{2t} \right] \right\}$$

$$\times \int_{Q_t}^{\infty} \frac{1}{\sqrt{(2\pi)}\sigma_1 \sigma_3/(\sigma_3^2 + \gamma^2 \sigma_1^2)^{1/2}} \exp\left\{ -\frac{(D_t - B_{1t})^2}{2\sigma_1^2 \sigma_3^2/(\sigma_3^2 + \gamma^2 \sigma_1^2)} \right\} dD_t$$

$$= \frac{|1 + \gamma(\alpha_2 - \alpha_1)|}{2\pi\sigma_2(\sigma_3^2 + \gamma^2 \sigma_1^2)^{1/2}} \exp\left\{ -\frac{1}{2} \left[\frac{(B_{2t} - B_{1t}^2)}{\sigma_1^2 \sigma_3^2/(\sigma_3^2 + \gamma^2 \sigma_1^2)} + A_{2t} \right] \right\}$$

$$\times \left[1 - \Phi\left(\frac{Q_t - B_{1t}}{\sigma_1 \sigma_3/(\sigma_3^2 + \gamma^2 \sigma_1^2)^{1/2}} \right) \right] \qquad (2.3.23)$$

By analogous reasoning, the first term of (2.3.20) is

$$\frac{|1 + \gamma(\alpha_2 - \alpha_1)|}{2\pi\sigma_1(\sigma_3^2 + \gamma^2 \sigma_2^2)^{1/2}} \exp\left\{ -\frac{1}{2} \left[\frac{(B_{4t} - B_{3t}^2)}{\sigma_2^2 \sigma_3^2/(\sigma_3^2 + \gamma^2 \sigma_2^2)} + A_{4t} \right] \right\}$$

$$\times \left[1 - \Phi \left(\frac{Q_t - B_{3t}}{\sigma_2 \sigma_3 / (\sigma_3^2 + \gamma^2 \sigma_2^2)^{1/2}} \right) \right] \qquad (2.3.24)$$

where

$$A_{4t} = \frac{(Q_t - \alpha_1 p_t - \beta_1' x_{1t})^2}{\sigma_1^2}$$

$$A_{5t} = \alpha_2 p_t + \beta_2' x_{2t}$$

$$A_{6t} = p_t - \gamma Q_t - \beta_3' x_{3t}$$

$$B_{3t} = \frac{\sigma_3^2 A_{5t} - \gamma A_{6t} \sigma_2^2}{\sigma_3^2 + \gamma^2 \sigma_2^2}$$

$$B_{4t} = \frac{\sigma_3^2 A_{5t}^2 + \sigma_2^2 A_{6t}^2}{\sigma_3^2 + \gamma^2 \sigma_2^2}$$

A FORTRAN subroutine evaluating the log-likelihood from (2.3.20) is given in appendix 2.B.

Three further modifications may be mentioned:

1   If there is asymmetric price adjustment (model D1), we must replace γ by γ_1 in (2.3.23), which corresponds to excess demand, and by γ_2 in (2.3.24), which corresponds to excess supply.

2   The formulas become substantially more complicated if the covariances in the error structure are nonzero. For reference, the formulas are presented in appendix 2.C.

3   Finally, if the price adjustment equation is $p_{t+1} = p_t + \gamma(D_t - S_t)$, as specified by Laffont and Garcia (1977), p_t is predetermined and the term Δp_t in (2.3.14) and (2.3.15) must be replaced by Δp_{t+1}. This also changes the Jacobian but leaves the derivation of the likelihood unchanged in principle from that of model C.

2.4   Unbounded Likelihood Functions

A well-behaved likelihood function encountered in practice is bounded from above. As a consequence, standard optimization algorithms have a fair chance of converging to a local maximum of the log-likelihood function.[1]

It is frequently the case in models involving unobservables that the boundedness property disappears. Four examples will be considered briefly.

---

[1]Convergence to a global maximum is, of course, not guaranteed even in these favorable cases. For procedures designed to locate the global maximum see Quandt (1983b), Timmer (1984), and Boender, Rinnooy Kan, Timmer and Stougie (1982).

Switching Regression Model

Consider the case introduced in chapter 1 in which observations on a dependent variable y are generated by the following mechanism:

$$y_i = \beta_1' x_{1i} + u_{1i} \qquad \text{with probability } \lambda$$
$$y_i = \beta_2' x_{2i} + u_{2i} \qquad \text{with probability } 1 - \lambda \qquad (2.4.1)$$

where u_{1i}, u_{2i} are i.i.d. $N(0, \sigma_1^2)$, $N(0, \sigma_2^2)$ respectively. The likelihood function is

$$L = \prod_{i=1}^{n} \left[\frac{\lambda}{\sqrt{(2\pi)}\sigma_1} \exp\left\{ -\frac{1}{2} \frac{(y_i - \beta_1' x_{1i})^2}{\sigma_1^2} \right\} \right.$$
$$\left. + \frac{1-\lambda}{\sqrt{(2\pi)}\sigma_2} \exp\left\{ -\frac{1}{2} \frac{(y_i - \beta_2' x_{2i})^2}{\sigma_2^2} \right\} \right] \qquad (2.4.2)$$

To show that the likelihood is unbounded, choose values of β_2 and σ_2 arbitrarily and choose β_1 so that a particular residual, say the kth, vanishes for the first regime, i.e. so that $y_k - \beta_1' x_{1k} = 0$. Then consider the behavior of the likelihood over a sequence of points with the chosen β_1, β_2, σ_2^2 values and values of $\sigma_1^2 \to 0$. For all terms of the likelihood, the second part in the bracket in (2.4.2) is > 0. For all terms such that $(y_i - \beta_1' x_{1i})^2$ is nonzero, the first part in the brackets converges to zero. But for the kth term the first part is $[\lambda/\sqrt{(2\pi)}\sigma_1] e^0$, which becomes arbitrarily large for σ_1 sufficiently close to 0. Hence the likelihood itself becomes arbitrarily large.[2]

Tobit Model

The model is given by

$$y_i = \beta' x_i + u_i \qquad \text{if } \beta' x_i + u_i > 0$$
$$y_i = 0 \qquad \text{otherwise}$$

and $u_i \sim N(0, \sigma^2)$. The likelihood function is

$$L = \prod_{y_i > 0} \frac{1}{\sqrt{(2\pi)}\sigma} \exp\left\{ -\frac{1}{2} \frac{(y_i - \beta' x_i)^2}{\sigma^2} \right\} \prod_{y_i = 0} \Phi\left(-\frac{\beta' x_i}{\sigma} \right) \qquad (2.4.3)$$

Assume that β is a $k \times 1$ vector and that $y_1, y_2, \ldots, y_{k-1} > 0$ and $y_k = \ldots = y_n = 0$. We again choose a vector β so as to make certain residuals equal to

---

[2] The reader should verify that the problem disappears if it is known *a priori* that $\sigma_1^2 = \sigma_2^2$. The reader should further convince himself that the problem is not due to our not knowing the true mixing probability λ.

zero; specifically choose β so that $\beta'x_i = y_i$ for $i = 1, \ldots, k-1$, and in addition so that $\beta'x_i \leq 0$ for $i = k, \ldots, n$. This can be done if the x_i ($i = 1, \ldots, k-1$) do not belong to the convex hull of $\{x_k, \ldots, x_n\}$, for then, if the equation $y = \beta'x$ contains a constant term, there exists a hyperplane separating the x_i ($i = 1, \ldots, k-1$) from $\{x_k, \ldots, x_n\}$ (see figure 2.2). As before, we let $\sigma_2 \to 0$. The first set of products in (2.4.3) becomes arbitrarily large and the second set converges to unity. Hence the likelihood is unbounded at such points.

Whereas in the switching regression problem the unboundedness always occurs as long as σ_1^2 and σ_2^2 can have arbitrary positive values, in the present case unboundedness occurs only when the data imply perfect classification. This is increasingly less likely to be encountered as n becomes large, similarly to the conditional logit case. The occurrence of this is also ruled out by the assumption that the first-order condition for a maximum holds (Olsen 1978). Differentiating log L,

$$\frac{\partial \log L}{\partial \beta} = \frac{1}{\sigma^2} \sum_{y_i > 0} (y_i - \beta'x_i)x_i - \sum_{y_i = 0} \frac{\phi(-\beta'x_i)x_i}{\Phi(-\beta'x_i/\sigma)\sigma}$$

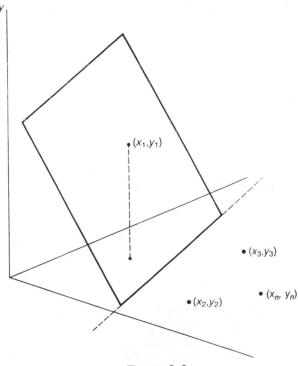

Figure 2.2

Unboundedness requires that the first term be zero, which contradicts the assumption (Quandt 1979).

Simple Disequilibrium Model

Write the likelihood function (2.3.8), into which (2.3.10) has been substituted, as

$$L = \prod_{t=1}^{T} (\alpha_t \beta_t + \gamma_t \delta_t)$$

where

$$\alpha_t = [1/\sqrt{(2\pi)}\sigma_1] \exp\{-(Q_t - \alpha_1 p_t - \beta_1' x_{1t})^2/2\sigma_1^2\}$$

$$\beta_t = 1 - \Phi[(Q_t - \alpha_2 p_t - \beta_2' x_{2t})/\sigma_2]$$

$$\gamma_t = [1/\sqrt{(2\pi)}\sigma_2] \exp\{-(Q_t - \alpha_2 p_t - \beta_2' x_{2t})^2/2\sigma_2^2\} \qquad (2.4.4)$$

$$\delta_t = 1 - \Phi[(Q_t - \alpha_1 p_t - \beta_1' x_{1t})/\sigma_1]$$

Consider a choice of values for α_1, β_1 such that $Q_k - \alpha_1 p_k - \beta_1' x_{1k} = 0$ and $Q_t - \alpha_1 p_t - \beta_1' x_{1t} < 0$ for all $t \neq k$. Such a choice is feasible in general if there is an intercept term in the demand function. Next choose arbitrary admissible values for α_2, β_2, σ_2^2. Again, as before, we consider the behavior of L over a sequence of σ_1^2 values converging to zero. It is evident that

(a) $\lim\limits_{\sigma_1^2 \to 0} \alpha_k = \infty$

(b) $\beta_t, \gamma_t \neq 0$ for all t

(c) $\lim\limits_{\sigma_1^2 \to 0} \delta_k = 1/2$

(d) $\lim\limits_{\sigma_1^2 \to 0} \delta_t = 1$ for $t \neq k$

It follows that the likelihood function is unbounded.

Harvest Model

For simplicity, we rewrite the equations of the harvest model of section 1.4 as follows:

$$q_t = b_1 z_{1t} + b_2 + u_{1t}$$

$$x_t = b_3 p_t + b_4 q_t + b_5 z_{2t} + b_6 + u_{2t}$$

$$p_t = b_7 z_{3t} + b_8 y_t + b_9 + u_{3t}$$

and assume that $b_4 = 0$. It can be shown (Goldfeld and Quandt 1975) that the density function for y_t, p_t is

$$h(y_t, p_t) = \frac{1}{2\pi} \frac{|1 - b_3 b_8|}{\sigma_2 \sigma_3} \exp\left\{ -\frac{1}{2}\left[\frac{(y_1 - b_3 p_t - b_5 z_{2t} - b_6)^2}{\sigma_2^2} \right.\right.$$

$$\left.\left. + \frac{(p_t - b_7 z_{3t} - b_8 y_t - b_9)^2}{\dot{\sigma}_3^2} \right]\right\} [1 - \Phi(I_t)]$$

$$+ \frac{1}{2\pi\sigma_1 \sigma_3} \exp\left\{ -\frac{1}{2}\left[\frac{(y_t - b_1 z_{1t} - b_2)^2}{\sigma_1^2} \right.\right.$$

$$\left.\left. + \frac{(p_t - b_7 z_{3t} - b_8 y_t - b_9)^2}{\sigma_3^2} \right]\right\} [1 - \Phi(I_t')]$$

$$\equiv \psi_{1t}(y_t, p_t)[1 - \Phi(I_t)] + \psi_{2t}(y_t, p_t)[1 - \Phi(I_t')]$$

where

$$I_t = \frac{y_t - b_1 z_{1t} - b_2}{\sigma_1}$$

$$I_t' = \frac{y_1 - b_3 p_t - b_5 z_{2t} - b_6}{\sigma_2}$$

and where the likelihood is the product over t of $h(y_t, p_t)$.

Consider the points $(y_1, p_1, z_{21}), \ldots, (y_n, p_n, z_{2n})$ and denote their convex hull by S. There exists a supporting hyperplane for S, defined by the coefficients $\alpha_1, \alpha_2, \alpha_3, \alpha_4$, such that $\alpha_1 \neq 0$ and

(a) $\alpha_1 y_k + \alpha_2 p_k + \alpha_3 z_{2k} + \alpha_4 = 0$ for some k
(b) $\alpha_1 y_t + \alpha_2 p_t + \alpha_3 z_{2t} + \alpha_4 \leq 0$ for all t
(c) $\alpha_1 y_j + \alpha_2 p_j + \alpha_3 z_{2j} + \alpha_4 = 0$ for $j \neq k$ occurs with probability
                                                     zero

The coefficients of the desired harvest equation correspond to ratios of αs: $b_3 = -\alpha_2/\alpha_1$, $b_5 = -\alpha_3/\alpha_1$, and $b_6 = -\alpha_4/\alpha_1$. Choose a hyperplane (this fixes b_3, b_5, and b_6) that satisfies conditions (a), (b), and (c); choose $\sigma_1^2 > 0$, and some values for the other coefficients; and now let $\sigma_2^2 \to 0$. Evidently it is the case that

(i) $1 - \Phi(I_{1t}) \neq 0$
(ii) $\psi_{2t}(y_t, p_t) \neq 0$
(iii) $\psi_{1k}(y_k, p_k) \to \infty$ as $\sigma_2^2 \to 0$
(iv) $1 - \Phi(I_k') = 1/2$
(v) $I_t' \to -\infty$ and hence $1 - \Phi(I_t') \to 1$ as $\sigma_2^2 \to 0$.

It follows that the likelihood function becomes arbitrarily large.

The practical consequence of this property in all the models discussed is that maximum likelihood estimation may become extremely difficult. In all cases the likelihood function has many points of singularity,[3] and there may therefore be substantial regions in parameter space in which the gradient points toward such singularities. Any effective optimization algorithm will tend to move in the direction of these "spikes" in the likelihood surface. Since these points lie on the boundaries of the parameter space ($\sigma_1^2 = 0$ or $\sigma_2^2 = 0$), computation will eventually break down (say, when one or another variance becomes $< 10^{-10}$). The parameter values at the point at which computation breaks down have, unfortunately, no desirable statistical properties. Although this difficulty arises only occasionally in practice, it does arise with sufficient persistence to be a matter of concern. We briefly discuss some estimating techniques that do not share this problem in sections 2.6 and 2.7.

In the context of maximum likelihood estimation, an effective way to avoid the region of unboundedness has been employed by Kooiman, van Dijk and Thurik (1985). They note that in the context of their model the region of unboundedness consists of almost all data points being assigned to one of the regimes with probability 1, the remaining points being assigned to the other regime with probability 1. To avoid straying into these regions they employ constrained optimization using a penalty function based on the average of the excess supply probabilities. In the context of model A such a penalty function might be set up by choosing parameters a and b and penalizing the maximand by $[a - (1-\bar{\delta})/(1-b)]/(1-\bar{\delta})$ if $\bar{\delta} \geq b$ or by 0 otherwise, where $\bar{\delta}$ is the average value of δ_t (see (2.4.4)) over the sample.

The unboundedness problem is a consequence of substantial elements of "latency" in models. In model A, for example, not only are demand and supply unobserved, but we do not even observe sample separation; that is, we do not even know when $D_t < S_t$ and conversely. Reducing the degree of "latency" may well eliminate the unboundedness problem. For example, it is not difficult to show that the problem does not arise in either model B or model C or in model A with prior sorting.

2.5   The Possibility of False Maxima

An additional difficulty may arise in even the simplest model, e.g. model A, if the error terms have a nonzero covariance. What may happen in these cases is that the gradient of the likelihood function may point in a direction in parameter space in which the covariance matrix ultimately becomes singular (Goldfeld and Quandt 1978). The covariance matrix can become singular (if all elements are bounded away from zero) in two ways: either $\rho = \sigma_{12}/\sigma_1\sigma_2$ has to become -1 or it has to become $+1$. Thus there are two cases to consider.

---

[3] Since there are many ways of satisfying the conditions under which unboundedness may occur.

Case 1: $\rho = -1.0$

Assume that in the process of estimation values of the parameters in (2.1.1) and (2.1.2) have been selected by an optimization algorithm such that

$$\frac{Q_t - \beta_1' x_{1t}}{\sigma_1} + \frac{Q_t - \beta_2' x_{2t}}{\sigma_2} < 0 \qquad (2.5.1)$$

for all t. Parameter values will always exist that insure that condition (2.5.1) holds if both equations contain constant terms or contain variables that never change sign over the observations. We now examine the behavior of the likelihood function over an infinite sequence of points such that $\rho \to -1.0$, holding σ_1, σ_2 constant. Consider what happens to the terms of the density function (2.3.9). Examination of the arguments of the $\Phi(\ )$ function shows that both these arguments approach $-\infty$. It follows that $h(Q_t)$ converges to

$$\frac{1}{\sqrt{(2\pi)}\sigma_1} \exp\{-(Q_t - \beta_1' x_{1t})^2/2\sigma_1^2\} + \frac{1}{\sqrt{(2\pi)}\sigma_2} \exp\{-(Q_t - \beta_2' x_{2t})^2/2\sigma_2^2\}$$

When ρ is near -1.0, the density and hence the likelihood must be increasing as ρ approaches -1.0. Denoting the two terms in the above sum by f_{1t}, f_{2t} respectively we have

$$\frac{\partial h(Q_t)}{\partial \rho} = f_{2t}\, \phi \left[\frac{Q_t - \beta_1' x_{1t} - \rho(\sigma_1/\sigma_2)(Q_t - \beta_2' x_{2t})}{\sigma_1(1-\rho^2)^{1/2}} \right]$$

$$\times \left[\frac{(Q_t - \beta_2' x_{2t})/\sigma_2 - \rho(Q_t - \beta_1' x_{1t})/\sigma_1}{(1-\rho^2)^{3/2}} \right]$$

$$+ f_{1t}\, \phi \left[\frac{Q_t - \beta_2' x_{2t} - \rho(\sigma_2/\sigma_1)(Q_t - \beta_1' x_{1t})}{\sigma_2(1-\rho^2)^{1/2}} \right]$$

$$\times \left[\frac{(Q_t - \beta_1' x_{1t})/\sigma_1 - \rho(Q_t - \beta_2' x_{2t})/\sigma_2}{(1-\rho^2)^{3/2}} \right] \qquad (2.5.2)$$

where $\phi(x) = d\Phi(x)/dx$. By condition (2.5.1) this is negative for ρ arbitrarily close to -1.0.

Case 2: $\rho = 1.0$

Now assume that values of the coefficients have been selected by the optimization algorithm such that

$$\frac{Q_t - \beta_2' x_{2t}}{\sigma_2} > \frac{Q_t - \beta_1' x_{1t}}{\sigma_1}$$

$$\text{if } \exp\{-(Q_t - \beta_2' x_{2t})^2/2\sigma_2^2\}/\sigma_2 > \exp\{-(Q_t - \beta_1' x_{1t})^2/2\sigma_1^2\}/\sigma_1$$

$$\frac{Q_t - \beta_2' x_{2t}}{\sigma_2} < \frac{Q_t - \beta_1' x_{1t}}{\sigma_1} \qquad \text{otherwise}$$

These conditions can also be satisfied if there is a constant term in the equations. We may construct a point in parameter space by setting $\sigma_1 = \sigma_2 = 1$ and choosing βs so that the demand equation produces all negative residuals with relatively large absolute values and the supply equation produces all positive residuals with relatively small absolute values.

The relevance of these conditions can again be seen from (2.5.2). When $\rho = 1.0$, the two ϕ terms in (2.5.2) have equal value (since their arguments are identical except for sign). If $f_{2t} > f_{1t}$, then $(Q_t - \beta_2' x_{2t})/\sigma_2 - (Q_t - \beta_1' x_{1t})/\sigma_1 > 0$ ensures that $\partial h(Q_t)/\partial \rho > 0$, and hence near $\rho = 1.0$ the likelihood function will increase with ρ.

An efficient optimization algorithm may in such a case drive the current estimate in the sequence of iterations to the point at which the likelihood function is not defined (i.e. $\rho \geq 1.0$ or $\rho \leq -1.0$). Computations have to break down at such a point. Breakdowns in computation should thus generally be examined to see if either unboundedness or the present section's false maxima have occurred.

2.6   Minimum Distance Methods of Estimation

Several methods other than maximum likelihood may be applied to some of the disequilibrium models discussed in this chapter, as well as to some of the related models. We consider some selected approaches.

Two-Stage Method for model A with Sample Separation

Model A can be rewritten as

$$Q_t = \begin{cases} \beta_1' x_{1t} + u_{1t} & \text{if } \beta_1' x_{1t} + u_{1t} < \beta_2' x_{2t} + u_{2t} \\ \beta_2' x_{2t} + u_{2t} & \text{otherwise} \end{cases} \tag{2.6.1}$$

with the sample separation known; that is, we know the subsets T_1 and T_2 of the time index t for which the first or second equation of (2.6.1) held. This is in effect a switching regression model in the general form of (1.3.23), where the condition determining which regime we are in, $\beta_3' x_{3t} \gtreqless u_{3t}$, has the specific form $\beta_1' x_{1t} - \beta_2' x_{2t} \gtreqless u_{2t} - u_{1t}$.

We can thus write the model as

$$Q_t = \begin{cases} \beta_1' x_{1t} + u_{1t} & \text{if } z_t < 0 \\ \beta_2' x_{2t} + u_{2t} & \text{otherwise} \end{cases} \tag{2.6.2}$$

$$z_t = \beta_3' x_{3t} - u_{3t} \tag{2.6.3}$$

It is convenient to normalize (2.6.3) by the standard deviation of u_{3t}, σ, which equals $(\sigma_1^2 + \sigma_2^2 - 2\sigma_{12})^{1/2}$. Then (2.6.3) becomes

$$w_t = \gamma' x_{3t} - v_t \tag{2.6.4}$$

where $w_t = z_t/\sigma$, $\gamma = \beta_3/\sigma$, $v_t = u_{3t}/\sigma$.

Now define a variable

$$\delta_t = \begin{cases} 1 & \text{if } w_t < 0 \\ 0 & \text{otherwise} \end{cases}$$

The pairs of error terms u_{1t}, v_t and u_{2t}, v_t are jointly normal and the variance of v_t is unity. (u_{1t}, u_{2t}, and v_t together have a singular normal distribution.) Let the joint density of u_{1t}, v_t be $f_1(u_{1t}, v_t)$ and that of u_{2t}, v_t be $f_2(u_{2t}, v_t)$. We need these bivariate densities for obtaining the density function of Q_t: either $Q_t - \beta_1'x_{1t}$ replaces u_{1t} or $Q_t - \beta_2'x_{2t}$ replaces u_{2t}, depending on δ_t; but δ_t depends on v_t and hence we must start with the appropriate bivariate densities. Since δ_t is observed, we can write the likelihood as

$$L = \prod_t \left\{ \int_{\gamma'x_{3t}}^{\infty} f_1(Q_t - \beta_1'x_{1t}, v_t) dv_t \right\}^{\delta_t} \left\{ \int_{-\infty}^{\gamma'x_{3t}} f_2(Q_t - \beta_2'x_{2t}, v_t) dv_t \right\}^{1-\delta_t} \quad (2.6.5)$$

It may be verified that this likelihood function is exactly the same as (2.3.11).

Since δ_t is in fact observable, the following two-stage procedure may also be employed. Remember that the reason that OLS cannot be applied to estimating a particular equation, say the demand equation, is that $E[u_{1t}|(\beta_1'x_{1t} - \beta_2'x_{2t})/\sigma < (u_{2t} - u_{1t})/\sigma] \neq 0$. Hence, if we were to compute this expected value, denoted for brevity by E_{1t}, and wrote the demand function as

$$Q_t = \beta_1 x_{1t} + E_{1t} + (u_{1t} - E_{1t})$$

we would have "corrected" the error term, in effect "purged" the error term of the part correlated with x_{1t}. But

$$E_{1t} = E[u_{1t}|(\beta_1'x_{1t} - \beta_2'x_{2t})/\sigma < (u_{2t} - u_{1t})/\sigma]$$
$$= E(u_{1t}|\gamma'x_{3t} < v_t)$$

If z_1 and z_2 are sets of normally distributed variables with mean vectors and covariance matrices $E(z_1) = \mu_1$, $E(z_2) = \mu_2$, $E(z_1 - \mu_1)(z_1 - \mu_1)' = \Sigma_{11}$, $E(z_1 - \mu_1)(z_2 - \mu_2)' = \Sigma_{12}$, $E(z_2 - \mu_2)(z_2 - \mu_2)' = \Sigma_{22}$, we have the conditional means and covariance matrices

$$E(z_1|z_2) = \mu_1 - \Sigma_{12}\Sigma_{22}^{-1}(\mu_2 - z_2)$$
$$E[(z_1 - \mu_1)(z_1 - \mu_1)'|z_2] = \Sigma_{11} - \Sigma_{12}\Sigma_{22}^{-1}\Sigma_{21}$$

It follows in the above example that

$$E(u_{1t}|v_t) = \sigma_{1v} v_t$$

where $\sigma_{1v} = (\sigma_{12} - \sigma_1^2)/\sigma$. Hence

$$E_{1t} = E(\sigma_{1v} v_t|\gamma'x_{3t} < v_t) = \sigma_{1v} \frac{\phi(\gamma'x_{3t})}{1 - \Phi(\gamma'x_{3t})}$$

by (2.3.4).

But γ can be estimated since δ_t is observed, and accordingly we may estimate the probit model

$$\delta_t = \begin{cases} 1 & \text{if } \gamma'x_{3t} < v_t \\ 0 & \text{otherwise} \end{cases}$$

Replacing γ by its estimate $\hat{\gamma}$, we may then consistently estimate a second stage by OLS from the regression:

$$Q_t = \beta_1'x_{1t} + \sigma_{1v}\frac{\phi(\hat{\gamma}'x_{3t})}{1 - \Phi(\hat{\gamma}'x_{3t})} + (u_{1t} - E_{1t}) \tag{2.6.6}$$

and similarly for the other equation:

$$Q_t = \beta_2'x_{2t} - \sigma_{2v}\frac{\phi(\hat{\gamma}'x_{3t})}{\Phi(\hat{\gamma}'x_{3t})} + (u_{2t} - E_{2t}) \tag{2.6.7}$$

For a more extensive treatment of two-stage methods of this type, the reader should consult Maddala (1983b).

Two-Stage Method for model C

Consider now the structural equations (2.3.16). They contain the jointly dependent variables Q_t, p_t, Δp_t^+, and Δp_t^-. They may therefore be estimated by conventional two-stage least squares by replacing in each equation the right hand jointly dependent variables by the predicted values of these variables from their regressions on all the exogenous variables in the model (Amemiya 1974a). The method was first suggested by Fair and Jaffee (1972) who proposed using the predictions for Δp_t^+ and Δp_t^- only when the corresponding Δp_t^+ and Δp_t^- are nonzero; when they are zero, they suggested using in fact zero in place of the predicted values. This procedure produces inconsistent estimates for the following reason. For simplicity, consider a single structural equation with a single right hand side endogenous variable

$$y = \alpha_1 y_1 + \beta_1'x_1 + u_1$$

The OLS predictions for y_1 are $X(X'X)^{-1}X'y_1$, where X is the $T \times K$ matrix of observations on all exogenous variables. Let X_1 denote the matrix of exogenous variables in this equation. If the OLS predictions are to be used for the subset indexed by a, and if the predictions are replaced by zero for the subset indexed by b, the second-stage equation is

$$y = \begin{bmatrix} y_a \\ y_b \end{bmatrix} = \begin{bmatrix} X_a(X'X)^{-1}X'y_1 & X_{1a} \\ 0 & X_{1b} \end{bmatrix} \begin{bmatrix} \alpha_1 \\ \beta_1 \end{bmatrix} + v$$

Two-stage least squares estimates are obtained by premultiplying by the transpose of the matrix on the right hand side. We have

$$
\begin{bmatrix} \hat{\alpha}_1 \\ \hat{\beta}_1 \end{bmatrix} = \left[\begin{pmatrix} X_a(X'X)^{-1}X'y_1 & X_{1a} \\ 0 & X_{1b} \end{pmatrix}' \begin{pmatrix} X_a(X'X)^{-1}X'y_1 & X_{1a} \\ 0 & X_{1b} \end{pmatrix} \right]^{-1}
$$

$$
\times \begin{bmatrix} y_1'X(X'X)^{-1}X_a'y_a \\ X_{1a}'y_a + X_{1b}'y_b \end{bmatrix}
$$

Substituting for y_a and y_b, and letting G be the matrix inverse above,

$$
\begin{pmatrix} \hat{\alpha}_1 \\ \hat{\beta}_1 \end{pmatrix} - \begin{pmatrix} \alpha \\ \beta \end{pmatrix} = G \begin{pmatrix} y_1'X(X'X)^{-1}X_a'u_a \\ X_{1a}'u_a + X_{1b}'u_b \end{pmatrix}
$$

Since the replacement of the predicted values by zero is *not exogenous*, the plim $X_a'u_a/T$ is not zero and hence $\hat{\alpha}_1$ cannot be consistent.

This difficulty does not arise if the predictions of the right hand side endogenous variables are used for all the observations. But even in this case, the estimates cannot be efficient since they fail to take advantage of (a) the cross-equation restriction due to γ, and (b) the fact that Δp_t^+, Δp_t^- are non-linear functions of a basic endogenous variable.

Nonlinear Least Squares Estimation

Some of the difficulties of maximum likelihood estimation may be avoided by the minimum distance estimators recommended by Nasim and Satchell (1982, 1984), Frei (1984), and Stalder (1984). We concentrate on (2.1.1) to (2.1.3) of model A, allowing for a covariance between u_{1t} and u_{2t}. The strategy of minimum distance estimation will be to express $E(Q_t)$ in terms of parameters and exogenous variables and to minimize $[Q - E(Q)]'S[Q-E(Q)]$, where Q and $E(Q)$ are vectors and S is some positive definite matrix. In practice, this makes the problem one of nonlinear least squares.

Define the (endogenous) dummy variable δ_t by

$$
\delta_t = \begin{cases} 0 & \text{if } D_t > S_t \\ 1 & \text{otherwise} \end{cases}
$$

Multiplying (2.1.1) by δ_t, (2.1.2) by $1 - \delta_t$, and adding, we obtain[4]

$$
Q_t = \delta_t\beta_1'x_{1t} + (1-\delta_t)\beta_2'x_{2t} + \delta_t u_{1t} + (1-\delta_t)u_{2t} \tag{2.6.8}
$$

since $Q_t = D_t$ if $D_t < S_t$ and conversely. Noting that $E(\delta_t) = \Pr\{D_t \leq S_t\} =$

---

[4] The reader may compare this to the switching regression technique in Goldfeld and Quandt (1972, chapter 8), Ginsburgh, Tishler and Zang (1980), and Tishler and Zang (1977, 1979).

$Pr\{u_{1t} - u_{2t} \leqq \beta_2' x_{2t} - \beta_1' x_{1t}\} = \Phi(v_t)$, where $v_t = (\beta_2' x_{2t} - \beta_1' x_{1t})/\sigma$, $\sigma^2 = \sigma_1^2 + \sigma_2^2 - 2\sigma_{12}$, and taking the expectation of (2.6.8),

$$E(Q_t) = \Phi(v_t)\beta_1' x_{1t} + [1 - \Phi(v_t)]\beta_2' x_{2t} + E[\delta_t u_{1t} + (1 - \delta_t)u_{2t}] \qquad (2.6.9)$$

To evaluate the last expectation in (2.6.9) we require $E(\delta_t u_{1t})$, $E[(1 - \delta_t)u_{2t}]$. Now

$$\delta_t u_{1t} = \begin{cases} u_{1t} & \text{if } u_{1t} - u_{2t} \leqq \beta_2' x_{2t} - \beta_1' x_{1t} \\ 0 & \text{otherwise} \end{cases}$$

Letting $\xi(u_{1t}, u_{1t} - u_{2t})$ be the joint p.d.f. of u_{1t}, $u_{1t} - u_{2t}$, we can write

$$E(\delta_t u_{1t}) = \int_{-\infty}^{v_t\sigma} \int_{-\infty}^{\infty} u_{1t}\xi(u_{1t}, u_{1t} - u_{2t})\,du_{1t}\,d(u_{1t} - u_{2t}) \qquad (2.6.10)$$

Since $\xi(u_{1t}, u_{1t} - u_{2t}) = \xi_1(u_{1t}|u_{1t} - u_{2t})\xi_2(u_{1t} - u_{2t})$
where

$$\xi_2(u_{1t} - u_{2t}) = \frac{1}{\sqrt{(2\pi)}\sigma} \exp\left\{-\frac{(u_{1t} - u_{2t})^2}{2\sigma^2}\right\}$$

and $\xi_1(u_{1t}|u_{1t} - u_{2t})$ is normal density with mean equal to $(\sigma_1^2 - \sigma_{12}) \times (u_{1t} - u_{2t})/\sigma^2$ and variance equal to $\sigma_1^2 - (\sigma_1^2 - \sigma_{12})^2/\sigma^2$, the integral in (2.6.10) becomes

$$E(\delta_t u_{1t}) = \int_{-\infty}^{v_t\sigma} \frac{(\sigma_1^2 - \sigma_{12})(u_{1t} - u_{2t})}{\sigma^2} \frac{1}{\sqrt{(2\pi)}\sigma}$$

$$\times \exp\left\{-\frac{(u_{1t} - u_{2t})^2}{2\sigma^2}\right\} d(u_{1t} - u_{2t})$$

Letting $(u_{1t} - u_{2t})/\sigma = r_t$,

$$E(\delta_t u_{1t}) = \frac{\sigma_1^2 - \sigma_{12}}{\sigma^2} \int_{-\infty}^{v_t} \frac{1}{\sqrt{(2\pi)}} \sigma r_t e^{-r_t^2/2}\,dr_t$$

$$= -\frac{(\sigma_1^2 - \sigma_{12})}{\sigma} \frac{1}{\sqrt{(2\pi)}} \exp\left\{-\frac{(\beta_2' x_{2t} - \beta_1' x_{1t})^2}{\sigma^2}\right\}$$

$$= -(\sigma_1^2 - \sigma_{12})\phi(v_t)/\sigma$$

Analogously,

$$E[(1 - \delta_t)u_{2t}] = -(\sigma_2^2 - \sigma_{12})\phi(v_t)/\sigma$$

and so

$$E[\delta_t u_{1t} + (1-\delta_t)u_{2t}] = -\sigma \phi(v_t)$$

Equation (2.6.9) then becomes

$$E(Q_t) = \Phi(v_t)\beta_1' x_{1t} + [1-\Phi(v_t)]\beta_2' x_{2t} - \sigma\phi(v_t) \qquad (2.6.11)$$

This immediately shows that $E(Q_t)$ is less than $\beta_2' x_{2t}$ (and, similarly, than $\beta_1' x_{1t}$). Equation (2.6.11) can be written as (see also Gourieroux, Laffont and Monfort 1984)

$$E(Q_t) = \beta_2' x_{2t} - \sigma[\Phi(v_t)v_t + \phi(v_t)]$$

If a random variable ν is distributed as $N(0,1)$ and truncated from above by v_t, then $E(\nu) = -\phi(v_t)/\Phi(v_t)$; but this expected value itself must not exceed the truncation value v_t, and hence $-\phi(v_t)/\Phi(v_t) \le v_t$. Hence the bracketed expression above is nonnegative, which proves the claim. In the first instance, then, estimation may be performed by selecting S to be the identity matrix and minimizing

$$\sum_{t=1}^{T} [Q_t - E(Q_t)]^2 \qquad (2.6.12)$$

which allows estimation of β_1, β_2, and σ^2, but not of σ_1^2, σ_2^2, σ_{12} separately.

Because of the heteroscedasticity of the terms $Q_t - E(Q_t)$ (see below for the variance of Q_t), the estimates are inefficient (albeit consistent) and the estimated covariance matrix is inconsistent. Hajivassiliou (1983) suggests applying White's (1980) covariance correction. Let $\beta' = (\beta_1', \beta_2')$ and denote $F = \partial E(Q)/\partial\beta$, a $T \times (k_1+k_2)$ matrix, and let $\hat{F}$ be the matrix F evaluated at the estimates that minimize (2.6.12). Then the appropriate covariance matrix is $V = (\hat{F}'\hat{F})^{-1}(\hat{F}' \hat{\Omega}\hat{F})(\hat{F}'\hat{F})^{-1}$, where $\hat{\Omega}$ is a diagonal matrix with $Q_t - \widehat{E(Q_t)}$ for diagonal elements.

Generalized or weighted least squares estimates may be obtained by minimizing $[Q - E(Q)]'S[Q - E(Q)]$, where S is a diagonal matrix with diagonal elements equal to the reciprocal of the tth term's relative contribution to the variance, i.e. to $[\sum_t \text{var}(Q_t)]/\text{var}(Q_t)$. Nasim and Satchell (1982) and Frei (1984) show that

$$\text{var}(Q_t) = \sigma_1^2\theta_{1t} + \sigma_2^2\theta_{2t} + \sigma_{12}\theta_{3t} + \theta_{4t}$$

where

$$\theta_{1t} = \Phi(v_t) + v_t\phi(v_t)$$

$$\theta_{2t} = 1 - \Phi(v_t) + v_t\phi(v_t)$$

$$\theta_{3t} = -2 v_t\phi(v_t)$$

$$\theta_{4t} = (\sigma v_t)^2\Phi(v_t)[1-\Phi(v_t)] - \sigma^2\phi(v_t)^2 - 2\sigma^2 v_t\phi(v_t)\Phi(v_t)$$

From the estimates obtained by minimizing (2.6.12) we can obtain estimates of $[Q_t - E(Q_t)]^2$, $\hat{\theta}_{1t}$, $\hat{\theta}_{2t}$, $\hat{\theta}_{3t}$, $\hat{\theta}_{4t}$. Nasim and Satchell suggest regressing $[Q_t - E(Q_t)]^2$ on $\hat{\theta}_{1t}, \ldots, \hat{\theta}_{4t}$ and using the estimated coefficients as estimates of $\hat{\sigma}_1^2$, $\hat{\sigma}_2^2$, $\hat{\sigma}_{12}$.

Moment Generating Function Method

The MGF method was developed by Quandt and Ramsey (1978) and Schmidt (1982), primarily for mixtures of normal distributions and switching regressions. The simplest problem is that of a mixture of normal densities: the observed random variable y is generated as

$$y \sim N(\mu_1, \sigma_1^2) \quad \text{with probability } \lambda$$

or $\qquad\qquad\qquad\qquad\qquad\qquad\qquad\qquad\qquad\qquad\qquad$ (2.6.13)

$$y \sim N(\mu_2, \sigma_2^2) \quad \text{with probability } 1 - \lambda$$

The switching regression model is obtained if the means μ_1, μ_2 are no longer constant but are replaced by $\beta_1' x_{1t}$, $\beta_2' x_{2t}$ respectively. The MGF method rests on choosing the unknown parameters in such a fashion as to minimize the generalized sum of squares of deviations between the theoretical and the sample moment generating functions. It follows from (2.6.13) that the theoretical moment generating function is

$$E(e^{\theta y}) = \lambda \exp(\mu_1 \theta + \sigma_1^2 \theta^2 / 2) + (1 - \lambda)\exp(\mu_2 \theta + \sigma_2^2 \theta^2 / 2) \qquad (2.6.14)$$

Imagine that we have chosen some particular values of θ, denoted by $\theta_1, \ldots, \theta_k$, where $k \geq 5$, the number of parameters to be estimated in the simple mixture model. Given a sample of y_i, $i = 1, \ldots, n$, we can define

$$x_{ij} = e^{\theta_j y_i}$$

$$\gamma = (\mu_1, \mu_2, \sigma_1^2, \sigma_2^2, \lambda)$$

$$G(\gamma, \theta_j) = \lambda \exp(\mu_1 \theta_j + \sigma_1^2 \theta_j^2 / 2) + (1 - \lambda)\exp(\mu_2 \theta_j + \sigma_2^2 \theta_j^2 / 2)$$

$$v_{ij} = x_{ij} - G(\gamma, \theta_j)$$

$$\bar{x}_j = \frac{1}{n} \sum_{i=1}^{n} x_{ij}$$

$$\bar{v}_j = \frac{1}{n} \sum_{i=1}^{n} v_{ij} = \bar{x}_j - G(\gamma, \theta_j)$$

Quandt and Ramsey propose to minimize

$$S_1 = \sum_{j=1}^{k} \bar{v}_j^2 \qquad\qquad\qquad\qquad\qquad\qquad\qquad (2.6.15)$$

with respect to γ, which is also equivalent to minimizing

$$S_2 = \sum_{j=1}^{k} \sum_{i=1}^{n} v_{ij}^2 / n$$

The consistency of the resulting estimates follows by applying the following:

Theorem (Rockafellar)   Let $h(x)$ be a closed proper convex function which attains its infimum at a unique x^0. If $x_1, x_2, \ldots$ is any sequence such that $h(x_1), h(x_2), \ldots$ converges to $\inf(h)$, then $x_1, x_2, \ldots$ converges to x^0.

In the present case, the x_{ij} are distributed identically with finite variance, and by the strong law of large numbers $\bar{x}_j \rightarrow G(\gamma, \theta_j)$ almost surely; hence $S_1 \rightarrow 0$ almost surely. Differentiating (2.6.15) twice, we obtain

$$\frac{\partial S_1}{\partial \gamma} = -2 \sum_{j=1}^{k} \bar{v}_j \frac{\partial G}{\partial \gamma} \tag{2.6.16}$$

$$\frac{\partial^2 S_1}{\partial \gamma \partial \gamma'} = -2 \sum_{j=1}^{k} \bar{v}_j \frac{\partial^2 G}{\partial \gamma \partial \gamma'} + 2 \sum_{j=1}^{k} \frac{\partial G}{\partial \gamma} \frac{\partial G}{\partial \gamma'} \tag{2.6.17}$$

Since the first term of the Hessian goes to zero, and $k \geq 5$, $\partial^2 S_1 / \partial \gamma \partial \gamma'$ has a positive definite limit. Hence S_1 satisfies the conditions of the theorem and it follows that $\hat{\gamma} \rightarrow \gamma$ almost surely.

It can also be shown that

$$\sqrt{(n)} \, (\hat{\gamma} - \gamma) \rightarrow N(0, V_1)$$

where

$$V_1 = (A'A)^{-1} A' \Omega A (A'A)^{-1}$$

$$\left. \begin{array}{l} A_{ij} = \dfrac{\partial G(\gamma, \theta_i)}{\gamma_j} \\[2ex] \Omega_{ij} = G(\gamma, \theta_i + \theta_j) - G(\gamma, \theta_i) G(\gamma, \theta_j) \end{array} \right\} \quad \begin{array}{l} i = 1, \ldots, k \\[2ex] j = 1, \ldots, 5 \end{array}$$

Schmidt (1982) has noted that the covariance matrix V_1 has the same form as the covariance matrix in OLS. It follows that if Ω is not a scalar matrix, as it is not in the present case, the ordinary least squares estimates will be inefficient. Schmidt therefore proposes estimation by minimizing the generalized least squares

$$S_3 = \bar{v}' \, \Omega^{-1} \, \bar{v}$$

where $\bar{v}' = (\bar{v}_1, \ldots, \bar{v}_k)$. The resulting estimator $\bar{\gamma}$ also has asymptotically normal distribution and

$$\sqrt{(n)} \, (\bar{\gamma} - \gamma) \rightarrow N(0, V_3)$$

where $V_3 = (A' \Omega^{-1} A)^{-1}$.

In all of this the choice of θs was arbitrary, subject to there being at least five different θs (without at least five, the normal equations obtained by setting equal to zero (2.6.16) become singular). Schmidt has explored a suggestion of Kiefer's (1978c) to choose the θs so as to minimize the determinant of the asymptotic covariance matrix, and found that the spread of optimal θs tended to be very small (within 0.03). It also appears that there is some sensitivity in the asymptotic variances to the θs, but relatively less so if their number is not too close to five. Computation of the estimates by the MGF method requires numerical optimization and is therefore more difficult than, say, OLS, but it is not more difficult than maximum likelihood estimation and avoids the unboundedness problem encountered occasionally by the latter.

The approach is similar but more complicated in the switching regression case. In these cases, as well as in other models, a similar approach would be to "fit" the characteristic function. This approach has been employed by Arad Wiener (1975) with respect to the stable Paretian family of distributions. Bowden (1979) has derived the characteristic function of the simple disequilibrium model as

$$\int_{-\infty}^{\infty} e^{i\theta Q} h(Q) dQ = \exp\{i\theta\beta_1' x_1 - \sigma_1^2\theta^2/2\}$$

$$\times \left[1 - \int_{-\infty}^{i\theta\sigma_1^2} \frac{1}{\sqrt{(2\pi)}\sigma} \exp\left\{ - \frac{[z - (\beta_2' x_2 - \beta_1' x_1)]^2}{2\sigma^2} \right\} dz \right]$$

$$+ \exp\{i\theta\beta_2' x_2 - \sigma_2^2\theta^2/2\}$$

$$\times \left[1 - \int_{-\infty}^{i\theta\sigma_2^2} \frac{1}{\sqrt{(2\pi)}\sigma} \exp\left\{ - \frac{[z - (\beta_1' x_1 - \beta_2' x_2)]^2}{2\sigma^2} \right\} dz \right]$$

where $\sigma^2 = \sigma_1^2 + \sigma_2^2$. Minimizing a sum of squares analogous to (2.6.15) requires power series approximations to the terms above so that the characteristic function can be approximated as $G_1(\gamma,\theta) + iG_2(\gamma,\theta)$, where γ represents all the unknown parameters. One may then form the sums of squares of deviations between these terms and their sample equivalents. This does not yet appear to have been tried out in practice.

2.7   The EM Algorithm

The EM algorithm, due to Dempster, Laird and Rubin (1977), is a computational method for obtaining maximum likelihood estimates in incomplete data problems such as the switching regression model, the tobit model, or the disequilibrium model. We assume that there exists a density function with parameter vector θ over the unobserved random variable $y*$

$$f(y*|\theta) \tag{2.7.1}$$

and a mapping $y^* \rightarrow y(y^*)$, where y represents the observed data. The density of y then is

$$g(y|\theta) = \int_{Y^*(y)} f(y^*|\theta)dy^* \qquad (2.7.2)$$

where $Y^*(y)$ denotes the region in y^*-space that maps into y. Thus, for example, in the tobit model

$$y_t^* = \beta'x_t + u_t$$

and

$$f(y_t^*|\beta,\sigma^2) = \frac{1}{\sqrt{(2\pi)}\sigma} \exp\left\{-\frac{(y_t^* - \beta'x_t)^2}{2\sigma^2}\right\}$$

$$y = \begin{cases} y^* & \text{if } y^* > 0 \\ 0 & \text{otherwise} \end{cases}$$

Hence

$$g(y|\theta) = \begin{cases} \dfrac{1}{\sqrt{(2\pi)}\sigma} \exp\left\{-\dfrac{(y_t - \beta'x_t)^2}{2\sigma^2}\right\} & \text{if } y^* > 0 \\ \phi\left(-\dfrac{\beta'x_t}{\sigma}\right) & \text{otherwise} \end{cases}$$

Restricting our attention to the exponential class of densities (see Dempster, Laird and Rubin 1977 for other cases), we can write the likelihood for the complete data problem as

$$L^*(y^*|\theta) = b(y^*)e^{\theta'T(y^*)}/a(\theta) \qquad (2.7.3)$$

where $T(y^*)$ is the vector of natural sufficient statistics by the factorization theorem (Rao 1973). It follows immediately that the likelihood for the incomplete data problem (i.e. when we observe only y) is

$$L(y|\theta) = \int_{Y^*(y)} L^*(y^*|\theta)dy^* \qquad (2.7.4)$$

Substituting from (2.7.3) and taking logarithms,

$$\log L(y|\theta) = \log \int_{Y^*(y)} b(y^*)e^{\theta'T(y^*)}dy^* - \log a(\theta) \qquad (2.7.5)$$

The key idea in the EM algorithm is that an iterative method of estimation emerges if we alternately maximize the complete and incomplete data likelihoods. Dealing first with the complete data case, taking logs of (2.7.3) and differentiating,

$$\frac{\partial \log L^*(y^*)}{\partial \theta} = T(y^*) - \frac{\partial \log a(\theta)}{\partial \theta} = 0 \tag{2.7.6}$$

Differentiating (2.7.5) and setting equal to zero yields

$$\frac{\partial \log L(y|\theta)}{\partial \theta} = \left[\int_{Y^*(y)} b(y^*)e^{\theta'T(y^*)}dy^*\right]^{-1}$$

$$\times \left[\int_{Y^*(y)} b(y^*)e^{\theta'T(y^*)}T(y^*)dy^*\right] - \frac{\partial \log a(\theta)}{\partial \theta} = 0 \tag{2.7.7}$$

Introduce $1/a(\theta)$ into the second bracket of (2.7.7) and a compensating $1/a(\theta)$ in the first. The first bracket is then the probability of observing y since it is the integral of the joint density of y^* over the region defined by the mapping $Y^*(y)$. The ratio of the two brackets is then the integral of $T(y^*)$ multiplied by the conditional density of y^*, and can be written formally as

$$\int_{Y^*(y)} T(y^*)h(y^*|y)dy^* = E[T(y^*)|y,\theta] \tag{2.7.8}$$

where $h(y^*|y)$ is the conditional density of y^*. We can then proceed as follows:

1   E-step: start with any value of θ, say θ^k. Use (2.7.7) to determine $E[T(y^*)|y,\theta^k]$.
2   M-step: replace $T(y^*)$ in (2.7.6) by $E[T(y^*)|y,\theta^k]$ and solve (2.7.6) for a new value of θ, say θ^{k+1}.
3   Continue iterating between steps 1 and 2 until convergence is reached.

It is clear that if convergence occurs, the first-order conditions (2.7.7) for a maximum are satisfied. If convergence occurs, $\theta^k = \theta^{k+1}$ and $E[T(y^*)|y,\theta^k] = \partial \log a(\theta^{k+1})/\partial \theta$ by the M-step; $\partial \log a(\theta^k)/\partial \theta = \partial \log a(\theta^{k+1})/\partial \theta$ by convergence; hence $E[T(y^*)|y,\theta^k] = \partial \log a(\theta^k)/\partial \theta$, which shows that (2.7.7) is satisfied.

Simple Example

Dempster, Laird and Rubin consider the multinomial case of five categories with the number of outcomes in each being given by y_i^*. Assuming that the probabilities of the five categories on a single trial are $1/2$, $p/4$, $(1-p)/4$, $(1-p)/4$, $p/4$, with p unknown, the complete data likelihood is

$$f^*(y^*|p) = \frac{\left(\sum_i y_i^*\right)!}{\prod_i y_i^*!} \left(\frac{1}{2}\right)^{y_1^*} \left(\frac{p}{4}\right)^{y_2^*} \left(\frac{1-p}{4}\right)^{y_3^*} \left(\frac{1-p}{4}\right)^{y_4^*} \left(\frac{p}{4}\right)^{y_5^*}$$

$$\tag{2.7.9}$$

If the first two categories are not observed separately, but only their sum, $y_1 = y_1^* + y_2^*, y_2 = y_3^*, y_3 = y_4^*, y_4 = y_5^*$, then the incomplete likelihood is

$$f^*(y^*|p) = \frac{\left(\sum\limits_{i=1}^{4} y_i\right)!}{\prod\limits_{i=1}^{4} y_i!} \left(\frac{1}{2} + \frac{p}{4}\right)^{y_1} \left(\frac{1-p}{4}\right)^{y_2} \left(\frac{1-p}{4}\right)^{y_3} \left(\frac{p}{4}\right)^{y_4}$$

$$(2.7.10)$$

The M-step is to use $E(y_1^*|y,p), E(y_2^*|y,p)$ and to compute p from (2.7.9) by maximizing with respect to p:

$$\hat{p} = \frac{E(y_2^*|y,p) + y_5^*}{E(y_2^*|y,p) + y_3^* + y_4^* + y_5^*}$$

The E-step is to compute the relevant expectations, using the value $\hat{p}$:

$$E(y_2^*|y,p) = E(y_2^*|y_1^* + y_2^*, p) = y_1 \Pr\{y_2^*|y_1\} = y_1 \left(\frac{p/4}{1/2+p/4}\right)$$

Convergence in the example is extremely rapid. Assume that $y_1 = 18$, $y_3^* = 5, y_4^* = 3, y_5^* = 6$. The course of iterations, starting at $p^0 = 0.375$, is as follows:

Iteration	$E(y_2^*|y,p)$	p
0	—	0.375 00
1	2.842 11	0.525 00
2	3.752 57	0.549 11
3	3.877 41	0.552 98
4	3.896 22	0.553 04
5	3.898 22	0.553 05
6	3.899 18	0.553 05

Switching Regressions

This model has been considered by Kiefer (1980b) as an example of the applicability of the EM algorithm. We employ the following form of the model:

$$y_i = \beta_1' x_i + u_{1i} \quad \text{with probability } \lambda$$

and

$$(2.7.11)$$

$$y_i = \beta_2' x_i + u_{2i} \quad \text{with probability } 1 - \lambda$$

where u_{1i} and u_{2i} are i.i.d. normal with zero means and variances σ_1^2, σ_2^2. The (incomplete) data density is

$$f(y_i) = \frac{\lambda}{\sqrt{(2\pi)}\sigma_1} \exp\left\{-\frac{(y_i-\beta_1'x_i)^2}{2\sigma_1^2}\right\} + \frac{1-\lambda}{\sqrt{(2\pi)}\sigma_2} \exp\left\{-\frac{(y_i-\beta_2'x_i)^2}{2\sigma_2^2}\right\}$$

$$i=1,\ldots,n$$

$$(2.7.12)$$

If we had a complete data problem, i.e. if the regime assignment were known, we could define w_i $(i=1,\ldots,n)$ as 1 if the ith observation belonged to the first regime of (2.7.11) and 0 otherwise. Forming the matrices $W_1 = \text{diag}(w_i)$ and $W_2 = I - W_1$, and denoting by X and Y and $n \times k$ and $n \times 1$ matrices of observations on x_i and y_i, we can write the maximum likelihood estimates for the complete data problem as

$$\hat{\beta}_j = (X'W_jX)^{-1}X'W_jY \qquad j=1,2 \tag{2.7.13}$$

$$\hat{\lambda} = \sum_{i=1}^{n} w_i/n \tag{2.7.14}$$

$$\mu_1 = \hat{\lambda}$$

$$\mu_2 = 1 - \hat{\lambda}$$

$$\hat{\sigma}_j^2 = \frac{1}{n\mu_j}(Y-X\hat{\beta}_j)'W_j(Y-X\hat{\beta}_j) \qquad j=1,2 \tag{2.7.15}$$

For given values of w_i, these estimates represent the M-step. Given the values of the parameters, we obtain $E(w|y)$ from the E-step:

$$\begin{aligned} E(w|y) &= (1)\Pr\{w=1|y\} + (0)\Pr\{w=0|y\} \\ &= \frac{f(y|w=1)\Pr\{w=1\}}{f(y)} \\ &= \frac{\lambda\exp\{(y-\beta_1'x)^2/2\sigma_1^2\}}{\lambda\exp\{-(y-\beta_1'x)^2/2\sigma_1^2\} + (1-\lambda)\exp\{-(y-\beta_2'x)^2/2\sigma_2^2\}} \end{aligned}$$

$$(2.7.16)$$

In the EM algorithm, the values of $E(w|y)$ are then used in the place of w in the M-step. It is clear that if convergence occurs, the resulting estimates are the maximum likelihood estimates of the incomplete data problem. To show this, add the logarithms of (2.7.12) to form the log-likelihood function and differentiate:

$$\frac{\partial \log L}{\partial \beta_j} = \sum_{i=1}^{n}\left(\frac{\lambda f_{ji}}{f_i}\right)\frac{(y_i-\beta_j'x_i)^2}{\sigma_j^2} = 0 \tag{2.7.17}$$

$$\frac{\partial \log L}{\partial \sigma_j^2} = \sum_{i=1}^{n}\left(\frac{\lambda f_{ji}}{f_i}\right)\left[-\frac{1}{2\sigma_j^2}+\frac{(y_i-\beta_j'x_i)^2}{2\sigma_j^4}\right] = 0 \tag{2.7.18}$$

$$\frac{\partial \log L}{\partial \lambda} = \sum_{i=1}^{n} \left(\frac{f_{1i} - f_{2i}}{f_i} \right) = 0 \qquad (2.7.19)$$

where we denote $f(y_i)$ from (2.7.12) by f_i and where

$$f_{ji} = \exp \left\{ - \frac{(y_i - \beta_j' x_i)^2}{2\sigma_j^2} \right\} \Big/ \sqrt{(2\pi)} \sigma_j$$

Since, from (2.7.16), $\lambda f_{1i}/f_i = w_i$, (2.7.17) is the same as (2.7.13). Substituting $f_{1i} = w_i f_i / \lambda$ and $f_{2i} = (1 - w_i) f_i / (1 - \lambda)$ in (2.7.19) yields

$$\hat{\lambda} = \sum_{i=1}^{n} w_i / n \qquad (2.7.20)$$

Finally, (2.7.18) can be simplified to

$$\sigma_1^2 = \frac{\sum_{i=1}^{n} w_i (y_i - \beta_1' x_i)^2}{\sum_{i=1}^{n} w_i}, \qquad \sigma_2^2 = \frac{\sum_{i=1}^{n} (1 - w_i)(y_i - \beta_2' x_i)^2}{\sum_{i=1}^{n} (1 - w_i)}$$

which, using (2.7.20), becomes (2.7.15).

Kiefer (1980b) has also derived the result that if $\sigma_1^2 = \sigma_2^2 = \sigma^2$ *a priori*, the quantity $E(w|y)$ has the logistic form $[1 + \exp(a + by)]^{-1}$, where a and b depend on parameters and on the xs.

Simple Disequilibrium Model

Consider once again the model given by (2.1.1) to (2.1.3). The EM algorithm was applied to this by Hartley (1977). If this were not an incomplete data problem, i.e. if D_t and S_t were observed, then the joint density of D_t, S_t would be

$$g(D_t, S_t) = \frac{1}{2\pi\sigma_1\sigma_2(1 - \rho^2)^{1/2}} \exp \left\{ - \frac{1}{2} [(D_t - \beta_1' x_{1t})^2 \sigma^{11} \right.$$

$$\left. - 2(D_t - \beta_1' x_{1t})(S_t - \beta_2' x_{2t}) \sigma^{12} + (S_t - \beta_2' x_{2t})^2 \sigma^{22}] \right\} \quad (2.7.21)$$

where σ^{ij} are the inverse elements of the covariance matrix and $\rho = \sigma_{12}/\sigma_1\sigma_2$. Thus the M-step involves maximizing the log-likelihood based on (2.7.21), which yields asymptotically the same estimates as the seemingly unrelated regression method.

In order to perform the E-step, we require the expected values $E(D_t|Q_t)$, $E(S_t|Q_t)$. We derive $E(D_t|Q_t)$; *mutatis mutandis*, this also gives us $E(S_t|Q_t)$. We first need the partial first moment of the normal density. We have

Lemma   Given the random variable $x \sim N(\mu, \sigma^2)$,

$$\int_q^\infty x\psi(x;\mu,\sigma^2)dx = \sigma^2\psi(q;\mu,\sigma^2) + \mu[1 - \Psi(q;\mu,\sigma^2)]$$

Proof   Using the substitution $(x-\mu)/\sigma = z$, we have

$$\int_q^\infty \frac{x}{\sqrt{(2\pi)}\sigma} \exp\left\{\frac{(x-\mu)^2}{2\sigma^2}\right\} dx = \frac{1}{\sqrt{(2\pi)}} \int_{(q-\mu)/\sigma}^\infty (\sigma z + \mu)\exp\{-z^2/2\}\,dz$$

$$= \frac{\sigma}{\sqrt{(2\pi)}} \exp\left\{-\frac{(q-\mu)^2}{2\sigma^2}\right\}$$

$$+ \mu \int_q^\infty \frac{1}{\sqrt{(2\pi)}\sigma} \exp\left\{-\frac{(x-\mu)^2}{2\sigma^2}\right\}dx$$

$$= \sigma^2\psi(q;\mu,\sigma^2) + \mu[1 - \Psi(q;\mu,\sigma^2)] \qquad \square$$

It is convenient to introduce the following notation to represent the density function $h(Q_t)$ in (2.3.9):

$$h(Q_t) = h_1(Q_t) + h_2(Q_t) \tag{2.7.22}$$

We continue to denote the joint p.d.f. of D_t, S_t by $g(D_t, S_t)$ as in (2.3.6) and (2.3.7). We can then write the density of D_t conditional on Q_t as

$$g(D_t|Q_t) = \begin{cases} 0 & \text{if } D_t < Q_t \\ h_1(Q_t)/h(Q_t) & \text{if } D_t = Q_t \\ g(D_t,Q_t)/h(Q_t) & \text{if } D_t > Q_t \end{cases} \tag{2.7.23}$$

The reasons are that:

1    $D_t < Q_t$ cannot occur by the statement of the disequilibrium model.
2   When $D_t = Q_t$, $g(D_t|Q_t)$ is given by the probability that $D_t < S_t$ conditional on Q_t, which is $h_1(Q_t)/h(Q_t)$.
3    $g(D_t,Q_t)/h(Q_t)$ is the definition of $g(D_t|Q_t)$ for $D_t > Q_t$.

It follows that

$$E(D_t|Q_t) = \frac{Q_t h_1(Q_t)}{h(Q_t)} + \int_{Q_t}^\infty \frac{D_t g(D_t,Q_t)}{h(Q_t)}\,dD_t \tag{2.7.24}$$

To simplify (2.7.24), we need to introduce some additional notation. First, we define

$$h_i(Q_t) = g_i(Q_t)[1 - G_j(Q_t)] \qquad i,j = 1,2 \text{ and } i \neq j \tag{2.7.25}$$

where g_i ($i = 1,2$) stands for the two densities and G_j for the normal integrals in (2.3.9). Inspection of (2.3.9) shows that $G_j(Q_t)$ is the cumulative distribution of demand (supply) *conditional on* supply (demand) and evaluated at Q_t. Letting $g_1(D_t|S_t)$ be the conditional density of D_t given S_t (and $g_2(S_t|D_t)$ that of S_t given D_t), we can write the conditional density of D_t, given that $S_t = Q_t$, as

$$h_1(D_t|S_t = Q_t) = \frac{g_1(D_t|Q_t)}{1 - G_1(Q_t)} \qquad (2.7.26)$$

because D_t is truncated at Q_t. Now define the weights

$$w_i(Q_t) = h_i(Q_t)/h(Q_t) = \frac{g_i(Q_t)[1 - G_j(Q_t)]}{h(Q_t)} \qquad i,j = 1,2 \qquad (2.7.27)$$

Hence, multiplying (2.7.26) by w_2 and evaluating at $D_t = Q_t$,

$$h_1(Q_t|Q_t) w_2(Q_t) = \frac{g_2(Q_t)g_1(Q_t|Q_t)}{h(Q_t)} = \frac{g(Q_t, Q_t)}{h(Q_t)} \qquad (2.7.28)$$

Now consider the integral on the right hand side of (2.7.24):

$$\int_{Q_t}^{\infty} \frac{D_t g(D_t, Q_t)}{h(Q_t)} \, \mathrm{d}D_t = \frac{1}{h(Q_t)} \int_{Q_t}^{\infty} D_t g_1(D_t|Q_t) g_2(Q_t) \mathrm{d}D_t$$

$$= \frac{g_2(Q_t)}{h(Q_t)} \int_{Q_t}^{\infty} D_t g_1(D_t|Q_t) \mathrm{d}D_t$$

$$= \frac{g_2(Q_t)}{h(Q_t)} \{\sigma_{1.2}^2 g_1(Q_t|Q_t) + \mu_{1.2t}[1 - G_1(Q_t)]\}$$

$$(2.7.29)$$

since $G_1(Q_t)$ is the cumulative of the conditional density $g_1(Q_t|Q_t)$ and by the lemma, and where $\mu_{1.2t}$ and $\sigma_{1.2}^2$ are the mean and variance of the conditional density g_1. (Note that $\mu_{1.2t}$ depends on t.) Replacing g_1 in (2.7.29) from (2.7.26), (2.7.29) becomes

$$\frac{g_2(Q_t)[1 - G_1(Q_t)]}{h(Q_t)} [\sigma_{1.2}^2 h_1(Q_t|Q_t) + \mu_{1.2t}] = \frac{h_2(Q_t)}{h(Q_t)} [\sigma_{1.2}^2 h_1(Q_t|Q_t) + \mu_{1.2t}]$$

$$= \sigma_{1.2}^2 \frac{g(Q_t, Q_t)}{h(Q_t)} + w_2(Q_t)\mu_{1.2t}$$

$$(2.7.30)$$

by (2.7.27) and (2.7.28). Combining (2.7.30) with (2.7.24) and noting that $\mu_{1.2t} = \beta_1' x_{1t} + \rho(\sigma_1/\sigma_2)(Q_t - \beta_2' x_{2t})$ and $\sigma_{1.2}^2 = \sigma_1^2(1 - \rho^2)$,

$$E(D_t|Q_t) = w_1(Q_t)Q_t + w_2(Q_t)\left[\beta_1'x_{1t} + \rho\,\frac{\sigma_1}{\sigma_2}\,(Q_t - \beta_2'x_{2t})\right]$$

$$+ \sigma_1^2(1-\rho^2)\,\frac{g(Q_t,Q_t)}{h(Q_t)} \tag{2.7.31}$$

with a corresponding expression for $E(S_t|Q_t)$.

The EM algorithm can thus, for each set of parameter values obtained in the previous M-step, compute the appropriate expectations in the E-step, from which the next M-step becomes possible. As Hartley (1977) has noted, the conditional expectation of demand (supply) is a weighted average of the transacted amount and the conditional mean demand (supply) plus a correction term for the conditional variance.

2.8   The Probabilities of Excess Demand

There are two main concepts of the probability that an observation corresponds to excess demand. These are the unconditional probability $\Pr\{D_t > S_t\}$ and the probability conditional on the observed transactions, $\Pr\{D_t > S_t|Q_t\}$.

The former is obtained as follows. In model A,

$$\Pr\{D_t > S_t\} = \Pr\{\beta_1'x_{1t} + u_{1t} > \beta_2'x_{2t} + u_{2t}\}$$

$$= \Pr\left\{\frac{\beta_1'x_{1t} - \beta_2'x_{2t}}{\sigma} > \frac{u_{2t} - u_{1t}}{\sigma}\right\}$$

$$= \Phi\left(\frac{\beta_1'x_{1t} - \beta_2'x_{2t}}{\sigma}\right) \tag{2.8.1}$$

where $\sigma^2 = \mathrm{var}(u_{2t} - u_{1t})$. Since $\beta_1'x_{1t}$ is the unconditional expectation $E(D_t)$ and $\beta_2'x_{2t}$ is $E(S_t)$, it follows immediately that $\Pr\{D_t > S_t\} > 0.5$ if and only if $E(D_t) > E(S_t)$ (Gersovitz 1980).

The conditional probability can be written formally as

$$\Pr\{D_t > S_t|Q_t\} = \frac{f(Q_t|D_t > S_t)\Pr\{D_t > S_t\}}{h(Q_t)} \tag{2.8.2}$$

By (2.3.5), this clearly turns out to be the second term of the density of Q_t divided by the density of Q_t or, from (2.3.7),

$$\Pr\{D_t > S_t|Q_t\} = \int_{Q_t}^{\infty} g(D_t,Q_t)\mathrm{d}D_t \left/ \left[\int_{Q_t}^{\infty} g(Q_t,S_t)\mathrm{d}S_t + \int_{Q_t}^{\infty} g(D_t,Q_t)\mathrm{d}D_t\right]\right.$$

$$\tag{2.8.3}$$

Gersovitz (1980) shows that if $\sigma_1^2 = \sigma_2^2$ and if $\beta_1' x_{1t} > \beta_2' x_{2t}$, then $\Pr\{D_t > S_t | Q_t\} > 0.5$. For set (2.8.3) greater than 0.5 and substitute in the expression from (2.3.10); this implies that

$$\int_{Q_t}^{\infty} \left[\exp\left\{ -\frac{1}{2} \left(\frac{y - \beta_1' x_{1t}}{\sigma_1} \right)^2 \right\} - \exp\left\{ -\frac{1}{2} \left[\left(\frac{y - \beta_2' x_{2t}}{\sigma_2} \right)^2 \right. \right. \right.$$
$$\left. \left. \left. + \left(\frac{Q_t - \beta_1' x_{1t}}{\sigma_1} \right)^2 \right] \right\} \right] dy > 0 \quad (2.8.4)$$

A sufficient condition for (2.8.4) to hold is that

$$\left(\frac{y - \beta_1' x_{1t}}{\sigma_1} \right)^2 + \left(\frac{Q_t - \beta_2' x_{2t}}{\sigma_2} \right)^2 < \left(\frac{y - \beta_2' x_{2t}}{\sigma_2} \right)^2 + \left(\frac{Q_t - \beta_1' x_{1t}}{\sigma_1} \right)^2$$

for all $y > Q_t$. It follows easily that if $\sigma_1^2 = \sigma_2^2$, then $\beta_1' x_{1t} > \beta_2' x_{2t}$ is sufficient for this condition to hold. Thus, if the two variances are sufficiently close to one another, the classification of regimes using the conditional and unconditional probabilities are likely to be close too. In Monte Carlo experiments, Gersovitz (1980) found that maximum likelihood estimation of the parameters leads to conditional probability estimates with small biases, although the probabilities tend to be overestimated when their true values are small and conversely when they are large. In one empirical study, Burkett (1981) has found no substantial differences between conditional and unconditional probabilities; in another, Quandt and Rosen (1985) have found that the conditional probabilities provide sharper discrimination between the regimes than the unconditional ones.

Exercises

2.1 Show that the likelihood function of the switching regressions model (2.4.2) is not unbounded if $\sigma_1^2 = k\sigma_2^2$, with k known *a priori*.
2.2 Derive the formulas in appendix 2.C.
2.3 Show that the likelihood function (2.3.11) is not unbounded.
2.4 Show that the likelihood function for model C, (2.3.17), is not unbounded.
2.5 Show that the likelihood functions (2.3.17) and (2.3.18) are the same.
2.6 Verify that (2.3.11) and (2.6.5) are the same by substituting in the latter the precise functional form and completing the square.
2.7 Show that minimizing S_1 in (2.6.15) is equivalent to minimizing S_2.
2.8 Show that $E(Q_t)$ in (2.6.11) can also be written as

$$E(Q_t) = \min(\beta_1' x_{1t}, \beta_2' x_{2t}) - \int_{-\infty}^{-|\beta_1' x_{1t} - \beta_2' x_{2t}|} \Phi(z)\mathrm{d}z$$

2.9 Derive the unconditional probability $\Pr\{D_t > S_t\}$ for model D in section 2.3.

Appendix 2.A
FORTRAN Program for the Likelihood Function of Model A

The likelihood function is evaluated by subroutine DISEQ1 and the first and second partial derivatives by subroutines DISEFP and DISESP respectively. The routines are compatible with the programming conventions of the numerical optimization package GQOPT4. In particular, the following should be noted:

1   If an optimization algorithm strays into a forbidden region (e.g. if σ_1^2 or σ_2^2 should become nonpositive), the computation does not necessarily terminate; a nonstandard return from the subroutine is executed and the algorithms in GQOPT4 then attempt different steps. If the reader's own optimization algorithms behave differently, the reader may wish to replace each occurrence of RETURN 1 with the setting of an error flag and then execute a normal return.

2   Error messages may be printed under control of print flags IPT and JPT and if positive will print on logical units NFILE and MFILE respectively (see COMMON/BPRINT/IPT,NFILE,NDIG,NPUNCH,JPT, MFILE). Unless the reader is using GQOPT4, the other variables in the common block may be safely ignored.

```
      SUBROUTINE DISEQ1(A,NP,FUN,*)
      IMPLICIT REAL*8 (A-H,O-Z)
      DIMENSION A(NP)
C
C     NP   = TOTAL NUMBER OF PARAMETERS
C     N    = NUMBER OF OBSERVATIONS
C     K1   = NUMBER OF COEFFICIENTS IN DEMAND EQUATION
C     K2   = NUMBER OF COEFFICIENTS IN SUPPLY EQUATION
C     A( ) = COEFFICIENTS TO BE ESTIMATED; A(1),...,A(K1) ARE DEMAND
C            EQUATION COEFFICIENTS, A(K1+1),...,A(K1+K2) ARE SUPPLY
C            EQUATION COEFFICIENTS, A(NP-1) IS DEMAND DISTURBANCE
C            VARIANCE, A(NP) IS SUPPLY DISTURBANCE VARIANCE (K1+K2=NP-2)
C     Q( ) = OBSERVATIONS ON TRANSACTED AMOUNT
C     X1( )= OBSERVATIONS ON RIGHT HAND VARIABLES IN DEMAND; MUST BE
C            DIMENSIONED X1(N,K1) IN MAIN PROGRAM
C     X2( )= OBSERVATIONS ON RIGHT HAND VARIABLES IN SUPPLY; MUST BE
C            DIMENSIONED X2(N,K2) IN MAIN PROGRAM
C
C     FUN  = THE FUNCTION VALUE CALCULATED
C
      COMMON/USER1/Q(1)
      COMMON/USER2/X1(1)
      COMMON/USER3/X2(1)
      COMMON/USER4/N,K1,K2
      COMMON/BPRINT/IPT,NFILE,NDIG,NPUNCH,JPT,MFILE
C
C     SQ2  = SQUAREROOT OF 2.0
C     S2PINV= RECIPROCAL OF SQUAREROOT OF 2.0*PI
C
      DATA SQ2/0.1414213562373D+01/,S2PINV/0.3989422804008D+00/
C
C     TEST FOR USER ERROR
C
      IF(K1+K2+2.EQ.NP.AND.K1.GT.0.AND.K2.GT.0 ) GOTO 5
      IF(IPT.GT.0) WRITE (NFILE,1000)
      IF(JPT.GT.0) WRITE (MFILE,1000)
1000  FORMAT(' ERROR IN K1 OR K2 OR NP...EXECUTION TERMINATED')
      STOP
C
C     CHECK FOR NONPOSITIVE VARIANCES; IF YES, TAKE NONSTANDARD RETURN
C
5     IF(A(NP-1).LE.0.0.OR.A(NP).LE.0.0) RETURN 1
      SIG1=DSQRT(A(NP-1))
      SIG2=DSQRT(A(NP))
      F1=S2PINV/SIG1
      F2=S2PINV/SIG2
      SUM=0.0
C     OBSERVATION LOOP BEGINS HERE
      DO 100 I=1,N
      S1=0.0
      S2=0.0
C     LOOP TO COMPUTE RIGHT HAND SIDE OF DEMAND EQUATION
      DO 10 J=1,K1
10    S1=S1+A(J)*X1((J-1)*N+I)
C     LOOP TO COMPUTE RIGHT HAND SIDE OF SUPPLY EQUATION
      DO 20 J=1,K2
20    S2=S2+A(K1+J)*X2((J-1)*N+I)
C     OBTAIN NORMALIZED RESIDUALS
      S1=(Q(I)-S1)/SIG1
      S2=(Q(I)-S2)/SIG2
C     OBTAIN COMPONENT PARTS OF DENSITY
      PHIS1=DEXP(-S1*S1/2.0)*F1
      PHIL2=0.5-0.5*DERF(S2/SQ2)
      PHIS2=DEXP(-S2*S2/2.0)*F2
      PHIL1=0.5-0.5*DERF(S1/SQ2)
C     DENSITY
      DENS=PHIS1*PHIL2+PHIS2*PHIL1
C     CHECK IF DENSITY POSITIVE; OTHERWISE TAKE NONSTANDARD RETURN
      IF(DENS.LE.0.0) RETURN 1
100   SUM=SUM+DLOG(DENS)
      FUN=SUM
      RETURN
      END
```

```
      SUBROUTINE DISEFP(A,NP,FUN,FPD,FUNC,*)
      IMPLICIT REAL*8 (A-H,O-Z)
      DIMENSION A(NP),FPD(NP),B(200)
C
C     TO CALCULATE FIRST PARTIAL DERIVATIVES
C
C     NP    = TOTAL NUMBER OF PARAMETERS
C     N     = NUMBER OF OBSERVATIONS
C     K1    = NUMBER OF COEFFICIENTS IN DEMAND EQUATION
C     K2    = NUMBER OF COEFFICIENTS IN SUPPLY EQUATION
C     A( )  = COEFFICIENTS TO BE ESTIMATED; A(1),...,A(K1) ARE DEMAND
C               EQUATION COEFFICIENTS, A(K1+1),...,A(K1+K2) ARE SUPPLY
C               EQUATION COEFFICIENTS, A(NP-1) IS DEMAND DISTURBANCE
C               VARIANCE, A(NP) IS SUPPLY DISTURBANCE VARIANCE (K1+K2=NP-2)
C     Q( )  = OBSERVATIONS ON TRANSACTED AMOUNT
C     X1( ) = OBSERVATIONS ON RIGHT HAND VARIABLES IN DEMAND; MUST BE
C               DIMENSIONED X1(N,K1) IN MAIN PROGRAM
C     X2( ) = OBSERVATIONS ON RIGHT HAND VARIABLES IN SUPPLY; MUST BE
C               DIMENSIONED X2(N,K2) IN MAIN PROGRAM
C
C     FPD( )=FIRST PARTIAL DERIVATIVES ARE RETURNED HERE
C
      COMMON/BPRINT/IPT,NFILE,NDIG,NPUNCH,JPT,MFILE
      COMMON/BOPT2/ACC,R,PM1,IVAL,ITERL,ITERC,MX,IER
      COMMON/USER1/Q(1)
      COMMON/USER2/X1(1)
      COMMON/USER3/X2(1)
      COMMON/USER4/N,K1,K2
C
C     SQ2   = SQUAREROOT OF 2.0
C     S2PINV= RECIPROCAL OF SQUAREROOT OF 2.0*PI
C
      DATA SQ2/0.14142135623730+01/,S2PINV/0.39894228040080+00/
C
C     TEST FOR USER ERROR
C
      IF(NP.LE.200) GOTO 3
      IF (JPT.GT.0) WRITE (MFILE,1001)
      IF(IPT.GT.0) WRITE (NFILE,1001)
1001  FORMAT(' NP MUST NOT EXCEED 200---EXECUTION TERMINATED')
      STOP
3     IF(K1+K2+2.EQ.NP) GOTO 5
      IF(JPT.GT.0) WRITE (MFILE,1000)
      IF(IPT.GT.0) WRITE (NFILE,1000)
1000  FORMAT(' K1+K2+2 MUST EQUAL NP...EXECUTION TERMINATED')
      STOP
C
C     CHECK FOR NONPOSITIVE VARIANCES; IF YES, TAKE NONSTANDARD RETURN
C
5     IF(A(NP-1).LE.0.0.OR.A(NP).LE.0.0) RETURN 1
      DO 1 I=1,NP
1     FPD(I)=0.
      SIG1=DSQRT(A(NP-1))
      SIG2=DSQRT(A(NP))
      F1=S2PINV/SIG1
      F2=S2PINV/SIG2
      SUM=0.0
C     OBSERVATION LOOP BEGINS HERE
      DO 100 I=1,N
      S1=0.0
      S2=0.0
C     LOOP TO COMPUTE RIGHT HAND SIDE OF DEMAND EQUATION
      DO 10 J=1,K1
10    S1=S1+A(J)*X1((J-1)*N+I)
C     LOOP TO COMPUTE RIGHT HAND SIDE OF SUPPLY EQUATION
      DO 20 J=1,K2
20    S2=S2+A(K1+J)*X2((J-1)*N+I)
C     OBTAIN NORMALIZED RESIDUALS
      S1=(Q(I)-S1)/SIG1
      S2=(Q(I)-S2)/SIG2
C     OBTAIN COMPONENT PARTS OF DENSITY
      PHIS1=DEXP(-S1*S1/2.0)*F1
```

```
        PHIL2=0.5-0.5*DERF(S2/SQ2)
        PHIS2=DEXP(-S2*S2/2.0)*F2
        PHIL1=0.5-0.5*DERF(S1/SQ2)
C       DENSITY
        G=PHIS1*PHIL2+PHIS2*PHIL1
C       CHECK IF DENSITY POSITIVE; OTHERWISE TAKE NONSTANDARD RETURN
        IF(G.LE.0.0) RETURN 1 *
35      F1F2=PHIS1*PHIS2
        F1LF2=PHIS1*PHIL2
        F2LF1=PHIL1*PHIS2
        B(NP-1)=F1LF2*(S1**2-1.)/(2.*A(NP-1))+F1F2*S1/(2.*SIG1)
        B(NP)=F2LF1*(S2**2-1.)/(2.*A(NP))+F1F2*S2/(2.*SIG2)
        DO 40 J=1,K1
40      B(J)=(F1LF2*S1/SIG1+F1F2)*X1((J-1)*N+I)
        DO 50 J=1,K2
50      B(K1+J)=(F2LF1*S2/SIG2+F1F2)*X2((J-1)*N+I)
        FPD(NP-1)=FPD(NP-1)+B(NP-1)/G
        FPD(NP)=FPD(NP)+B(NP)/G
        DO 60 J=1,K1
60      FPD(J)=FPD(J)+B(J)/G
        DO 70 J=1,K2
70      FPD(K1+J)=FPD(K1+J)+B(K1+J)/G
100     CONTINUE
        RETURN
        END
```

```
      SUBROUTINE DISESP(A,NP,FUN,FPD,SPD,FUNC,*)
      IMPLICIT REAL*8 (A-H,O-Z)
      DIMENSION A(NP),FPD(NP),B(200),SPD(NP,NP)
C
C     TO CALCULATE SECOND PARTIAL DERIVATIVES
C
C     NP    = TOTAL NUMBER OF PARAMETERS
C     N     = NUMBER OF OBSERVATIONS
C     K1    = NUMBER OF COEFFICIENTS IN DEMAND EQUATION
C     K2    = NUMBER OF COEFFICIENTS IN SUPPLY EQUATION
C     A( )  = COEFFICIENTS TO BE ESTIMATED; A(1),...,A(K1) ARE DEMAND
C             EQUATION COEFFICIENTS, A(K1+1),...,A(K1+K2) ARE SUPPLY
C             EQUATION COEFFICIENTS, A(NP-1) IS DEMAND DISTURBANCE
C             VARIANCE, A(NP) IS SUPPLY DISTURBANCE VARIANCE (K1+K2=NP-2)
C     Q( )  = OBSERVATIONS ON TRANSACTED AMOUNT
C     X1( ) = OBSERVATIONS ON RIGHT HAND VARIABLES IN DEMAND; MUST BE
C             DIMENSIONED X1(N,K1) IN MAIN PROGRAM
C     X2( ) = OBSERVATIONS ON RIGHT HAND VARIABLES IN SUPPLY; MUST BE
C             DIMENSIONED X2(N,K2) IN MAIN PROGRAM
C
C     SPD( , )=SECOND PARTIAL DERIVATIVES ARE RETURNED HERE
C
      COMMON/BPRINT/IPT,NFILE,NDIG,NPUNCH,JPT,MFILE
      COMMON/BOPT2/ACC,R,PM1,IVAL,ITERL,ITERC,MX,IER
      COMMON/USER1/Q(1)
      COMMON/USER2/X1(1)
      COMMON/USER3/X2(1)
      COMMON/USER4/N,K1,K2
C
C     SQ2   = SQUAREROOT OF 2.0
C     S2PINV= RECIPROCAL OF SQUAREROOT OF 2.0*PI
C
      DATA SQ2/0.14142135623730+01/,S2PINV/0.3989422804008D+00/
C
C     TEST FOR USER ERROR
C
      IF(NP.LE.200) GOTO 3
      IF (JPT.GT.0) WRITE (MFILE,1001)
      IF(IPT.GT.0) WRITE (NFILE,1001)
 1001 FORMAT(' NP MUST NOT EXCEED 200---EXECUTION TERMINATED')
      STOP
 3    IF(K1+K2+2.EQ.NP) GOTO 5
      IF(JPT.GT.0) WRITE (MFILE,1000)
      IF(IPT.GT.0) WRITE (NFILE,1000)
 1000 FORMAT(' K1+K2+2 MUST EQUAL NP...EXECUTION TERMINATED')
      STOP
C
C     CHECK FOR NONPOSITIVE VARIANCES; IF YES, TAKE NONSTANDARD RETURN
C
 5    IF(A(NP-1).LE.0.0.OR.A(NP).LE.0.0) RETURN 1
      DO 2 I=1,NP
      DO 2 J=1,NP
 2    SPD(I,J)=0.
      SIG1=DSQRT(A(NP-1))
      SIG2=DSQRT(A(NP))
      F1=S2PINV/SIG1
      F2=S2PINV/SIG2
      SUM=0.0
C     OBSERVATION LOOP BEGINS HERE
      DO 200 I=1,N
      R1=0.0
      R2=0.0
C     LOOP TO COMPUTE RIGHT HAND SIDE OF DEMAND EQUATION
      DO 10 J=1,K1
```

```
10      R1=R1+A(J)*X1((J-1)*N+I)
C       LOOP TO COMPUTE RIGHT HAND SIDE OF SUPPLY EQUATION
        DO 20 J=1,K2
20      R2=R2+A(K1+J)*X2((J-1)*N+I)
C       OBTAIN NORMALIZED RESIDUALS
        R1=(Q(I)-R1)/SIG1
        R2=(Q(I)-R2)/SIG2
        R1R2=R1*R2
        R1P2=R1*R1
        R1P4=R1P2*R1P2
        R2P2=R2*R2
        R2P4=R2P2*R2P2
        SIG1P4=A(NP-1)*A(NP-1)
        SIG2P4=A(NP)*A(NP)
        SIG1P3=A(NP-1)*SIG1
        SIG2P3=A(NP)*SIG2
C       OBTAIN COMPONENT PARTS OF DENSITY
        PHIS1=DEXP(-R1*R1/2.0)*F1
        PHIL2=0.5-0.5*DERF(R2/SQ2)
        PHIS2=DEXP(-R2*R2/2.0)*F2
        PHIL1=0.5-0.5*DERF(R1/SQ2)
C       DENSITY
        G=PHIS1*PHIL2+PHIS2*PHIL1
C       CHECK IF DENSITY POSITIVE; OTHERWISE TAKE NONSTANDARD RETURN
        IF(G.LE.0.0) RETURN 1
35      GSQ=G*G
        F1F2=PHIS1*PHIS2
        F1LF2=PHIS1*PHIL2
        F2LF1=PHIL1*PHIS2
        B(NP-1)=F1LF2*(R1**2-1.)/(2.*A(NP-1))+F1F2*R1/(2.*SIG1)
        B(NP)=F2LF1*(R2**2-1.)/(2.*A(NP))+F1F2*R2/(2.*SIG2)
        DO 40 J=1,K1
40      B(J)=(F1LF2*R1/SIG1+F1F2)*X1((J-1)*N+I)
        DO 50 J=1,K2
50      B(K1+J)=(F2LF1*R2/SIG2+F1F2)*X2((J-1)*N+I)
        SPD(NP-1,NP-1)=SPD(NP-1,NP-1)+(G*(F1LF2*(R1P4-6.*R1P2+3.)/(4.*
     1  SIG1P4)+F1F2*R1*(R1P2-3.)/(4.*SIG1P3))-B(NP-1)*B(NP-1))/GSQ
        SPD(NP,NP)=SPD(NP,NP)+(G*(F2LF1*(R2P4-6.*R2P2+3.)/(4.*SIG2P4)+
     1  F1F2*R2*(R2P2-3.)/(4.*SIG2P3))-B(NP)*B(NP))/GSQ
        SPD(NP-1,NP)=SPD(NP-1,NP)+(G*(F1F2*(R2*(R1P2-1.)/SIG1+R1*(R2P2-1.)
     1  /SIG2)/(4.*SIG1*SIG2))-B(NP)*B(NP-1))/GSQ
        DO 110 J=1,K1
        DO 110 K=J,K1
110     SPD(J,K)=SPD(J,K)+(G*(F1LF2*(R1P2-1.)/A(NP-1)+F1F2*R1/SIG1)*
     1  X1((J-1)*N+I)*X1((K-1)*N+I)-B(J)*B(K))/GSQ
        DO 120 J=1,K1
        DO 120 K=1,K2
120     SPD(J,K1+K)=SPD(J,K1+K)+(G*F1F2*(R1/SIG1+R2/SIG2)*
     1  X1((J-1)*N+I)*X2((K-1)*N+I)-B(J)*B(K1+K))/GSQ
        DO 130 J=1,K1
        SPD(J,NP-1)=SPD(J,NP-1)+(G*(F1LF2*R1*(R1P2-3.)/(2.*SIG1P3)+F1F2*
     1  (R1P2-1.)/(2.*A(NP-1)))*X1((J-1)*N+I)-B(J)*B(NP-1))/GSQ
130     SPD(J,NP)=SPD(J,NP)+(G*(F1F2*(R2P2-1.)/(2.*A(NP))+F1F2*R1R2/(2.*
     1  SIG1*SIG2))*X1((J-1)*N+I)-B(J)*B(NP))/GSQ
        DO 140 J=1,K2
        DO 140 K=J,K2
        SPD(K1+J,K1+K)=SPD(K1+J,K1+K)+(G*(F2LF1*(R2P2-1.)/A(NP)+
     1  F1F2*R2/SIG2)*X2((J-1)*N+I)*X2((K-1)*N+I)-B(K1+J)*B(K1+K))/GSQ
140     CONTINUE
        DO 150 J=1,K2
        SPD(K1+J,NP-1)=SPD(K1+J,NP-1)+(G*(F1F2*(R1P2-1.)/(2.*A(NP-1))+
     1  F1F2*R1R2/(2.*SIG1*SIG2))*X2((J-1)*N+I)-B(K1+J)*B(NP-1))/GSQ
150     SPD(K1+J,NP)=SPD(K1+J,NP)+(G*(F2LF1*R2*(R2P2-3.)/(2.*SIG2P3)+
     1  F1F2*(R2P2-1.)/(2.*A(NP)))*X2((J-1)*N+I)-B(K1+J)*B(NP))/GSQ
200     CONTINUE
        DO 250 I=1,NP
```

```
      DO 250 J=I,NP
250   SPD(J,I)=SPD(I,J)
      RETURN
      END
```

Appendix 2.B
FORTRAN Program for the Likelihood Function of Model D

The likelihood function is evaluated by subroutine DISEQ2.

```
      SUBROUTINE DISEQ2(A,NP,FUN,*)
      IMPLICIT REAL*8 (A-H,O-Z)
      DIMENSION A(NP)
      COMMON/USER0/Q(1)
      COMMON/USER1/P(1)
      COMMON/USER2/X1(1)
      COMMON/USER3/X2(1)
      COMMON/USER4/X3(1)
      COMMON/USER5/N,K1,K2,K3
      COMMON/BPRINT/IPT,NFILE,NDIG,NPUNCH,JPT,MFILE
C
C     NP    = TOTAL NUMBER OF PARAMETRS
C     N     = NUMBER OF OBSERVATIONS
C     K1    = NUMBER OF PARAMETERS IN DEMAND EQUATION
C     K2    = NUMBER OF PARAMETERS IN SUPPLY EQUATION
C     K3    = NUMBER OF PARAMETERS IN ADJUSTMENT EQUATION (INCLUDES GAMMA
C     A( )  = PARAMETERS TO BE ESTIMATED:
C                 A(1),....,A(K1)  DEMAND PARAMETERS
C                     A(1) = COEFFICIENT OF PRICE
C                 A(K1+1),....,A(K1+K2) SUPPLY PARAMETERS
C                     A(K1+1) = COEFFICIENT OF PRICE
C                 A(K1+K2+1),....,A(K1+K2+K3) ADJUSTMENT EQUATION PARAMETERS
C                     WITH A(K1+K2+1) REPRESENTING GAMMA
C                 A(NP-2) = DEMAND ERROR TERM VARIANCE
C                 A(NP-1) = SUPPLY ERROR TERM VARIANCE
C                 A(NP)   = ADJUSTMENT EQUATION VARIANCE
C
C                 DATA ARRAYS:
C     NAME     CONTENT                            DIMENSION IN MAIN PROGRAM
C     Q        QUANTITY                           Q(N)
C     P        PRICE                              P(N)
C     X1       EXOGENOUS VARIABLES IN             X1(N,K1-1)
C                 DEMAND EQUATION
C     X2       EXOGENOUS VARIABLES IN             X2(N,K2-1)
C                 SUPPLY EQUATION
C     X3       EXOGENOUS VARIABLES IN             X3(N,K3-1)
C                 ADJUSTMENT EQUATION
C
C     OUTPUT: FUNCTION VALUE RETURNED IN FUN
C
C     SQ2   = SQUAREROOT OF 2.0
C     PI2IN = RECIPROCAL OF 2.0*PI
C
      DATA SQ2/0.1414213562373D+01/,PI2IN/0.1591549431D+0/
C
C     TEST FOR USER ERROR
C
      IF(K1+K2+K3+3.EQ.NP) GOTO 5
      IF(IPT.GT.0) WRITE (NFILE,1000)
      IF(JPT.GT.0) WRITE (MFILE,1000)
1000  FORMAT(' K1+K2+K3+3 MUST EQUAL NP...EXECUTION TERMINATED')
      GOTO 9
5     IF(K1.GE.1.AND.K2.GE.1.AND.K3.GE.1) GOTO 10
      IF(IPT.GT.0) WRITE (NFILE,1001)
      IF(JPT.GT.0) WRITE (MFILE,1001)
```

```
1001    FORMAT(' K1, K2, K3 MUST BE .GE. 1')
9       STOP
C
C       TEST FOR NONPOSITIVE VARIANCES; IF YES, TAKE NONSTANDARD RETURN
C
10      IF(A(NP).LE.0..OR.A(NP-1).LE.0..OR.A(NP-2).LE.0.) RETURN 1
        S1=DSQRT(A(NP-2))
        S2=DSQRT(A(NP-1))
        S3=DSQRT(A(NP))
        V1=A(NP)+A(K1+K2+1)**2*A(NP-2)
        V2=A(NP)+A(K1+K2+1)**2*A(NP-1)
        RV1=DSQRT(V1)
        RV2=DSQRT(V2)
        R1=A(NP-2)*A(NP)/V1
        R2=A(NP-1)*A(NP)/V2
        XJAC=DABS(1.D0+A(K1+K2+1)*(A(K1+1)-A(1)))
C
C       IF JACOBIAN = 0 TAKE NONSTANDARD RETURN
C
        IF(XJAC.EQ.0) RETURN 1
        SUM=0.
        DO 800 I=2,N
        G1=0.
        G2=0.
        G3=P(I-1)
        IF(K1.EQ.1) GOTO 20
        DO 15 J=2,K1
15      G1=G1+A(J)*X1((J-2)*N+I)
20      IF(K2.EQ.1) GOTO 30
        DO 25 J=2,K2
25      G2=G2+A(K1+J)*X2((J-2)*N+I)
30      IF(K3.EQ.1) GOTO 40
        DO 35 J=2,K3
35      G3=G3+A(K1+K2+J)*X3((J-2)*N+I)
40      AA1=A(1)*P(I)+G1
        AA2=(Q(I)-A(K1+1)*P(I)-G2)**2/A(NP-1)
        AA3=P(I)+A(K1+K2+1)*Q(I)-G3
        AA4=(Q(I)-A(1)*P(I)-G1)**2/A(NP-2)
        AA5=A(K1+1)*P(I)+G2
        AA6=P(I)-A(K1+K2+1)*Q(I)-G3
        EX1=AA2+(AA3-A(K1+K2+1)*AA1)**2/V1
        EX2=AA4+(AA6-A(K1+K2+1)*AA5)**2/V2
        BB1=(AA1*A(NP)+A(K1+K2+1)*AA3*A(NP-2))/V1
        BB3=(AA5*A(NP)+A(K1+K2+1)*AA6*A(NP-1))/V2
        XL1=(Q(I)-BB1)/(SQ2*R1)
        XL2=(Q(I)-BB3)/(SQ2*R2)
        DEN=DEXP(-0.5D0*EX1)*(0.5-0.5*DERF(XL1))/(S1*RV1)+
     1      DEXP(-0.5D0*EX2)*(0.5-0.5*DERF(XL2))/(S2*RV2)
C
C       IF DENSITY = 0, TAKE NONSTANDARD RETURN
C
        IF(DEN.LE.0.) RETURN 1
800     SUM=SUM+DLOG(DEN)
        FUN=SUM+(N-1)*(DLOG(XJAC)+DLOG(PI2IN))
        RETURN
        END
```

Appendix 2.C
Likelihood Function for Model D

Write the joint p.d.f. of D_t, S_t, p_t as

$$g(D_t, S_t, p_t) = \frac{|1 + \gamma(\alpha_2 - \alpha_1)|}{(2\pi)^{3/2}\,|\Sigma|^{1/2}}\,\exp\left\{-\frac{1}{2}\,u_t'\,\Sigma^{-1}u_t\right\} \tag{2.C.1}$$

where $u_t' = (u_{1t}, u_{2t}, u_{3t})$ is to be replaced from (2.1.5), (2.1.6) and (2.1.9). Denoting the elements of Σ^{-1} by σ^{ij} and defining

$$A_1 = \sigma^{11} + \gamma^2\sigma^{33} - 2\gamma\sigma^{13}$$

$$\begin{aligned}
A_{2t} ={}& (\alpha_1 p_t + \beta_1' x_{1t})(\gamma\sigma^{13} - \sigma^{11}) + (Q_t - \alpha_2 p_t - \beta_2' x_{2t})(\sigma^{12} - \gamma\sigma^{23}) \\
&+ (\gamma Q_t + p_t - \beta_3' x_{3t})(\sigma^{13} - \gamma\sigma^{33})
\end{aligned}$$

$$\begin{aligned}
A_{3t} ={}& \sigma^{11}(\alpha_1 p_t + \beta_1' x_{1t})^2 + \sigma^{22}(Q_t - \alpha_2 p_t - \beta_2' x_{2t})^2 \\
&+ \sigma^{33}(\gamma Q_t + p_t - \beta_3' x_{3t})^2 + 2\sigma^{12}(Q_t - \alpha_2 p_t - \beta_2' x_{2t})(-\alpha_1 p_t - \beta_1' x_{1t}) \\
&+ 2\sigma^{13}(-\alpha_1 p_t - \beta_1' x_{1t})(\gamma Q_t + p_t - \beta_3' x_{3t}) \\
&+ 2\sigma^{23}(Q_t - \alpha_2 p_t - \beta_2' x_{2t})(\gamma Q_t + p_t - \beta_3' x_{3t})
\end{aligned}$$

$$A_4 = \sigma^{22} + \gamma^2\sigma^{33} + 2\gamma\sigma^{23}$$

$$\begin{aligned}
A_{5t} ={}& (\alpha_2 p_t + \beta_2' x_{2t})(-\sigma^{22} - \gamma\sigma^{23}) + (p_t - \beta_3' x_{3t} - \gamma Q_t)(\gamma\sigma^{33} + \sigma^{23}) \\
&+ (Q_t - \alpha_1 p_t - \beta_1' x_{1t})(\sigma^{12} + \gamma\sigma^{13})
\end{aligned}$$

$$\begin{aligned}
A_{6t} ={}& \sigma^{11}(Q_t - \alpha_1 p_t - \beta_1' x_{1t})^2 + \sigma^{22}(\alpha_2 p_t + \beta_2' x_{2t})^2 + \sigma^{33}(p_t - \gamma Q_t - \beta_3' x_{3t})^2 \\
&+ 2\sigma^{12}(Q_t - \alpha_1 p_t - \beta_1' x_{1t})(-\alpha_2 p_t - \beta_2' x_{2t}) \\
&+ 2\sigma^{13}(Q_t - \alpha_1 p_t - \beta_1' x_{1t})(p_t - \gamma Q_t - \beta_3' x_{3t}) \\
&+ 2\sigma^{23}(-\alpha_2 p_t - \beta_2' x_{2t})(p_t - \gamma Q_t - \beta_3' x_{3t})
\end{aligned}$$

$$B_{1t} = A_{3t} - A_{2t}^2/A_1$$

$$B_{2t} = A_{6t} - A_{5t}^2/A_4$$

$$L_{1t} = A_1^{1/2}\,(Q_t + A_{2t}/A_1)$$

$$L_{2t} = A_4^{1/2}\,(Q_t + A_{5t}/A_4)$$

we obtain the density

$$\begin{aligned}
h(Q_t, p_t) ={}& \frac{|1 + \gamma(\alpha_2 - \alpha_1)|}{2\pi\,|\Sigma|^{1/2}} \\
&\times \big[\exp(-B_{1t}/2)[1 - \Phi(L_{1t})]/A_1^{1/2} \\
&\quad + \exp(-B_{2t}/2)[1 - \Phi(L_{2t})]/A_4^{1/2}\big]
\end{aligned} \tag{2.C.2}$$

3

Equilibrium, Disequilibrium, and Testing

3.1 Introduction

When markets clear, the economy is said to be in a state of equilibrium; otherwise it is in a state of disequilibrium, according to one prevalent use of terms.[1] This dichotomy raises three somewhat related questions:

1   Since it does not appear plausible to argue that all economic systems must always be in equilibrium or always in disequilibrium, how do we characterize systems that may switch back and forth between those two states?

2   Since it may be desirable to know whether an equilibrium or a disequilibrium specification is more appropriate in a particular case, how do we test the null hypothesis of equilibrium versus the alternative of disequilibrium?

3   If we were to find that a disequilibrium specification is more appropriate, is it possible to test hypotheses about the prevalence of excess demand as contrasted with excess supply?

These are the questions to be investigated in the present chapter. In section 3.2 we consider the case when price ceilings or floors might be imposed, which leads to a modification of the standard models discussed in chapter 2. In section 3.3 we allow for endogenous switching between equilibrium and disequilibrium states. In section 3.4 we deal with testing the hypothesis that the equilibrium specification is correct. In section 3.5 we characterize models in which there has always been excess demand, and in section 3.6 we consider tests in these models.

---

[1] We reiterate that in this sense disequilibrium need not be interpreted as a state in which forces are acting to change the current values of the endogenous variables. The "disequilibrium" state may, in fact, represent the solution to a general equilibrium model in which agents are acting optimally, given the set of constraints they face.

3.2 The Case of Controlled Prices

In some markets it may occasionally be the case that institutional prohibi-
tions prevent the price from attaining certain values. Thus, in the case of
some agricultural commodities the price may not be allowed to fall below a
government-imposed price support level. In other cases, there may be a price
ceiling above which the price may not rise, while in still others both price
floors and ceilings may be present. Models of this type have been developed
in detail by Maddala (1983a, 1983b) and Gourieroux and Monfort
(1980).

Consider the case of a price ceiling. We assume that the demand and supply
functions are given by

$$D_t = \alpha_1 p_t + \beta_1' x_{1t} + u_{1t}$$
$$S_t = \alpha_2 p_t + \beta_2' x_{2t} + u_{2t}$$
(3.2.1)

and that we are presented with exogenously determined constraints

$$p_t \leq \bar{p}_t$$
(3.2.2)

where the $\bar{p}_t$ are observed and exogenous. If we posit market clearing,
$D_t = S_t = Q_t$ and the solution of (3.2.1) yields an equilibrium price p_t^*.
(Q_t, p_t^*) will be the observed quantity and price respectively, if and only if
$p_t^* < \bar{p}_t$. In the contrary event, there will be excess demand and we observe

$$Q_t = \min(D_t, S_t) = S_t$$

The situation is shown graphically in figures 3.1a and 3.1b. In figure 3.1a the
intersection of demand and supply occurs at a price less than $\bar{p}_t$ and accordingly we observe Q_t and the equilibrium price p_t^*. In figure 3.1b we observe $\bar{p}_t$
and the minimum of D_t, S_t which in fact is S_t. Maddala (1983b) refers to such a
model as a rationing model because potential purchasers cannot buy as much
as they would like and, hence, are rationed.

We now consider several specific cases.

Case 1

In this case $\bar{p}_t$ is exogenous, p_t and Q_t are observed. Assume, as usual, that the
errors u_{1t}, u_{2t} are jointly normally distributed with density function
$f(u_{1t}, u_{2t})$. Then if $p_t < \bar{p}_t$, the jointly dependent variables are p_t and Q_t
with density function $|\alpha_1 - \alpha_2| f(Q_t - \alpha_1 p_t - \beta_1' x_{1t}, Q_t - \alpha_2 p_t - \beta_2' x_{2t})$,
where $|\alpha_1 - \alpha_2|$ is the absolute value of the Jacobian of the transformation
$(u_{1t}, u_{2t}) \rightarrow (Q_t, p_t)$. On the other hand, if $p_t = \bar{p}_t$, the observed price is
exogenous and the jointly dependent variables are D_t and $S_t = Q_t$ with
density function $f(D_t - \alpha_1 \bar{p}_t - \beta_1' x_{1t}, S_t - \alpha_2 \bar{p}_t - \beta_2' x_{2t})$. From this
latter, the density of the only observable random variable is

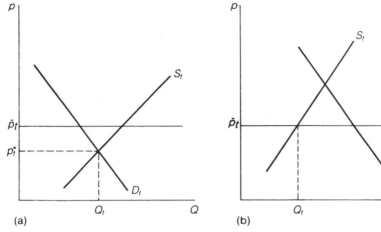

Figure 3.1

$$\int_{Q_t}^{\infty} f(D_t - \alpha_1 \bar{p}_t - \beta_1' x_{1t}, \quad Q_t - \alpha_2 \bar{p}_t - \beta_2' x_{2t}) \, dD_t \qquad (3.2.3)$$

If T_1 and T_2 denote index sets such that $p_t < \bar{p}_t$ for $t \in T_1$ and $p_t = \bar{p}_t$ for $t \in T_2$, the likelihood function is

$$L = \prod_{T_1} |\alpha_1 - \alpha_2| f(Q_t - \alpha_1 p_t - \beta_1' x_{1t}, \quad Q_t - \alpha_2 p_t - \beta_2' x_{2t})$$

$$\times \prod_{T_2} \int_{Q_t}^{\infty} f(D_t - \alpha_1 \bar{p}_t - \beta_1' x_{1t}, \quad Q_t - \alpha_2 \bar{p}_t - \beta_2' x_{2t}) \, dD_t \qquad (3.2.4)$$

In the special case when u_{1t} and u_{2t} are independent, (3.2.4) becomes

$$L = \prod_{T_1} \frac{|\alpha_1 - \alpha_2|}{2\pi\sigma_1\sigma_2} \exp\left\{ -\frac{1}{2}\left[\frac{(Q_t - \alpha_1 p_t - \beta_1' x_{1t})^2}{\sigma_1^2} + \frac{(Q_t - \alpha_2 p_t - \beta_2' x_{2t})^2}{\sigma_2^2} \right] \right\}$$

$$\times \prod_{T_2} \frac{1}{\sqrt{(2\pi)}\sigma_2} \exp\left\{ -\frac{(Q_t - \alpha_2 \bar{p}_t - \beta_2' x_{2t})^2}{2\sigma_2^2} \right\}$$

$$\times \left[1 - \Phi\left(\frac{Q_t - \alpha_1 \bar{p}_t - \beta_1' x_{1t}}{\sigma_1} \right) \right] \qquad (3.2.5)$$

The likelihood function may be maximized by numerical methods as usual.

This model can also be estimated by the two-stage method originally due to Heckman (1978). For the index set T_1 we can obtain the reduced form equation[2]

---

[2] Remember that $D_t = S_t = Q_t$ for $t \in T_1$.

$$p_t = \frac{\beta_2' x_{2t} - \beta_1' x_{1t}}{\alpha_1 - \alpha_2} + \frac{u_{2t} - u_{1t}}{\alpha_1 - \alpha_2} \tag{3.2.6}$$

or more simply,

$$p_t = \pi' x_t + v_t \tag{3.2.7}$$

where $\pi' = [\beta_2'/(\alpha_1 - \alpha_2), \; -\beta_1'/(\alpha_1 - \alpha_2)]$, $x_t' = (x_{2t}', x_{1t}')$ and $v_t = (u_{2t} - u_{1t})/(\alpha_1 - \alpha_2)$. Obviously also for $t \, \epsilon \, T_2$, the reduced form for p_t is

$$p_t = \bar{p}_t \tag{3.2.8}$$

Rewriting these last two equations together with the conditions under which they hold,

$$p_t = \begin{cases} \pi' x_t + v_t & \text{if } p_t^* < \bar{p}_t \\ \bar{p}_t & \text{if } p_t^* \geq \bar{p}_t \end{cases} \tag{3.2.9}$$

where the equilibrium price p_t^* is in fact given by (3.2.6). Equations (3.2.9) are a tobit model, the parameters of which can be estimated consistently by maximizing the likelihood

$$L = \prod_{T_1} \frac{1}{\sqrt{(2\pi)}\sigma_v} \exp\left\{ -\frac{(p_t - \pi' x_t)^2}{2\sigma_v^2} \right\} \prod_{T_2} \left[1 - \Phi\left(\frac{\bar{p}_t - \pi' x_t}{\sigma_v} \right) \right]$$

The first structural equation in (3.2.1) does not have an error term with zero expectation conditionally on $p_t^* < \bar{p}_t$. We can write from (3.2.9)

$$E(p_t | t \, \epsilon \, T_1) = \pi' x_t + E(v_t | v_t < \bar{p}_t - \pi' x_t)$$

$$= \pi' x_t + \sigma_v E\left(\frac{v_t}{\sigma_v} \, \bigg| \, \frac{v_t}{\sigma_v} < \frac{\bar{p}_t - \pi' x_t}{\sigma_v} \right)$$

$$= \pi' x_t - \sigma_v \frac{\phi(z_t)}{\Phi(z_t)} \tag{3.2.10}$$

where $z_t = (\bar{p}_t - \pi' x_t)/\sigma_v$ (see appendix 3.A). Using (3.2.10) allows us to form consistent predictions $\hat{p}_t$ of p_t. The conditional expectation of the error term in the first structural equation is (again from appendix 3.A)

$$E(u_{1t} | t \, \epsilon \, T_1) = E(u_{1t} | v_t/\sigma_v < z_t) = -\frac{\sigma_{1v}}{\sigma_v} \frac{\phi(z_t)}{\Phi(z_t)} \tag{3.2.11}$$

where σ_{1v} represents the covariance between u_{1t} and v_t. We can thus write the first structural equation as

$$Q_t = \alpha_1 p_t + \beta_1' x_{1t} - \frac{\sigma_{1v}}{\sigma_v} \frac{\phi(z_t)}{\Phi(z_t)} + \epsilon_t \tag{3.2.12}$$

Replacing p_t by $\hat{p}_t$ from above and the parameters σ_v and those occurring in z_t by their tobit estimates, we can estimate (3.2.12) consistently by applying

OLS as a second-stage estimation. Gourieroux and Monfort (1980) suggest that it suffices to replace p_t by $\hat{\pi}'x_t$ rather than by (3.2.10) in the second stage.

Case 2

Additional variations on the model can be obtained by positing the $\bar{p}_t$ itself depends on some variables, e.g.

$$\bar{p}_t = \beta_3'x_{3t} + u_{3t} \tag{3.2.13}$$

Gourieroux and Monfort (1980) consider various special cases. First, if D_t, S_t, p_t and $\bar{p}_t$ are all observed, then (3.2.1) and (3.2.13) determine two joint density functions. If $p_t < \bar{p}_t$, we have

$$Q_t = \alpha_1 p_t + \beta_1'x_{1t} + u_{1t}$$

$$Q_t = \alpha_2 p_t + \beta_2'x_{2t} + u_{2t}$$

$$\bar{p}_t = \beta_3'x_{3t} + u_{3t}$$

from which we obtain $|\alpha_2 - \alpha_1| f(Q_t - \alpha_1 p_t - \beta_1'x_{1t}, Q_t - \alpha_2 p_t - \beta_2'x_{2t}, \bar{p}_t - \beta_3'x_{3t})$, which we abbreviate as $g_1(Q_t, p_t, \bar{p}_t)$. If $p_t = \bar{p}_t$, we have

$$D_t = \alpha_1 \bar{p}_t + \beta_1'x_{1t} + u_{1t}$$

$$S_t = \alpha_2 \bar{p}_t + \beta_2'x_{2t} + u_{2t}$$

$$\bar{p}_t = \beta_3'x_{3t} + u_{3t}$$

from which we get $f(D_t - \alpha_1 \bar{p}_t - \beta_1'x_{1t}, S_t - \alpha_2 \bar{p}_t - \beta_2'x_{2t}, \bar{p}_t - \beta_3'x_{3t})$, which we abbreviate as $g_2(D_t, S_t, \bar{p}_t)$. Thus in one case the random variables are Q_t, p_t, $\bar{p}_t$ and in the other D_t, S_t, $\bar{p}_t$. The likelihood function is then the product of appropriate terms as in

$$L = \prod_{p_t < \bar{p}_t} g_1(Q_t, p_t, \bar{p}_t) \prod_{p_t = \bar{p}_t} g_2(D_t, S_t, \bar{p}_t) \tag{3.2.14}$$

Case 3

If only Q_t and p_t are observed, then to obtain the density function for the observable variables we must integrate $\bar{p}_t$ out of $g_1(\ )$ and D_t out of $g_2(\ )$, yielding

$$h(Q_t, p_t) = \int_{p_t}^{\infty} g_1(Q_t, p_t, \bar{p}_t)\,d\bar{p}_t + \int_{Q_t}^{\infty} g_2(D_t, Q_t, \bar{p}_t)\,dD_t \tag{3.2.15}$$

Perhaps the most plausible scenario is that D_t and S_t are not always observed but $\bar{p}_t$ is. Then the sample can be sorted by comparing p_t with $\bar{p}_t$ and the likelihood is analogous to (3.2.4):

$$L = \prod_{p_t < \bar{p}_t} g_1(Q_t, p_t, \bar{p}_t) \prod_{p_t = \bar{p}_t} \int_{Q_t}^{\infty} g_2(D_t, Q_t, \bar{p}_t) \, dD_t \qquad (3.2.16)$$

3.3 Endogenous Switching Between Equilibrium and Disequilibrium

Instead of letting exogenous price limits determine whether we have an equilibrium or disequilibrium regime in effect, we may consider the possibility that the "system" itself chooses the regime so as to minimize certain adjustment costs (Quandt 1983a). Write the hypothetical equilibrium model as

$$Q_t = \alpha_1 p_t + \beta_1' x_{1t} + u_{1t}$$
$$Q_t = \alpha_2 p_t + \beta_2' x_{2t} + u_{2t} \qquad (3.3.1)$$

and the corresponding hypothetical disequilibrium model as

$$D_t = \alpha_1 p_t + \beta_1' x_{1t} + u_{1t}$$
$$S_t = \alpha_2 p_t + \beta_2' x_{2t} + u_{2t}$$
$$Q_t = \min(D_t, S_t) \qquad (3.3.2)$$
$$p_t = p_{t-1} + \gamma(D_t - S_t) + u_{3t}$$

where in the first case u_{1t}, u_{2t} are distributed as $N(0, \Sigma_1)$ and in the second case u_{1t}, u_{2t}, u_{3t} are distributed as $N(0, \Sigma_2)$. The density functions of Q_t, p_t in the two cases are well known by now and will be denoted by $f_e(Q_t, p_t)$ and $f_d(Q_t, p_t)$ respectively. Finally, denote the solution value of price, i.e. the equilibrium price, in (3.3.1) by p_t^* and the solution value in (3.3.2) by p_t^{**}. As a first approximation we might posit that price change imposes adjustment costs that are proportional to the magnitude of the change, and that regimes are so chosen as to minimize these costs. Then the choice of equilibrium and disequilibrium regimes obeys the following:

select equilibrium model   if $|p_{t-1} - p_t^*| < |p_{t-1} - p_t^{**}|$
select disequilibrium model   otherwise   (3.3.3)

It is readily apparent, however, that this will bias the model against choosing the equilibrium regime. Writing the price adjustment equation in the Bowden (1978a, 1978b) manner as

$$p_t^{**} = \mu p_{t-1} + (1 - \mu) p_t^* + \mu u_{3t} \qquad (3.3.4)$$

and applying (3.3.3), equilibrium will be selected if

$$|p_{t-1} - p_t^*| < |(1 - \mu)(p_{t-1} - p_t^*) - \mu u_{3t}| \qquad (3.3.5)$$

Replacing $p_{t-1} - p_t^*$ by Δ_t, squaring both sides of (3.3.5) and factoring yields the equivalent expression (if $\mu > 0$ as is required)

$$(u_{3t} + \Delta_t)\left[u_{3t} - \frac{\Delta_t(2-\mu)}{\mu}\right] > 0 \qquad (3.3.6)$$

Hence equilibrium is chosen either if

$$u_{3t} > -\Delta_t \quad \text{and} \quad u_{3t} > \frac{\Delta_t(2-\mu)}{\mu}$$

or if

$$u_{3t} < -\Delta_t \quad \text{and} \quad u_{3t} < \frac{\Delta_t(2-\mu)}{\mu}$$

There are thus two asymmetric intervals about the origin (since $0 \leq \mu \leq 1$ and depending on the sign of Δ_t) with the property that if u_{3t} falls within the interval, disequilibrium will be chosen. Hence, if σ_3^2 is small, disequilibrium will be chosen predominantly.

A less restrictive approach is to

select equilibrium model   if $|p_{t-1} - p_t^*| < |k_1(p_{t-1}-p_t^{**}) + k_2|$

select disequilibrium model   otherwise   (3.3.7)

where $k_1 (\geq 0)$ and k_2 are parameters to be determined. We first determine that (3.3.7) is free of the difficulty encountered above. Proceeding as in (3.3.5) and (3.3.6) yields for the choice of equilibrium the following conditions: when $\Delta_t > 0$, either

$$u_{3t} > \frac{k_1(1-\mu)\Delta_t + k_2 + \Delta_t}{k_1\mu} \qquad (3.3.8)$$

or

$$u_{3t} < \frac{k_1(1-\mu)\Delta_t + k_2 - \Delta_t}{k_1\mu}$$

and when $\Delta_t < 0$, either

$$u_{3t} < \frac{k_1(1-\mu)\Delta_t + k_2 + \Delta_t}{k_1\mu} \qquad (3.3.9)$$

or

$$u_{3t} > \frac{k_1(1-\mu)\Delta_t + k_2 - \Delta_t}{k_1\mu}$$

It is clear from (3.3.8) and (3.3.9) that if, say, $k_2 = 0$ and $k_1 \to 0$ then $\Pr\{E\} \to 0$, while if $k_1 \to \infty$ then $\Pr\{E\} \to 1$. Hence the choice of k_1 and k_2 allows equilibrium to occur with any probability between 0 and 1. We now derive the likelihood function for this model.

Let $f(Q_t, p_t|M)$ be the joint p.d.f. of the observable random variables conditional on the model selected where $M = (E(\text{quilibrium}),$ $D(\text{isequilibrium}))$. Then $f(Q_t, p_t|E) = f_e(Q_t, p_t)$ and $f(Q_t, p_t|D) = f_d(Q_t, p_t)$, and the p.d.f. of Q_t, p_t is

$$g(Q_t, p_t) = f(Q_t, p_t|E)\Pr\{E\} + f(Q_t, p_t|D)\Pr\{D\} \tag{3.3.10}$$

We require $\Pr\{E\}$ and $\Pr\{D\} = 1 - \Pr\{E\}$. The criteria for model selection are

$$|p_{t-1} - p_t^*| = \left| p_{t-1} - \frac{1}{\Delta_1}[\beta_1' x_{1t} - \beta_2' x_{2t} + u_{1t} - u_{2t}] \right| \tag{3.3.11}$$

and

$$|k_1(p_{t-1} - p_t^{**}) + k_2| = \left| k_1 \left\{ p_{t-1} - \frac{1}{\Delta_2}[\gamma(\beta_1' x_{1t} - \beta_2' x_{2t}) + p_{t-1} \right.\right.$$
$$\left.\left. + \gamma(u_{1t} - u_{2t}) + u_{3t}] \right\} + k_2 \right| \tag{3.3.12}$$

where $\Delta_1 = \alpha_2 - \alpha_1$ and $\Delta_2 = 1 + \gamma(\alpha_2 - \alpha_1)$. Denote the arguments of the absolute value functions on the right hand sides of (3.3.11) and (3.3.12) by v_{1t} and v_{2t} respectively. Conditional on p_{t-1}, v_{1t} and v_{2t} are jointly normally distributed with mean vector

$$\mu_v = \begin{bmatrix} p_{t-1} - \dfrac{1}{\Delta_1}(\beta_1' x_{1t} - \beta_2' x_{2t}) \\[2ex] k_1 \left\{ p_{t-1} - \dfrac{1}{\Delta_2}[\gamma(\beta_1' x_{1t} - \beta_2' x_{2t}) + p_{t-1}] \right\} + k_2 \end{bmatrix} \tag{3.3.13}$$

and covariance matrix

$$\Sigma_v = \begin{bmatrix} (\sigma_1^2 + \sigma_2^2 - 2\sigma_{12})/\Delta_1^2 & k_1[\gamma(\sigma_1^2 + \sigma_2^2 - 2\sigma_{12}) + \sigma_{13} - \sigma_{23}]/\Delta_1\Delta_2 \\[2ex] \bullet & k_1^2[\gamma^2(\sigma_1^2 + \sigma_2^2 - 2\sigma_{12}) + 2\gamma(\sigma_{13} - \sigma_{23}) + \sigma_3^2]/\Delta_2^2 \end{bmatrix} \tag{3.3.14}$$

The probability $\Pr\{|v_{1t}| < |v_{2t}|\}$ is

$$\begin{aligned} \Pr\{|v_{1t}| < |v_{2t}|\} = &\Pr\{v_{1t} < v_{2t}|v_{1t} \geq 0, v_{2t} \geq 0\} \\ &+ \Pr\{v_{1t} < -v_{2t}|v_{1t} \geq 0, v_{2t} < 0\} \\ &+ \Pr\{-v_{1t} < v_{2t}|v_{1t} < 0, v_{2t} \geq 0\} \\ &+ \Pr\{-v_{1t} < -v_{2t}|v_{1t} < 0, v_{2t} < 0\} \end{aligned} \tag{3.3.15}$$

The required probability is the sum of the integrals of the normal p.d.f. over two wedge-shaped areas bounded by $|v_1| = |v_2|$ and extending from the origin to $\pm \infty$. It is evaluated most easily by rotating the coordinate system in the positive sense through an angle $\pi/4$ according to the transformation

$$\begin{bmatrix} y_{1t} \\ y_{2t} \end{bmatrix} = A \begin{bmatrix} v_{1t} \\ v_{2t} \end{bmatrix}$$

where A is the orthogonal matrix

$$A = \frac{1}{\sqrt{2}} \begin{bmatrix} 1 & -1 \\ 1 & 1 \end{bmatrix}$$

The required probability is

$$\Pr\{E\} = \Pr\{|v_{1t}| < |v_{2t}|\}$$

$$= \int_0^\infty \int_{-\infty}^0 \frac{1}{2\pi |\Sigma_y|^{1/2}} \exp\left\{ -\frac{1}{2} [(y - \mu_y)' \Sigma_y^{-1} (y - \mu_y)] \right\} dy_1 dy_2$$

$$+ \int_{-\infty}^0 \int_0^\infty \frac{1}{2\pi |\Sigma_y|^{1/2}} \exp\left\{ -\frac{1}{2} [(y - \mu_y)' \Sigma_y^{-1} (y - \mu_y)] \right\} dy_1 dy_2$$

$$(3.3.16)$$

where $\mu_y = A\mu_v$ and $\Sigma_y = A\Sigma_v A'$. The integrals in (3.3.16) are easily evaluated.[3] The likelihood function then is

$$L = \sum_{t=1}^T g(Q_t, p_t) \tag{3.3.17}$$

It is tedious but straightforward to verify that (3.3.17) shares the well-known unboundedness property of disequilibrium likelihood functions in the neighborhood of certain points on the boundaries $\sigma_1^2 = 0$ and $\sigma_2^2 = 0$.

It is not easy to make the choice mechanism more realistic by complicating it in various ways. One might argue that in the disequilibrium regime costs are incurred owing to both price change and to the existence of disequilibrium. Thus the choice mechanism in (3.3.7) would involve both $|p_{t-1} - p_t^{**}|$ and $|D_t - S_t|$. However, it is not clear that this is useful since the joint density of $p_{t-1} - p_t^*$, $p_{t-1} - p_t^{**}$, $D_t - S_t$ is singular (see exercise 3.1). Making the choice criterion depend on proportionate price changes and on the percentage of excess demand would solve this problem, but the likelihood function is then intractable.

A related approach that does not rest on a behavioral assumption concerning the system's choice between equilibrium and disequilibrium has been suggested by Deville (1982). The underlying idea is that the market is more likely to be in equilibrium when the systematic parts of demand and supply (i.e. $\alpha_1 p_t + \beta_1' x_{1t}$ and $\alpha_2 p_t + \beta_2' x_{2t}$ in (3.3.2)) are close in value than when they are far apart. Define for this purpose a function $P(\epsilon)$ with the properties

---

[3] See the modification of Hausman and Wise (1978) of Owen's (1956) method. The FORTRAN program for bivariate integration of the normal density is in appendix 6.B.

$P(0) = 1, 0 \leq P(\epsilon) \leq 1$ for $\epsilon \neq 0$, and $P'(\epsilon)\epsilon < 0$ for $\epsilon \neq 0$, and let

$$\Pr\{E\} = P(\alpha_1 p_t + \beta_1' x_{1t} - \alpha_2 p_t - \beta_2' x_{2t})$$
$$\Pr\{D\} = 1 - \Pr\{E\}$$

The density of Q_t is then claimed to have the same general form as (3.3.10). The difficulty is that the probability of equilibrium depends on p_t, which is endogenous and cannot be known until "nature" has tossed the appropriate die to determine whether p_t is to be generated from the equilibrium or disequilibrium regimes.

3.4   Testing for Equilibrium

A question of considerable practical importance is whether one can use the data to choose between an equilibrium and a disequilibrium specification. Before we begin to treat this question in detail, two general observations are worth noting:

1   It is probably not of great interest to be able to choose between an arbitrary member of the class of equilibrium models and an equally arbitrary member of the disequilibrium class, since members of both classes may be very badly chosen or since, as is more probable, the member of the one class is chosen with very much greater care than that of the other. What one should presumably aim at is effective test procedures when the respective members of the two classes are reasonably "well matched."

2   Disequilibrium models can differ substantially among themselves and it is certainly not clear that the same or even similar techniques will be applicable to all. What we can hope to achieve is to identify some major types of models in which testing can be accomplished.

Testing in model D

The relatively most complicated of the standard disequilibrium models is model D, which is reproduced for convenience in (3.3.2). A natural equilibrium counterpart is obtained by setting $D_t = S_t = Q_t$ and the model then is (3.3.1). It is clear that the price adjustment equation can play no role in the equilibrium version. The p.d.f. for the disequilibrium model was derived in chapter 2 and is given by (2.3.20). The p.d.f. for the equilibrium case and uncorrelated normal errors is

$$h_e(Q_t, p_t) = \frac{|\alpha_2 - \alpha_1|}{2\pi\sigma_1\sigma_2} \exp\left\{-\frac{1}{2}\left[\frac{(Q_t - \alpha_1 p_t - \beta_1' x_{1t})^2}{\sigma_1^2}\right.\right.$$
$$\left.\left. + \frac{(Q_t - \alpha_2 p_t - \beta_2' x_{2t})^2}{\sigma_2^2}\right]\right\} \tag{3.4.1}$$

A relevant question is the relationship of (3.4.1) to the p.d.f. of the disequilibrium model. Denote the p.d.f. in this model (given by (2.3.20) into which (2.3.23) and (2.3.24) have been substituted) by $h_d(Q_t, p_t)$. We then have the following:

Theorem

$$\lim_{\gamma \to \infty} h_d(Q_t, p_t) = h_e(Q_t, p_t)$$

Proof   Consider first the leading terms $|1 + \gamma(\alpha_2 - \alpha_1)|/2\pi\sigma_2(\sigma_3^2 + \gamma^2\sigma_1^2)^{1/2}$ and $|1 + \gamma(\alpha_2 - \alpha_1)|/2\pi\sigma_1(\sigma_3^2 + \gamma^2\sigma_2^2)^{1/2}$ in (2.3.23) and (2.3.24). Dividing numerator and denominator in both by γ and letting $\gamma \to \infty$ shows that both have the identical limit $|\alpha_2 - \alpha_1|/2\pi\sigma_1\sigma_2$, which is in fact the leading term of (3.4.1).

Next consider the terms $(B_{2t} - B_{1t}^2)(\sigma_3^2 + \gamma^2\sigma_1^2)/\sigma_1^2\sigma_3^2$ and $(B_{4t} - B_{3t}^2)(\sigma_3^2 + \gamma^2\sigma_2^2)/\sigma_2^2\sigma_3^2$ in the exp{ } terms in (2.3.23) and (2.3.24). After simplifying the expressions and dividing numerator and denominator by γ^2, they can be written as

$$\frac{(A_{1t} - A_{3t}/\gamma)^2}{\sigma_3^2/\gamma^2 + \sigma_1^2}$$

and   (3.4.2)

$$\frac{(A_{5t} + A_{6t}/\gamma)^2}{\sigma_3^2/\gamma^2 + \sigma_2^2}$$

The first of these has the limit $(Q_t - \alpha_1 p_t - \beta_1' x_{1t})^2/\sigma_1^2$ as $\gamma \to \infty$ and the second has the limit $(Q_t - \alpha_2 p_t - \beta_2' x_{2t})^2/\sigma_2^2$. Given the definitions of A_{2t} and A_{4t} (see immediately following (2.3.22) and (2.3.24)), both exp{ } terms have the identical limit of $\exp\{-(1/2)[(Q_t - \alpha_1 p_t - \beta_1' x_{1t})^2/\sigma_1^2 + (Q_t - \alpha_2 p_t - \beta_2' x_{2t})^2/\sigma_2^2]\}$.

Finally we turn to the $1 - \Phi(\ )$ terms in (2.3.23) and (2.3.24). The arguments of the two $\Phi(\ )$ functions become after simplification

$$\frac{Q_t\sigma_3^2 - A_{1t}\sigma_3^2 - \gamma(p_t - p_{t-1})\sigma_1^2}{\sigma_1\sigma_3(\sigma_3^2 + \gamma^2\sigma_1^2)^{1/2}}$$

and   (3.4.3)

$$\frac{Q_t\sigma_3^2 - A_{5t}\sigma_3^2 + \gamma(p_t - p_{t-1})\sigma_2^2}{\sigma_2\sigma_3(\sigma_3^2 + \gamma^2\sigma_2^2)^{1/2}}$$

Dividing numerator and denominator in both by γ and letting $\gamma \to \infty$ shows that the respective limits are $-(p_t - p_{t-1})/\sigma_3$ and $(p_t - p_{t-1})/\sigma_3$. Thus the limit of $h_d(Q_t, p_t)$ is

$$\lim h_d(Q_t, p_t) = \frac{|\alpha_2 - \alpha_1|}{2\pi\sigma_1\sigma_2} \exp\left\{ -\frac{1}{2}\left[\frac{(Q_t - \alpha_1 p_t - \beta_1' x_{1t})^2}{\sigma_1^2} \right. \right.$$

$$+ \frac{(Q_t - \alpha_2 p_t - \beta_2' x_{2t})^2}{\sigma_2^2} \Big] \Big\} \Big[1 - \Phi\left(-\frac{p_t - p_{t-1}}{\sigma_3}\right)$$

$$+ 1 - \Phi\left(\frac{p_t - p_{t-1}}{\sigma_3}\right) \Big] \tag{3.4.4}$$

but the terms in the last bracket clearly add to unity, thus proving the contention. □

Another way of looking at this phenomenon is to substitute the demand and supply functions in (3.3.2) into the price adjustment equation, which upon further backward substitution becomes

$$p_t = \mu^j p_{t-j} + (1-\mu)[p_t^* + \mu p_{t-1}^* + \ldots + \mu^{j-1} p_{t-j+1}^*]$$
$$+ \mu u_{3t} + \mu^2 u_{3t-1} + \ldots + \mu^j u_{3t-j+1} \tag{3.4.5}$$

where p_t^* is the equilibrium price and $\mu = 1/[1 + \gamma(\alpha_2 - \alpha_1)]$. It is readily apparent that if $\gamma \to \infty$, $p_t \to p_t^*$ as long as the equilibrium prices are bounded by functions going to infinity slower than μ goes to zero and if the distribution of u_{3t} is stationary. It thus appears reasonable to test for equilibrium as against the alternative of disequilibrium in two ways:

1   By computing the likelihood ratio λ for the equilibrium and disequilibrium models and comparing $-2\log\lambda$ with the critical values of the χ^2 distribution
2   By examining whether γ is large.

We first examine the likelihood ratio approach. It appears from the limit argument above and from (3.4.4) that the equilibrium counterpart obtained from the disequilibrium model by letting $\gamma \to \infty$ involves two fewer parameters, since σ_3^2 disappears as well (Mouchart and Orsi 1986). Hence, applying asymptotic theory for testing, $\chi^2(2)$ is the appropriate distribution for critical values.

In the second approach, we must make clear what it means to say that γ is large. It therefore seems more plausible to examine whether $1/\gamma$ is small or not. We would thus make equilibrium the null hypothesis (as in the likelihood ratio test) and reject H_0 if $1/\gamma$ is significantly different from zero. The relationship between the present test and the previous one is illuminated by noting that the present test is a Wald test. The size of $1/\gamma$ can be examined in at least three ways:

1   We could parameterize the model so that we estimate $\delta = 1/\gamma$ rather than γ.
2   We could parameterize the model in the Bowden manner (see (2.1.11)) and test whether μ is significantly different from zero.
3   We could estimate the model parameterized by γ and then use an approximation to estimate the (asymptotic) standard error of $1/\hat{\gamma}$.

In the Bowden parameterization we can estimate μ directly by maximizing the likelihood function or, provided that the demand and supply functions do not contain the lagged price, we can obtain the reduced form for p_t by substituting in the adjustment equation and using OLS. If $\hat{\theta}$ is a consistent and asymptotically normal estimator of a scalar parameter θ such that $\sqrt{(T)}(\hat{\theta} - \theta^0) \xrightarrow{a} N(0, V)$ and if $g(\theta)$ is a differentiable function of θ, then the asymptotic distribution of $\sqrt{(T)}[g(\hat{\theta}) - g(\theta^0)]$ is $N(0, g'(\theta^0)^2 V)$ and the variance can be consistently estimated by $g'(\theta)^2 V$. Now consider $1/\gamma$ as the particular case in point and let $\hat{\sigma}^2$ denote the asymptotic variance of $\hat{\gamma}$. Then the test statistic for $1/\hat{\gamma}$ is $(1/\hat{\gamma})/(\hat{\sigma}^2/\hat{\gamma}^4)^{1/2} = \hat{\gamma}/\hat{\sigma}$.

It is easy to verify that this is in fact the Wald test. If the parameter vector is $\theta = (\theta_1, \ldots, \theta_k)'$ and the null hypothesis is expressed $h(\theta) = [h_1(\theta), \ldots, h_m(\theta)]' = 0$, the Wald test statistic is given by

$$W = h(\theta)' \left[\frac{\partial h(\theta)'}{\partial \theta} J^{-1} \frac{\partial h(\theta)}{\partial \theta} \right]^{-1} h(\theta)$$

where J represents the information matrix. Letting $h(\theta) = 1/\gamma$ and evaluating W at the unrestricted estimates gives the test statistic in question.

The test is exactly the same as the test statistic for the null hypothesis that γ is zero. This may appear paradoxical, but in fact is not. A significant $1/\hat{\gamma}$ is equivalent to a significant $\hat{\gamma}$ and rejects the null hypothesis of equilibrium. But a significant $\hat{\gamma}$ should not be interpreted to mean that $\hat{\gamma}$ is large and therefore the equilibrium regime must hold. Large γs in the sense of implying near equilibrium by (3.4.5) are not indicated by statistically significant γs; that is a $\hat{\gamma}$ could be 0.1 and have an asymptotic standard deviation of 0.01, yet (3.4.5) would not even approximately suggest that $p_t = p_t^*$. The important part in the interpretation is that equilibrium is the null hypothesis; we can only reject it or fail to reject it, but γ is not used to confirm its existence.

Testing in model C

It is immediate from the density function or likelihood function of this model (see (2.3.17)) that here, too, the equilibrium model is the limit as $\gamma \to \infty$ (Gourieroux, Laffont and Monfort 1980c). Denoting the density function of the observable random variables in model C by $h_c(Q_t, p_t)$, we have the following:

Theorem

$$\lim_{\gamma \to \infty} h_c(Q_t, p_t) = h_e(Q_t, p_t)$$

Proof The density function underlying (2.3.18) can be written as

$$h_c(Q_t, p_t) = \delta_t f_2(Q_t, p_t) + (1 - \delta_t) f_1(Q_t, p_t)$$

where $\delta_t = 1$ if $\Delta p_t > 0$ and zero otherwise. But it is straightforward to verify that

$$\lim_{\gamma \to \infty} f_1(Q_t, p_t) = \lim_{\gamma \to \infty} f_2(Q_t, p_t) = h_e(Q_t, p_t)$$

from which the result follows.   □

Finally, we also have the further theorem (Goldfeld and Quandt 1981b):

Theorem

$$\lim_{\sigma_3^2 \to 0} h_d(Q_t, p_t) = h_c(Q_t, p_t)$$

Proof   We again consider the Jacobian terms in (2.3.23) and (2.3.24) first, but with the proviso that, to make the models strictly comparable, we first replace $\beta_3' x_{3t}$ by p_{t-1}. In both cases the limits as $\sigma_3^2 \to 0$ are $|1/\gamma + \alpha_2 - \alpha_1|/2\pi\sigma_1\sigma_2$, which is the Jacobian term in (2.3.17). Simplifying the exp $\{\ \}$ terms in (2.3.23) and (2.3.24) shows that their limits as $\sigma_3^2 \to 0$ are

$$\exp\left\{-\frac{1}{2}\left[\frac{(Q_t - \alpha_1 p_t - \beta_1' x_{1t} + \Delta p_t/\gamma)^2}{\sigma_1^2} + \frac{(Q_t - \alpha_2 p_t - \beta_2' x_{2t})^2}{\sigma_2^2}\right]\right\}$$

(3.4.6)

and

$$\exp\left\{-\frac{1}{2}\left[\frac{(Q_t - \alpha_1 p_t - \beta_1' x_{1t})^2}{\sigma_1^2} + \frac{(Q_t - \alpha_2 p_t - \beta_2' x_{2t} - \Delta p_t/\gamma)^2}{\sigma_2^2}\right]\right\}$$

(3.4.7)

respectively. Finally, it can be seen that the argument of $\Phi(\ )$ in (2.3.23) goes to $-\infty$ if $\Delta p_t > 0$ and to $+\infty$ if $\Delta p_t < 0$, with the reverse holding for (2.3.24). Thus, (3.4.6) vanishes from the density when $\Delta p_t < 0$, and the second term of the remaining term (3.4.7) is, by the definition of Δp_t^+ and Δp_t^- (section 2.3), just $(Q_t - \alpha_2 p_t - \beta_2' x_{2t} + \Delta p^-/\gamma)^2/\sigma_2^2$. For similar reasons (3.4.7) vanishes from the density when $\Delta p_t > 0$, and the first term of (3.4.6) becomes $(Q_t - \alpha_1 p_t - \beta_1' x_{1t} + \Delta p_t^+/\gamma)^2/\sigma_1^2$. Finally, if $\Delta p_t = 0$, the argument of both $\Phi(\ )$ functions is zero.   □

But this shows that the density function of the stochastic price adjustment case converges to that of the nonstochastic price adjustment model as $\sigma_3^2 \to 0$. Hence we can test the null hypothesis of a nonstochastic price adjustment equation against the more general case by a likelihood ratio test. Since this is a test of a null hypothesis on the boundary of the parameter space, the significance level needs to be adjusted up by a factor of 2 to get a test of correct size (Gourieroux, Holly and Monfort 1982).

Testing the hypothesis of equilibrium versus disequilibrium can thus employ similar techniques as for model D. In addition, in the present case, a Lagrange multiplier test due to Upcher (1982) is straightforward. We first reparameterize the model by setting $1/\gamma = \delta$ and write (2.3.17) using the parameter δ. The null hypothesis is $H_0 : \delta = 0$.

L is the log-likelihood, and we define the second partial derivative matrix with respect to the parameter vector $\theta = (\delta,$ all other parameters$)$ as

$$- \frac{\partial^2 L}{\partial \theta \, \partial \theta'} = H = \begin{bmatrix} H_{11} & H_{12} \\ H_{21} & H_{22} \end{bmatrix}$$

where obviously the subscript 1 refers to δ and the subscript 2 to the remaining parameters in the model. The Lagrange multiplier test statistic is given by

$$\text{LM} = \left(\frac{\partial L}{\partial \delta} \right) (H_{11} - H_{12} H_{22}^{-1} H_{21})^{-1} \left(\frac{\partial L}{\partial \delta} \right) \tag{3.4.8}$$

where all quantities on the right hand side are evaluated under the null hypothesis. These are

$$\frac{\partial L}{\partial \delta} = \frac{T}{|\alpha_2 - \alpha_1 + \delta|} - \sum_{t=1}^{T} [\Delta p_t^+, \Delta p_t^-] \, \Sigma^{-1} \, u_t$$

and evaluating at $\delta = 0$,

$$\left. \frac{\partial L}{\partial \delta} \right|_{\delta = 0} = \frac{T}{|\alpha_2 - \alpha_1|} - \sum_{t=1}^{T} \widetilde{\Delta p_t'} \, \Sigma^{-1} \, \tilde{u}_t$$

where $\widetilde{\Delta p_t}$ represents the two-vector $[\Delta p_t^+, \Delta p_t^-]$ and $\tilde{u}_t$ is the vector of residuals for the tth observation from the equilibrium model. Similarly,

$$\left. \frac{\partial^2 L}{\partial \delta^2} \right|_{\delta = 0} = - \frac{T}{(\alpha_2 - \alpha_1)^2} - \sum_{t=1}^{T} \widetilde{\Delta p_t'} \, \Sigma^{-1} \, \widetilde{\Delta p_t}$$

$$\left. \frac{\partial^2 L}{\partial \delta \, \partial \alpha_1} \right|_{\delta = 0} = - \frac{T}{(\alpha_2 - \alpha_1)^2} - \sum_{t=1}^{T} \widetilde{\Delta p_t'} \, \Sigma^{-1} \binom{p_t}{0}$$

$$\left. \frac{\partial^2 L}{\partial \delta \, \partial \alpha_2} \right|_{\delta = 0} = - \frac{T}{(\alpha_2 - \alpha_1)^2} - \sum_{t=1}^{T} \widetilde{\Delta p_t'} \, \Sigma^{-1} \binom{0}{p_t}$$

$$\left. \frac{\partial^2 L}{\partial \delta \, \partial \beta_1'} \right|_{\delta = 0} = - \sum_{t=1}^{T} \widetilde{\Delta p_t'} \, \Sigma^{-1} \binom{x_{1t}'}{0'}$$

$$\left. \frac{\partial^2 L}{\partial \delta \, \partial \beta_2'} \right|_{\delta = 0} = \sum_{t=1}^{T} \widetilde{\Delta p_t'} \, \Sigma^{-1} \binom{0'}{x_{2t}'}$$

$$\left. \frac{\partial^2 L}{\partial \delta \, \partial \sigma^{ij}} \right|_{\delta = 0} = \sum_{t=1}^{T} \widetilde{\Delta p_t'} \, D_{ij} \, \tilde{u}_t$$

where D_{ij} is a matrix that has unity in the ijth and jith positions and zeros elsewhere. Finally, H_{22} is just obtained as the negative of the matrix of second partial derivatives of the equilibrium log-likelihood function.

Testing in model A

In this model, the equilibrium and disequilibrium versions have exactly the same parameters. Writing (2.1.1) and (2.1.2) so as to exhibit explicitly the dependence of demand and supply on price, we have

$$D_t = \alpha_1 p_t + \beta_1' x_{1t} + u_{1t} \tag{3.4.9}$$

$$S_t = \alpha_2 p_t + \beta_2' x_{2t} + u_{2t} \tag{3.4.10}$$

When $Q_t = \min(D_t, S_t)$ and D_t, S_t are unobserved, we have disequilibrium. When $D_t = S_t = Q_t$, with Q_t observed, we have equilibrium. Hence there is no parameter restriction implied by either hypothesis and the usual Wald, Lagrange multiplier, and likelihood ratio tests are not appropriate. Hwang (1980) has designed a test procedure that can be effective in this situation.

First obtain the reduced form from the *equilibrium* version of the model. This is

$$\begin{bmatrix} Q_t \\ p_t \end{bmatrix} = \begin{bmatrix} -\alpha_2\beta_1'/(\alpha_1-\alpha_2) & \alpha_1\beta_2'/(\alpha_1-\alpha_2) \\ -\beta_1'/(\alpha_1-\alpha_2) & \beta_2'/(\alpha_1-\alpha_2) \end{bmatrix} \begin{bmatrix} x_{1t} \\ x_{2t} \end{bmatrix} + \begin{bmatrix} v_{1t} \\ v_{2t} \end{bmatrix} \tag{3.4.11}$$

Denote the covariance matrix of the normal errors u_{1t}, u_{2t} by Σ and the matrix of coefficients of the endogenous variables in the structural equations by Γ. Let $v_t \sim N(0,\Omega)$, with $\Omega = \|\omega_{ij}\| = \Gamma^{-1}\Sigma\Gamma'^{-1}$. Since v_{1t} and v_{2t} are jointly normal, the normal regression relation holds, according to which $v_{1t} = (\omega_{12}/\omega_{22})v_{2t} + \epsilon_t$. The error term ϵ_t is normal and independent of v_{2t} and, since p_t depends only on the error v_{2t} (and not on v_{1t}), ϵ_t is also independent of p_t. From $u_t = \Gamma v_t$ we have $u_{1t} = v_{1t} - \alpha_1 v_{2t}$, and substituting for v_{1t} from the normal regression relation above, then replacing v_{2t} from (3.4.11), and finally using this value of u_{1t} in the first structural equation, we obtain

$$Q_t = (\omega_{12}/\omega_{22})p_t + [(\omega_{12}/\omega_{22}-\alpha_2)\beta_1'/(\alpha_1-\alpha_2)]x_{1t}$$
$$+ [(\alpha_1 - \omega_{12}/\omega_{22})\beta_2'/(\alpha_1-\alpha_2)]x_{2t} + \epsilon_t \tag{3.4.12}$$

This equation is a hybrid between the structural and reduced form equations and has the properties that (a) all variables other than Q_t appear on the right hand side; (b) its error term is uncorrelated with any of the right hand variables and may thus be consistently estimated by OLS; (c) its coefficients are complicated but *constant* functions of the original structural parameters. The actual estimates for these coefficients are of no particular interest.

If the disequilibrium model is appropriate, we can write

$$Q_t = \delta_t D_t + (1-\delta_t)S_t$$

with $\delta_t = 1$ if $D_t < S_t$ and 0 otherwise (as in (2.6.8)), and further obtain

$$Q_t = [\delta_t\alpha_1 + (1-\delta_t)\alpha_2]p_t + \delta_t\beta_1'x_{1t} + (1-\delta_t)\beta_2'x_{2t} + w_t$$

which is similar to (3.4.12) except that it contains time-varying parameters.

Hwang suggests therefore computing for an equation of the general form $Q_t = \theta_0 p_t + \theta_1' x_{1t} + \theta_2' x_{2t} + \epsilon_t$ the Brown, Durbin and Evans (1975) recursive residuals and using the cusum or cusum of squares test[4] for testing the null hypothesis that the regression coefficients are constant. Rejecting H_0 is then equivalent to rejecting the equilibrium hypothesis.

Several qualifications have to be noted:

1   Under the alternative hypothesis the errors are heteroscedastic and this may have an effect on the power of the test.

2   If the alternative hypothesis involves a price adjustment equation (as in model C), a similar test is still possible in principle but is likely to be less satisfactory. In this case, the price adjustment equation (most easily thought to be in Bowden form here) has to be used for backward substitution to obtain an equation with an infinite distributed lag in the exogenous variables; to estimate such an equation under the null already involves a specification error.

3   The power of the test even in the ideal case of model A is likely to be considerably affected by the pattern of excess demands and supplies. Thus, for example, the power is likely to be greater if there are relatively few alternations between long periods of excess demand and supply rather than relatively frequent and random alternations between the two regimes. Sampling experiments by Hwang (1980) find that the test is generally satisfactory, although the power decreases with the sample size.

Testing Model A Price Endogeneity

Hajivassiliou (1986a) introduced a Lagrange multiplier test of model A against the alternative that price is endogenous (e.g. determined as in model D). We again start from (3.3.1). If price were endogenous in reality, the reduced form equation could be written as

$$p_t = \beta_3' x_{3t} + v_t \tag{3.4.13}$$

where x_{3t} incorporates all predetermined variables and v_t is the reduced form error. Thus, with a model D price adjustment equation, this reduced form is

$$p_t = (\gamma \beta_1' x_1 - \gamma \beta_2' x_2 + p_{t-1})/[1 + \gamma(\alpha_2 - \alpha_1)] + v_t$$

The three error terms u_{1t}, u_{2t}, v_t have a covariance matrix that may be written as

---

[4] See appendix 3.B for a derivation of the recursive residuals and the cusum test. Obviously there are also other ways of testing, using models of time-varying parameters. Note that δ_t is endogenous in the equation, which is an additional reason why the null hypothesis may be rejected.

$$\begin{bmatrix} \Sigma_{uu} & \Sigma_{uv} \\ \Sigma_{uv} & \sigma_v^2 \end{bmatrix}$$

and allows us to deduce the joint density $f(D_t, S_t, p_t)$. As in chapter 2,

$$h(Q_t, p_t) = \int_{Q_t}^{\infty} f(D_t, Q_t, p_t)\,dD_t + \int_{Q_t}^{\infty} f(Q_t, S_t, p_t)\,dS_t \equiv f_1 + f_2 \qquad (3.4.14)$$

We can write formally $f(D_t, S_t, p_t) = f(D_t, S_t | p_t)g(p_t)$, and then

$$f_1 = g(p_t)\int_{Q_t}^{\infty} f(D_t, Q_t | p_t)\,dD_t$$

and similarly for f_2. In order to utilize this we need $f(p_t)$, which is immediate from (3.4.13) and $f(D_t, S_t | p_t)$. This is a bivariate conditional normal with mean vector

$$\mu_t = \begin{bmatrix} \mu_{1t} \\ \mu_{2t} \end{bmatrix} = \begin{bmatrix} \alpha_1 p_t + \beta_1' x_{1t} \\ \alpha_2 p_t + \beta_2' x_{2t} \end{bmatrix} + \Sigma_{uv}\,(p_t - \beta_3' x_{3t})/\sigma_v^2$$

and covariance matrix

$$\Sigma = \Sigma_{uu} - \Sigma_{uv}\Sigma_{uv}'/\sigma_v^2$$

Testing for the exogeneity of price is then accomplished by testing for $\Sigma_{uv} = 0$. To obtain a Lagrange multiplier test, we need the first partial derivatives of the log-likelihood evaluated at $\Sigma_{uv} = 0$.

From (3.4.14) we have for f_1

$$f_1 = g(p_t)\int_{Q_t}^{\infty} \frac{1}{2\pi |\Sigma|^{1/2}} \exp\left\{-\frac{1}{2} r_{1t}' \Sigma^{-1} r_{1t}\right\} dD_t$$

where $r_{1t}' = (D_t - \mu_{1t}, Q_t - \mu_{2t})$, and

$$f_2 = g(p_t)\int_{Q_t}^{\infty} \frac{1}{2\pi |\Sigma|^{1/2}} \exp\left\{-\frac{1}{2} r_{2t}' \Sigma^{-1} r_{2t}\right\} dS_t$$

where $r_{2t}' = (Q_t - \mu_{1t}, S_t - \mu_{2t})$. Using the facts that

$$\left.\frac{\partial |\Sigma|^{-1/2}}{\partial \Sigma_{uv}}\right|_{\Sigma_{uv}=0} = 0, \qquad \left.\frac{\partial \Sigma^{-1}}{\partial \Sigma_{uv}}\right|_{\Sigma_{uv}=0} = 0 \qquad (3.4.15)$$

it follows that

$$\left.\frac{\partial f_1}{\partial \Sigma_{uv}}\right|_{\Sigma_{uv}=0} = g(p_t) \int_{Q_t}^{\infty} \left[\frac{1}{2\pi |\Sigma_{uv}|^{1/2}} \exp\left\{ -\frac{1}{2} r'_{1t} \Sigma_{uu}^{-1} r_{1t} \right\} \right.$$

$$\left. \times r_{1t} \Sigma_{uu}^{-1} (p_t - \beta'_3 x_{3t})/\sigma_v^2 \right] dD_t$$

with a similar expression holding for $\partial f_2 / \partial \Sigma_{uv}$ (where r_{2t} replaces r_{1t} and dS_t replaces dD_t). From this, $(\partial \log h_t / \partial \Sigma_{uv})_{\Sigma_{uv}=0}$ is obtained immediately. Hajivassiliou shows that, as is generally the case for the Lagrange multiplier test, only the restricted likelihood needs to be maximized, which can also be obtained from the artificial model

$$D_t = \alpha_1 p_t + \beta'_1 x_{1t} + \xi_1 (p_t - \beta'_3 x_{3t}) + u_{1t}$$

$$S_t = \alpha_2 p_t + \beta'_2 x_{2t} + \xi_2 (p_t - \beta'_3 x_{3t}) + u_{2t}$$

$$Q_t = \min(D_t, S_t)$$

where p_t is treated as exogenous. The corresponding density has (except for a factor σ_v^2) the same partial derivatives with respect to ξ_1, ξ_2 evaluated at $\xi_1 = \xi_2 = 0$ as $(\partial \log h_t / \partial \Sigma_{uv})_{\Sigma_{uv}=0}$ obtained earlier.

Testing in Other Models

In models that do not conform to the canonical forms emphasized in chapter 2, it may not be obvious what an appropriate test of equilibrium and disequilibrium should be based on. However, if the equilibrium and disequilibrium modes of such a model are derived from minimizing some loss functions, insight may be gained into the appropriate test criterion by comparing it with some canonical case such as models C or D. In those models, the parameter γ corresponds to the parameter θ in the loss function $C = (p_t - p_{t-1})^2 + \theta(D_t - S_t)^2$ (see also (2.2.1) and the discussion following). If γ, that is θ, were very large, even a slight discrepancy between demand and supply would generate a sizeable loss and hence, with optimization, the system would behave as an equilibrium system. As an illustration, consider the loss function discussed in section 1.4 which purports to represent the objective of the Federal Home Loan Bank Board. With the possibility of rationing, this loss function is $V = (R - C)^2 + v_1(R - R_{-1})^2 + v_2(H - H^*)^2 + v_3(A^d - A)^2$, where the last term measures the loss caused by a discrepancy between the demand for advances and their actual volume. If v_3 is very large, it will be costly to ration and the system will tend to behave in market-clearing mode. Hence a test on v_3 is appropriate.

3.5 The Problem of All-Excess-Demand: Estimability

If it is deemed appropriate to model a market as a disequilibrium phenomenon, we may wish to know whether we can assert that the market in question always exhibits excess demand or always exhibits excess supply. This type of view is stressed by Kornai (1979, 1980a), who believes that socialist, planned economies *always* exhibit excess demand. A corresponding question would arise in the context of a free-enterprise economy if we asked whether the labor market might always exhibit excess supply. Cases of this type have been investigated by Hartley and Mennemeyer (1974) who concentrate the model with respect to the unobserved demand or supply and deduce the values of the structural parameters from FIML estimates from the concentrated (partially reduced form) model.

In this section we investigate under what circumstances the parameters of the model remain estimable if there is always excess demand or excess supply. This approach highlights the reasons why estimability cannot be achieved in certain cases.

Case of No Price Adjustment

The model is described by (2.1.1)–(2.1.3) and the appropriate likelihood function can be obtained in two ways:

1   Since in the all-excess-demand case we claim prior knowledge that the index set for which $D_t > S_t$ is the set of all index values, the likelihood function becomes one that is formally similar to the directional method (2.3.11) with all terms allocated to excess demand, i.e.

$$L = \prod_{t=1}^{T} \int_{Q_t}^{\infty} g(D_t, Q_t)\,\mathrm{d}D_t \qquad (3.5.1)$$

2   Alternatively, we may start with the density for model A and claim that $\int_{Q_t}^{\infty} g(Q_t, S_t)\,\mathrm{d}S_t$ in (2.3.7) is small relative to $h(Q_t)$; as a limiting case this term is neglected and we again obtain (3.5.1). For the case given by (3.2.1) the specific form of the likelihood is

$$L = \prod_{t=1}^{T} \frac{1}{\sqrt{(2\pi)}\,\sigma_2} \exp\left\{ -\frac{1}{2} \frac{(Q_t - \alpha_2 p_t - \beta_2' x_{2t})^2}{\sigma_2^2} \right\}$$
$$\times \left[1 - \Phi\left(\frac{Q_t - \alpha_1 p_t - \beta_1' x_{1t}}{\sigma_1} \right) \right] \qquad (3.5.2)$$

From the form of (3.5.2) we immediately derive the following:

Proposition 1   If the demand function contains a constant term, the parameters α_1, β_1, σ_1^2 are not estimable.

Proof   The likelihood is the product over t of a density term and the $1 - \Phi(\ )$ term. These terms share no parameters. Hence L can be maximized by independently maximizing with respect to $\alpha_1, \beta_1, \sigma_1^2$ on the one hand, and $\alpha_2, \beta_2, \sigma_2^2$ on the other. But the value of $1 - \Phi(\ )$ can be made arbitrarily close to its upper bound of 1.0 by assigning arbitrary values to the nonconstant term coefficients $\beta_{11}, \ldots, \beta_{1k}$ and making the constant term β_{10} arbitrarily large. $\square$

The intuition behind this is quite simple: if we are certain that all data points lie along the supply curve, they contain no information concerning the shape of the demand curve. It is clear that the same result holds if there is no constant term in the equation but there is a variable that does not change sign over the observations. The fact that makes estimation impossible if there is a constant term or a variable that does not change sign is that we can increase the relevant coefficient value and thus make the long side of the market even 'longer'; that is, by increasing some particular coefficient we push the demand function outward (north-east), and all hypothetical alternative positions occupied by the demand function are compatible with the *a priori* restriction. This does not occur if the relevant variable changes sign, for then arbitrary increases in the corresponding coefficient move the demand function in the opposite direction for some observations which eventually contradicts the prior information. For simplicity we posit henceforth that all relevant equations contain a constant term.

The typical term of the likelihood function (3.5.1) (and, for that matter, the typical term for many other types of disequilibrium model) can always be written as

$$\psi(\theta_1, \theta_2)[1 - \Phi(\theta_2, \theta_3)] \tag{3.5.3}$$

where $\psi(\ )$ is the density or density-like term, θ_1 is the subset of parameters occurring only in $\psi(\ )$, θ_3 is the subset occurring only in $\Phi(\ )$, and θ_2 is the subset occurring in both. A necessary condition for the estimability of the equation describing the long side of the market is then given by the following:

Proposition 2   A necessary condition for estimability is either that the set of coefficients θ_3 be empty or that they be the coefficients of variables that change sign over the sample period.

It should be noted that sufficient conditions for estimability are in general harder to obtain. Consider the following (artificial) case in which we know *a priori* that $\alpha_1 = \alpha_2$, $\beta_1 = \beta_2$, the variance of u_{1t} is σ_1^2 and the variance of u_{2t} is $\sigma_1^2 + \sigma_2^2$. Let $\hat{\alpha}_1$, $\hat{\beta}_1$ be the OLS estimates of α_1, β_1 from the *supply* equation (having replaced S_t by Q_t) and imagine that it is the case that the residuals $Q_t - \hat\alpha_1 p_t - \hat\beta_1' x_{1t}$ are all negative. Then it is clear from (3.5.2) that the global maximum of the likelihood is obtained at $\hat\alpha_1$, $\hat\beta_1$ with σ_1 being set arbitrarily close to zero; hence σ_1 is not estimable, even though there are no parameters in $\Phi(\ )$ of (3.5.2) that do not also appear in $\psi(\ )$.

We conclude this section by relaxing the assumption that the covariance σ_{12} between u_{1t} and u_{2t} is zero. Equation (3.5.2) then becomes, from (2.3.9),

$$L = \prod_{t=1}^{T} \frac{1}{\sqrt{(2\pi)}\sigma_2} \exp\left\{ -\frac{1}{2} \frac{(Q_t - \alpha_2 p_2 - \beta_2' x_{2t})^2}{\sigma_2^2} \right\}$$

$$\times \left[1 - \Phi\left(\frac{Q_t - \alpha_{1t} - \beta_1' x_{1t} - \rho(\sigma_1/\sigma_2)(Q_t - \alpha_2 p_t - \beta_2' x_{2t})}{\sigma_1(1-\rho^2)^{1/2}} \right) \right]$$

$$(3.5.4)$$

where $\rho = \sigma_{12}/\sigma_1\sigma_2$, and it is clear that introducing a nonzero covariance is not sufficient to estimate the demand equation, although, as before, the supply equation is estimable.

Model with Price Adjustment

We write the model as

$$D_t = \alpha_1 p_t + \beta_1' x_{1t} + u_{1t} \tag{3.5.5}$$

$$S_t = \alpha_2 p_t + \beta_2' x_{2t} + u_{2t} \tag{3.5.6}$$

$$Q_t = \min(D_t, S_t) \tag{3.5.7}$$

$$p_t = \gamma_1 D_t + \gamma_2 S_t + \beta_3' x_{3t} + u_{3t} \tag{3.5.8}$$

where we now allow separate γ coefficients for demand and supply. We continue to assume for simplicity that u_{1t}, u_{2t}, u_{3t} are independent of one another. Given the joint p.d.f. $g(D_t, S_t, p_t)$, the likelihood function under the prior restriction that excess supply has always occurred is

$$L = \prod_{t=1}^{T} \int_{Q_t}^{\infty} g(Q_t, S_t, p_t) \, dS_t \tag{3.5.9}$$

and is

$$L = \prod_{t=1}^{T} \int_{Q_t}^{\infty} g(D_t, Q_t, p_t) \, dD_t \tag{3.5.10}$$

for the case of perpetual excess demand.

The all-excess-demand and all-excess-supply density functions, i.e. the terms of (3.5.9) and (3.5.10) are

$$h_D(Q_t, p_t) = \frac{|1 - \alpha_1\gamma_1 - \alpha_2\gamma_2|}{2\pi\sigma_2(\sigma_3^2 + \gamma_1^2\sigma_1^2)^{1/2}}$$

$$\times \exp\left\{ -\frac{1}{2} \left[\frac{B_{2t} - B_{1t}^2}{\sigma_1^2\sigma_3^2/(\sigma_3^2 + \gamma_1^2\sigma_1^2)} + A_{2t} \right] \right\}$$

$$\times \left[1 - \Phi\left(\frac{Q_t - B_{1t}}{\sigma_1\sigma_3/(\sigma_3^2 + \gamma_1^2\sigma_1^2)^{1/2}} \right) \right] \qquad (3.5.11)$$

and

$$h_S(Q_t, p_t) = \frac{|1 - \alpha_1\gamma_1 - \alpha_2\gamma_2|}{2\pi\sigma_1(\sigma_3^2 + \gamma_2^2\sigma_2^2)^{1/2}}$$

$$\times \exp\left\{ -\frac{1}{2} \left[\frac{B_{4t} - B_{3t}^2}{\sigma_2^2\sigma_3^2/(\sigma_3^2 + \gamma_2^2\sigma_2^2)} + A_{4t} \right] \right\}$$

$$\times \left[1 - \Phi\left(\frac{Q_t - B_{3t}}{\sigma_2\sigma_3/(\sigma_3^2 + \gamma_2^2\sigma_2^2)^{1/2}} \right) \right] \qquad (3.5.12)$$

where the $A_{jt}, j = 1, \ldots, 6$, and $B_{jt}, j = 1, \ldots, 4$, have the same definitions as in (2.3.23) and (2.3.24) *except* that in A_{3t}, B_{1t}, B_{2t} the γ is replaced by γ_1 and in A_{6t}, B_{3t}, B_{4t} the γ is replaced by $-\gamma_2$. It is clear that the necessary condition for estimability of proposition 2 is met. In particular, it is met in the ordinary case when $\gamma_1 = -\gamma_2$. However, this does not ensure that all parameters can be estimated. Consider, for example, (3.5.12), in which the exp{ } term can be simplified as

$$\exp\left\{ -\frac{1}{2} \left[A_{4t} + (A_{6t} - \gamma_2 A_{5t})^2/(\sigma_3^2\sigma_2^2) \right] \right\}$$

If $Q_t - B_{3t}$ is negative for all observations, as is possible if the values of the error terms are small but the excess supply is large, the likelihood may be monotone increasing as $\sigma_2^2 \to 0$ and this parameter cannot be estimated. Hence, even if the necessary condition is met, estimation may require an *a priori* assumption about the value of the variance associated with the variable that is never observed. We now consider some special cases:

Case 1: $\gamma_1 = 0$. In this event $h_S(Q_t, p_t)$ in (3.5.12) remains unchanged, but (3.5.11) becomes

$$h_D(Q_t, p_t) = \frac{|1 - \gamma_2\alpha_2|}{2\pi\sigma_2\sigma_3}$$

$$\times \exp\left\{ -\frac{1}{2} \left[A_{2t} + \frac{(p_t - \gamma_2 Q_t - \beta_3'x_{3t})^2}{\sigma_3^2} \right] \right\}$$

$$\times \left[1 - \Phi \left(\frac{Q_t - \alpha_1 p_t - \beta_1' x_{1t}}{\sigma_1} \right) \right] \tag{3.5.13}$$

It is clear that the condition of proposition 2 is violated for h_D but not for h_S. Hence, if $\gamma_1 = 0$ and the all-excess-demand restriction is imposed, the demand function is not estimable, whereas if the all-excess-supply restriction is imposed, both functions are. It is easy to verify that the converse statement holds if $\gamma_2 = 0$.

Case 2: $\gamma_1 = \gamma_2 = 0$. Function $h_D(Q_t, p_t)$ is the same as (3.5.13) except for γ_2 being zero. Function $h_S(Q_t, p_t)$ becomes

$$h_S(Q_t, p_t) = \frac{1}{2\pi\sigma_1\sigma_3} \exp\left\{ -\frac{1}{2}\left[A_{4t} + \frac{(p_t - \beta_3' x_{3t})^2}{\sigma_3^2} \right] \right\}$$

$$\times \left[1 - \Phi\left(\frac{Q_t - \alpha_2 p_t - \beta_2' x_{2t}}{\sigma_2} \right) \right]$$

and the equation representing the long side of the market cannot be estimated.

Case 3: $\gamma_1 = \gamma_2 = 0$, but $\sigma_{ij} \neq 0$ for $i \neq j$. In this case the formulas for the density function become much more complicated (see appendix 2.C). It is tedious to verify that in the case of perpetual excess demand, the $\Phi(\ )$ in (3.5.3) is a function of α_1 and $\beta_1' x_{1t}$, whereas all terms involving α_1 and $\beta_1' x_{1t}$ cancel out in $\psi(\ )$. The necessary condition for estimability thus fails again.

Estimation from a Condensed Model

In the case of perpetual excess demand, the model in (3.5.5) to (3.5.8) may be condensed according to Hartley and Mennemeyer (1974) by replacing S_t by Q_t and substituting from (3.5.5) into (3.5.8), yielding

$$Q_t = \alpha_2 p_t + \beta_2' x_{2t} + u_{2t} \tag{3.5.14}$$

$$p_t = \gamma_1(\alpha_1 p_t + \beta_1' x_{1t} + u_{1t}) + \gamma_2 Q_t + \beta_3' x_{3t} + u_{3t} \tag{3.5.15}$$

The density function for the observable variables is

$$g_D(Q_t, p_t) = \frac{|1 - \alpha_1\gamma_1 - \alpha_2\gamma_2|}{2\pi\sigma_2(\sigma_3^2 + \gamma_1^2\sigma_1^2)^{1/2}}$$

$$\times \exp\left\{ -\frac{1}{2}\left[\frac{(Q_t - \alpha_2 p_t - \beta_2' x_{2t})^2}{\sigma_2^2} \right. \right.$$

$$\left. \left. + \frac{((1 - \alpha_1\gamma_1)p_t - \gamma_2 Q_t - \gamma_1\beta_1' x_{1t} - \beta_3' x_{3t})^2}{\sigma_3^2 + \gamma_1^2\sigma_1^2} \right] \right\} \tag{3.5.16}$$

By substituting in B_{1t} in (3.5.11), it is immediately evident that $g_D(Q_t, p_t)$ is the same as $h_D(Q_t, p_t)$ *without the $1 - \Phi(\ )$ term*. Thus, basing estimation on this condensation is equivalent to the interpretation of the all-excess-demand hypothesis that $\Phi(\ )$ in (3.5.11) is equal to zero, this latter being the integral of the density of D_t, conditional on S_t and p_t, all evaluated at Q_t (see also (2.7.25)). It is clear from (3.5.16) that the necessary condition for the estimability of demand is the same, i.e. γ_1 must be nonzero; it is further clear that σ_1 can never be separately identified from the condensed model.

The failure to achieve estimability in the model subject to the restriction that there is always excess demand (supply) is due to inadequate feedbacks in the structural equations. Thus, for example, if in the price adjusting model $\gamma_1 = 0$, there is no feedback in the model through D_t, although there is through S_t. The consequence is that arbitrary demand parameters are compatible with the restrictions and the data. Nor does it help to have covariances present in the error structure; hence, it is not necessary to have a fully recursive model in order to encounter estimability failure. Therefore, it appears useful in empirical work, prior to estimation, to check if at least the necessary condition for estimability is met in cases subject to the all-excess-demand restriction.

3.6   The Problem of All-Excess-Demand: Testing

We can now ask the question whether the data support the null hypothesis that excess demand (supply) has always occurred. Various tests, some only suggestive rather than definitive, are possible and differ in the interpretation given to the notion of all-excess-demand. These interpretations are analogous to those discussed in section 3.5 in connection with the various ways of estimating the model in the presence of chronic excess demand. We emphasize that the issue here is not only whether excess demand can *conceivably* occur but whether the sample at hand corresponds to excess demand for every data point.

Heuristic Tests

Assume that the parameters of the model are identified and estimable on the assumption of all-excess-demand. Then, denoting the likelihood function by $L_0(\theta)$ under the all-excess-demand restriction, it may be maximized, yielding $\hat{\theta}_0$, the restricted maximum likelihood estimate.[5] It is also possible, of course, to maximize the general likelihood $L_1(\theta)$ that admits the possibility of both excess demand and excess supply; the resulting estimates are denoted by θ_1. If

---

[5] This can be accomplished in principle either by maximizing the appropriate analog of (3.5.1) or the likelihood function corresponding to the condensed model. These two approaches differ by having somewhat different interpretations of what all-excess-demand means.

one were given an arbitrary null hypothesis $H_0:\theta = \bar{\theta}$, an appropriate test statistic would be $-2[\log L_1(\bar{\theta}) - \log L_1(\hat{\theta})]$ which is asymptotically distributed as χ^2 with degrees of freedom equal to the number of parameters. In the present situation one might pretend that $\hat{\theta}_0$ is given *a priori* and use as the test statistic $-2[\log L_1(\hat{\theta}_0) - \log L_1(\hat{\theta}_1)]$. Under the null hypothesis $\hat{\theta}_0$ and $\hat{\theta}_1$ are in general both consistent and the log-likelihood ratio will be small; under the alternative hypothesis it will tend to be large. This test has been applied by Portes, Quandt and Yeo (1985).

Rogers Test

Rogers (1984) considers the general problem of testing for "latency" in several categories of qualitative dependent variable models such as the tobit model, the truncated regression model, and the disequilibrium model. The tests presuppose stochastic exogenous variables x and latent (at least partially unobserved) variables y^*. The joint density of y^* and x can be written as $f^*(y^*|x;\theta)h(x)$, where θ is the unknown parameter vector and where the density $h(x)$ is usually not specified by the investigator. In such a model we observe y and the model specifies the relationship between y and y^*. Thus in the tobit model $y_i^* = \beta'x_i + u_i$, and $y_i = y_i^*$ if $y_i^* > 0$ and $y_i = 0$ otherwise. In the simple disequilibrium model $y_{1t}^* = \beta_1'x_{1t} + u_{1t}$, $y_{2t}^* = \beta_2'x_{2t} + u_{2t}$, and $y_t = y_{1t}^*$ if $y_{1t}^* < y_{2t}^*$ and $y_t = y_{2t}^*$ otherwise. In any event, given the particular rules of the model at hand, one can derive in general the density function of y_t and x_t as $f(y|x;\theta)h(x)$. If we wish to test the all-excess-demand hypothesis, we are really concerned about the probability that $y_t^* = y_{2t}^* - y_{1t}^*$ (excess supply) is negative; we would be inclined to reject the null hypothesis of chronic excess demand if the probability that $y_t^* < 0$ fell short, on the average, of some preselected number c. The Rogers test makes these ideas precise.

First of all, we note that from the joint density of y_{1t}^* and y_{2t}^* we can easily obtain the density of excess supply y_t^*: if the joint p.d.f. of y_{1t}^*, y_{2t}^* is $\psi(y_{1t}^*, y_{2t}^*|x_i;\theta)$, we make the transformation $y_t^* = y_{2t}^* - y_{1t}^*$, and obtain $g(y_t^*|x_i; \theta)$ as

$$\int_{-\infty}^{\infty} \psi(y_{1t}^*, y_t^* + y_{1t}^*|x_i;\theta)\,dy_{1t}^*$$

From this we can obtain

$$\Pr\{y_t^* < 0|x_t, \theta)\} = \int_{-\infty}^{0} g(y_t^*|x_i;\theta)\,dy_t^* \equiv p(x_i;\theta) \tag{3.6.1}$$

and

$$\Pr\{y_t^* < 0|\theta\} = \int_{x} p(x_i;\theta)h(x_t)\,dx_t = E[p(x_i;\theta)] \tag{3.6.2}$$

The hypothesis is really about (3.6.2). Since $\sum_{t=1}^{T} p(x_t; \hat{\theta})/T$ converges almost surely to $E[p(x; \theta_0)]$, where $\hat{\theta}$ is the maximum likelihood estimated of θ and θ_0 the true value, a test can be based on the statistic

$$R_1 = T^{-1/2} \sum_{t=1}^{T} [p(x_t; \hat{\theta}) - c]/\hat{v} \tag{3.6.3}$$

where $\hat{v}^2$ is a variance that appropriately normalizes R_1 to have asymptotic variance of unity. This is developed below, where we employ the notation $\overset{a}{=}$ to mean "converges in probability to" and $\overset{a}{\sim}$ to mean "is asymptotically distributed as."

Since $\hat{\theta}$ is the maximum likelihood estimate, we can write

$$0 = \frac{\partial \log L(\hat{\theta})}{\partial \theta} = \frac{\partial \log L(\theta_0)}{\partial \theta} + \frac{\partial^2 \log L(\theta_*)}{\partial \theta \, \partial \theta'} (\hat{\theta} - \theta_0)$$

where θ_* is between $\hat{\theta}$ and θ_0. It therefore follows that

$$T^{1/2}(\hat{\theta} - \theta_0) - T^{-1/2} V^{-1} \sum_{i=1}^{T} \frac{\partial \log f(y_t | x_t; \theta_0)}{\partial \theta} \overset{a}{=} 0 \tag{3.6.4}$$

and

$$\sqrt{(T)}(\hat{\theta} - \theta_0) \overset{a}{\sim} N(0, V^{-1})$$

where $V = - E_x \{ E_y [\partial^2 \log f(y | x; \theta)/\partial \theta \, \partial \theta'] \}$. Expanding $p(x; \theta)$ in Taylor series, we also have

$$\sum_{t=1}^{T} p(x_t; \hat{\theta}) = \sum_{t=1}^{T} p(x_t; \theta_0) + \sum_{t=1}^{T} \frac{\partial p(x_t; \theta_*)}{\partial \theta'} (\hat{\theta} - \theta_0)$$

from which it follows that

$$T^{-1/2} \sum_{t=1}^{T} p(x_t; \hat{\theta}) - T^{-1/2} \sum_{t=1}^{T} p(x_t; \theta_0) - T^{1/2} G'(\hat{\theta} - \theta_0) \overset{a}{=} 0 \tag{3.6.5}$$

where $G = E_x [\partial p(x_t; \theta_0)/\partial \theta]$. Substituting out $T^{1/2}(\hat{\theta} - \theta_0)$ in (3.6.5) from (3.6.4), we obtain

$$T^{-1/2} \sum_{t=1}^{T} p(x_t; \hat{\theta}) - T^{-1/2} \sum_{t=1}^{T} p(x_t; \theta_0)$$

$$- T^{-1/2} G' V^{-1} \sum_{t=1}^{T} \frac{\partial \log f(y_t | x_t; \theta_0)}{\partial \theta} \overset{a}{=} 0 \tag{3.6.6}$$

Adding and subtracting $T^{-1/2}$ times $E[p(x; \theta_0)]$ in (3.6.6) shows that

$$T^{-1/2} \sum_{t=1}^{T} \{ p(x_t; \hat{\theta}) - E[p(x; \theta_0)] \}$$

is asymptotically normally distributed with mean zero and variance

$$\hat{v}^2 = E\left\{p(x;\theta_0) - E[p(x;\theta_0)] - G'V^{-1}\frac{\partial \log f(y|x;\theta_0)}{\partial\theta}\right\}^2$$

$$= \operatorname{var}[p(x;\theta_0)] + G'V^{-1}G \qquad (3.6.7)$$

since

$$E\left[\frac{\partial \log f(y|x;\theta_0)}{\partial\theta}\frac{\partial \log f(y|x;\theta_0)}{\partial\theta'}\right] = V$$

and the cross-product term has zero expectation. Thus, under the null hypothesis of $c = E[p(x;\theta_0)]$, the statistic R_1 in (3.6.3) is asymptotically distributed as $N(0,1)$.

In the simple disequilibrium model we have

$$P_t \equiv \Pr\{D_t > S_t\} = \Pr\{\beta_1'x_{1t} - \beta_2'x_{2t} > u_{2t} - u_{1t}\} = \Phi(v_t)$$

where $v_t = (\beta_1'x_{1t} - \beta_2'x_{2t})/\sigma$, $\sigma = (\sigma_1^2 + \sigma_2^2 - 2\sigma_{12})^{1/2}$. In the simplified case in which $\sigma_{12} = 0$, the G vector has as its components

$$\frac{\partial P_t}{\partial\beta_1} = \frac{\phi(v_t)x_{1t}}{\sigma}, \qquad \frac{\partial P_t}{\partial\beta_2} = -\frac{\phi(v_t)x_{2t}}{\sigma}$$

$$\frac{\partial P_t}{\partial\sigma_1^2} = \phi(v_t)\left[\frac{\beta_2'x_{2t} - \beta_1'x_{1t}}{2(\sigma_1^2 + \sigma_2^2)^{1/2}}\right], \qquad \frac{\partial P_t}{\partial\sigma_1^2} = \frac{\partial P_t}{\partial\sigma_2^2}$$

It is also possible to test hypotheses about the conditional probability $\Pr\{y_t^* < 0|y_t\}$. This case is substantially more complicated. Rogers shows that $E[\Pr\{y_t^* < 0|y_t, x; \theta_0\}]$ is not equal to the probability of interest, $\Pr\{y_t^* < 0|y_t\}$. Define

$$p(x;\theta|y) = \Pr\{y^* < 0|y,x;\theta\}$$

$$F(y;\theta) = \int_x f(y|x;\theta)h(x)dx$$

$$p^*(x;\theta|y) = f(y|x;\theta)p(x;\theta|y)$$

Then it follows that the quantity $E[f(y|x;\theta)p(x;\theta|y)/F(y;\theta)] = \Pr\{y^* > 0|y;\theta\}$. Denoting $E[p^*(x;\theta_0|y)]$ by E^*, Rogers shows that under the null hypothesis the quantity

$$R_2 = \left\{\left[\sum_{t=1}^{T}f(y_t|x_t;\hat{\theta})/T\right]^{-1}T^{-1/2}\sum_{t=1}^{T}[p^*(x_t;\hat{\theta}|y_t) - E^*]\right\}\bigg/\hat{v} \qquad (3.6.8)$$

is asymptotically distributed as $N(0,1)$, where

$$\hat{v}^2 = \left[\sum_{t=1}^{T} f(y_t|x_t; \hat{\theta})/T \right]^{-2} \sum_{t=1}^{T} [p^*(x_t; \hat{\theta}|y_t) - E^*]^2/T + G'V^{-1}G$$

$$(3.6.9)$$

and where G is $[\Sigma \partial p^*(x_t; \hat{\theta}|y_t)/\partial \theta]/T$.

In the simple disequilibrium model, $f(y_t|x_t; \hat{\theta})$ is given by (2.3.10) and $p^*(x_t; \hat{\theta}|y_t)$ is just one of the terms of $f(y_t|x_t; \hat{\theta})$, given by

$$\frac{1}{\sqrt{(2\pi)}\sigma_2} \exp\left\{ -\frac{(y_t - \beta_2' x_{2t})^2}{2\sigma_2^2} \right\} \left[1 - \Phi\left(\frac{y_t - \beta_1' x_{1t}}{\sigma_1} \right) \right]$$

Its derivatives, required for the calculation of $\hat{v}$, are

$$\frac{\partial p^*}{\partial \beta_1} = \frac{1}{\sqrt{(2\pi)}\sigma_2} \exp\left\{ -\frac{(y_t - \beta_2' x_{2t})^2}{2\sigma_2^2} \right\}$$

$$\times \frac{1}{\sqrt{(2\pi)}\sigma_1} \exp\left\{ -\frac{(y_t - \beta_1' x_{1t})^2}{2\sigma_1^2} \right\} x_{1t}$$

$$\frac{\partial p^*}{\partial \beta_2} = \frac{1}{\sqrt{(2\pi)}\sigma_2} \exp\left\{ -\frac{(y_t - \beta_2' x_{2t})^2}{2\sigma_2^2} \right\} \left[\frac{y_t - \beta_2' x_{2t}}{\sigma_2^2} \right]$$

$$\times \left[1 - \Phi\left(\frac{y_t - \beta_1' x_{1t}}{\sigma_1} \right) \right] x_{2t}$$

$$\frac{\partial p^*}{\partial \sigma_1^2} = \frac{1}{\sqrt{(2\pi)}\sigma_2} \exp\left\{ -\frac{(y_t - \beta_2' x_{2t})^2}{2\sigma_2^2} \right\}$$

$$\times \frac{1}{\sqrt{(2\pi)}\sigma_1} \exp\left\{ -\frac{(y_t - \beta_1' x_{1t})^2}{2\sigma_1^2} \right\} \left(\frac{y_t - \beta_1' x_{1t}}{2\sigma_1^2} \right)$$

$$\frac{\partial p^*}{\partial \sigma_2^2} = \frac{1}{\sqrt{(2\pi)}\sigma_2} \exp\left\{ -\frac{(y_t - \beta_2' x_{2t})^2}{2\sigma_2^2} \right\} \frac{1}{2\sigma_2^2} \left[\left(\frac{y_t - \beta_2' x_{2t}}{\sigma_2} \right)^2 - 1 \right]$$

$$\times \left[1 - \Phi\left(\frac{y_t - \beta_1' x_{1t}}{\sigma_1} \right) \right]$$

Some Sampling Experiments

The Rogers test employing R_1 has been applied in Portes, Quandt and Yeo (1985) and in Quandt and Rosen (1985). There does not exist extensive experience as to the behavior of the test in finite samples. We briefly investigate this question here with the aid of some small-scale Monte Carlo experiments, intended to be suggestive rather than conclusive. For this purpose we take the model given by

$$D_t = 100 - x_{1t} + x_{2t} + u_{1t}$$

$$S_t = -20 + x_{1t} + x_{3t} + u_{2t}$$

$$Q_t = \min(D_t, S_t)$$

In all experiments x_{1t}, x_{2t}, x_{3t} were generated from the uniform distribution and u_{1t}, u_{2t} from the normal distributions $N(0, \sigma_1^2)$, $N(0, \sigma_2^2)$. The salient characteristics of the experiments are displayed in table 3.1. Thus, for example, in experiment 1 the sample size was 20; the experiment was replicated 50 times; the ranges of the exogenous variables were 55 to 105 for x_1, 50 to 150 for x_2, 0 to 100 for x_3; the error variances were 25; the expected value of the probability that $D_t > S_t$ (the expectation being taken over x_1, x_2, x_3) was 0.5742; the sample mean over the replications of the relative frequency that demand exceeded supply was 0.5720.[6] We note from table 3.1 that the sample averages are excellent estimates of the true expectations. For each replication a new set of exogenous variable values were obtained.

For each experiment and each replication we computed R_1 for five values of c: 0.99, 0.95, 0.90, 0.80, and the value $E[\Pr\{D > S|x\}]$. In table 3.2 we give the power of the test based on R_1 using a one-sided test with a significance level of 0.05. The different c values were chosen to represent different alternative views of what one might mean by "chronic excess demand." For the two largest values of c, we have power equal to 1.0 in all cases except experiment 4 in which the sample size is only 20 and the expected probability of excess demand as high as 0.75. In general, the power is still very good for $c = 0.90$ (except for experiment 4) and acceptable even when $c = 0.80$ (except for experiments 4, 5, and 6). Power increases with sample size and decreases as the true $E[\Pr\{D > S|x\}]$ or the error variance increases, as one would expect. When $c = E[\Pr\{D > S|x\}]$, we expect to reject the null hypothesis with a frequency equal to the significance level; on average we reject the null hypothesis when it is in fact true with a frequency of 0.05, which is identical to the theoretically expected figure. Finally, we test the normality of the R_1 values generated under H_0. Table 3.3 displays the Kolmogorov-Smirnov statistics and the Smirnov limit probability that the sample cumulative distribution will depart from the theoretical one by as much as or less than was observed. We would reject the null hypothesis of normality at the 0.05 level if the Smirnov limit probability exceeded 0.95. Obviously, we cannot reject the null hypothesis of normality at the 0.05 level for any experiment. We conclude in general that the test based on R_1 has good power and has a finite sample distribution under H_0 that departs only in minor ways from the asymptotic distribution.

---

[6] The expected value

$$E[\Pr\{D > S|x\} = \int\limits_{x_1} \int\limits_{x_2} \int\limits_{x_3} \Phi\left(\frac{120 - 2x_1 + x_3 - x_3}{(\sigma_1^2 + \sigma_2^2)^{1/2}}\right) \Big/ r_1 r_2 r_3 \, dx_1 \, dx_2 \, dx_3$$

where r_1, r_2, r_3 are the ranges of the xs, was obtained by trivariate Gaussian quadrature.

Table 3.1 Characteristics of experiments

Experiment	Sample size	No. of replications	x_1	x_2	x_3	σ_1^2, σ_2^2	$E[Pr\{D > S\}]$	Average fraction $D_t > S_t$	Average $Pr\{D_t > S_t | Q_t\}$
1	20	50	55–105	50–150	0–100	25.0	0.5742	0.5720	0.5759
2	40	50	55–105	50–150	0–100	25.0	0.5742	0.5735	0.5743
3	60	50	55–105	50–150	0–100	25.0	0.5742	0.5720	0.5704
4	20	50	55–105	75–175	0–100	25.0	0.7465	0.7540	0.7405
5	40	50	55–105	75–175	0–100	25.0	0.7465	0.7520	0.7435
6	60	50	55–105	75–175	0–100	25.0	0.7465	0.7457	0.7372
7	40	50	55–105	50–150	0–100	100.0	0.5723	0.5655	0.5730
8	40	50	65–95	70–130	20–80	25.0	0.6211	0.6190	0.6211

Table 3.2   Power of R_1 test of $H_0: E[\Pr\{D > S\}] \geq c$.
Size of test = 0.05

Experiment	0.99	0.95	0.90	0.80	$E[\Pr\{D > S\}]$
1	1.00	1.00	0.96	0.52	0.08
2	1.00	1.00	2.00	0.92	0.08
3	1.00	1.00	1.00	1.00	0.04
4	0.92	0.72	0.38	0.14	0.02
5	1.00	0.98	0.76	0.20	0.04
6	1.00	1.00	0.98	0.22	0.04
7	1.00	1.00	0.96	0.60	0.04
8	1.00	0.96	0.86	0.44	0.06

Table 3.3   Kolmogorov-Smirnov test of normality for R_1

Experiment	Kolmogorov-Smirnov statistic	Smirnov limit probability
1	0.0988	0.2860
2	0.1039	0.3464
3	0.0799	0.0927
4	0.0760	0.0648
5	0.0675	0.0232
6	0.0854	0.1406
7	0.0870	0.1567
8	0.0764	0.0679

To examine the finite-sample behavior of R_2, we slightly rewrite (3.6.8) and (3.6.9). First, make the notation more compact by writing $\sum_{t=1}^{T} f(y_t|x_t;\ \theta)/T$ as $\Sigma f/T$ and by abbreviating $p^*(x_t;\theta|y_t)$ by p^*. Then the numerator of (3.6.8) is

$$\frac{T^{-1/2}\Sigma(p^* - E^*)}{\Sigma f/T} = \frac{T^{-1/2}\Sigma p^*}{\Sigma f/T} - \frac{T^{1/2}E^*}{\Sigma f/T}$$

The null hypothesis concerns the expected value of the conditional (on y_t) probability that demand exceeds supply: over the sample this is appropriately measured by $E^*/\Sigma f/T$. Thus the researcher must specify a hypothesized value c that will replace $E^*/\Sigma f/T$ above. The first term of (3.6.9) can then be written as

$$\Sigma \left[\frac{p^*}{\Sigma f/T} - \frac{E^*}{\Sigma f/T} \right]^2 \bigg/ T = \Sigma \left[\frac{p^*}{\Sigma f/T} - c \right]^2 \bigg/ T$$

R_2 then becomes

$$R_2 = \left(\frac{T^{-1/2}\Sigma p^*}{\Sigma f/T} - T^{1/2}c\right) \Bigg/ \left[\Sigma\left(\frac{p^*}{\Sigma f/T} - c\right)^2 \Bigg/ T + G'V^{-1}G\right]^{1/2}$$

where, as in the previous case, reasonable values of c for expressing the all-excess-demand hypothesis might be in the range of 0.8 to 0.99.

The power of R_2 was examined using the same set of experiments as in table 3.1. It is interesting to note from that table that the average over data points and replications of the conditional probability that demand exceeds supply is very close to the unconditional expectation and to the average fraction of data points in which demand exceeded supply; this tends to underscore Burkett's (1981) observation of this phenomenon. It is clear from table 3.4 that the power of the R_2 test is roughly comparable with that of R_1 but is fairly consistently a little less. The last column of table 3.4 gives the power when $c = 0.70$; for experiments 4, 5, and 6 this value is very close to the null hypothesis. Hence the corresponding powers should be close to the significance level 0.05, which they are.

Exercises

3.1 Show that the joint density of $D_t - S_t$, $p_{t-1} - p_t^*$, and $p_{t-1} - p_t^{**}$ of section 3.3 is singular.

3.2 Consider the regression model $Y = X\beta + u$ where X is $n \times k$. Assume that an additional $m \leq k$ observations on all variables become available. Use the recursive residuals for a direct demonstration that the numerator and denominator of Chow's test for the constancy of regression coefficients have independent χ^2 distributions and that the Chow statistic is thus F-distributed.

3.3 Assume that you want to estimate μ in the Bowden parameterization by OLS from the reduced form of the price adjustment equation. Why is this not appropriate if either demand or supply contains the lagged price?

3.4 Prove that ϵ_t is independent of v_{2t} in the derivation of the test for model A in section 3.4.

Table 3.4   Power of R_2 test of $H_0: E[\Pr\{D > S \mid Q\}] \geq c$

Experiment	0.99	0.95	0.90	0.80	0.70
1	1.00	0.98	0.92	0.60	0.26
2	1.00	1.00	1.00	0.86	0.42
3	1.00	1.00	1.00	0.98	0.56
4	0.88	0.74	0.42	0.14	0.02
5	1.00	0.98	0.60	0.12	0.04
6	1.00	1.00	0.88	0.20	0.02
7	1.00	1.00	1.00	0.90	0.42
8	1.00	1.00	0.98	0.74	0.24

3.5 Verify that the likelihood function in (3.3.17) is unbounded in parameter space.

3.6 Verify theorem 1 of appendix 3.B in detail.

3.7 Prove (3.4.15).

Appendix 3.A
The Conditional Expectation in a Joint Normal Density

Consider the vector $u' = (u_1, u_2)$ and assume that it is normally distributed with mean vector $\mu = (0,0)$ and covariance matrix

$$\Sigma = \begin{bmatrix} \sigma_1^2 & \sigma_{12} \\ \sigma_{12} & \sigma_2^2 \end{bmatrix}$$

Then

$$f(u_1, u_2) = \frac{1}{2\pi\Delta^{1/2}} \exp\left\{ -\frac{1}{2\Delta} (\sigma_2^2 u_1^2 + \sigma_1^2 u_2^2 - 2\sigma_{12} u_1 u_2) \right\}$$

where $\Delta = \sigma_1^2\sigma_2^2 - \sigma_{12}^2$. We wish to find $E(u_1 | u_2 < w)$. Letting $z = w/\sigma_2$, this is the same as finding $E(u_1 | u_2/\sigma_2 < z)$.

We first obtain the joint density of u_1, u_2 conditional on $u_2/\sigma_2 < z$. This is

$$f(u_1, u_2 | u_2/\sigma_2 < z) = f(u_1, u_2)/\Pr\{u_2/\sigma_2 < z\}$$

$$= f(u_1, u_2) \bigg/ \int_{-\infty}^{\sigma_2 z} \int_{-\infty}^{\infty} f(u_1, u_2) du_1 du_2$$

$$= f(u_1, u_2)/\Phi(z)$$

The required expectation can now be written as

$$E(u_1 | u_2/\sigma_2 < z)$$

$$= \int_{-\infty}^{\sigma_2 z} \int_{-\infty}^{\infty} \frac{u_1}{2\pi\Delta^{1/2}} \exp\left\{ -\frac{1}{2\Delta} [\sigma_2^2 u_1^2 + \sigma_1^2 u_2^2 - 2\sigma_{12} u_1 u_2] \right\} du_1 du_2 / \Phi(z)$$

Completing the square on u_1 in the square bracket in the exponent, the latter can be written as

$$\left(u_1 - \frac{\sigma_{12}}{\sigma_2^2} u_2 \right)^2 \sigma_2^2 + u_2^2 \left(\sigma_1^2 - \frac{\sigma_{12}^2}{\sigma_2^2} \right)$$

or

$$v_1^2 \sigma_2^2 + v_2^2 \left(\sigma_1^2 - \frac{\sigma_{12}^2}{\sigma_2^2} \right)$$

where we have used the transformation

$$v_1 = u_1 - \frac{\sigma_{12}}{\sigma_2^2} u_2$$

$$v_2 = u_2$$

which has Jacobian equal to unity. Substituting in $E(u_1 | u_2/\sigma_2 < z)$ gives

$$E(u_1 | u_2/\sigma_2 < z)$$

$$= \frac{1}{\Phi(z)} \int_{-\infty}^{\sigma_2 z} \int_{-\infty}^{\infty} \frac{v_1 + \sigma_{12} v_2/\sigma_2^2}{2\pi\Delta^{1/2}} \exp\left\{ -\frac{v_1^2 \sigma_2^2}{2\Delta} \right\}$$

$$\times \exp\left\{ -\frac{v_2^2 (\sigma_1^2 - \sigma_{12}^2/\sigma_2^2)}{2\Delta} \right\} dv_1 dv_2$$

$$= \frac{1}{\Phi(z)} \int_{-\infty}^{\sigma_2 z} \left[\int_{-\infty}^{\infty} \frac{v_1 \exp\{ -v_1^2/(2\Delta/\sigma_2^2) \}}{\sqrt{(2\pi)}\, \Delta^{1/2}/\sigma_2} dv_1 \right.$$

$$\left. + \int_{-\infty}^{\infty} \frac{(\sigma_{12} v_2/\sigma_2^2)\exp\{ -v_1^2/(2\Delta/\sigma_2^2) \}}{\sqrt{(2\pi)}\, \Delta^{1/2}/\sigma_2} dv_1 \right]$$

$$\times \frac{1}{\sqrt{(2\pi)}\sigma_2} \exp\left\{ -\frac{v_2^2(\sigma_1^2 - \sigma_{12}^2/\sigma_2^2)}{2\Delta} \right\} dv_2$$

It is clear that the first integral in the square bracket has value $= 0$ and the second has value $= \sigma_{12} v_2/\sigma_2^2$. The conditional expectation therefore is

$$E(u_1 | u_2/\sigma_2 < z) = \frac{1}{\Phi(z)} \int_{-\infty}^{\sigma_2 z} \frac{\sigma_{12} v_2/\sigma_2^2}{\sqrt{(2\pi)}\sigma_2} \exp\left\{ -\frac{v_2^2}{2\sigma_2^2} \right\} dv_2$$

$$= -\frac{\sigma_{12}}{\sigma_2} \frac{\phi(z)}{\Phi(z)}$$

Appendix 3.B
Recursive Residuals

Consider the regression $Y = X\beta + u$, with X being $n \times k$ and nonstochastic. Let X_j denote the submatrix of X consisting of its first j rows and let x_j' denote the jth row itself. Let Y_j similarly refer to the first j rows of the vector Y, with y_j representing its jth row, i.e. the element y_j. We define the recursive regression coefficient vectors

$$\tilde{\beta}_j = (X_j' X_j)^{-1} X_j' Y_j \qquad \text{for } j = k, \ldots, n \tag{3.B.1}$$

We also define the recursive residuals as

$$\tilde{u}_j = \frac{y_j - x_j' \tilde{\beta}_{j-1}}{[1 + x_j' (X_{j-1}' X_{j-1})^{-1} x_j]^{1/2}} \qquad \text{for } j = k+1, \ldots, n \tag{3.B.2}$$

We now derive their principal properties (see Brown, Durbin and Evans 1975; Johnston 1984).

Lemma (Bartlett's identity)   If A and B are nonsingular matrices of order n and u and v are n-vectors such that $B = A + uv'$, then

$$B^{-1} = A^{-1} - \frac{A^{-1} u v' A^{-1}}{1 + v' A^{-1} u}$$

Proof   Multiplying $B^{-1} B$ we have

$$B^{-1} B = \left(A^{-1} - \frac{A^{-1} u v' A^{-1}}{1 + v' A^{-1} u} \right) (A + uv')$$

$$= I + [(-A^{-1} uv' + A^{-1} uv' + A^{-1} uv' (v' A^{-1} u)$$
$$- A^{-1} u (v' A^{-1} u) v')]/(1 + v' A^{-1} u)$$

Since $v' A^{-1} u$ is a scalar, it commutes with v' in the last term of the numerator which therefore equals zero, showing that $B^{-1} B = I$ as is required (obviously also $BB^{-1} = I$). □

Theorem 1   The recursive regression coefficients obey

$$\tilde{\beta}_j = \tilde{\beta}_{j-1} + \frac{(X_{j-1}' X_{j-1}) x_j (y_j - x_j' \tilde{\beta}_{j-1})}{1 - x_j' (X_{j-1}' X_{j-1})^{-1} x_j} \qquad \text{for } j = k+1, \ldots, n$$

Proof   By definition,

$$X_j' X_j = X_{j-1}' X_{j-1} + x_j x_j' \tag{3.B.3}$$

and

$$X_j' Y_j = X_{j-1}' Y_{j-1} + x_j y_j \tag{3.B.4}$$

Write

$$\tilde{\beta}_j = (X_j' X_j)^{-1} X_j' Y_j \tag{3.B.5}$$

Because of (3.B.3), the inverse of $X_j' X_j$ can be obtained from Bartlett's identity. Replace $(X_j' X_j)^{-1}$ with this and replace $X_j' Y_j$ from (3.B.5). The result follows from simplifying the resulting expression. □

Theorem 2   The $(n-k)$-vector $\tilde{u}$ defined by (3.B.2) has the following properties:

(a) $\tilde{u}$ is linear in Y, i.e. $\tilde{u} = GY$ for some matrix G

(b) $GX = 0$

(c) $E(\tilde{u}) = 0$

(d) $GG' = I_{n-k}$

(e) $\tilde{u}'\tilde{u} = \hat{u}'\hat{u}$, where $\hat{u}$ is the vector of ordinary least squares residuals.

Proof Property (a) is obvious from the definition of (3.B.2); the matrix G is given by

$$
G = \begin{bmatrix}
\dfrac{-x'_{k+1}(X'_k X_k)^{-1} X'_k}{d_{k+1}} & \dfrac{1}{d_{k+1}} & 0 \\
\cdots\cdots\cdots & & \ddots \\
\dfrac{-x'_n(X'_{n-1}X_{n-1})^{-1}X'_{n-1}}{d_n} & & \dfrac{1}{d_n}
\end{bmatrix}
$$

where $d_j = [1 + x'_j(X'_{j-1}X_{j-1})^{-1}x_j]^{1/2}$, 0 is a triangular block of zeros and the matrix is of order $(n-k) \times n$. Property (b) follows immediately by post-multiplying G by X. From this (c) follows since $E(\tilde{u}) = E(GY) = E[G(X\beta + u)] = E(u) = 0$. Property (d) follows by multiplying G by G'. Finally, (e) is obtained by writing $\tilde{u}'\tilde{u} = Y'G'GY$ and noting that $G'G = I_n - X(X'X)^{-1}X'$ as is the case for the matrix employed in the definition of all linear unbiased, scalar-covariance estimators of error terms (Theil 1971).   □

Two tests of the constancy of regression parameters have been suggested by Brown, Durbin and Evans: the cusum test and the cusum of squares test. The former is based on

$$
C_{1i} = \frac{\displaystyle\sum_{j=k+1}^{i} u_j}{S} \qquad i = k+1, \ldots, n
$$

where[7]

$$
S^2 = \sum_{j=k+1}^{n} \tilde{u}_j^2/(n-k)
$$

The null hypothesis is rejected if the sequence of $C_{1i}s$ $(i = k+1, \ldots, n)$ exceeds in absolute value $a(n - 3k + 2i)/(n - k)^{1/2}$, where $a = 0.948$ or 1.143 for 0.05 and 0.01 levels of significance respectively.

The cusum of squares test is based on

---

[7] A. Harvey (1975) has suggested using $n - k - 1$ instead of $n - k$ to increase the power of the test.

$$C_{2i} = \frac{\sum_{j=k+1}^{i} \tilde{u}_j^2}{S^2} \qquad i = k+1, \ldots, n$$

It is straightforward to verify that under the null hypothesis of no switch in regression parameter values, $1 - C_{2i}$ has beta distribution with parameters $\alpha = -1 + (n-k)/2$, $\beta = -1 + (i-k)/2$. Since

$$C_{2i}^{-1} - 1 = \frac{\sum_{j=i+1}^{n} \tilde{u}_j^2}{\sum_{j=k+1}^{i} \tilde{u}_j^2}$$

by the properties of recursive residuals, numerator and denominator are independent and $(C_{2i}^{-1} - 1)(i-k)/(n-k) \sim F(n-i, i-k)$. The conclusion follows by noting that if R is any F-distributed variable with m and n degrees of freedom, $(mR/n)/(1+mR/n)$ has beta distribution, since applying this transformation yields $1 - C_{2i}$. It follows that $E(C_{2i}) = (i-k)/(n-k)$. Brown, Durbin and Evans construct confidence intervals of C_{2i} as $(i-k)/(n-k) \pm c_0$, where c_0 is chosen from table 1 in Durbin (1969).

4

Alternative Specifications

4.1 Introduction

In the previous chapter we considered a variety of departures from the canonical disequilibrium model, but these departures were generally modest and tended not to alter the basic character of the model. In the present chapter, we consider some more substantial departures. We start out by introducing some modifications of the min condition in section 4.2 and then, in section 4.3, we analyze the case in which the presence of rationing itself affects demand or supply. In section 4.4, we introduce another modification of the min condition that deals with the question of aggregation. In section 4.5 we reconsider the adjustment process, and in section 4.6 we introduce serial correlation of the error terms and lagged dependent variables. In section 4.7 we discuss testing for serial correlation, and in section 4.8 we briefly consider rational expectations. In section 4.9 we finally consider a particular rationing model.

4.2 The Ginsburgh-Tishler-Zang Model

In a series of papers, Ginsburgh, Tishler and Zang (1980) and Tishler and Zang (1977, 1979) have suggested that the disequilibrium model (model A of chapter 2) may be reformulated as follows:

$$D_t = \beta_1' x_{1t} \tag{4.2.1}$$

$$S_t = \beta_2' x_{2t} \tag{4.2.2}$$

$$Q_t = \min(D_t, S_t) + u_t \tag{4.2.3}$$

The suggestion has been employed in empirical work by Sneessens (1981a, 1983). Two formally identical interpretations are possible: (1) "nature" generates a nonstochastic demand and supply and the observed quantity is the minimum of these plus a stochastic error term; or (2) "nature" pays attention only to the *expected* demand and supply and thus the min condition is applied to expected demand and supply, to which then an error term is added, as before. Alternatively, we can write the model as

$$Q_t = \begin{cases} \beta_1' x_{1t} + u_t & \text{if } \beta_1' x_{1t} < \beta_2' x_{2t} \\ \beta_2' x_{2t} + u_t & \text{otherwise} \end{cases} \tag{4.2.4}$$

which shows that it is formally a deterministic switching regression model. In a more general form this can be written as

$$y_t = \begin{cases} \beta_1' x_{1t} + u_{1t} & \text{if } \pi' x_{3t} < 0 \\ \beta_2' x_{2t} + u_{2t} & \text{if } \pi' x_{3t} \geq 0 \end{cases} \tag{4.2.5}$$

where π is a vector of unknown coefficients and x_{3t} a vector of exogenous variables. In the present case, $\pi' x_{3t} = \beta_1' x_{1t} - \beta_2' x_{2t}$ and $u_{1t} = u_{2t} = u_t$. Defining $\delta_t = 0$ if $\pi' x_{3t} < 0$ and $\delta_t = 1$ otherwise, (4.2.5) can also be written as

$$y_t = (1 - \delta_t)\beta_1' x_{1t} + \delta_t \beta_2' x_{2t} + (1 - \delta_t)u_{1t} + \delta_t u_{2t} \tag{4.2.6}$$

In principle, one would want to estimate the parameters of (4.2.6), i.e. β_1, β_2, σ_1^2, σ_2^2, and the δ_t. Without further restrictions or simplifications this is an intractable problem because (1) estimation involves choosing one of 2^T different possible δ-vectors, and (2) even if the appropriate δ-vector were given, the π vector would, in the general case, not be identified since the mapping between δ and π simply says that for some values of t the π vector must subtend an acute angle with x_{3t} and for others an obtuse angle.[1] Possible solutions to the problem of estimating (4.2.6) involve elimination of the discreteness of δ_t by various types of smoothing. Goldfeld and Quandt (1972, 1976) suggest replacing δ_t with the approximation

$$\delta_t = \int_{-\infty}^{\pi' x_{3t}} \frac{1}{\sqrt{(2\pi)}\sigma} \exp\left\{-\frac{\xi^2}{2\sigma^2}\right\} d\xi \tag{4.2.7}$$

where σ^2 is a new parameter and may be interpreted to measure the "fuzziness" of discrimination between the two regimes. Alternatively, δ_t could be defined in terms of cumulative distribution of the Cauchy ($\delta_t = 0.5 + (1/\pi\sigma)\tan^{-1}(\pi' x_{3t}/\sigma)$) or logistic ($\delta_t = 1 + \exp(-\pi' x_{3t}/\sigma)^{-1}$) distributions.

Tishler and Zang (1979) point out that smoothing methods based on cumulative distribution functions never actually allocate 0 or 100 per cent of an observation to a regime. To cope with this problem they recommend a variety of approximations. All of these involve the choice of a parameter α

---

[1] This second difficulty is obviously not present in the disequilibrium model (4.2.4). It is also clear that if x_{3t} is random, then as $T \to \infty$ the range of indeterminacy for π diminishes. See Tishler and Zang (1979).

which determines a range outside of which the smoothing yields $\delta_t = 0$ or 1. Denoting for simplicity $\pi' x_{3t}$ by r_t, the simplest smoothing formula is

$$\delta_t(r_t) = \begin{cases} 0 & \text{if} \quad r_t < -\alpha \\ 0.5 + r_t/2\alpha & \text{if} \quad -\alpha \leq r_t \leq \alpha \\ 1 & \text{if} \quad \alpha < r_t \end{cases}$$

where $\alpha > 0$ and chosen to be small. At $r_t = \pm\alpha$ the approximation is not differentiable with respect to π. If this is to be avoided, one may employ the differentiable formulas

$$\delta_t(r_t) = \begin{cases} 0 & \text{if} \quad r_t \leq -\alpha - 2\alpha\beta \\ (0.5 + r_t/2\alpha + \beta)^2/4\beta & \text{if} \quad -\alpha - 2\alpha\beta \leq r_t \leq -\alpha + 2\alpha\beta \\ 0.5 + r_t/2\alpha & \text{if} \quad -\alpha + 2\alpha\beta \leq r_t \leq \alpha - 2\alpha\beta \\ 1 - (0.5 - r_t/2\alpha + \beta)^2/4\beta & \text{if} \quad \alpha - 2\alpha\beta \leq r_t \leq \alpha + 2\alpha\beta \\ 1 & \text{if} \quad \alpha + 2\alpha\beta \leq r_t \end{cases}$$

where $\alpha > 0$ and $0 < \beta < 0.5$ are parameters to be chosen. The employment of a cubic yields a once continuously differentiable smoothing according to

$$\delta_t(r_t) = \begin{cases} 0 & \text{if} \quad r_t \leq -\alpha \\ -r_t^3/4\alpha^3 + 3r_t/4\alpha + 0.5 & \text{if} \quad -\alpha \leq r_t \leq \alpha \\ 1 & \text{if} \quad \alpha \leq r_t \end{cases}$$

Finally, to obtain a twice continuously differentiable smoothing, Tishler and Zang (1979) recommend

$$\delta_t = \begin{cases} 0 & \text{if} \quad r_t \leq -\alpha \\ \dfrac{3}{16}(r_t/\alpha)^5 - \dfrac{5}{8}(r_t/\alpha)^3 + \dfrac{15}{16}(r_t/\alpha) + 0.5 & \text{if} \quad -\alpha \leq r_t \leq \alpha \\ 1 & \text{if} \quad \alpha \leq r_t \end{cases}$$

As a practical matter, they recommend an iterative adjustment of α. The initial value is chosen to be fairly large and the problem is solved using this value. Then α is to be reset to $0.99 \min_t|r_t|$ (unless it is already the case that $\alpha \leq \min_t|r_t|$) and the problem solved again with the new value. This process is to be repeated until convergence is attained (i.e. until at the kth iteration of this α is already $\leq \min_t|r_t|$). Tishler and Zang report good results with this procedure.

Attacking directly the problem of estimating (4.2.1) to (4.2.3), we obtain for the density function of Q_t

$$f(Q_t|x_{1t},x_{2t}) = \begin{cases} \dfrac{1}{\sqrt{(2\pi)}\sigma} \exp\left\{ -\dfrac{(Q_t - \beta_1' x_{1t})^2}{2\sigma^2} \right\} & \text{if } \beta_1' x_{1t} < \beta_2' x_{2t} \\[2ex] \dfrac{1}{\sqrt{(2\pi)}\sigma} \exp\left\{ -\dfrac{(Q_t - \beta_2' x_{2t})^2}{2\sigma^2} \right\} & \text{if } \beta_1' x_{1t} \geq \beta_2' x_{2t} \end{cases}$$

$$(4.2.8)$$

Hence the likelihood function is

$$
L = \prod_{\beta_1' x_{1t} < \beta_2' x_{2t}} \frac{1}{\sqrt{(2\pi)}\,\sigma} \; \exp\left\{ - \frac{(Q_t - \beta_1' x_{1t})^2}{2\sigma^2} \right\}
$$

$$
\times \prod_{\beta_1' x_{1t} \geq \beta_2' x_{2t}} \frac{1}{\sqrt{(2\pi)}\,\sigma} \; \exp\left\{ - \frac{(Q_t - \beta_2' x_{2t})^2}{2\sigma^2} \right\} \tag{4.2.9}
$$

A FORTRAN program for evaluating (4.2.9) is given in appendix 4.A, and L may be maximized by numerical methods.

The obvious and immediate advantage of specification (4.2.1) to (4.2.3) is that (4.2.9) is not prone to the same problems as the standard disequilibrium likelihood (2.3.10). Moreover, Sneessens (1981b, 1985) reports good results in maximizing (4.2.9) and finds that its estimates are reasonable even if the true model is model A of chapter 2.

Against that are at least two difficulties. The first is that the likelihood function tends to have numerous local maxima. Condensing the log-likelihood, it can be written as

$$
\log L = -\frac{T}{2}\,(\log 2\pi + 1)
$$

$$
-\frac{T}{2}\,\log\left\{ \left[\sum_{\beta_1' x_{1t} < \beta_2' x_{2t}} (Q_t - \beta_1' x_{1t})^2 + \sum_{\beta_1' x_{1t} \geq \beta_2' x_{2t}} (Q_t - \beta_2' x_{2t})^2 \right] \Big/ T \right\}
$$

$$
\tag{4.2.10}
$$

Maximizing this is equivalent to minimizing the sum of squared deviations with respect to β_1, β_2 and with respect to the "sorting" of observations between terms of the two types in the large bracket in (4.2.10). Consider as an example the (highly artificial) case in which both demand and supply depend only on price and the observed data are as follows:

Observation	Q_t	p_t
1	9.9	90.0
2	20.1	80.0
3	29.9	70.0
4	29.9	30.0
5	20.1	20.0
6	9.9	10.0
7	40.0	50.0

Observations 1 through 3 are plausibly from the demand function and 4 through 6 from the supply function. If observation 7 is grouped with the first three, the estimated demand and supply functions are $Q_t = 78.894 - 0.744p_t$ and $Q_t = 0.033 + 1.000p_t$, respectively, and these parameter estimates provide a local minimum (since for the given allocation of observation 7 the partial derivatives of the log-likelihood are zero and the

Hessian negative definite. If observation 7 is grouped with observations 4 through 6, we obtain $Q_t = 99.967 - 1.000p_t$ and $Q_t = 4.523 + 0.744p_t$, which again represents a local minimum. Finally we note that the coefficient estimates obtained from these two possible allocations of observation 7 are compatible with the allocation. When this observation is grouped with 1 through 3 for the demand function,

$$\beta_1' x_1 = 41.694 < 49.967 = \beta_2' x_2$$

for the seventh observation and it properly belongs to the demand function. When it is grouped with observations 4 through 6 for the supply function,

$$\beta_1' x_1 = 49.967 > 41.723 = \beta_2' x_2$$

and it properly belongs to the supply function.

The second disadvantage is that the rather substantial simplicity of (4.2.10) is rapidly diminished if the model becomes at all more complicated. Thus if a price adjustment equation is introduced, the model becomes

$$D_t = \alpha_1 p_t + \beta_1' x_{1t}$$

$$S_t = \alpha_2 p_t + \beta_2' x_{2t}$$

$$Q_t = \min(D_t, S_t) + u_{1t}$$

$$p_t = p_{t-1} + \gamma(D_t - S_t) + u_{1t}$$

Letting $y_t' = (Q_t, p_t)$ and

$$A_i = \begin{bmatrix} 1 & -\alpha_i \\ 0 & 1 + \gamma(\alpha_2 - \alpha_1) \end{bmatrix}$$

$$b_{it} = \begin{bmatrix} \beta_i' x_{it} \\ p_{t-1} + \gamma(\beta_1' x_{1t} - \beta_2' x_{2t}) \end{bmatrix}$$

we can write the model as

$$A_1 y_t = b_{1t} + u_t \quad \text{if } \alpha_1 p_t + \beta_1' x_{1t} < \alpha_2 p_t + \beta_2' x_{2t}$$

$$A_2 y_t = b_{2t} + u_t \quad \text{if } \alpha_1 p_t + \beta_1' x_{1t} \geq \alpha_2 p_t + \beta_2' x_{2t}$$

(4.2.11)

In principle, one would have to ascertain that for each equation system in (4.2.11) the (reduced form) solution for p_t is compatible with the inequality condition under which that equation system holds. (This is the problem of coherency, and it will be discussed in more detail in chapters 5 and 6.) In fact, it can be shown that this is the case (see exercise 4.1). The likelihood is then the product of the simultaneous equations likelihoods corresponding to the two parts of (4.2.11):

$$L = \prod_{a_1 p_t + \beta_1' x_{1t} < \alpha_2 p_t + \beta_2' x_{2t}} \frac{|A_1|}{2\pi |\Sigma|^{1/2}} \exp\left\{ -\frac{1}{2}(A_1 y_t - b_{1t})' \Sigma^{-1}(A_1 y_t - b_{1t}) \right\}$$

$$\times \prod_{\alpha_1 p_t + \beta_1' x_{1t} \geq \alpha_2 p_t + \beta_2' x_{2t}} \frac{|A_2|}{2\pi |\Sigma|^{1/2}} \exp\left\{-\frac{1}{2}(A_2 y_t - b_{2t})' \Sigma^{-1}(A_2 y_t - b_{2t})\right\}$$

(4.2.12)

A final minor difficulty, not likely to create great problems in practice, is that the partial derivatives of the likelihood are not continuous at the points at which particular observations switch their position between the two regimes. Although this may conceivably be bothersome for optimization algorithms employing derivatives, in practice it is not likely to be so.

Sneessens (1981a) has examined the performance of the maximum likelihood estimator for the Ginsburgh-Tishler-Zang model based on the fifth-degree smoothing of Tishler and Zang. Specifically, the logarithm of (4.2.9) can be written as

$$\log L = \sum_{t=1}^{T} \log \left[(1 - \delta_t) \frac{1}{\sqrt{(2\pi)}\sigma} \exp\left\{-\frac{(Q_t - \beta_1' x_{1t})^2}{2\sigma^2}\right\}\right.$$
$$\left. + \delta_t \frac{1}{\sqrt{(2\pi)}\sigma} \exp\left\{\frac{(Q_t - \beta_2' x_{2t})^2}{2\sigma^2}\right\}\right]$$

where in principle δ_t equals 0 if $\beta_1' x_{1t} < \beta_2' x_{2t}$ and equals 1 otherwise. In practice $\delta_t(\beta_1' x_{1t} - \beta_2' x_{2t})$ is replaced by the fifth-degree smoothing as a function of $\beta_1' x_{1t} - \beta_2' x_{2t}$. Sneessens examines the root mean square errors of the estimates when estimation is by this method as well as by the likelihood maximization procedure appropriate for method A. He generally finds the Ginsburgh-Tishler-Zang approach to be robust to misspecification: it appears to yield smaller root mean square errors often even when it is the "incorrect" method.

A More General Error Specification

Model A and the Ginsburgh-Tishler-Zang specification may be combined as in

$$D_t = \beta_1' x_{1t} + u_{1t} \tag{4.2.13}$$

$$S_t = \beta_2' x_{2t} + u_{2t} \tag{4.2.14}$$

$$Q_t = \min(D_t, S_t) + u_{3t} \tag{4.2.15}$$

Superficially, the derivation of the density function for Q_t may appear to be difficult, for one might argue that under the specification (4.2.13) and (4.2.14), $y_t = \min(D_t, S_t)$ has the density given by (2.3.5) or (2.3.10); the density of Q_t is then the convolution of the densities of y_t and u_{3t} (see exercise 4.2). However, it is clear that (4.2.13)–(4.2.15) can also be written as

$$D_t^* = \beta_1' x_{1t} + u_{1t} + u_{3t}$$

$$S_t^* = \beta_t' x_{2t} + u_{2t} + u_{3t} \qquad (4.2.16)$$

$$Q_t = \min(D_t^*, S_t^*)$$

which is formally identical with model A with error covariance $= \sigma_3^2$ if u_{1t}, u_{2t}, u_{3t} are uncorrelated and a covariance equal to $\sigma_{12} + \sigma_{13} + \sigma_{23} + \sigma_3^2$ if all cross-correlations are present. The appropriate density is then given by (2.3.9) and no new difficulties arise.

Bowden's Fuzzy Min Condition

Bowden (1979) has generalized the min conditions employed up to this point by introducing the delta (impulse) function $\delta(z)$ and the unit step function $u(z)$ given by

$$u(z) = \begin{cases} 0 & \text{if } z \leqq 0 \\ 1 & \text{if } z > 0 \end{cases}$$

and

$$\delta(z) = \begin{cases} 0 & \text{if } z \neq 0 \\ \text{undefined} & \text{if } z = 0 \end{cases}$$

with the further property that for any continuous function $\xi(z)$,

$$\int_{-\infty}^{\infty} \delta(z)\xi(z)\,dz = \xi(0) \qquad (4.2.17)$$

The joint density of Q_t, D_t, S_t in model A may then be written as

$$f(Q_t, D_t, S_t) = \{\delta(Q_t - S_t)u(D_t - S_t) + \delta(Q_t - D_t)u(S_t - D_t)\}g(D_t, S_t) \qquad (4.2.18)$$

where $g(D_t, S_t)$ is the joint p.d.f. of D_t, S_t. Of course, $f(\ )$ is not well defined since $\delta(z)$ is not defined for $z = 0$. However, if for interpretative purposes we were to take $\delta(0) = 1$, the interpretation of (4.2.18) becomes clear and it also says that points Q, D, S for which Q is not equal to either D or S have zero density, as is required in the standard min condition. The point here is that if, in the notation of (4.2.18), $u(\ )$ and δ were defined in some *suitable but different* manner, (4.2.18) would in general allow nonzero densities to be associated with points in (Q, D, S) space at which Q is equal neither to D nor to S. Even under the stricter interpretation where $\delta(0)$ is undefined, $f(Q, D, S)$ is sensible in the sense that its marginal density with respect to D and S is the correct density $h(Q)$:

$$h(Q) = \int_{-\infty}^{\infty} \int_{-\infty}^{\infty} f(Q, D, S)\,dD\,dS$$

$$= \int_{-\infty}^{\infty} u(D-Q)g(D,Q)\,\mathrm{d}D + \int_{-\infty}^{\infty} u(S-Q)g(Q,S)\,\mathrm{d}S$$

$$= \int_{Q}^{\infty} g(D,Q)\,\mathrm{d}D + \int_{Q}^{\infty} g(Q,S)\,\mathrm{d}S \tag{4.2.19}$$

Other types of min conditions may be obtained by generalizing the expression in { } in (4.2.18). This expression, referred to as a membership function, can be generalized by letting both δ and u depend on a parameter. In this more general approach we would write

$$f(Q_t,D_t,S_t) = \{\delta(Q_t-S_t;\theta_1)u(D_t-S_t,\theta_3)$$
$$+ \delta(Q_t-D_t;\theta_2)u(S_t-D_t,\theta_3)\}\,g(D_t,\,S_t) \tag{4.2.20}$$

It may be convenient to assume that the $\delta(\ )$ now represent normal densities with means zero and variances θ_1, θ_2, and $u(\ )$ represents cumulative normals with means zero and variance θ_3. As θ_1, $\theta_2 \to 0$ the δs converge to the impulse function, and as $\theta_3 \to 0$ the u converges to the unit step function. Under the above assumptions about u we have $u(D_t-S_t,\theta_3) = 1 - u(S_t-D_t,\theta_3)$, and various benchmark cases may be described.

1   $\theta_1 = \theta_2 = 0$ but $\theta_3 \neq 0$. In this case, zero density is assigned to Q, D, S combinations unless Q is either equal to D or to S, but the min condition does not hold strictly, i.e. even though $Q = D$, S might be less than D. (Note, however, that if S is much smaller than D then $u(S-D,\theta_3)$ will be very small and such events will occur with only small probability.)
2   θ_1, $\theta_2 \neq 0$ but $\theta_3 = 0$. Then it is possible for points at which Q is neither D nor S to contribute to the density of Q, D, S.

In the former case the density of Q_t is

$$h(Q_t) = \int_{-\infty}^{\infty} g(D_t,Q_t)u(D_t-Q_t,\theta_3)\,\mathrm{d}D_t + \int_{-\infty}^{\infty} g(Q_t,S_t)u(S_t-Q_t,\theta_3)\,\mathrm{d}S_t \tag{4.2.21}$$

which is also the density function for the tobit-type model given by

$$Q_t = \begin{cases} S_t & \text{if } D_t - S_t > \epsilon_t \\ D_t & \text{if } D_t - S_t \leq \epsilon_t \end{cases}$$

where ϵ_t is distributed as $N(0,\theta_3)$.

Bowden derives the characteristic function for the random variable Q in the general case. If D_t and S_t are given, as usual, by $\beta_1' x_{1t} + u_{1t}$, $\beta_2' x_{2t} + u_{2t}$, the characteristic function is

$$f(\tau) = \exp\{-\mathrm{i}\beta_2' x_{2t}\tau - (\sigma_2^2+\theta_1)\tau^2/2\}$$

$$\times \, [1 - \Psi(-i\tau\sigma_2^2; \beta_1' x_{1t} - \beta_2' x_{2t}, \theta_3 + \sigma_1^2 + \sigma_2^2)]$$
$$+ \, \exp\{-i\beta_1' x_{1t}\tau - (\sigma_1^2 + \theta_2)\tau^2/2\}$$
$$\times \, [1 - \Psi(-i\tau\sigma_1^2; \beta_2' x_{2t} - \beta_1' x_{1t}, \theta_3 + \sigma_1^2 + \sigma_2^2)] \qquad (4.2.22)$$

where $\Psi(a; \mu, \sigma^2)$ is the cumulative normal integral from $-\infty$ to a of a normal density with mean μ and variance σ^2. The density function is not known, but estimation by fitting the sample characteristic function (see section 2.6, which discusses the simpler moment generating function method) is at least conceivable. However, the practical difficulties of estimation in the general case are likely to be severe enough to make the usefulness of the present approach questionable, particularly in the absence of compelling economic reasons for the formulation. Needless to say, the fuzzy min approach is likely to be even more difficult if there is a price adjustment equation present.

4.3   Models in Which Rationing Affects Demand or Supply

It has been observed that the demand (supply) of a good may be influenced by the expectations of the buyer (seller) that he may be rationed. Thus, a potential buyer, noticing that a long queue exists, may modify his purchase intentions and forgo entering the queue. Alternatively, the buyer may make an estimate that he will end up being rationed in the marketplace; if it is not costless for him to attempt to obtain the good, he may decide to forgo the attempt altogether if the probability that he will be rationed is high enough. Models of this general type have been discussed by Eaton and Quandt (1983) in the context of an individual's labor supply decision and by Katz and Owen (1984), Lindsay and Feigenbaum (1984), and Charemza, Gronicki and Quandt (1985) in the context of socialist, planned economies.

Consider now model A with the modification that the demand in each period t is assumed to depend on the probability P_t that buyers will be rationed (Eaton and Quandt 1983). We then write

$$D_t = \beta_1' x_{1t} + \delta P_t + u_{1t} \qquad (4.3.1)$$

$$S_t = \beta_2' x_{2t} \qquad\quad + u_{2t} \qquad (4.3.2)$$

$$Q_t = \min(D_t, S_t)$$

So far the specification is vague with respect to whether P_t should be taken to be the unconditional probability $P_t = \Pr\{D_t \geqq S_t\}$ or the conditional probability $\Pr\{D_t \geqq S_t | Q_t\}$. For two reasons the former is preferable. First, when purchase intentions are formed, Q_t is generally not yet observable. Secondly, the density of Q_t depends on P_t, but if P_t is taken to be the conditional probability, it itself depends on the density in question. It is unclear whether the resulting functional equation can be solved for the density. For both of these reasons, we take P_t to be $\Pr\{D_t \geq S_t\}$. From (4.3.1) and (4.3.2) we have

$$P_t = \Pr\{D_t \geq S_t\} = \Pr\{\beta_1' x_{1t} + \delta P_t + u_{1t} \geq \beta_2' x_{2t} + u_{2t}\}$$

$$= \int_{-\infty}^{\beta_1' x_{1t} + \delta P_t - \beta_2' x_{2t}} \frac{1}{\sqrt{(2\pi)}\sigma} \exp\{-v^2/2\sigma^2\}\,dv \qquad (4.3.4)$$

where $\sigma^2 = \sigma_1^2 + \sigma_2^2 - 2\sigma_{12}$.

Proposition If $\delta < 0$, (4.3.4) determines a unique value of P_t such that $0 < P_t < 1$.

Proof For $P_t = 0$ the right hand side of (4.3.4) is positive but less than 1.0 and exceeds the left hand side. As P_t increases, the left hand side increases, reaching unity when $P_t = 1.0$; at the same time the right hand side decreases. Hence there exists a value of P_t between 0 and 1 when the left and right hand sides are equal. □

In the case when $\delta > 0$, a unique solution is not guaranteed. At $P_t = 0$ the right hand side is again positive and < 1.0. At $P_t = 1$, the right hand side is also positive and < 1.0. In between, the right hand side is increasing in P_t. The second derivative is

$$\frac{d^2(\text{RHS})}{dP_t^2} = \frac{\delta^2}{\sqrt{(2\pi)}\sigma} \exp\left\{ -\frac{(\beta_1' x_{1t} + \delta P_t - \beta_2' x_{2t})^2}{2\sigma^2} \right\}$$

$$\times \left[-\frac{(\beta_1' x_{1t} + \delta P_t - \beta_2' x_{2t})}{\sigma^2} \right]$$

which is either always positive (if $\beta_1' x_{1t} + \delta P_t$ is small relative to $\beta_2' x_{2t}$ for all P_t), or always negative (if the reverse is true), or is positive for small P_t and negative for large P_t. In the first two of these subcases the solution is unique, but in the third one it need not be because the right hand side starts out convex and then becomes concave. Hence up to three solutions might exist. This is an example of a case in which several sets of values of the endogenous variables (D_t, S_t) may be compatible with a given set of exogenous variable values. This represents a fundamental inconsistency in a model and is referred to as the problem of coherency, which will be discussed in more detail in chapters 5 and 6. Fortunately, only $\delta < 0$ is sensible from the economic point of view and we shall restrict ourselves to that case.

Clearly, the solution to (4.3.4) depends entirely on exogenous variables and parameters and (if u_{1t}, u_{2t} are independent) we can then write the p.d.f. of Q_t as

$$h(Q_t) = \frac{1}{\sqrt{(2\pi)}\sigma_1} \exp\left\{ -\frac{(Q_t - \beta_1' x_{1t} - \delta P_t)^2}{2\sigma_1^2} \right\} \left[1 - \Phi\left(\frac{Q_t - \beta_2' x_{2t}}{\sigma_2} \right) \right]$$

$$+ \frac{1}{\sqrt{(2\pi)}\sigma_2} \exp\left\{ - \frac{(Q_t - \beta_2' x_{2t})^2}{\sigma_2^2} \right\} \left[1 - \Phi\left(\frac{Q_t - \beta_1' x_{1t} - \delta P_t}{\sigma_1} \right) \right]$$

(4.3.5)

and the likelihood function is obtained in the usual way by multiplication.

Lastly, we discuss briefly an effective solution method, *regula falsi*, for equations of the type (4.3.4) in which we are assured that a unique root exists in an interval between two values a and b (Acton 1970). Consider the function $f(x)$ in figure 4.1. Since a unique root is known to exist between a and b, the function values $f(a)$, $f(b)$ must be of opposite sign. Connect them by a straight line and find the first approximation to the root, x_1, where it intersects the horizontal axis. If $f(x_1)$ has the same sign as $f(b)$, drop point b and repeat the procedure, yielding x_2 in figure 4.1. If $f(x_1)$ has the same sign as $f(a)$, drop point a and repeat the procedure. (Obviously, if $f(x_1)$ is zero, x_1 is the root.) Proceed in this fashion until acceptable accuracy is achieved. The algorithm then generates x values according to

$$x_i = x_{i-2} + f_{i-2} \left[\frac{x_{i-1} - x_{i-2}}{f_{i-1} - f_{i-2}} \right]$$

(4.3.6)

where f_i denotes the function value $f(x_i)$. It generally converges quite rapidly, and in appendix 4.B we present a FORTRAN program to implement this algorithm with an enhancement to speed convergence in unusual cases.

4.4   The Problem of Aggregation

So far, all models considered were implicitly based on the assumption that we

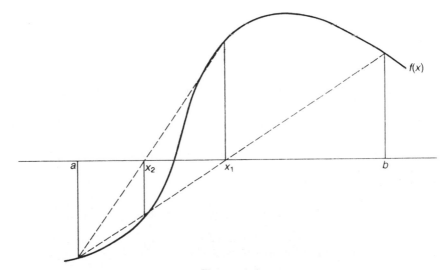

Figure 4.1

are dealing with a single market; in effect, with a single marketplace in which traders meet and in which, after trading is concluded, an excess demand or supply materializes. Muellbauer (1978) was the first to question this assumption by noting that in many situations, e.g. the labor market, the observation on the aggregate quantity transacted may be thought to be the sum of the outcomes of several (or numerous) local markets that may operate independently of one another. This requires a substantial reformulation of the model.

Muellbauer-Hajivassiliou Model

Assume that markets are indexed by j and that the demand and supply functions can be written as

$$D_t^j = D_t^* + \epsilon_{1jt} \tag{4.4.1}$$

$$S_t^j = S_t^* + \epsilon_{2jt} \tag{4.4.2}$$

where D_t^* and S_t^* represent the mean demand and supply (i.e. $D_t^* = \beta_1' x_{1t}$, $S_t^* = \beta_2' x_{2t}$) and ϵ_{1jt} and ϵ_{2jt} are error terms. For simplicity, all markets are assumed to have the same mean (i.e. the same size). If this were not the case, scale factors would have to be introduced to account for basic size differences. A further simplification is to assume that the error terms do not depend on the market and on the time index t, so that their joint density can be written as $f(\epsilon_1, \epsilon_2)$ (Hajivassiliou 1983). If there are n markets, the aggregate demand and supply are

$$\sum_j D_t^j = n D_t^* + \sum_j \epsilon_{1jt}$$

and

$$\sum_j S_t^j = n S_t^* + \sum_j \epsilon_{2jt}$$

where we retain the subscript j on the error terms to indicate that a separate realization of ϵs is thought to be drawn for each market (albeit from a common distribution). The standard approach then specifies the observed aggregate Q_t as $Q_t = \min(\sum_j D_t^j, \sum_j S_t^j)$. In reality, however, some markets may exhibit excess demand while others show excess supply. The observed aggregate then is

$$Q_t = \sum_{D_t^j < S_t^j} D_t^j + \sum_{D_t^j \geq S_t^j} S_t^j \tag{4.4.3}$$

Denote by E_t^* the (average) excess demand $E_t^* = D_t^* - S_t^*$, let $\epsilon_{2t} - \epsilon_{1t} = \eta_t$, and let $F(\epsilon_1, \epsilon_2)$ be the joint distribution of ϵ_1, ϵ_2. Assuming a continuum of markets, (4.4.3) is replaced by

$$Q_t = \iint\limits_{\eta_t \geq E_t^*} (D_t^* + \epsilon_1) dF(\epsilon_1, \epsilon_2) + \iint\limits_{\eta_t < E_t^*} (S_t^* + \epsilon_t) dF(\epsilon_1, \epsilon_2)$$

$$= D_t^* \iint\limits_{\eta_t \geq E_t^*} dF(\epsilon_1, \epsilon_2) + S_t^* \iint\limits_{\eta_t < E_t^*} dF(\epsilon_1, \epsilon_2)$$

$$+ \iint\limits_{\eta_t \geq E_t^*} \epsilon_1 dF(\epsilon_1, \epsilon_2) + \iint\limits_{\eta_t < E_t^*} \epsilon_2 dF(\epsilon_1, \epsilon_2) \qquad (4.4.4)$$

Since the double integral

$$\iint\limits_{\eta_t < E_t^*} dF(\epsilon_1, \epsilon_2)$$

is the probability P that excess demand occurs in a market, (4.4.4) can also be written as

$$Q_t = D_t^*(1 - P_t) + S_t^* P_t + E(\epsilon_1 | \eta_t \geq E_t^*)(1 - P_t) + E(\epsilon_2 | \eta_t < E_t^*) P_t \qquad (4.4.5)$$

Consider now model A for the whole market and the expected value of Q in that model as expressed in (2.6.9) and (2.6.11). Since in that model

$$E(Q_t) = E(D_t | D_t < S_t) \Pr\{D_t < S_t\} + E(S_t | D_t \geq S_t) \Pr\{D_t \geq S_t\}$$

and since (a) $D_t^* + E(\epsilon_1 | \eta_t \geq E_t^*)$ in (4.4.5) is formally identical with $E(D_t | D_t < S_t)$ and (b) $1 - P_t$ is $\Pr\{D_t < S_t\}$, expression (4.4.5) is formally identical to (2.6.9) and, on the assumption of normality, Q_t in the present model is given by

$$Q_t^a = \Phi(v_t)\beta_1' x_{1t} + [1 - \Phi(v_t)]\beta_2' x_{2t} - \sigma\phi(v_t) \qquad (4.4.6)$$

where $v_t = (\beta_2' x_{2t} - \beta_1' x_{1t})/\sigma$ and $\sigma^2 = \sigma_1^2 + \sigma_2^2 - 2\sigma_{12}$.

The locus of realizations in the present model of aggregation is thus equal to $E(Q_t)$ in the standard simple disequilibrium model. It is interesting to note that this locus lies to the left of the wedge-shaped locus given by the standard min condition (see figure 4.2). This is plausible since the conditional expectations in (4.4.5) both involve truncating the range of the relevant error terms from above and hence these expectations are negative. More formally, we can proceed as follows. If we apply the minimum condition for each market and then "aggregate," we obtain (4.4.6). If we first aggregate and then take the min, we obtain $Q_t = \min(D_t^*, S_t^*)$. If the claim that Q_t from (4.4.6) is always smaller than $\min(D_t^*, S_t^*)$ were false, we would have to have

$$D_t^* \Phi(v_t) + S_t^*[1 - \Phi(v_t)] - \sigma\phi(v_t) > D_t^* \qquad \text{if } D_t^* < S_t^* \qquad (4.4.7)$$

and

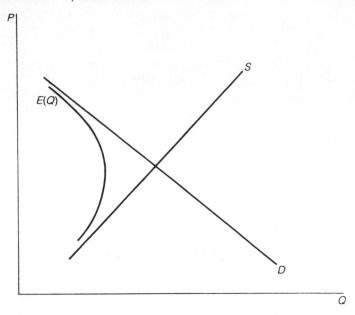

Figure 4.2

$$D_t^* \, \Phi(v_t) + S_t^* [1 - \Phi(v_t)] - \sigma\phi(v_t) > S_t^* \qquad \text{if } S_t^* \leq D_t^* \qquad (4.4.8)$$

Consider (4.4.7) and, noting that $(S_t^* - D_t^*)/\sigma = v_t$, rewrite it as

$$v_t > \frac{\phi(v_t)}{1 - \Phi(v_t)} \qquad (4.4.9)$$

But the right hand side is the conditional mean $E(y|y > v_t)$ from a standard normal density truncated at v_t and cannot be smaller than v_t; hence (4.4.9) implies a contradiction. A similar construction works for (4.4.8) and the previous claim is thus true. The estimation of this model involves therefore the same formulas as the nonlinear least squares method of section 2.6.

Effect of Demand Shifts on Q_t

As we showed before, the realization of Q_t in the Muellbauer-Hajivassiliou model is the same as the expected realization in the standard model. It is interesting to examine how this changes with the expected demand D^*. Differentiating (4.4.6) with respect to $D_t^* \ (= \beta_1' x_{1t})$ yields

$$\frac{\partial Q_t^a}{\partial D_t^*} = \Phi(v_t) + D_t^* \phi(v_t) \left(-\frac{1}{\sigma} \right) + S_t^* \phi(v_t) \left(\frac{1}{\sigma} \right) - \sigma\phi(v_t) v_t \left(\frac{1}{\sigma} \right)$$

$$= \Phi(v_t)$$

which is the probability that excess supply will occur. This proposition, originally due to Malinvaud (1980), expresses what one can reasonably expect: if the probability of excess supply is large, an increase in D^* will translate itself approximately unit for unit into transactions; if the probability of excess demand is very large, then essentially none of the demand increase gets translated into an increase in Q.

Estimation in the Muellbauer-Hajivassiliou Model

To estimate the parameters under the Muellbauer-Hajivassiliou specification, one could employ any one of several methods (Quandt 1986b):

1   ML: one could disregard the aggregation problem and employ the maximum likelihood method based on the density (2.3.10).
2   NLS: one could employ nonlinear least squares by minimizing $\Sigma_t (Q_t - Q_t^a)^2$ with respect to the parameters. Unlike ML, which represents a misspecification in the Muellbauer-Hajivassiliou case, this method is "appropriate" even if there is no aggregation problem.
3   NLSH: recognizing that the implicit model of the NLS method, namely $Q_t = Q_t^a + \epsilon_t$, is heteroscedastic, one could apply to it White's (1980) heteroscedastic covariance matrix estimator. Denoting by D the $k \times T$ matrix with elements $\partial Q_t^a / \partial \theta_k$, where θ denotes the k-vector of all parameters, and by ω_t the estimated residual $Q_t - Q_t^a$, the appropriate heteroscedasticity-consistent covariance matrix estimator for $\hat{\theta}$ is $(D'D)^{-1} W(D'D)^{-1}$, where W is a $k \times k$ matrix, the ijth element of which is $W_{ij} = \Sigma_{t=1}^{T} \omega_t^2 D_t' D_t$ and where D_t is the tth row of D.
4   WNLS: one could employ weighted nonlinear least squares. Defining σ_t^2 to represent the variance of Q_t, and h_t as $\sigma_t^2 / \Sigma_{t=1}^{T} \sigma_t^2$, WNLS minimizes $\Sigma_{t-1}^{T} [Q_t - E(Q_t)]^2 / h_t$. The variance of Q_t is given, in turn (see Nasim and Satchell 1982), by

$$\sigma_t^2 = \sigma_1^2 A_{1t} + \sigma_2^2 A_{2t} + A_{3t}$$

where

$$A_{1t} = \Phi(v_t) + v_t \phi(v_t)$$

$$A_{2t} = 1 - \Phi(v_t) + v_t \phi(v_t)$$

$$A_{3t} = (\sigma v_t)^2 \Phi(v_t)[1 - \Phi(v_t)] - \sigma^2 \phi(v_t)^2 - 2\sigma^2 v_t \phi(v_t) \Phi(v_t)$$

(since σ_{12} was assumed to be zero, we exclude it from the formulas). Whereas method NLSH estimates a heteroscedastic model and corrects the covariance estimates, WNLS attempts to find "correct" residuals for the objective function, purged of heteroscedasticity.

It is interesting to compare these estimators with some Monte Carlo experiments in which alternately the Muellbauer-Hajivassilliou specification or the standard "no-aggregation problem" specification is true. We posit that there exists a number m of submarkets and that in the jth market the demand and supply are set as follows:

$$D_t^j = (\beta_{10} + \beta_{11}x_{1t} + \beta_{12}x_{2t})/m + u_{1t}^j/\sqrt{m}$$

$$S_t^j = (\beta_{20} + \beta_{21}x_{1t} + \beta_{22}x_{3t})/m + u_{2t}^j/\sqrt{m}$$

where u_{1t} and u_{2t} are normally distributed with mean 0 and variances σ_1^2, σ_2^2 and are independent of one another and over time. We assume that the min condition holds in each submarket, and the properly aggregated quantity of transactions is, as before,

$$Q_t^a = \sum_{D_t^j < S_t^j} D_t^j + \sum_{D_t^j \geq S_t^j} S_t^j$$

If we ignore the partitioning into submarkets, the not properly aggregated total transacted quantity is

$$Q_t^n = \min \left(\sum_j D_t^j, \sum_j S_t^j \right)$$

From summation we obtain the aggregate demand and supply as

$$D_t = \beta_{10} + \beta_{11}x_{1t} + \beta_{12}x_{2t} + \sum_j u_{1t}^j/\sqrt{m}$$

$$S_t = \beta_{20} + \beta_{21}x_{1t} + \beta_{22}x_{3t} + \sum_j u_{2t}^j/\sqrt{m}$$

and hence the error terms in the implied aggregate equations have variances σ_1^2, σ_2^2 respectively.

The true values of the coefficients in the principal experiments were $\beta_{10} = 100$, $\beta_{11} = -1$, $\beta_{12} = 1$, $\beta_{20} = -20$, $\beta_{21} = 1$, $\beta_{22} = 1$, $\sigma_1^2 = 25$, $\sigma_2^2 = 25$. Values of the xs were generated once and for all for each jt combination in a given set of replications of the experiment. The xs were drawn from uniform distributions: from 55–105 for x_1, 50–150 for x_2, and 0–100 for x_3. It follows that the expected number of observations characterized by excess demand is 0.4. Experiments were performed for values of $m = 3$ and 10 and for sample sizes $n = 30$ and 60. In one experiment, σ_1^2 and σ_2^2 were set to 250.0.

Tables 4.1 through 4.12 in appendix C contain (a) the mean square errors of the estimates, (b) the results of testing the sampling distribution of $(\hat{\beta}_i - \beta_i^0)/\hat{\sigma}_i$ for normality ($N(0,1)$) with the Kolmogorov-Smirnov test (where β_i^0 denotes the true values), and (c) the results of comparing across methods the fraction of times that a method gives parameter estimates closest to the true values. In experiments 1, 2, and 4 the sample size is 30 and in experiment 3 it is 60. In experiments 1, 3, and 4 the assumed number of submarkets m is 10 and in experiment 2 it is 3. Experiment 4 differs from 1 by having $\sigma_1^2 = \sigma_2^2 = 250$. The rationale for using large variances in one experiment is that with small variances the different aggregation schemes will not yield materially different Q values except very near the equilibrium point of demand and supply. Thus differences between ML and the other methods ought to become more prominent in experiment 4. The number of replications was 40 in experiments 1, 2, and 3 and was 32 in experiment 4. "Data $Q = Q^a$" corresponds to the case in which the data are correctly aggregated, and "data $Q = Q^n$" refers to the case in which we pretend that they come from a single market. Methods NLS, NLSH, and WNLS are "appropriate" in all cases, but ML represents a misspecification in the former case and is the preferred method in the latter. Since NLS and NLSH differ only by the estimated covariance matrix, their coefficient mean square errors are identical. Also, since in the "closest-to-true-value" calculations in tables 4.3, 4.6, 4.9 and 4.12 these two methods would invariably tie with each other, we compare only ML, NLS, and WNLS.

We first compare experiments 1, 2, and 3. We note that the mean square errors for ML are smaller on the whole than for the other methods when $n = 30$, even when ML is not the appropriate estimating method. NLS and WNLS are reasonably similar. All methods improve when $n = 60$ but NLS is, on balance, better than ML when ML is inappropriate, with the reverse holding when ML is appropriate. For the larger sample size, WNLS improves relative to NLS when $Q = Q^a$.

Tables 4.2, 4.5, and 4.8 exhibit the Kolmogorov-Smirnov statistics and the Smirnov limit probability that under the null hypothesis of normality a value as great or greater is observed. First compare tables 4.2 and 4.8 where the difference is in the sample size. Using a significance level of 0.05 we invariably reject normality for ML when ML is inappropriate and accept normality in all but one instance in the reverse case. Normality tends to be rejected for NLS frequently, whether $Q - Q^a$ or $Q - Q^n$ and whether the sample size is small or large. Normality is accepted for NLSH for both sample sizes, whether $Q = Q^a$ or not. For WNLS normality is accepted for the small but not for the larger samples. These results are not surprising since:

1   ML represents a misspecification for $Q = Q^a$.
2   The estimated standard errors from NLS on the mistaken assumption of homoscedasticity are incorrect for both $Q = Q^a$ and $Q = Q^n$.
3   The estimated standard errors for NLSH are "correct" for both $Q = Q^a$ and $Q = Q^n$ (although for $Q = Q^n$ ML would be the generally preferred method).
4   For WNLS the estimated standard errors are again incorrect.

Comparing tables 4.2 and 4.5, the most interesting finding is that in the latter the ML estimates do not significantly depart from normality for $Q = Q^a$. The reason is that when the number of submarkets is small, as is the case in experiment 2, the "correct" aggregation will yield the same result as the "incorrect" aggregation with higher probability than when m is large; hence ML will be less inappropriate in these cases than for large m. Apparently this effect manifests itself quite substantially when $m = 3$.

Finally, we compare tables 4.3, 4.6, and 4.9. Comparing the fraction of times that each method "wins," ML beats NLS and WNLS for the small sample sizes whether $Q = Q^a$ or $Q = Q^n$, although by small margins when $Q = Q^a$ (and thus ML is inappropriate). When $n = 60$, ML wins easily for $Q = Q^n$ and all methods are fairly comparable in performance when $Q = Q^a$. However, with minor exceptions we cannot reject the null hypothesis that all methods are equally good.

Comparing experiment 1 with experiment 4 we note that the larger error variances lead to a slight deterioration of mean square errors for ML whether $Q = Q^a$ or not. The nonlinear least squares methods tend to perform very poorly in terms of mean square errors, owing to some very large outliers. It should be noted that the comparison is not nearly as unfavorable to these methods when the mean bias or midspread is the basis of comparison. From the point of view of the normality of estimates, ML behaves very much as in experiment 1. For NLS and WNLS, normality improves marginally, but for NLSH with $Q = Q^a$ it deteriorates significantly. The comparison of the fraction of times that each method produces an estimate closest to the true value (table 4.2) again favors ML, and in somewhat more pronounced fashion than in table 4.3.

Sampling experiments based on as few replications as those reported here must necessarily be treated with caution. Nevertheless, some tentative conclusions may be formed:

1　Unlike NLS, the method NLSH produces estimates the sampling distribution of which is, on the whole, approximately normal. Hence standard significance tests based on NLSH will be more reliable as a rule.

2　Maximum likelihood estimation does well against the other methods, even when it represents a misspecification, when the sample size is small or when the misspecification is not too severe, as in the case in which the number of submarkets is small. This is, clearly, not to be interpreted as an argument in favor of using an estimating method based on a misspecification; rather, it says that under certain circumstances the costs of the misspecification are small, particularly when, as in the case of a small number of submarkets, the alternative method also involves an approximation.

3　For relatively large sample sizes the advantage of ML tends to disappear when ML is inappropriate, but even for $n = 60$ it is not clear on absolute grounds that, say, NLS is to be preferred.

4　When error variances are large, the nonlinear least squares methods tend to produce large outliers and the advantage of ML tends to increase.

Lambert Model

Instead of assuming that demands and supplies in micromarkets are normally distributed, Lambert (1984) posits that their logarithms are normally distributed. Equations (4.4.1) and (4.4.2) are then written as

$$\log D_t^j = D_t^* + \epsilon_{1t} \tag{4.4.10}$$

$$\log S_t^j = S_t^* + \epsilon_{2t} \tag{4.4.11}$$

where $\epsilon_{1t}, \epsilon_{2t}$ are distributed as $N(0, \Sigma)$ and independently of t. It follows that:

$$E(D_t^j) = e^{D_t^* + \sigma_1^2/2}$$

$$E(S_t^j) = e^{S_t^* + \sigma_2^2/2}$$

Lambert aggregates the individual markets by multiplying their demands and supplies by the number of markets n, yielding

$$\log D_t = D_t^* + \log n + \epsilon_{1t} \tag{4.4.12}$$

$$\log S_t = S_t^* + \log n + \epsilon_{2t} \tag{4.4.13}$$

Since summing the individual market demands yields

$$D_t = \sum_j D_t^j = e^{D_t^*} \sum_j e^{\epsilon_{1t}}$$

(and similarly for supply), (4.4.12) and (4.4.13) are contingent on the implicit assumption that either each submarket experiences the same drawing ϵ_{1t} or that, at least, the scale condition $\Sigma_j\, e^{\epsilon_{1t}} = ne^{\epsilon_{1t}}$ always holds. The former possibility is not entirely reasonable and the latter violates the independence of errors across markets, although it may hold to an approximation. It seems most reasonable, therefore, to interpret the consequences of this as approximate results.

For simplicity we now drop the subscript t and denote $D^* + \log n$, $S^* + \log n$ by D_n^*, S_n^* respectively. Lambert takes the transacted quantity to be the average value of the minimum of aggregate demand and supply, i.e.

$$Q = E[\min(D, S)] \tag{4.4.14}$$

This is $E(S|D>S)\Pr\{D>S\} + E(D|D\leq S)\Pr\{D\leq S\}$, which can also be written as

$$Q = \int_{-\infty}^{\infty} \int_{S_n^* - D_n^* + \epsilon_2}^{\infty} \exp(S_n^* + \epsilon_2)\psi(\epsilon; 0, \Sigma)d\epsilon_1 d\epsilon_2$$

$$+ \int_{-\infty}^{\infty} \int_{D_n^* - S_n^* + \epsilon_1}^{\infty} \exp(D_n^* + \epsilon_1)\psi(\epsilon; 0, \Sigma)d\epsilon_2 d\epsilon_1 \tag{4.4.15}$$

where $\psi(\epsilon; 0, \Sigma)$ is the joint normal p.d.f. of $\epsilon' = (\epsilon_1, \epsilon_2)$ with mean zero and covariance matrix Σ. The two terms yield similar results; we concentrate on the first term. Denoting it by Q_1, we have

$$Q_1 = e^{S_n^*} \int\limits_{-\infty}^{\infty} \int\limits_{S_n^* - D_n^* + \epsilon_2}^{\infty} \frac{1}{2\pi \, |\Sigma|^{1/2}} \exp\left\{ -\frac{1}{2} \, [\epsilon'\Sigma^{-1}\epsilon - 2\epsilon_2] \right\} d\epsilon_1 d\epsilon_2$$

$$(4.4.16)$$

when $\epsilon' = (\epsilon_1, \epsilon_2)$. Then Q_1 can be written as

$$Q_1 = e^{S_n^* + \sigma_2^2/2} \int\limits_{-\infty}^{\infty} \int\limits_{S_n^* - D_n^* + \sigma_2^2 - \rho_1\sigma_1\sigma_2 + \eta_2}^{\infty} \psi(\eta; 0, \Sigma) d\eta_1 d\eta_2$$

$$= E(S) \Pr\{\eta_1 > S_n^* - D_n^* + \sigma_2^2 - \rho\sigma_1\sigma_2 + \eta_2\} \qquad (4.4.17)$$

since $e^{S_n^* + \sigma_2^2/2} = E(S)$ from (4.4.13) and the definition of S_n^*. Defining $\sigma^2 = \sigma_1^2 + \sigma_2^2 - 2\rho\sigma_1\sigma_2$, we note that $(\eta_2 - \eta_1)/\sigma \sim N(0,1)$ and that

$$Q_1 = E(S)\Phi\left(\frac{D_n^* - S_n^* + \rho\sigma_1\sigma_2 - \sigma_2^2}{\sigma} \right) \qquad (4.4.18)$$

Finally, let

$$R = \frac{D_n^* - S_n^* + (\sigma_1^2 - \sigma_2^2)/2}{\sigma} \qquad (4.4.19)$$

which equals $\log[E(D)/E(S)]/\sigma$. Then the argument of $\Phi(\ )$ in (4.4.18) is $R - \sigma/2$ and

$$Q_1 = E(S)\Phi(R - \sigma/2) \qquad (4.4.20)$$

By similar reasoning, the second term in (4.4.15) is

$$Q_2 = E(D)\Phi(-R - \sigma/2) \qquad (4.4.21)$$

From the joint density of ϵ_1, ϵ_2 and (4.4.12), (4.4.13) we can obtain the joint density of D and S; denote this by $g(D,S)$. The probability that $D > S$ is $\int_0^\infty \int_S^\infty g(D,S)dDdS$ and is an estimate of the proportion of micromarkets in which demand exceeds supply. Lambert also introduces the weighted proportion

$$P_w = \int\limits_0^{\infty} \int\limits_S^{\infty} Sg(D,S)dDdS/Q$$

$$= \frac{Q_1}{Q_1 + Q_2} = 1 \left/ \left[\frac{E(D)\Phi(-R-\sigma/2)}{E(S)\Phi(R-\sigma/2)} \right] \right. \qquad (4.4.22)$$

By (4.4.12), (4.4.13), (4.4.19) we can write $E(D)/E(S) = e^{R\sigma}$ and

$$P_w = \frac{1}{1 + e^{R\sigma}\Phi(-R-\sigma/2)/\Phi(R-\sigma/2)} \tag{4.4.23}$$

Since $P_w = 1/2$ for $R = 0$, and

$$\lim_{R\to-\infty} P_w = 0, \qquad \lim_{R\to\infty} P_w = 1$$

Lambert approximates P_w by the logistic, so that to an approximation

$$P_w = \frac{1}{1 + e^{-\gamma(R-\alpha)}} \tag{4.4.24}$$

which is obtained by equating the true P_w to its approximation and by equating the derivative of the true P_w with respect to R to the derivative of the approximation, both evaluated at $R = 0$. This yields $\alpha = 0$ and $\gamma = -\sigma + 2\phi(-\sigma/2)\Phi(-\sigma/2)$. Hence P_w can be written as

$$P_w = \frac{1}{1 + \left[\dfrac{E(D)}{E(S)}\right]^{-\gamma/\sigma}} \tag{4.4.25}$$

By exercise 4.4., $P_w = \partial \log Q/\partial \log E(S)$ which also equals $\partial \log Q/\partial S^*$, and $1 - P_w = \partial \log Q/\partial D^*$. We can thus write

$$P_w = \frac{\partial \log Q}{\partial S^*} = \frac{1}{1 + \exp\{-(\gamma/\sigma)(D^* + \sigma_1^2/2 - S^* - \sigma_2^2/2)\}} \tag{4.4.26}$$

Integrating both sides of (4.4.26) with respect to S^* yields

$$Q = k\left[\exp\left\{-\frac{\gamma}{\sigma}\left(D^* + \frac{\sigma_1^2}{2}\right)\right\} + \exp\left\{-\frac{\gamma}{\sigma}\left(S^* + \frac{\sigma_2^2}{2}\right)\right\}\right]^{-\sigma/\gamma}$$

$$= k[E(D)^{-\gamma/\sigma} + E(S)^{-\gamma/\sigma}]^{-\sigma/\gamma}$$

Since

$$\lim_{E(D)/E(S)\to\infty} L = E(S) \qquad \text{and} \qquad \lim_{E(D)/E(S)\to 0} L = E(D)$$

k must be 1 and

$$Q = [E(D)^{-\gamma/\sigma} + E(S)^{-\gamma/\sigma}]^{-\sigma/\gamma} \tag{4.4.27}$$

This is a CES function and, as such, familiar in econometric practice. It has the attractive feature of providing a locus that, as in the case of the Muellbauer-Hajivassiliou formulation, lies to the left of the wedge given by the min condition applied to the standard model. By including in (4.4.27) an error term, that equation becomes a reasonable estimating equation. Finally, it is interesting to note that the CES function has been suggested before, on a more *ad hoc* basis, as an approximation to the min condition by Ginsburgh, Tishler and Zang (1980).

Spencer Model

An approach that is superficially similar to the previous ones was suggested by Spencer (1975), who proposed that one take

$$Q_t = \lambda_t D_t + (1 - \lambda_t) S_t \tag{4.4.28}$$

and

$$\lambda_t = \frac{\exp\{(S_t - D_t)/\sigma\}}{1 + \exp\{(S_t - D_t)/\sigma\}} \tag{4.4.29}$$

The similarity comes from the appearance of a convex combination of D and S in (4.4.28) and (4.4.5). However, the locus (4.4.28) does not lie to the left of the wedge given by the standard min condition, although it does share the property with (4.4.6) that when excess demand (supply) is large, Q_t is close to supply (demand). Also, as $\sigma \to 0$, the Spencer model coincides with the standard disequilibrium model. Nevertheless, the economic justification for the model is not clear.[2]

4.5 Disequilibrium as Partial Adjustment

Prior to the seminal papers discussed in chapter 2 (e.g. Fair and Jaffee 1972), the study of disequilibrium phenomena employed the partial adjustment model. The partial adjustment and the min condition approaches are carefully compared in Chow (1977), who considers the former a more satisfactory formulation. We summarize his observations below and note that applications of the partial adjustment approach to aggregate labor markets are due to Sarantis (1981) and Briguglio (1984).

It is assumed that a system of structural equations determines the equilibrium values of the endogenous variables as in

$$\Gamma y_t^* = B x_t + u_t \tag{4.5.1}$$

where y_t^* is a $G \times 1$ vector of equilibrium values, x_t is a vector of predetermined variables, and u_t is a vector of error terms. These endogenous y_t^* are not observed. What is observed is a set of y_t values given by

$$y_t - y_{t-1} = \Lambda(y_t^* - y_{t-1}) \tag{4.5.2}$$

---

[2] Hajivassiliou (1983) shows that the Spencer model is obtained if ϵ_1 and ϵ_2 are assumed to have identical extreme value distributions.

where Λ is a matrix of speeds of adjustment. In the context of a single market we might write

$$Q_t^* - \alpha_1 p_t^* = \beta_1' x_{1t} + u_{1t}$$
$$Q_t^* - \alpha_2 p_t^* = \beta_2' x_{2t} + u_{2t}$$
$$Q_t - Q_{t-1} = \lambda_1(Q_t^* - Q_{t-1})$$
$$p_t - p_{t-1} = \lambda_2(p_t^* - p_{t-1})$$

The partial adjustment approach clearly generates a different time path for the endogenous variables and is an intrinsically different specification. It leads to more routine estimation problems than the numerous variants of the disequilibrium model with a min condition. To see this, substitute from (4.5.1) into (4.5.2), yielding

$$y_t = \Lambda\Gamma^{-1} Bx_t + (I - \Lambda)y_{t-1} + v_t \tag{4.5.3}$$

which is a standard simultaneous equations model with lagged dependent variables and may be estimated by standard methods.

Chow advances three reasons for preferring the partial adjustment model:

1 The time path generated by the partial adjustment model is more reasonable. In figure 4.3, starting from an equilibrium position defined by D_1 and S, assume that demand shifts to D_2. The new equilibrium would be at (Q_2^*, p_2^*). The partial adjustment model predicts a partial

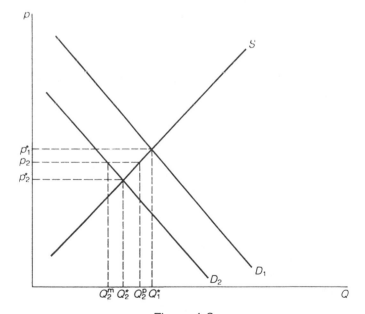

Figure 4.3

move from (Q_1^*, p_1^*) to a point such as (Q_2^p, p_2). The min condition predicts a move to a point such as (Q_2^m, p_2) at which the quantity is even smaller than at the new equilibrium position, which is suggested to be unreasonable.

2   If the min-type disequilibrium model is specified with a price adjustment equation, the partial adjustment model is again claimed to be more satisfactory, because "given the same difference $D_t - S_t$ between the two desired quantities at the existing price, the role of change in price would depend on how far the actual price is from disequilibrium" (Chow 1977).

3   The min-based disequilibrium model treats prices and quantities asymmetrically in that price adjustment is but quantity adjustment is not explicitly modelled.

In spite of these cogent observations, it is difficult to compare conclusively the models with respect to plausibility since they are such different specifications. The partial adjustment model, while relying on the notions of costly adjustments, does not really speak to the question of rationing and there are cases for which it is difficult to find a partial adjustment analog, to wit model A which posits exogenous and rigid prices. The most defensible position would seem to be that both are reasonably plausible models and that ultimately the data will have to decide in each concrete case which is the more appropriate formulation. A systematic test in which hypothetical data are generated from one or the other model and in which both models are estimated and the estimates compared appears to be lacking at this time, although it is possible in principle to apply the various nonnested hypothesis tests.

4.6   Serial Correlation of Error Terms and Lagged Dependent Variables

New estimation problems arise either if error terms are autocorrelated or if lagged values of the unobservable endogenous variables appear in some of the equations. The manner in which these difficulties arise and the methods of coping with some of the problems will be discussed in the present section. We start out by providing some general motivation and description of the problem.

Preliminary Considerations

Consider first model A given by

$$D_t = \beta_1' x_{1t} + u_{1t} \tag{4.6.1}$$

$$S_t = \beta_2' x_{2t} + u_{2t} \tag{4.6.2}$$

$$Q_t = \min(D_t, S_t) \tag{4.6.3}$$

and assume that u_{1t}, u_{2t} are generated by the first-order Markov process

$$u_{1t} = \rho_1 u_{1t-1} + \epsilon_{1t} \tag{4.6.4}$$

$$u_{2t} = \rho_2 u_{2t-1} + \epsilon_{2t} \tag{4.6.5}$$

where ϵ_{1t}, ϵ_{2t} are spherical normal errors. Then multiplying (4.6.1) and (4.6.2) by ρ_1 and ρ_2 respectively, lagging one period and subtracting, we obtain

$$D_t = \beta_1' x_{1t} + \rho_1 D_{t-1} - \rho_1 \beta_1' x_{1t-1} + \epsilon_{1t} \tag{4.6.6}$$

$$S_t = \beta_2' x_{2t} + \rho_2 S_{t-1} - \rho_2 \beta_2' x_{2t-1} + \epsilon_{2t} \tag{4.6.7}$$

and these two equations, together with (4.6.3), almost form a standard model A, except for the fact that lagged values of the unobserved variables appear. Hence the problem of autocorrelation of error terms can easily be transformed into a problem of lagged dependent variables, although it may raise the same kind of problem as the Cochrane-Orcutt transformation in the linear regression model in its treatment of the first observation.

Lagged unobserved endogenous variables can occur in structural equations for a variety of economic reasons. Dagenais (1980) considers a model in which sellers can hold inventories and the quantity supplied depends on the discrepancy between desired and actual inventories, and in which purchasers experience intertemporal spillovers:

$$D_t = \alpha_1 p_t + \beta_1' x_{1t} + \phi_1(D_{t-1} - Q_{t-1}) + u_{1t} \tag{4.6.8}$$

$$S_t = \alpha_2 p_t + \beta_2' x_{2t} + \phi_2(I_{t-1} - I_t^d) + u_{2t} \tag{4.6.9}$$

$$Q_t = \min(D_t, S_t) \tag{4.6.10}$$

$$p_t = p_t + \gamma(D_{t-1} - S_{t-1}) + u_{3t} \tag{4.6.11}$$

where I_t represents inventories and I_t^d desired inventories. The term $\phi_1(D_{t-1} - Q_{t-1})$ in the demand function represents the spillover into current demand of any unsatisfied demand from the last period. The term $\phi_2(I_{t-1} - I_t^d)$ is the adjustment to current supply due to inventories not being at the "right" level. Dagenais posits that desired inventories are a linear function of the supply without the inventory adjustment term; in general we could write it as

$$I_t^d = \alpha_3 p_t + \beta_3' x_{3t} + u_{4t} \tag{4.6.12}$$

Dagenais suggests the following method for estimation:

1   Substitute (4.6.12) in (4.6.9) to write S_t in terms of p_t, xs and I_{t-1}.
2   Lag the equation obtained in 1 and combine it with (4.6.11) to get an expression for D_{t-1}.
3   Use this expression to eliminate D_{t-1} from (4.6.8).

This procedure yields a demand and a supply function from which lagged latent variables have been eliminated. These two functions, together with (4.6.10) and (4.6.11), form a system from which maximum likelihood estimates can be computed. However, the resulting estimates will not be efficient since they do not utilize the information implicit in $Q_{t-1} = \min(D_{t-1}, S_{t-1})$.

Orsi (1984) discusses a labor market model of the following form:

$$D_t = \alpha_1 w_t + \beta_1' x_{1t} + \phi_1(D_{t-1} - L_{t-1}) + u_{1t} \tag{4.6.13}$$

$$S_t = \alpha_2 w_t + \beta_2' x_{2t} + \phi_2(S_{t-1} - L_{t-1}) + u_{2t} \tag{4.6.14}$$

$$L_t = \min(D_t, S_t) \tag{4.6.15}$$

where w_t is the wage. The wage adjustment equation is stated in the Bowden form (see (2.1.11)) as

$$w_t = \delta_t[\mu_1 w_{t-1} + (1 - \mu_1)w_t^*] + (1 - \delta_t)[\mu_2 w_{t-1} + (1 - \mu_2)w_t^*] \tag{4.6.16}$$

where $\delta_t = 1$ if $w_t \geq w_{t-1}$ and $= 0$ otherwise and where w_t^* is the equilibrium wage. The terms $\phi_1(D_{t-1} - L_{t-1})$, $\phi_2(S_{t-1} - L_{t-1})$ represent the intertemporal spillovers, with the obvious restrictions $0 \leq \phi_1, \phi_2 < 1$. Orsi estimates the reduced form of a structure derived from the above by eliminating the latent variables (see exercise 4.7).

It is noteworthy that both models have particular features that make it possible to eliminate at least the lagged values of the latent variables. In the Dagenais model, no lagged latent variable appears in the supply function. In the Orsi model, the adjustment equation is specified without an error term. If neither of these features is present, as in

$$D_t = \alpha_1 p_t + \beta_1' x_{1t} + \phi_1(D_{t-1} - Q_{t-1}) + u_{1t} \tag{4.6.17}$$

$$S_t = \alpha_2 p_t + \beta_2' x_{2t} + \phi_2(S_{t-1} - Q_{t-1}) + u_{2t} \tag{4.6.18}$$

$$Q_t = \min(D_t, S_t) \tag{4.6.19}$$

$$p_t = p_{t-1} + \gamma(D_t - S_t) + u_{3t} \tag{4.6.20}$$

the situation is as follows. If we lag (4.6.20) one period and solve (4.6.17), (4.6.18), and the one-period lagged form of (4.6.20) for D_{t-1}, S_{t-1}, and p_t, we obtain in matrix form

$$
\begin{bmatrix} D_{t-1} \\ S_{t-1} \\ p_{t-1} \end{bmatrix} = \frac{-1}{\gamma(\alpha_1\phi_2 - \alpha_2\phi_1)} \begin{bmatrix} \gamma\alpha_2 & -\gamma\alpha_1 & -\alpha_1\phi_2 \\ \gamma\alpha_2 & -\gamma\alpha_1 & -\alpha_2\phi_1 \\ -\gamma\phi_2 & \gamma\phi_1 & \phi_1\phi_2 \end{bmatrix} \begin{bmatrix} D_t - \beta_1' x_{1t} + \phi_1 Q_{t-1} - u_{1t} \\ S_t - \beta_2' x_{2t} + \phi_2 Q_{t-1} - u_{2t} \\ p_{t-1} - p_{t-2} - u_{3t-1} \end{bmatrix} \tag{4.6.21}
$$

and substituting from (4.6.21) into (4.6.17) and (4.6.18) for D_{t-1} and S_{t-1} causes the error structure to be serially correlated.

Maximum Likelihood Estimation for model C

Laffont and Monfort (1979) have developed the appropriate estimation method when model C has lagged latent endogenous variables. A general form of such a model is[3]

$$D_t = \alpha_1 p_t + \beta_1' x_{1t} + \phi_{11} D_{t-1} + \phi_{12} S_{t-1} + u_{1t} \tag{4.6.22}$$

$$S_t = \alpha_2 p_t + \beta_2' x_{2t} + \phi_{21} D_{t-1} + \phi_{22} S_{t-1} + u_{2t} \tag{4.6.23}$$

$$Q_t = \min(D_t, S_t) \tag{4.6.24}$$

$$p_t = p_{t-1} + \gamma(D_t - S_t) \tag{4.6.25}$$

As a first step, substitute (4.6.25) in (4.6.22) and (4.6.23):

$$D_t = \alpha_1 [p_{t-1} + \gamma(D_t - S_t)] + \beta_1' x_{1t} + \phi_{11} D_{t-1} + \phi_{12} S_{t-1} + u_{1t}$$

$$S_t = \alpha_2 [p_{t-1} + \gamma(D_t - S_t)] + \beta_2' x_{2t} + \phi_{21} D_{t-1} + \phi_{22} S_{t-1} + u_{2t}$$

We can also write this as

$$\begin{bmatrix} w_{1t} \\ w_{2t} \end{bmatrix} \equiv \begin{bmatrix} 1 - \alpha_1 \gamma & \alpha_1 \gamma \\ -\alpha_2 \gamma & 1 + \alpha_2 \gamma \end{bmatrix} \begin{bmatrix} D_t \\ S_t \end{bmatrix} - \begin{bmatrix} z_{1t} \\ z_{2t} \end{bmatrix} = \begin{bmatrix} u_{1t} \\ u_{2t} \end{bmatrix} \tag{4.6.26}$$

which defines w_{1t}, w_{2t} and where it was convenient to introduce the notation $z_{1t} = \beta_1' x_{1t} + \phi_{11} D_{t-1} + \phi_{12} S_{t-1}$, $z_{2t} = \beta_2' x_{2t} + \phi_{21} D_{t-1} + \phi_{22} S_{t-1}$. If u_{1t}, u_{2t} are distributed as $N(0, \Sigma)$ and are uncorrelated over time, we obtain the p.d.f. of D_t, S_t, given D_{t-1}, S_{t-1}, as

$$f(D_t, S_t | D_{t-1}, S_{t-1}) = \frac{|1 + \gamma(\alpha_2 - \alpha_1)|}{2\pi |\Sigma|^{1/2}} \exp\left\{ -\frac{1}{2} [w_t' \Sigma^{-1} w_t] \right\} \tag{4.6.27}$$

where $w_t' = (w_{1t}, w_{2t})$, and where $1 + \gamma(\alpha_2 - \alpha_1)$ is the Jacobian of the transformation.

We now transform from a density of D_t, S_t to one of Q_t, Δp_t. As before in model C,

$$\Delta p_t = \begin{cases} \gamma(D_t - Q_t) & \text{if } D_t > S_t \\ \gamma(Q_t - S_t) & \text{otherwise} \end{cases}$$

Thus the transformation from D_t, S_t to Q_t, Δp_t is

$$D_t = Q_t + \Delta p_t / \gamma$$

$$S_t = Q_t \tag{4.6.28}$$

if $D_t > S_t$ and

$$D_t = Q_t$$

---

[3] Laffont and Monfort actually discuss for p_t (see (4.6.25)) the case in which there are different speeds of adjustment γ_1, γ_2 corresponding to excess demand and excess supply. This complicates the algebra slightly but does not alter the essence of the argument.

$$S_t = Q_t - \Delta p_t / \gamma \qquad (4.6.29)$$

in the converse case. The Jacobians of the transformations are $1/\gamma$ in either case.[4]

Equation (4.6.27) then becomes

$$f(Q_t, \Delta p_t \mid D_{t-1}, S_{t-1}) = \frac{|1 + \gamma(\alpha_2 - \alpha_1)|}{2\pi |\gamma| |\Sigma|^{1/2}} \exp\left\{ -\frac{1}{2} [w_t' \Sigma^{-1} w_t] \right\}$$

$$(4.6.30)$$

where we must make sure that the D_t, S_t appearing in w_t are replaced by either (4.6.28) or (4.6.29), depending on whether $\Delta p_t > 0$ or not.

The last step is to replace the lagged values of demand and supply by their mappings into lagged Q and lagged Δp, depending on the sign of lagged Δp. The density thus has four different possible forms, depending on the signs of Δp_t and Δp_{t-1}. We can summarize the result in the following manner.

Define the vectors

$$w_t^{++} = \begin{bmatrix} 1 - \alpha_1 \gamma & \alpha_1 \gamma \\ -\alpha_2 \gamma & 1 + \alpha_2 \gamma \end{bmatrix} \begin{bmatrix} Q_t + \Delta p_t / \gamma \\ Q_t \end{bmatrix}$$

$$- \begin{bmatrix} \beta_1' x_{1t} + \phi_{11}(Q_{t-1} + \Delta p_{t-1}/\gamma) + \phi_{12} Q_{t-1} \\ \beta_2' x_{2t} + \phi_{21}(Q_{t-1} + \Delta p_{t-1}/\gamma) + \phi_{22} Q_{t-1} \end{bmatrix}$$

$$w_t^{+-} = \begin{bmatrix} 1 - \alpha_1 \gamma & \alpha_1 \gamma \\ -\alpha_2 \gamma & 1 + \alpha_2 \gamma \end{bmatrix} \begin{bmatrix} Q_t + \Delta p_t / \gamma \\ Q_t \end{bmatrix}$$

$$- \begin{bmatrix} \beta_1' x_{1t} + \phi_{11} Q_{t-1} + \phi_{12}(Q_{t-1} - \Delta p_{t-1}/\gamma) \\ \beta_2' x_{2t} + \phi_{21} Q_{t-1} + \phi_{22}(Q_{t-1} - \Delta p_{t-1}/\gamma) \end{bmatrix}$$

$$w_t^{-+} = \begin{bmatrix} 1 - \alpha_1 \gamma & \alpha_1 \gamma \\ -\alpha_2 \gamma & 1 + \alpha_2 \gamma \end{bmatrix} \begin{bmatrix} Q_t \\ Q_t - \Delta p_t / \gamma \end{bmatrix}$$

$$- \begin{bmatrix} \beta_1' x_{1t} + \phi_{11}(Q_{t-1} + \Delta p_{t-1}/\gamma) + \phi_{12} Q_{t-1} \\ \beta_2' x_{2t} + \phi_{21}(Q_{t-1} + \Delta p_{t-1}/\gamma) + \phi_{22} Q_{t-1} \end{bmatrix}$$

$$w_t^{--} = \begin{bmatrix} 1 - \alpha_1 \gamma & \alpha_1 \gamma \\ -\alpha_2 \gamma & 1 + \alpha_2 \gamma \end{bmatrix} \begin{bmatrix} Q_t \\ Q_t - \Delta p_t / \gamma \end{bmatrix}$$

$$- \begin{bmatrix} \beta_1' x_{1t} + \phi_{11} Q_{t-1} + \phi_{12}(Q_{t-1} - \Delta p_{t-1}/\gamma) \\ \beta_2' x_{2t} + \phi_{21} Q_{t-1} + \phi_{22}(Q_{t-1} - \Delta p_{t-1}/\gamma) \end{bmatrix}$$

Then the density function is

---

[4] If separate γ_1, γ_2 are employed, γ is replaced by γ_1 in the first and by γ_2 in the second of these transformations.

$$f(Q_t, \Delta p_t \mid Q_{t-1}, \Delta p_{t-1}) = \begin{cases} \dfrac{|1+\gamma(\alpha_2-\alpha_1)|}{2\pi|\gamma||\Sigma|^{1/2}} \ \exp\left\{-\dfrac{1}{2}\ (w_t^{++})'\Sigma^{-1}w_t^{++}\right\} \\ \qquad\qquad \text{if} \ \ \Delta p_t > 0 \\ \qquad\qquad\qquad \Delta p_{t-1} > 0 \\[6pt] \dfrac{|1+\gamma(\alpha_2-\alpha_1)|}{2\pi|\gamma||\Sigma|^{1/2}} \ \exp\left\{-\dfrac{1}{2}\ (w_t^{+-})'\Sigma^{-1}w_t^{+-}\right\} \\ \qquad\qquad \text{if} \ \ \Delta p_t > 0 \\ \qquad\qquad\qquad \Delta p_{t-1} \leqq 0 \\[6pt] \dfrac{|1+\gamma(\alpha_2-\alpha_1)|}{2\pi|\gamma||\Sigma|^{1/2}} \ \exp\left\{-\dfrac{1}{2}\ (w_t^{-+})'\Sigma^{-1}w_t^{-+}\right\} \\ \qquad\qquad \text{if} \ \ \Delta p_t \leqq 0 \\ \qquad\qquad\qquad \Delta p_{t-1} > 0 \\[6pt] \dfrac{|1+\gamma(\alpha_2-\alpha_1)|}{2\pi|\gamma||\Sigma|^{1/2}} \ \exp\left\{-\dfrac{1}{2}\ (w_t^{--})'\Sigma^{-1}w_t^{--}\right\} \\ \qquad\qquad \text{if} \ \ \Delta p_t \leqq 0 \\ \qquad\qquad\qquad \Delta p_{t-1} \leqq 0 \end{cases}$$

$$(4.6.31)$$

The likelihood function is then the product of terms such as (4.6.31).

This approach will also handle the case of serial correlation of error terms. Assume that $\phi_{11} = \phi_{12} = \phi_{21} = \phi_{22} = 0$, but $u_t = Ru_{t-1} + \epsilon_t$, where u_t, ϵ_t are vectors and R is a matrix. Let $Y_t' = (D_t, S_t)$, $A' = (\alpha_1, \alpha_2)$, $X_t' = (x_{1t}', x_{2t}')$ and

$$B = \begin{bmatrix} \beta_1' & 0 \\ 0 & \beta_2' \end{bmatrix}$$

Then (4.6.22) and (4.6.23) can be written as

$$Y_t = Ap_t + BX_t + u_t$$

Lagging this, multiplying by R and subtracting yields

$$Y_t = RY_{t-1} + Ap_t - RAp_{t-1} + BX_t - RBX_{t-1} + \epsilon_t$$

which is in the general form of model C with lagged latent variables.

Finally, two-stage least squares can also be employed and this is fully analogous to the case of two-stage least squares in model C without lagged latent variables. Define Δp_t^+ and Δp_t^- as in (2.3.16). Then demand may be written as

$$Q_t = \alpha_1 p_t + \beta_1' x_{1t} - \Delta p_t^+/\gamma + \begin{cases} \phi_{11}(Q_{t-1}+\Delta p_{t-1}/\gamma)+\phi_{12}Q_{t-1}+u_{1t} \\ \qquad\qquad \text{if} \ \Delta p_{t-1} > 0 \\ \phi_{11}Q_{t-1}+\phi_{12}(Q_{t-1}-\Delta p_{t-1}/\gamma)+u_{1t} \\ \qquad\qquad \text{otherwise} \end{cases}$$

and supply is

$$Q_t = \alpha_2 p_t + \beta_2' x_{2t} - \Delta p_t^- / \gamma + \begin{cases} \phi_{21}(Q_{t-1} + \Delta p_{t-1}/\gamma) + \phi_{12}Q_{t-1} + u_{2t} \\ \qquad\qquad\qquad\qquad \text{if } \Delta p_{t-1} > 0 \\ \phi_{21}Q_{t-1} + \phi_{22}(Q_{t-1} - \Delta p_{t-1}/\gamma) + u_{2t} \\ \qquad\qquad\qquad\qquad \text{otherwise} \end{cases}$$

Using the Δp_{t-1}^+, Δp_{t-1}^- notation, we can finally write demand and supply in the general form

$$Q_t = \alpha_1 p_t + \beta_1' x_{1t} - \Delta p_t^+ / \gamma + (\phi_{11} + \phi_{12})Q_{t-1} + \phi_{11}\Delta p_{t-1}^+ / \gamma$$
$$+ \phi_{12}\Delta p_{t-1}^- / \gamma + u_{1t}$$

$$Q_t = \alpha_2 p_t + \beta_2' x_{2t} - \Delta p_t^- / \gamma + (\phi_{21} + \phi_{22})Q_{t-1} + \phi_{21}\Delta p_{t-1}^+ / \gamma$$
$$+ \phi_{22}\Delta p_{t-1}^- / \gamma + u_{2t}$$

which contains, in addition to Q_t, Q_{t-1}, and p_t, the nonlinear endogenous variables Δp_t^+, Δp_t^- as well as their lagged values, and may be estimated directly by two-stage least squares.

Estimation in model A

We briefly consider the problem of estimation in model A with serially correlated errors. We first write the model as usual,

$$D_t = \beta_1' x_{1t} + u_{1t}$$

$$S_t = \beta_2' x_{2t} + u_{2t}$$

$$Q_t = \min(D_t, S_t)$$

and add the relationships

$$u_{1t} = \rho_1 u_{1t-1} + \epsilon_{1t}$$

$$u_{2t} = \rho_2 u_{2t-1} + \epsilon_{2t}$$

where $|\rho_1|$, $|\rho_2| < 1$ and where $\epsilon_{it} \sim N(0, \sigma_i^2)$ and independent over time. (For a more general framework, see section 4.7.) Define $k_{1t} = -\beta_1' x_{1t} + \rho_1 \beta_1' x_{1t-1}$, $k_{2t} = -\beta_2' x_{2t} + \rho_2 \beta_2' x_{2t-1}$ and let C_{1t} stand for D_t and C_{2t} for S_t. The joint conditional p.d.f. $g(D_t, S_t | D_{t-1}, S_{t-1}) = g_1(D_t | D_{t-1}) g_2(S_t | S_{t-1})$ is obtained by substituting for $g_1(\ )$ and $g_2(\ )$:

$$g_i(C_{it} | C_{it-1}) = \frac{1}{\sqrt{(2\pi)}\sigma_i} \exp\left\{ -\frac{1}{2}\left(\frac{C_{it} - \rho_i C_{it-1} + k_{it}}{\sigma_i} \right)^2 \right\} \qquad (4.6.32)$$

The joint density of D_T, S_T, $\ldots$, D_1, S_1 is $\Pi_{t=1}^T g(D_t, S_t | D_{t-1}, S_{t-1})$ where D_0, S_0 are assumed known. The conditional density $h(Q_t | D_{t-1}, S_{t-1})$ is

$$h(Q_t|D_{t-1}, S_{t-1}) = \int_{Q_t}^{\infty} g(Q_t, S_t|D_{t-1}, S_{t-1})\,dS_t + \int_{Q_t}^{\infty} g(D_t, Q_t|D_{t-1}, S_{t-1})\,dD_t$$

$$= \sum_{i=1}^{2} \frac{1}{\sqrt{(2\pi)}\,\sigma_i} \exp\left\{-\frac{1}{2}\left(\frac{Q_t - \rho_i C_{it-1} + k_{it}}{\sigma_i}\right)^2\right\}$$

$$\times \frac{1}{\sqrt{(2\pi)}\,\sigma_{3-i}}$$

$$\times \int_{Q_t}^{\infty} \exp\left\{-\frac{1}{2}\left(\frac{C_{3-i,t} - \rho_{3-i} C_{3-i,t-1} + k_{3-i,t}}{\sigma_{3-i}}\right)^2\right\}\,dC_{3-i,t}$$

$$(4.6.33)$$

From (4.6.33) we can obtain

$$h(Q_t|D_{t-2}, S_{t-2}) = \int_{Q_{t-1}}^{\infty} h(Q_t|Q_{t-1}, S_{t-1})g_1(Q_{t-1}|D_{t-2})g_2(S_{t-1}|S_{t-2})\,dS_{t-1}$$

$$+ \int_{Q_t}^{\infty} h(Q_t|D_{t-1}, Q_{t-1})g_1(D_{t-1}|D_{t-2})g_2(Q_{t-1}|S_{t-2})\,dD_{t-1}$$

$$(4.6.34)$$

Out of repeated applications of (4.6.34) we can build up the likelihood $h(Q_t)$; unfortunately it involves a T-fold multiple integral of the normal density and is intractable for that reason. A quasi-likelihood approach for this is suggested in Quandt (1981) where in evaluating the term for Q_t it is assumed that knowledge of previous Qs is not utilized. This leads to

$$h(Q_t) = \int_{-\infty}^{\infty} \int_{-\infty}^{\infty} h(Q_t|D_{t-1}, S_{t-1})f_1(D_{t-1}|D_0)f_2(S_{t-1}|S_0)\,dD_{t-1}\,dS_{t-1}$$

where

$$f_i(C_{it-1}|C_{i0}) = \int \cdots \int g_i(C_{it-1}|C_{it-2}) \cdots g_i(C_{i1}|C_{i0})\,dC_{it-2} \cdots dC_{i1}$$

Then

$$f_i(C_{it-1}|C_{i0}) = (2\pi)^{-1/2}\,\sigma_i^{-1}[1 + \rho_i^2 + \ldots + \rho_i^{2(t-2)}]^{-1/2}$$

$$\times \exp\left\{-\frac{(C_{it-1} - \rho_i^{t-1}C_{i0} + k_{it-1} + \rho_i k_{it-2} + \ldots + \rho_i^{t-2}k_{i1})^2}{2\sigma_i^2[1 + \rho_i^2 + \ldots + \rho_i^{2(t-2)}]}\right\}$$

and

$$h(Q_t) = \sum_{i=1}^{2} B_{it} \int_{-\infty}^{\infty} \left[1 - \Phi\left(\frac{Q_t - \rho_{3-i} C_{3-i,t-1} + k_{3-i,t}}{\sigma_{3-i}} \right) \right]$$

$$\times f_{3-i}(C_{3-i,t-1} | C_{3-i,0}) \, dC_{3-i,t-1}$$

where

$$B_{it} = (2\pi)^{-1/2} \sigma_i^{-1} [1 + \rho_i^2 + \ldots + \rho_i^{2(t-1)}]^{-1/2}$$

$$\times \exp\left\{ - \frac{(Q_t - \rho_i^t C_{i0} + k_{it} + \ldots + \rho_i^{t-1} k_{i1})^2}{2\sigma_i^2 [1 + \rho_i^2 + \ldots + \rho_i^{2(t-2)}]} \right\}$$

The likelihood is then the product of all $h(Q_t)$. Even with the simplifying assumption this is a complicated function to maximize. One might feel that it is not worth the trouble in the light of the theorem by Gourieroux, Monfort and Trognon (1983, 1985) that the usual maximum likelihood estimates obtained on the assumption of no serial correlation are consistent anyway (although the asymptotic covariance matrix is not). This is dangerous in general, for consistency almost certainly does not go through if there are also lagged dependent variables in the model.

4.7   Testing for First-Order Serial Correlation

An important question is how one might test for the presence of serial correlation of the error terms. This issue has been considered by Robinson (1982) with respect to the tobit model and by Lee (1984b) and Gourieroux, Monfort and Trognon (1983, 1985) with respect to general limited dependent variable models and the disequilibrium model. We first discuss Gourieroux, Monfort and Trognon's Lagrange multiplier test in general and then apply it briefly to model A.

General Theory

For the sake of generality, we write the model for the latent variables as follows:

$$f(y_t^*, x_t; \beta) = u_t \tag{4.7.1}$$

$$u_t = R u_{t-1} + \epsilon_t \tag{4.7.2}$$

where f is a vector function, y_t^* is a vector of latent endogenous variables, x_t represents exogenous variables, u_t is a vector of p error terms, R is a square matrix with roots inside the unit circle, and $\epsilon_t \sim N(0, \Sigma)$ and temporally uncorrelated. In the context of model A, $f(y_t^*, x_t; \beta) = u_t$ represents the usual specification of demand and supply. In addition to (4.7.1) and (4.7.2) we require a mapping $y_t^* \to y_t$, e.g. $y_t = g(y_t^*)$, which in the disequilibrium context is given by $Q_t = \min(D_t, S_t)$. It will also be convenient to abbreviate $f(y_t^*, x_t; \beta)$ by f_t.

The following statements can be derived in straightforward fashion:

1　The joint density of the u_t is

$$\Psi(u_1, \ldots, u_T) = \frac{1}{(2\pi)^{p/2} |\Omega|^{1/2}} \exp\left\{-\frac{1}{2} u_1' \Omega^{-1} u_1\right\}$$

$$\times \prod_{t=2}^{T} \frac{1}{(2\pi)^{p/2} |\Sigma|^{1/2}}$$

$$\times \exp\left\{-\frac{1}{2}(u_t - Ru_{t-1})' \Sigma^{-1}(u_t - Ru_{t-1})\right\}$$

$$(4.7.3)$$

where

$$\Omega = \sum_{j=0}^{\infty} R^j \Sigma R^{j'} \qquad (4.7.4)$$

2　The joint density of the y_t^* is

$$L^* = \frac{|\partial(u_1)/\partial(y_1^*)|}{(2\pi)^{p/2} |\Omega|^{1/2}} \exp\left\{-\frac{1}{2} f_1' \Omega^{-1} f_1\right\}$$

$$\times \prod_{t=2}^{T} \frac{|\partial(u_t)/\partial(y_t^*)|}{(2\pi)^{p/2} |\Sigma|^{1/2}}$$

$$\times \exp\left\{-\frac{1}{2}(f_t - Rf_{t-1})' \Sigma^{-1}(f_t - Rf_{t-1})\right\} \qquad (4.7.5)$$

where $|\partial(u_t)/\partial(y_t^*)|$ denotes the absolute value of the Jacobian of the transformation from u_t to y_t^*. Equation (4.7.5) is a product of t terms; for convenience we denote the tth term by m_t.

3　The likelihood function of the observable y_t is

$$L = \int_{Y^*} \ldots \int L^* \, dy_1^* \ldots dy_T^* = \int_{Y^*} \ldots \int \prod_t m_t \, dy_t^* \ldots dy_t^*$$

$$(4.7.6)$$

where Y^* denotes the domain of integration.

The null hypothesis to be tested is $H_0 : R = 0$, and to develop a Lagrange multiplier test we accordingly require the score vector

$$\frac{\partial \log L}{\partial \mathrm{vec}\, R} = \left(\frac{\partial \log L}{\partial r_{11}} \quad \frac{\partial \log L}{\partial r_{21}} \quad \frac{\partial \log L}{\partial r_{12}} \quad \frac{\partial \log L}{\partial r_{22}}\right)'$$

evaluated at $R = 0$ and at the estimates $\hat{\beta}$, $\hat{\Sigma}$ obtained under H_0. We shall work on differentiating (4.7.6), with (4.7.5) replacing L^* in the formula. Since the regularity conditions hold, we can interchange the order of differentiation and integration, and we have

$$\frac{\partial L}{\partial \mathrm{vec}\, R} = \int \cdots \int_{Y^*} \frac{\partial \left(\prod_t m_t \right)}{\partial \mathrm{vec}\, R} \, dy_1^* \ldots dy_T^*$$

$$= \sum_{t=1}^{T} \int \cdots \int_{Y^*} \frac{\partial m_t}{\partial \mathrm{vec}\, R} \prod_{\tau \neq t} m_\tau \, dy_1^* \ldots dy_T^* \qquad (4.7.7)$$

by the product rule of differentiation. In evaluating the partial derivatives $\partial m_t / \partial \mathrm{vec}\, R$, there are two cases to distinguish, $t = 1$ and $t \neq 1$. If $t \neq 1$, we immediately have

$$\frac{\partial m_t}{\partial \mathrm{vec}\, R} = m_t \frac{\partial}{\partial \mathrm{vec}\, R} \left[-\frac{1}{2} (f_t - R f_{t-1})' \Sigma^{-1} (f_t - R f_{t-1}) \right]$$

$$= m_t \Sigma^{-1} (f_t - R f_{t-1}) \otimes f_{t-1} \qquad (4.7.8)$$

where $\otimes$ notes the Kronecker product. Evaluating at $R = 0$,

$$\left. \frac{\partial m_t}{\partial \mathrm{vec}\, R} \right|_{R=0} = m_t^0 \Sigma^{-1} f_t \otimes f_{t-1} \qquad (4.7.9)$$

where care must be taken to evaluate m_t at $R = 0$ as well, denoted by m_t^0. If $t = 1$, $\partial m_1 / \partial \mathrm{vec}\, R|_{R=0} = 0$ since m_1 contains only even-powered terms of R. Combining these results,[5]

$$\left. \frac{\partial m_t}{\partial \mathrm{vec}\, R} \right|_{R=0} = \sum_{t=2}^{T} \int \cdots \int_{Y^*} \Sigma^{-1} f_t \otimes f_{t-1} \prod_{\tau=1}^{T} m_\tau^0 \, dy_1^* \ldots dy_T^* \quad (4.7.10)$$

Gourieroux, Monfort and Trognon note that when $R = 0$, the error terms, the y_t^*s and y_ts are independent, from which it follows that $\int_{y_t^*} m_t^0 dy_t^*$ is the marginal density of y_t and depends only on y_t. Denote this marginal density by M_t^0. Then

$$\frac{\partial L}{\partial \mathrm{vec}\, R} = \sum_{t=2}^{T} \int_{y_t^*} \int_{y_{t-1}^*} \Sigma^{-1} f_t \otimes f_{t-1} \, m_t^0 m_{t-1}^0 dy_t^* dy_{t-1}^* \prod_{\tau \neq t, t-1} \int_{y_\tau^*} m_\tau^0 dy_\tau^*$$

$$(4.7.11)$$

Since $L|_{R=0} = \prod_{t=1}^{T} M_t^0$ and since $\partial \log L / \partial \mathrm{vec}\, R = (\partial L / \partial \mathrm{vec}\, R)/L$, we have

---

[5] Note that (4.7.10) contains $\prod_{\tau=1}^{T} m_\tau$ whereas (4.7.7) has $\prod_{\tau \neq t} m_\tau$. The reason is that in (4.7.8) m appears in the tth term. This "restores" the missing m.

$$\frac{\partial \log L}{\partial \text{vec } R}\bigg|_{R=0} = \sum_{t=2}^{T} \frac{\displaystyle\int_{y_t^*}\int_{y_{t-1}^*} \Sigma^{-1} f_t \otimes f_{t-1} m_t^0 m_{t-1}^0 \mathrm{d}y_t^* \mathrm{d}y_{t-1}^*}{\displaystyle\int_{y_t^*}\int_{y_{t-1}^*} m_t^0 m_{t-1}^0 \mathrm{d}y_t^* \mathrm{d}y_{t-1}^*} \tag{4.7.12}$$

It is apparent that

$$m_t^0 m_{t-1}^0 \bigg/ \int_{y_t^*}\int_{y_{t-1}^*} m_t^0 m_{t-1}^0 \mathrm{d}y_t^* \mathrm{d}y_{t-1}^*$$

is a density function and that it is, in fact, the density of y_t^*, y_{t-1}^* conditional on y_t, y_{t-1} under H_0. Expression (4.7.12) is therefore the sum of the expectations (under H_0) of the terms $\Sigma^{-1} f_t \otimes f_{t-1}$ and can be written as

$$\frac{\partial \log L}{\partial \text{vec } R} = \sum_{t=2}^{T} E(\Sigma^{-1} f_t \otimes f_{t-1} | y_t, y_{t-1})$$

$$= \Sigma^{-1} \otimes I \sum_{t=2}^{T} E(f_t | y_t) \otimes E(f_{t-1} | y_{t-1}) \tag{4.7.13}$$

For the Lagrange multiplier test the score vector must be evaluated at the estimates obtained by imposing H_0; the expectations in (4.7.13) are then estimated by the appropriate residuals (see (4.7.1) for the definition of f). The estimated score vector can then be written as

$$\hat{s} \equiv \widehat{\frac{\partial \log L}{\partial \text{vec } R}}\bigg|_{R=0} = (\hat{\Sigma}^0)^{-1} \otimes I \sum_{t=2}^{T} \hat{u}_t(\hat{\beta}^0, \hat{\Sigma}^0 | y_t) \otimes \hat{u}_{t-1}(\hat{\beta}^0, \hat{\Sigma}^0 | y_{t-1})$$

$$\tag{4.7.14}$$

where $\hat{u}(\;|\;)$ will simply be abbreviated as $\hat{u}_t$.

Gourieroux, Monfort and Trognon show that $\hat{s}/T^{1/2}$ converges in distribution to $N(0, V)$, where

$$V = (\Sigma^{-1} \otimes I) \left(\text{plim} \frac{1}{T} \sum_{t=2}^{T} C_t \otimes C_{t-1} \right) (\Sigma^{-1} \otimes I)$$

and

$$C_t = E(\hat{u}_t \hat{u}_t')$$

with the expectation again being taken under H_0. The test statistic therefore is

$$S = \left[\sum_{t=2}^{T} \hat{u}_t \otimes \hat{u}_{t-1} \right]' [(\hat{\Sigma}^0)^{-1} \otimes I]$$

$$\times \left\{ [(\hat{\Sigma}^0)^{-1} \otimes I] \left[\sum_{t=2}^{T} (\hat{u}_t \hat{u}_t') \otimes (\hat{u}_{t-1} \hat{u}_{t-1}') \right] [(\hat{\Sigma}^0)^{-1} \otimes I] \right\}^{-1}$$

$$\times [(\hat{\Sigma}^0)^{-1} \otimes I] \left[\sum_{t=2}^{T} \hat{u}_t \otimes \hat{u}_{t-1} \right] \qquad (4.7.15)$$

which is asymptotically distributed as χ^2 with degrees of freedom equal to the order of V.[6]

Application to model A

The crucial step of applying the general approach of Gourieroux, Monfort and Trognon is to derive $E(u_{1t}|y_t)$ and $E(u_{2t}|y_t)$. We have from model A, (2.1.1)–(2.1.3),

$$\begin{aligned}
E(u_{1t}|Q_t) &= E(u_{1t}|Q_t, D_t > S_t) \Pr\{D_t > S_t|Q_t\} \\
&\quad + E(u_{1t}|Q_t, D_t \leq S_t) \Pr\{D_t \leq S_t|Q_t\} \\
&= E(u_{1t}|Q_t, D_t > S_t) \Pr\{D_t > S_t|Q_t\} \\
&\quad + (Q_t - \beta_1' x_{1t}) \Pr\{D_t \leq S_t|Q_t\}
\end{aligned} \qquad (4.7.16)$$

The conditional probabilities in (4.7.16) are given by (2.8.3) and are easily obtained from the density function for D_t, S_t. The only remaining part of (4.7.16) to be obtained is $E(u_{1t}|Q_t, D_t > S_t)$.

We first note that it is always possible to write $u_{1t} = (\sigma_{12}/\sigma_2^2)u_{2t} + v_{1t}$, where v_{1t} has mean zero, variance $\sigma_1^2 - \sigma_{12}^2/\sigma_2^2$ and is independent of u_{2t} (see the discussion before (3.4.12)). Then

$$\begin{aligned}
E(u_{1t}|Q_t, D_t > S_t) &= E(u_{1t}|Q_t = \beta_2' x_{2t} + u_{2t}, \beta_1' x_{1t} + u_{1t} > Q_t) \\
&= E\left[\frac{\sigma_{12}}{\sigma_2^2} u_{2t} + v_{1t} \middle| u_{2t} = Q_t - \beta_2' x_{2t}, u_{1t} > Q_t - \beta_1' x_{1t} \right] \\
&= \frac{\sigma_{12}}{\sigma_2^2} E(u_{2t}|u_{2t} = Q_t - \beta_2' x_{2t}, u_{1t} > Q_t - \beta_1' x_{1t}) \\
&\quad + E(v_{1t}|u_{2t} = Q_t - \beta_2' x_{2t}, u_{1t} > Q_t - \beta_1' x_{1t})
\end{aligned} \qquad (4.7.17)$$

The first term is simply $(\sigma_{12}/\sigma_2^2)(Q_t - \beta_2' x_{2t})$. The second term can be written as

$$E\left[v_{1t} \middle| \frac{\sigma_{12}}{\sigma_2^2} u_{2t} = \frac{\sigma_{12}}{\sigma_2^2}(Q_t - \beta_2' x_{2t}), u_{1t} > Q_t - \beta_1' x_{1t} \right]$$

---

[6] If V or Ω is not of full rank, a similar argument produces comparable results with the obvious provisos that matrix inverses must be replaced by generalized inverses and that the degrees of freedom for χ^2 are not the order but the rank of V.

$$= E\left[v_{1t}\,\middle|\,u_{1t} - v_{1t} = \frac{\sigma_{12}}{\sigma_2^2}(Q_t - \beta_2' x_{2t}),\ u_{1t} > Q_t - \beta_1' x_{1t}\right]$$

$$= E\left[v_{1t}\,\middle|\,v_{1t} > Q_t - \beta_1' x_{1t} - \frac{\sigma_{12}}{\sigma_2^2}(Q_t - \beta_2' x_{2t})\right]$$

Denoting $Q_t - \beta_1' x_{1t} - (\sigma_{12}/\sigma_2^2)(Q_t - \beta_2' x_{2t})/\sigma_1(1-\rho^2)^{1/2}$ as z, where $\rho = \sigma_{12}/\sigma_1\sigma_2$, and employing appendix 3.A, we can write (4.7.16) as

$$E(u_{1t}|Q_t) = \left[\frac{\sigma_{12}}{\sigma_2^2}(Q_t - \beta_2' x_{2t}) + \sigma_1(1-\rho^2)^{1/2}\frac{\phi(z)}{1-\Phi(z)}\right]$$

$$\times \Pr\{D_t > S_t|Q_t\} + (Q_t - \beta_1' x_{1t})\Pr\{D_t \le S_t|Q_t\} \quad (4.7.18)$$

A comparable development holds for $E(u_{2t}|Q_t)$ (see exercise 4.9).

In the unidimensional case the statistic S becomes

$$\left[\sum_{t=2}^{T} \hat{u}_t\,\hat{u}_{t-1}\right]^2 \Bigg/ \sum_{t=2}^{T} \hat{u}_{t-1}^2$$

which is not asymptotically equal, in general, to the squared autocorrelation coefficient

$$\left[\sum_{t=2}^{T} \hat{u}_t\,\hat{u}_{t-1}\right]^2 \Bigg/ \sum_{t=2}^{T} \hat{u}_t^2 \sum_{t=2}^{T} \hat{u}_{t-1}^2$$

Gouricroux, Monfort and Trognon show that the two are asymptotically equivalent if the x_t are i.i.d. random variables or if $y_t = y_t^*$ (i.e. there is no latency).

4.8   Models with Rational Expectations

Several of the models discussed previously may be extended to include expected variables of endogenous variables, where the expectation formation is

$$p_t^e = E_{t-1}(p_t) \qquad\qquad (4.8.1)$$

i.e. as the mathematical expectation of p_t taken on the basis of information available through period $t-1$. Models with rational expectations have been discussed by Quandt (1985a) and Chanda and Maddala (1983a, 1983b). However, there seem to be no analyses of models involving $E_{t-1}(p_{t+1})$, which are likely to be much harder.

One of the simplest models with rationally expected prices is obtained from (4.6.22) to (4.6.25) if the supply equation is posited to depend on p_t^e rather than p_t. This is then exactly the Laffont–Monfort model with the additional proviso of rational expectations. Substituting demand and supply into the price adjustment equation and taking expectations, yields

$$p_t^e = \lambda_1' x_{1t}^e + \lambda_2' x_{2t}^e + \lambda_3 p_{t-1} + \lambda_4 D_{t-1} + \lambda_5 S_{t-1}$$

where x_{1t}^e, x_{2t}^e are themselves the rational expectations at time $t-1$ of x_{1t}, x_{2t}. Substituting this value in the supply function and assuming that we can replace x_{1t}^e and x_{2t}^e by the forecasts of x_{1t}, x_{2t} from some appropriate ARIMA model, we obtain a transformed version that is exactly in the form of the Laffont–Monfort model of section 4.6 and may be obtained from the Dagenais model (4.6.8)–(4.6.12) with the following changes effected by Chanda and Maddala (1983a, 1983b):

1   The price adjustment equation (4.6.11) is written without an error term and with $D_t - S_t$ on the right hand side.
2   The price terms in the supply and desired inventories equations (4.6.9) and (4.6.12) are replaced by expected price terms.
3   A partial adjustment equation governing the evolution of inventories

$$I_t - I_{t-1} = \delta(I_t^d - I_{t-1}) \tag{4.8.2}$$

is introduced, reflecting the effect of costly adjustments.

This model can also be reduced to one that can be estimated by techniques analogous to those applied to the Laffont–Monfort model. Keeping in mind that (4.6.9) and (4.6.12) both contain p_t^e on the right hand side, substitute (4.6.12) in (4.8.2) and (4.6.9). That yields equations of the general form

$$I_t = \theta_0 + \theta_1' x_{2t} + \theta_2 p_t^e + \theta_3 I_{t-1} + v_{1t} \tag{4.8.3}$$

$$S_t = \theta_4 + \theta_5' x_{2t} + \theta_6 p_t^e + \theta_7 I_{t-1} + v_{2t} \tag{4.8.4}$$

Substituting (4.6.8) and (4.8.4) into (4.6.11) (without an error term), then taking expectations, yields

$$p_t^e = \theta_8 + \theta_9' x_{1t}^e + \theta_{10}' x_{2t}^e + \theta_{11}(D_{t-1} - Q_{t-1}) + \theta_{12} I_{t-1} + \theta_{13} p_{t-1} \tag{4.8.5}$$

Now we substitute (4.8.5) in (4.8.3) and (4.8.4) and replace p_t in (4.6.8) by $p_{t-1} + \gamma(D_t - S_t)$. We then end up with a three-equation system with the endogenous variables D_t, S_t, and I_t plus the min condition; the reader may verify that a straightforward extension of the method of section 4.6 can be used to derive the likelihood function.[7]

A final model considered by Chanda and Maddala (1983b) is a modi-

---

[7] Chanda and Maddala point out that the inventory and supply equations will contain both x_{2t} and x_{2t}^e which may well be highly correlated with one another. Severe multicollinearity may well cause estimation problems not only in linear models but also in nonlinear models such as the present one.

fication of the model with an exogenously fixed ceiling price given (3.2.1)–(3.2.2). With rational expectations this model is

$$D_t = \alpha_1 p_t + \beta_1' x_{1t} + u_{1t} \tag{4.8.6}$$

$$S_t = \alpha_2 p_t^e + \beta_2' x_{2t} + u_{2t} \tag{4.8.7}$$

$$p_t \leqq \bar{p}_t \tag{4.8.8}$$

with

$$Q_t = S_t \qquad \text{if } p_t \geqq \bar{p}_t \tag{4.8.9}$$

$$Q_t = D_t = S_t \qquad \text{otherwise} \tag{4.8.10}$$

If the price is less than $\bar{p}$ then equilibrium holds and the expected price conditional on information at time $t-1$ is $(\beta_2' x_{2t}^e - \beta_1' x_{1t}^e)/(\alpha_1 - \alpha_2)$. Otherwise the expected price is $\bar{p}_t$. Hence p_t^e is

$$p_t^e = \frac{\beta_2' x_{2t}^e - \beta_1' x_{1t}^e}{\alpha_1 - \alpha_2} \ \Pr\{p_t < \bar{p}_t\} + \bar{p}_t \Pr\{p_t \geqq \bar{p}_t\} \tag{4.8.11}$$

Denoting $\Pr\{p_t < \bar{p}_t\}$ by P_t, we have

$$P_t = \Pr\left\{\frac{1}{\alpha_1}\left[\beta_2' x_{2t} - \beta_1' x_{1t} + \alpha_2\right.\right.$$

$$\left.\left. \times \left(P_t \frac{\beta_2' x_{2t}^e - \beta_1' x_{1t}^e}{\alpha_1 - \alpha_2} + (1 - P_t)\bar{p}_t\right) + u_{2t} - u_{1t}\right] < \bar{p}_t\right\}$$

$$= \Pr\left\{u_{1t} - u_{2t} < \beta_2' x_{2t} - \beta_2' x_{1t} + \bar{p}_t(\alpha_2 - \alpha_1) + P_t \alpha_2 \left(\frac{\beta_2' x_{2t}^e - \beta_1' x_{1t}^e}{\alpha_1 - \alpha_2} - \bar{p}_t\right)\right\}$$

$$\tag{4.8.12}$$

Since the right hand side is monotone decreasing in P_t (the expected equilibrium price is exceeded by $\bar{p}_t$) and is positive and < 1 at $P_t = 0$, a unique solution exists for P_t which is a function of exogenous variables and their rational expectations. (A similar fixed point argument was employed in section 4.3.) Then p_t^e in (4.8.11) depends only on exogenous variables and their rational expectations. Replacing it in (4.8.7) then allows the methods of section 3.2 to be employed for estimation.

4.9   A Rationing Model with A Policy Variable

The models in this chapter so far have all been standard demand–supply models, including that of section 4.3 in which the idea of rationing was explicitly introduced. In the present section we consider the possibility of rationing as the outcome of a conscious policy by a central authority that can set the value of some policy variable. This makes the model of this section differ from the demand–supply models discussed before, in that the rationing in this section is the explicit consequence of choice exercised by an agent. Models of this type contain a rich array of possible approaches. We consider briefly only one of these; for more details on this approach as well as for other approaches see Goldfeld and Quandt (1986a, 1986b).

In the model of Goldfeld and Quandt the following mechanism is posited. There exists a central authority (e.g. a bank) with a policy instrument x_t (e.g. the rate of interest). The public's demand for borrowing is given by

$$y_t^d = \gamma_1 x_t + \gamma_2' z_{3t} + \epsilon_{3t} \tag{4.9.1}$$

where z_{3t} denotes some exogenous variables. The amount of funds made available by the authority is y_t and its desired values of x_t, y_t are given by

$$x_t^* = \alpha' z_{1t} + \epsilon_{1t} \tag{4.9.2}$$

$$y_t^* = \beta' z_{2t} + \epsilon_{2t} \tag{4.9.3}$$

where z_{1t}, z_{2t} are again exogenous and where x_t^*, y_t^* are known to the authority. The authority has a loss function given by

$$L = (x_t - x_t^*)^2 + v_1(y_t - y_t^*)^2 + v_2(y_t - y_t^d)^2 \tag{4.9.4}$$

The authority sets x_t and y_t; in the final analysis it must be true that

$$y_t \leqq y_t^d \tag{4.9.5}$$

Various possibilities exist for specifying the details of the decision mechanism and for the estimation method appropriate for that mechanism. For example, Goldfeld and Quandt (1986a) explore the consequences, among others, of expected loss minimization. Here we show the consequences of their two-stage approach:

1   First the authority minimizes (4.9.4) with respect to x_t, y_t subject to (4.9.1), (4.9.2), (4.9.3), and (4.9.5) on the preliminary assumption that ϵ_{3t} is zero.
2   The resulting x_t is then announced, y_t^d materializes and is then observed by the authority.
3   The authority then disregards the preliminary y_t value obtained in 1 and minimizes (4.9.4) with respect to y_t subject to (4.9.5), where the right hand side of the inequality is the actual value of y_t^d.

Goldfeld and Quandt show that this leads to the following determination of endogenous variable values:

$$x_t = \begin{cases} \dfrac{\alpha' z_{1t} + v_1 \gamma_1 \beta' z_{2t} - v_1 \gamma_1 \gamma_2' z_{3t}}{1 + v_1 \gamma_1^2} + \dfrac{\epsilon_{1t} + v_1 \gamma_1 \epsilon_{2t}}{1 + v_1 \gamma_1^2} \\ \quad \text{if } S_t \equiv \beta' z_{2t} - \gamma_1 \alpha' z_{1t} - \gamma_2' z_{3t} + \epsilon_{2t} - \gamma_1 \epsilon_{1t} \geqq 0 \\[2ex] \dfrac{(v_1 + v_2)\alpha' z_{1t} + \gamma_1 v_1 v_2 \beta' z_{2t} - \gamma_1 v_1 v_2 \gamma_2' z_{3t}}{v_1 + v_2 + \gamma_1^2 v_1 v_2} + \dfrac{(v_1 + v_2)\epsilon_{1t} + \gamma_1 v_1 v_2 \epsilon_{2t}}{v_1 + v_2 + \gamma_1^2 v_1 v_2} \\ \quad \text{if } S_t < 0 \end{cases}$$
$$\text{(4.9.6)}$$

$$y_t = \min[y_t^d, (v_1 y_t^* + v_2 y_t^d)/(v_1 + v_2)] \tag{4.9.7}$$

and where, of course, y_t^d, x_t^*, y_t^* are given by (4.9.1), (4.9.2), (4.9.3). For maximum likelihood estimation we require the density function of $h(x_t, y_t)$. To simplify this, we follow Goldfeld and Quandt (1986a) and (a) omit the subscript t, (b) define $\delta = v_1/(v_1 + v_2)$, (c) define the composite variable $y^c = \delta y^* + (1-\delta)y^d$, and (d) assume that ϵ_1, ϵ_2, ϵ_3 are independently distributed. The steps of the derivation (Goldfeld and Quandt 1986a) are as follows:

1   Equation (4.9.2) and the definition of S (in (4.9.6)) yield a linear transformation $\{\epsilon_1, \epsilon_2\} \to \{x^*, S\}$ from which the density $f\{x^*, S\}$ can be determined.

2   From (4.9.6) we obtain

$$x = \begin{cases} x^* + \gamma_1 k_1 S & \text{if } S \geqq 0 \\ x^* + \gamma_1 k_2 S & \text{otherwise} \end{cases} \tag{4.9.8}$$

where $k_1 = v_1/(1 + v_1 \gamma_1^2)$, $k_2 = v_1 v_2/(v_1 + v_2 + \gamma_1^2 v_1 v_2)$. Given the density $h(\epsilon_3)$, we obtain the p.d.f. $g(x, S, y^d)$ as

$$g(x, S, y^d) = \begin{cases} g_1(x, S, y^d) = f(x - \gamma_1 k_1 S, S) h(y^d - \gamma_1 x - \gamma_2' z_3) \\ \quad \text{if } S \geqq 0 \\ g_2(x, S, y^d) = f(x - \gamma_1 k_2 S, S) h(y^d - \gamma_1 x - \gamma_2' z_3) \\ \quad \text{otherwise} \end{cases}$$
$$\text{(4.9.9)}$$

3   From (4.9.8) and the definition of S,

$$y^* = \begin{cases} S + \gamma_1(x - \gamma_1 k_1 S) + \gamma_2' z_3 & \text{if } S \geqq 0 \\ S + \gamma_1(x - \gamma_1 k_2 S) + \gamma_2' z_3 & \text{otherwise} \end{cases} \tag{4.9.10}$$

Hence, from the definition of y^c,

$$\tilde{S} \equiv y^c - (1-\delta)y^d - \delta(\gamma_1 x + \gamma_2' z_3) = \begin{cases} \delta S(1 - \gamma_1^2 k_1) & \text{if } S \geqq 0 \\ \delta S(1 - \gamma_1^2 k_2) & \text{otherwise} \end{cases}$$
$$\text{(4.9.11)}$$

4   It is easy to verify that $1 - \gamma_1^2 k_i > 0$, $i = 1, 2$. Thus the signs of $\tilde{S}$ and S always agree (see (4.9.11)). Equation (4.9.11) implies two solutions for S, namely

$$S_i = [y^c - (1-\delta)y^d - \delta(\gamma_1 x + \gamma_2' z_3)]/\delta(1 - \gamma_1^2 k_i) \quad i = 1, 2 \quad (4.9.12)$$

5   Substituting (4.9.12) in (4.9.9) leads to

$$\psi(x, y^c, y^d) = \begin{cases} \psi_1(x, y^c, y^d) = J_1 g_1(x, S_1, y^d) & \text{if } \tilde{S} \geq 0 \\ \psi_2(x, y^c, y^d) = J_2 g_2(x, S_2, y^d) & \text{otherwise} \end{cases}$$

$$(4.9.13)$$

where $J_i = 1/\delta(1 - \gamma_1^2 k_i)$ is the relevant Jacobian.

6   Equation (4.9.13) gives the joint density of x, y^c, y^d from which we need to integrate out y^c or y^d as indicated by the min condition. The appropriate regions of integration are most easily shown with the aid of figure 4.4 in which a 45° line and the equation $\tilde{S} = 0$ are plotted. Note that at the intersection of the two, $y^d = \gamma_1 x + \gamma_2' z_3$.

(a) (i) $y^d < y^c$ and thus $y = y^d$ and $y < \gamma_1 x + \gamma_2' z_3$ as at point A_1. Then y^c must be integrated from the 45° line to the line $\tilde{S} = 0$ using ψ_2 (from A_2 to A_3, $\tilde{S} < 0$) and from the line $\tilde{S} = 0$ to infinity using ψ_1 (because above A_3, $\tilde{S} > 0$). Letting the value of y^c at A_3 be $L_1 = (1-\delta)y + \delta(\gamma_1 x + \gamma_2' z_3)$, the part of the p.d.f. here is

$$\int_y^{L_1} \psi_2(x, y^c, y)\,dy^c + \int_{L_1}^{\infty} \psi_1(x, y^c, y)\,dy^c$$

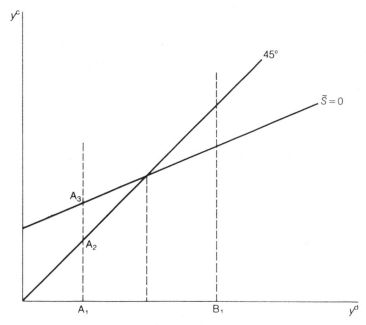

Figure 4.4

(a) (ii) $y > \gamma_1 x + \gamma_2' z_3$ as at B_1. Then we integrate out y^c from y to ∞, using ψ_1; thus yielding

$$\int_y^\infty \psi_1(x, y^c, y) \, dy^c$$

(b) $y^d \geqq y^c = y$. Letting $L_2 = [y - \delta(\gamma_1 x + \gamma_2' z_3)/(1 - \delta)$, an analogous argument yields the pieces

$$\int_{L_2}^\infty \psi_2(x, y, y^d) \, dy^d + \int_y^{L_2} \psi_1(x, y, y^d) \, dy^d$$

and

$$\int_y^\infty \psi_2(x, y, y^d) \, dy^d$$

for the cases when $y \geqq \gamma_1 x + \gamma_2' z_3$ and $y < \gamma_1 x + \gamma_2' z_3$ respectively.

7   Combining pieces according to whether $y \lesseqgtr \gamma_1 x + \gamma_2' z_3$, we have

$$h(x,y) = \begin{cases} h_1(x,y) = \displaystyle\int_y^\infty \psi_2(x, y, y^d) \, dy^d + \int_y^{L_1} \psi_2(x, y^c, y) \, dy^c \\[2em] \qquad\qquad + \displaystyle\int_{L_1}^\infty \psi_1(x, y^c, y) \, dy^c \qquad \text{if } y < \gamma_1 x + \gamma_2' z_3 \\[3em] h_2(x,y) = \displaystyle\int_y^\infty \psi_1(x, y^c, y) \, dy^c + \int_{L_2}^\infty \psi_2(x, y, y^d) \, dy^d \\[2em] \qquad\qquad + \displaystyle\int_y^{L_2} \psi_1(x, y, y^d) \, dy^d \qquad \text{if } y \geqq \gamma_1 x + \gamma_2' z_3 \end{cases}$$

$$(4.9.14)$$

The likelihood function is then

$$L = \prod_{y_t < \gamma_1 x_t + \gamma_2' z_{3t}} h_1(x_t, y_t) \prod_{y_t \geqq \gamma_1 x_t + \gamma_2' z_{3t}} h_2(x_t, y_t)$$

This "sorting" will generally change during the course of numerical optimization and suggests that, as in the Ginsburgh-Tishler-Zang model, the likelihood function may have numerous local maxima.

Exercises

4.1 Show that the reduced form solutions for p_t in the two equation systems in (4.2.11) are compatible with the inequalities under which these equations hold.

4.2 Show that the density of Q_t from (4.2.16) is the same as that derived from (4.2.13)–(4.2.15) by convoluting the densities of u_{3t} and of $\min(D_t, S_t)$. (For simplicity you may want to assume that $\sigma_{12} = \sigma_{13} = \sigma_{23} = 0$).

4.3 Show that (4.4.8) cannot hold.

4.4 Assume that $\log D = D^* + \epsilon_1$, $\log S = S^* + \epsilon_2$ and $Q = E[\min(D, S)]$ as in the Lambert model, and express $Q = Q_1 + Q_2$ as in (4.4.15). Show that $\partial \log Q / \partial \log E(D) = 1 - P_w$, the weighted proportion of markets in which supply exceeds demand (see also (4.4.21)).

4.5 Show that if the true P_w (4.4.23) and its approximation (4.4.24) are set to be equal at $R = 0$, then $\alpha = 0$. Show that if in addition their derivatives are set to be equal, $\gamma = -\sigma + 2\phi(-\sigma/2)/\Phi(-\sigma/2)$.

4.6 Show that (4.4.27) follows from (4.4.26) by integration.

4.7 Show for the Orsi model in section 4.6 that the following hold:

$$D_t - S_t = (\alpha_2 - \alpha_1)(w_t^* - w_t)$$

$$w_t - w_{t-1} \gtreqless 0 \text{ iff } w_t^* \gtreqless w_t \quad \text{iff } w_t^* \gtreqless w_{t-1}$$
$$\text{iff } D_t \gtreqless S_t$$

$$D_t - L_t = \delta_t(\alpha_2 - \alpha_1)\mu_1(w_t - w_{t-1})/(1 - \mu_1)$$

$$S_t - L_t = -(1 - \delta_t)(\alpha_2 - \alpha_1)\mu_2(w_t - w_{t-1})/(1 - \mu_2)$$

Use these relationships to reduce the model to one containing only observable variables.

4.8 Derive the equivalent of (4.6.31) for the case when the speeds of adjustment are different for positive and negative excess demand.

4.9 In analogy with (4.7.18), derive $E(u_{2t} | Q_t)$.

4.10 Derive the specific form of (4.9.14) for the case in which $\epsilon_{1t}, \epsilon_{2t}, \epsilon_{3t}$ are normally distributed with zero means and variances $\sigma_1^2, \sigma_2^2, \sigma_3^2$.

Appendix 4.A
FORTRAN Program for the Likelihood Function of the
Ginsburgh-Tishler-Zang Model

```
      SUBROUTINE DISEQ3(A,NP,FUN,*)
      IMPLICIT REAL*8 (A-H,O-Z)
      DIMENSION A(NP)
C
C     LIKELIHOOD FUNCTION FOR GINSBURG-TISHLER-ZANG MODEL
C
C
C     NP   = TOTAL NUMBER OF PARAMETERS
C     N    = NUMBER OF OBSERVATIONS
C     K1   = NUMBER OF COEFFICIENTS IN DEMAND EQUATION
C     K2   = NUMBER OF COEFFICIENTS IN SUPPLY EQUATION
C     A( ) = COEFFICIENTS TO BE ESTIMATED; A(1),....,A(K1) ARE DEMAND
C            EQUATION COEFFICIENTS, A(K1+1),....,A(K1+K2) ARE SUPPLY
C            EQUATION COEFFICIENTS, A(NP) IS THE DISTURBANCE
C            VARIANCE.
C     Q( ) = OBSERVATIONS ON TRANSACTED AMOUNT
C     X1( )= OBSERVATIONS ON RIGHT HAND VARIABLES IN DEMAND; MUST BE
C            DIMENSIONED X1(N,K1) IN MAIN PROGRAM
C     X2( )= OBSERVATIONS ON RIGHT HAND VARIABLES IN SUPPLY; MUST BE
C            DIMENSIONED X2(N,K2) IN MAIN PROGRAM
C
C     FUN  = THE FUNCTION VALUE CALCULATED
C
      COMMON/USER1/Q(1)
      COMMON/USER2/X1(1)
      COMMON/USER3/X2(1)
      COMMON/USER4/N,K1,K2
      COMMON/BPRINT/IPT,NFILE,NDIG,NPUNCH,JPT,MFILE
C
C     SQ2PLG= LOG OF SQUAREROOT OF 2*PI
C
      DATA SQ2PLG/0.9689385400/
C
C     TEST FOR USER ERROR
C
      IF(K1+K2+1.EQ.NP.AND.K1.GT.0.AND.K2.GT.0 ) GOTO 5
      IF(IPT.GT.0) WRITE (NFILE,1000)
      IF(JPT.GT.0) WRITE (MFILE,1000)
1000  FORMAT(' ERROR IN K1 OR K2 OR NP...EXECUTION TERMINATED')
      STOP
C
C     CHECK FOR NONPOSITIVE VARIANCE; IF YES, TAKE NONSTANDARD RETURN
C
5     IF(A(NP).LE.0.0) RETURN 1
      SIG=DSQRT(A(NP))
      SUM=0.0
C     OBSERVATION LOOP BEGINS HERE
      DO 100 I=1,N
      S1=0.0
      S2=0.0
C     LOOP TO COMPUTE RIGHT HAND SIDE OF DEMAND EQUATION
      DO 10 J=1,K1
10    S1=S1+A(J)*X1((J-1)*N+I)
C     LOOP TO COMPUTE RIGHT HAND SIDE OF SUPPLY EQUATION
      DO 20 J=1,K2
20    S2=S2+A(K1+J)*X2((J-1)*N+I)
      IF(S1.LT.S2) GOTO 40
      SUM=SUM-SIG-(Q(I)-S2)**2/(2.*A(NP))
      GOTO 100
40    SUM=SUM-SIG-(Q(I)-S1)**2/(2.*A(NP))
100   CONTINUE
      FUN=SUM-N*SQ2PLG
      RETURN
      END
```

Appendix 4.B
FORTRAN Program for Solving (4.3.4) by False Position Method

```
      SUBROUTINE REGFAL(A,B,SOL,FUNC,ACC,ITLIM,IER)
C
C     THIS SOLVES THE EQUATION FUNC(X)=0 BY THE METHOD OF FALSE
C     POSITION. IT MAY BE USED ONLY IF THERE EXISTS A UNIQUE
C     ROOT BETWEEN A AND B (A.LT.B). IF IT IS APPLIED TO EQUA-
C     TIONS THAT DO NOT SATISFY THESE REQUIREMENTS, UNPREDICTABLE
C     RESULTS WILL ENSUE. IF THE FUNCTION IS CONTINUOUS AND
C     SATISFIES THE REQUIREMENTS, CONVERGENCE IS GUARANTEED
C
C     A = LOWER BOUND OF REGION CONTAINING ROOT
C     B = UPPER BOUND OF REGION CONTAINING ROOT
C     SOL = THE SOLUTION FOUND
C     FUNC = THE NAME OF THE FUNCTION (MUST BE A FUNCTION
C              SUBPROGRAM
C     ACC = DESIRED ACCURACY
C     ITLIM = THE NUMBER OF PERMITTED ITERATIONS
C     IER = 0   CONVERGENCE OBTAINED
C         = -3  A IS NOT LESS THAN B
C         = -42 FUNC(A) AND FUNC(B) DO NOT HAVE OPPOSITE SIGNS, I.E.,
C               THERE IS EITHER NO ROOT OR THERE ARE SEVERAL ROOTS
C               IN THE INTERVAL
C         = -1  ITERATION LIMIT REACHED BEFORE CONVERGENCE
C
      IMPLICIT REAL*8 (A-H,O-Z)
      ITC=0
      IER=0
      IF(A.LT.B) GOTO 5
      IER=-3
1     RETURN
5     FA=FUNC(A)
      FB=FUNC(B)
      IF(FA.NE.0.) GOTO 10
      SOL=A
      GOTO 1
10    IF(FB.NE.0.) GOTO 20
      SOL=B
      GOTO 1
20    IF(FA.LT.0..AND.FB.GT.0.) GOTO 30
      IF(FA.GT.0..AND.FB.LT.0.) GOTO 30
      IER=-42
      GOTO 1
30    DO 400 K=1,10
      D=(B-A)/2.+A
      FD=FUNC(D)
      IF(FD) 310,305,320
305   SOL=D
      GOTO 1
310   IF(FA.LT.0.) GOTO 312
311   B=D
      FB=FD
      GOTO 400
312   A=D
      FA=FD
      GOTO 400
320   IF(FA.LT.0.) GOTO 311
      GOTO 312
400   CONTINUE
      TST=B
32    SOL=(B*FA-A*FB)/(FA-FB)
      FNEW=FUNC(SOL)
      IF(DABS(SOL-TST)/DMAX1(DABS(SOL),1.D-15).LT.ACC) GOTO 1
      ITC=ITC+1
      IF(ITC.LT.ITLIM) GOTO 35
      IER=-1
      GOTO 1
```

```
35      TST=SOL
        IF(FNEW) 40,1,50
40      IF(FA.LT.0.) GOTO 45
42      B=SOL
        FB=FNEW
        GOTO 32
45      A=SOL
        FA=FNEW
        GOTO 32
50      IF(FA.GT.0.) GOTO 45
        GOTO 42
        END
```

Appendix 4.C
Results of Sampling Experiments[8]

Table 4.1   Mean square errors: experiment 1

	ML	NLS	NLSH	WNLS
Data $Q = Q^a$				
β_{10}	135.2062	338.9785	338.9785	368.1489
β_{11}	0.0235	0.0523	0.0523	0.0574
β_{12}	0.0083	0.0096	0.0096	0.0094
β_{20}	138.3084	120.3416	120.3416	122.6050
β_{21}	0.0212	0.0201	0.0201	0.0213
β_{22}	0.0046	0.0047	0.0047	0.0042
Data $Q = Q^n$				
β_{10}	123.8717	251.2298	251.2298	242.9739
β_{11}	0.0208	0.0409	0.0409	0.0403
β_{12}	0.0059	0.0066	0.0066	0.0065
β_{20}	95.1316	102.3093	102.3093	108.4771
β_{21}	0.0148	0.0171	0.0171	0.0185
β_{22}	0.0024	0.0022	0.0022	0.0022

Table 4.2   Normality test: experiment 1

	ML		NLS		NLSH		WNLS	
	KS	$Pr\{>KS\}$	KS	$Pr\{>KS\}$	KS	$Pr\{>KS\}$	KS	$Pr\{>KS\}$
Data $Q = Q^a$								
β_{10}	0.2975	0.0017	0.2122	0.0544	0.1278	0.5310	0.1998	0.0821
β_{11}	0.2563	0.0104	0.2496	0.0137	0.1355	0.4551	0.1982	0.0863
β_{12}	0.2956	0.0018	0.1421	0.3942	0.0778	0.9687	0.1356	0.4534
β_{20}	0.3402	0.0002	0.2289	0.0302	0.1050	0.7699	0.1979	0.0871
β_{21}	0.3866	0.0000	0.2497	0.0136	0.1188	0.6244	0.2003	0.0807
β_{22}	0.3168	0.0007	0.2324	0.0266	0.1877	0.1195	0.2185	0.0439
Data $Q = Q^n$								
β_{10}	0.0931	0.8788	0.1760	0.1676	0.1527	0.3087	0.1348	0.4618
β_{11}	0.1410	0.4037	0.2406	0.0194	0.1456	0.3643	0.2031	0.0737
β_{12}	0.0831	0.9448	0.2147	0.0501	0.1018	0.8013	0.1835	0.1353
β_{20}	0.1549	0.2927	0.2026	0.0748	0.1156	0.6591	0.1667	0.2162
β_{21}	0.1394	0.4184	0.2087	0.0614	0.1125	0.6921	0.1650	0.2264
β_{22}	0.2030	0.0740	0.2885	0.0026	0.1912	0.1075	0.2601	0.0089

[8] Reproduced by permission from Quandt (1986b).

Table 4.3   Fraction of times that method gives parameter estimate closest to true value: experiment 1

	ML	NLS	WNLS	χ^2 for H_0: methods equal	$Pr\{>\chi^2\}$
Data $Q = Q^a$					
β_{10}	0.4500	0.2250	0.3250	3.07	0.2154
β_{11}	0.3750	0.3750	0.2500	1.31	0.5187
β_{12}	0.3750	0.2250	0.4000	2.29	0.3178
β_{20}	0.3000	0.2500	0.4500	2.52	0.2835
β_{21}	0.3750	0.2500	0.3750	1.31	0.5186
β_{22}	0.3250	0.3750	0.3000	0.35	0.8410
Average	0.3667	0.2833	0.3500		
Data $Q = Q^n$					
β_{10}	0.4000	0.4250	0.1750	5.07	0.0791
β_{11}	0.5000	0.4000	0.1000	12.42	0.0020
β_{12}	0.5250	0.1750	0.3000	7.53	0.0231
β_{20}	0.4750	0.2750	0.2500	3.47	0.1762
β_{21}	0.4500	0.2500	0.3000	2.52	0.2835
β_{22}	0.3500	0.3000	0.3500	0.20	0.9033
Average	0.4500	0.3042	0.2458		

Table 4.4   Mean square errors: experiment 2

	ML	NLS	NLSII	WNLS
Data $Q = Q^a$				
β_{10}	260.8579	247.4805	247.4805	258.5725
β_{11}	0.0299	0.0308	0.0308	0.0324
β_{12}	0.0052	0.0059	0.0059	0.0063
β_{20}	123.7501	141.7834	141.7834	139.8975
β_{21}	0.0184	0.0238	0.0238	0.0207
β_{22}	0.0037	0.0039	0.0039	0.0040
Data $Q = Q^n$				
β_{10}	221.8751	213.7350	213.7350	221.8272
β_{11}	0.0264	0.0268	0.0268	0.0287
β_{12}	0.0057	0.0063	0.0063	0.0070
β_{20}	101.2357	133.9347	133.9347	131.0062
β_{21}	0.0153	0.0216	0.0216	0.0214
β_{22}	0.0033	0.0037	0.0037	0.0035

Table 4.5   Normality test: experiment 2

	ML		NLS		NLSH		WNLS	
	KS	$Pr\{>KS\}$	KS	$Pr\{>KS\}$	KS	$Pr\{>KS\}$	KS	$Pr\{>KS\}$
Data $Q = Q^a$								
β_{10}	0.1673	0.2129	0.1546	0.2946	0.1403	0.4105	0.1151	0.6633
β_{11}	0.1517	0.3158	0.2071	0.0647	0.1331	0.4783	0.2000	0.0815
β_{12}	0.1797	0.1508	0.1898	0.1120	0.1961	0.0923	0.1312	0.4968
β_{20}	0.1321	0.4876	0.2088	0.0610	0.1533	0.3040	0.1762	0.1669
β_{21}	0.1386	0.4258	0.2091	0.0606	0.1494	0.3342	0.1864	0.1242
β_{22}	0.1184	0.6288	0.1805	0.1476	0.1319	0.4892	0.1567	0.2797
Data $Q = Q^n$								
β_{10}	0.1395	0.4178	0.1543	0.2970	0.1131	0.6861	0.1250	0.5598
β_{11}	0.1401	0.4123	0.2754	0.0046	0.1630	0.2384	0.2375	0.0219
β_{12}	0.2060	0.0670	0.1804	0.1482	0.1983	0.0861	0.1520	0.3138
β_{20}	0.1471	0.3521	0.2048	0.0698	0.1556	0.2876	0.1947	0.0963
β_{21}	0.1084	0.7347	0.1740	0.1773	0.1635	0.2354	0.1985	0.0855
β_{22}	0.1226	0.5845	0.2130	0.0530	0.1601	0.2567	0.1928	0.1021

Table 4.6   Fraction of times that method gives parameter estimate closest to true value: experiment 2

	ML	NLS	WNLS	χ^2 for H_0: methods equal	$Pr\{>\chi^2\}$
Data $Q = Q^a$					
β_{10}	0.3750	0.2250	0.4000	2.15	0.3413
β_{11}	0.2750	0.4000	0.3250	0.95	0.6219
β_{12}	0.4500	0.2666	0.2833	2.47	0.2908
β_{20}	0.4250	0.3750	0.2000	3.35	0.1873
β_{21}	0.4500	0.2750	0.2750	2.45	0.2938
β_{22}	0.3750	0.4666	0.1583	6.02	0.0493
Average	0.3917	0.3348	0.2736		
Data $Q = Q^n$					
β_{10}	0.4250	0.3500	0.2250	2.45	0.2938
β_{11}	0.4500	0.3500	0.2000	3.80	0.1496
β_{12}	0.4750	0.2666	0.2583	3.62	0.1637
β_{20}	0.4500	0.3500	0.2000	3.80	0.1496
β_{21}	0.4500	0.2500	0.3000	2.60	0.2725
β_{22}	0.3750	0.3166	0.2917	0.42	0.8105
Average	0.4375	0.3166	0.2458		

Table 4.7   Mean square errors: experiment 3

	ML	NLS	NLSH	WNLS
Data $Q = Q^a$				
β_{10}	111.3221	115.8564	115.8564	116.9315
β_{11}	0.0202	0.0217	0.0217	0.0218
β_{12}	0.0040	0.0063	0.0063	0.0037
β_{20}	85.1755	62.5559	62.5559	58.6954
β_{21}	0.0136	0.0095	0.0095	0.0090
β_{22}	0.0031	0.0027	0.0027	0.0025
Data $Q = Q^n$				
β_{10}	53.0787	83.8728	83.8728	86.0124
β_{11}	0.0102	0.0157	0.0157	0.0161
β_{12}	0.0020	0.0024	0.0024	0.0026
β_{20}	50.4933	50.0482	50.0482	53.0049
β_{21}	0.0070	0.0072	0.0072	0.0079
β_{22}	0.0018	0.0018	0.0018	0.0018

Table 4.8   Normality test: experiment 3

	ML		NLS		NLSH		WNLS	
	KS	Pr{>KS}	KS	Pr{>KS}	KS	Pr{>KS}	KS	Pr{>KS}
Data $Q = Q^a$								
β_{10}	0.3509	0.0001	0.2633	0.0078	0.1163	0.6515	0.2351	0.0210
β_{11}	0.3227	0.0005	0.2565	0.0103	0.1802	0.1487	0.2543	0.0113
β_{12}	0.3891	0.0000	0.2723	0.0053	0.0919	0.8882	0.2256	0.0340
β_{20}	0.4280	0.0000	0.2268	0.0326	0.1300	0.5080	0.2274	0.0319
β_{21}	0.4095	0.0000	0.3434	0.0174	0.0816	0.9529	0.2304	0.0286
β_{22}	0.4734	0.0000	0.3332	0.0003	0.2043	0.0709	0.3122	0.0008
Data $Q = Q^n$								
β_{10}	0.1248	0.5615	0.2609	0.0086	0.1456	0.3648	0.2516	0.0126
β_{11}	0.1890	0.1148	0.2697	0.0059	0.1767	0.1645	0.2374	0.0221
β_{12}	0.1293	0.5154	0.3210	0.0005	0.1078	0.7413	0.2838	0.0032
β_{20}	0.1802	0.1490	0.2470	0.0152	0.1674	0.2121	0.2340	0.0251
β_{21}	0.1443	0.3751	0.2764	0.0044	0.1003	0.8160	0.2431	0.0177
β_{22}	0.2521	0.0124	0.2740	0.0049	0.1935	0.1000	0.2721	0.0053

Table 4.9 Fraction of times that method gives parameter estimates closest to true value: experiment 3

	ML	NLS	WNLS	χ^2 for H_0: methods equal	$Pr\{>\chi^2\}$
Data $Q = Q^a$					
β_{10}	0.3750	0.3250	0.3000	0.35	0.8410
β_{11}	0.4250	0.2500	0.3250	1.85	0.3969
β_{12}	0.4000	0.2750	0.3250	0.94	0.6239
β_{20}	0.2750	0.4500	0.2750	2.34	0.3105
β_{21}	0.3000	0.4000	0.3000	0.77	0.6782
β_{22}	0.2000	0.3500	0.4500	3.99	0.1356
Average	0.3292	0.3417	0.3292		
Data $Q = Q^n$					
β_{10}	0.5250	0.1500	0.3250	8.84	0.0121
β_{11}	0.5500	0.3000	0.1500	9.92	0.0070
β_{12}	0.4500	0.3000	0.2500	2.52	0.2835
β_{20}	0.4000	0.3000	0.3000	0.78	0.6782
β_{21}	0.4000	0.3000	0.3000	0.78	0.6782
β_{22}	0.3250	0.3000	0.3750	0.35	0.8410
Average	0.4417	0.2750	0.2833		

Table 4.10 Mean square errors: experiment 4

	ML	NLS	NLSH	WNLS
Data $Q = Q^a$				
β_{10}	428.2969	6353.484	6353.484	5204.262
β_{11}	0.4510	4.5924	4.5924	4.6072
β_{12}	0.0809	24.0998	24.0998	8.7467
β_{20}	175.0826	411.6215	411.6215	1165.907
β_{21}	0.3342	4.4740	4.4740	16.6986
β_{22}	0.0686	1.0484	1.0484	5.7170
Data $Q = Q^n$				
β_{10}	231.6877	7216.520	7216.520	6409.828
β_{11}	0.2588	0.8279	0.8279	0.8053
β_{12}	0.1192	7.7370	7.7370	1.5321
β_{20}	102.9930	4250.562	4250.562	5919.301
β_{21}	0.1433	0.9944	0.9944	7.0688
β_{22}	0.0396	0.2509	0.2509	1.1519

Table 4.11   Normality test: experiment 4

	ML		NLS		NLSH		WNLS	
	KS	$Pr\{>KS\}$	KS	$Pr\{>KS\}$	KS	$Pr\{>KS\}$	KS	$Pr\{>KS\}$
Data $Q = Q^a$								
β_{10}	0.3954	0.0001	0.2281	0.0715	0.2426	0.0463	0.2192	0.0921
β_{11}	0.3441	0.0100	0.2235	0.0817	0.2561	0.0300	0.1890	0.2032
β_{12}	0.3870	0.0001	0.2842	0.0114	0.2565	0.0296	0.2443	0.0439
β_{20}	0.3959	0.0001	0.1790	0.2569	0.2470	0.0402	0.1669	0.3345
β_{21}	0.4615	0.0000	0.2320	0.0638	0.2746	0.0160	0.2213	0.0871
β_{22}	0.3814	0.0002	0.3076	0.0047	0.2693	0.0193	0.3064	0.0049
Data $Q = Q^n$								
β_{10}	0.2324	0.0630	0.2304	0.0670	0.1997	0.1556	0.1819	0.2403
β_{11}	0.2675	0.0205	0.2705	0.0185	0.2390	0.0516	0.2428	0.0460
β_{12}	0.1456	0.5062	0.1981	0.1621	0.1358	0.5969	0.1292	0.6591
β_{20}	0.1487	0.4789	0.1823	0.2377	0.1105	0.8290	0.1044	0.8765
β_{21}	0.2056	0.1336	0.2179	0.0958	0.0828	0.9807	0.1825	0.2371
β_{22}	0.1485	0.4808	0.2982	0.0068	0.1531	0.4409	0.2531	0.0331

Table 4.12   Fraction of times that method gives parameter estimate closest to true value: experiment 4

	ML	NLS	WNLS	χ^2 for H_0: methods equal	$Pr\{>\chi^2\}$
Data $Q = Q^a$					
β_{10}	0.4375	0.2813	0.2813	1.56	0.4578
β_{11}	0.4688	0.3750	0.1563	4.94	0.0847
β_{12}	0.4375	0.3125	0.2500	1.75	0.4169
β_{20}	0.5938	0.2500	0.1563	10.19	0.0061
β_{21}	0.4688	0.3125	0.2188	3.06	0.2163
β_{22}	0.4063	0.3750	0.2188	1.94	0.3796
Average	0.4687	0.3177	0.2135		
Data $Q = Q^n$					
β_{10}	0.5625	0.2188	0.2188	7.56	0.0228
β_{11}	0.5313	0.1563	0.3125	6.81	0.0332
β_{12}	0.4375	0.2500	0.3125	1.75	0.4169
β_{20}	0.5313	0.3438	0.1250	7.94	0.0189
β_{21}	0.5313	0.2813	0.1875	6.06	0.0483
β_{22}	0.3750	0.3438	0.2813	0.44	0.8035
Average	0.4948	0.2656	0.2396		

5

Multimarket Models and Coherency

5.1 Introduction

All the models discussed up to this point have been models of a single market. Although restricting our attention to single markets makes the analysis as well as the computational burden substantially simpler, the results have to be taken with the same grain of salt as those of any partial equilibrium model when contrasted with a general equilibrium model. We devote the present and the next chapters to a discussion of the issues that emerge when we adopt a more general viewpoint. In section 5.2 we discuss some basic concepts such as effective demand and supply. We introduce the notion of coherency in section 5.3 and apply it to simultaneous markets models in section 5.4. The uniqueness of the solution for the endogenous variables is further considered in section 5.5, and necessary and sufficient conditions are discussed in section 5.6.

5.2 Effective Demands, Supplies, and Multimarket Systems

It is convenient to consider initially a specification in which prices are completely rigid and in which the consumers' side and producers' side of the market are given by a single representative consumer and producer respectively. Although everything below can be generalized to economies with many goods, it will also be convenient to restrict our attention to the case of two goods, an input and an output, plus the *numéraire* good, money, the price of which may be normalized to unity or in any other convenient way.

If prices are flexible, the demands and supplies of agents are obtained from utility maximization subject only to a budget constraint (for consumers) and from profit maximization subject only to a production function (for firms). The resulting demands and supplies are referred to as Walrasian (or notional) and will be denote by $\sim$ over the functions. If they are rationed in some markets by quantity restrictions, it would be rational to take these restrictions into account in utility or profit maximization; the demand and supply functions obtained while observing quantity restrictions are known as effective demand and supply functions. Considerable effort has been devoted to discussing the appropriate way of deriving effective demands and supplies.

Optimization on the Micro Level

We assume, as does Ito (1980), that there are three goods: a consumption good x_1, hours of labor offered for sale x_2, and the real money balances x_m. T is the total amount of time available, and the consumer maximizes the Cobb-Douglas utility function

$$U = x_1^\alpha (T - x_2)^\beta x_m^\gamma \tag{5.2.1}$$

subject to the budget constraint

$$p_2 x_2 = p_1 x_m + p_1 x_1 \tag{5.2.2}$$

where we assume for simplicity that initial money balances are zero. It follows from (5.2.2) that real money balances are expressed in units of the consumer good. The Lagrangian is

$$\bar{U} = x_1^\alpha (T - x_2)^\beta x_m^\gamma + \lambda (p_2 x_2 - p_1 x_m - p_1 x_1)$$

and the first-order conditions for a constrained optimum are

$$\frac{\partial \bar{U}}{\partial x_1} = \alpha x_1^{\alpha-1} (T - x_2)^\beta x_m^\gamma - \lambda p_1 = 0$$

$$\frac{\partial \bar{U}}{\partial x_2} = -\beta x_1^\alpha (T - x_2)^{\beta-1} x_m^\gamma + \lambda p_2 = 0$$

$$\frac{\partial \bar{U}}{\partial x_m} = \gamma x_1^\alpha (T - x_2)^\beta x_m^{\gamma-1} - \lambda p_1 = 0$$

Hence the Walrasian functions are

$$\tilde{x}_1 = \frac{\alpha p_2 T}{p_1 (\alpha + \beta + \gamma)} \tag{5.2.3}$$

$$\tilde{x}_2 = \frac{(\alpha + \gamma) T}{(\alpha + \beta + \gamma)} \tag{5.2.4}$$

$$\tilde{x}_m = \frac{\gamma p_2 T}{p_1 (\alpha + \beta + \gamma)} \tag{5.2.5}$$

Now consider the case in which the consumer knows that his labor offer will be rationed to an amount $\bar{x}_2 < \tilde{x}_2$. He now maximizes

$$U = x_1^\alpha (T - \bar{x}_2)^\beta x_m^\gamma$$

subject to $p_2\bar{x}_2 = p_1 x_m + p_1 x_1$ with respect to x_1 and x_m. The first-order conditions are

$$\frac{\partial \bar{U}}{\partial x_1} = \alpha x_1^{\alpha-1}(T-\bar{x}_2)^\beta x_m^\gamma - \lambda p_1 = 0$$

$$\frac{\partial \bar{U}}{\partial x_m} = \gamma x_1^\alpha (T-\bar{x}_2)^\beta x_m^{\gamma-1} - \lambda p_1 = 0$$

and

$$x_1^e = \frac{p_2 \bar{x}_2 \alpha}{p_1(\alpha+\gamma)} \tag{5.2.6}$$

$$x_m^e = \frac{p_2 \bar{x}_2 \gamma}{(\alpha+\gamma)} \tag{5.2.7}$$

We first note that the effective demand for goods x_1^e must be less than the Walrasian $\tilde{x}_1$. For asserting the opposite, we have from (5.2.3) and (5.2.6)

$$\frac{\alpha p_2 T}{p_1(\alpha+\beta+\gamma)} < \frac{\alpha p_2 \bar{x}_2}{p_1(\alpha+\gamma)}$$

which leads to $\bar{x}_2 > T(\alpha+\gamma)/(\alpha+\beta+\gamma)$, a contradiction since the right hand side is $\tilde{x}_2$ by (5.2.4) and was assumed to exceed $\bar{x}_2$. Next, from (5.2.3) and (5.2.6) we can write

$$x_1^e = \tilde{x}_1 + \frac{\alpha}{\alpha+\gamma} \frac{p_2}{p_1} (\bar{x}_2 - \tilde{x}_2) \tag{5.2.8}$$

which shows that the effective demand for goods equals the notional or Walrasian demand plus a *spillover term* that is proportional to the discrepancy between the Walrasian supply of labor and the amount consumers are rationed to. This is the type of argument that has led to specifications of effective demand in which simple linear spillover terms from the other market(s) appear. However, as we shall see, this does not eliminate all disagreement about how effective demands and supplies should be formulated; nor is the situation quite as simple as (5.2.8) would make it appear. Consider the case of an entrepreneur producing x_1 with the input x_2 and production function $x_1 = x_2^\delta$, where $\delta < 1$. He maximizes

$$\Pi = p_1 x_2^\delta - p_2 x_2$$

yielding the Walrasian demand and supply

$$\tilde{x}_2 = \left(\frac{p_1 \delta}{p_2}\right)^{1/(1-\delta)}$$

and

$$\bar{x}_1 = \left(\frac{p_1\delta}{p_2}\right)^{\delta/(1-\delta)}$$

If he is rationed in his output market to a quantity $\bar{x}_1 < \tilde{x}_1$, his effective demand for labor is given by the inverse of the production function, $x_2^e = \bar{x}_1^{1/\delta}$. Expressing $x_2^e - \tilde{x}_2$ yields

$$x_2^e - \tilde{x}_2 = \bar{x}_1^{1/\delta} - \left(\frac{p_1\delta}{p_2}\right)^{1/(1-\delta)} = \bar{x}_1^{1/\delta} - \tilde{x}_1^{1/\delta} \tag{5.2.9}$$

Equation (5.2.9) is analogous to (5.2.8) for the consumer, and it is evident that the effective and Walrasian demands for labor are related by a spillover term that is no longer linear in $\bar{x}_1 - \tilde{x}_1$ (Meade 1985).

It is nevertheless the case that, to an approximation, effective demands can be taken to be linear in spillover terms, which is a consequence of employing a Taylor series expansion. Let us consider maximizing a general utility function $U(x_1, x_2, x_m)$ subject to the budget constraint. The Walrasian solutions are $\tilde{x}_1(p_1, p_2)$ and $\tilde{x}_2(p_1, p_2)$, i.e. functions of prices only. The constrained solution for x_1, given the constraint $x_2 \leqq \bar{x}_2$, is $x_1^e(p_1, p_2, \bar{x}_2)$, a function of $\bar{x}_2$ as well. Clearly,

$$x_1^e(p_1, p_2, \tilde{x}_2) = \tilde{x}_1$$

since constraining a person to his Walrasian choice does not impose an effective constraint. Then expanding x_1^e about $\tilde{x}_2$ we have

$$x_1^e(p_1, p_2, \bar{x}_2) = x_1^e(p_1, p_2, \tilde{x}_2) + \left[\frac{\partial}{\partial \tilde{x}_2} x_1^e(p_1, p_2, \tilde{x}_2)\right](\bar{x}_2 - \tilde{x}_2)$$

as claimed (see Gourieroux, Laffont and Monfort 1980a).

Effective Demand Concepts

In specifying the effective demands and supplies, it is necessary to take into account the quantity restrictions to which consumers and producers are subject. But to specify precisely which quantity restrictions the agent does take into account and which he does not in formulating his optimization problem is a matter involving behavioral assumptions in an area in which common sense may be a less than perfect guide. Two approaches have been principally employed.

Consider for the moment the case of the consumer. Drèze demands (Drèze 1975) are derived if we maximize the utility function subject to the budget constraint and *all* quantity restrictions that are known to exist. Thus, if the restrictions are $x_1 \leqq \bar{x}_1$, $x_2 \leqq \bar{x}_2$ and the ration quantities are so small that $\bar{x}_i < \tilde{x}_i$ for both $i = 1, 2$, then $x_1^e = \bar{x}_1$ and $x_2^e = \bar{x}_2$. If, on the other hand, $\bar{x}_2 < \tilde{x}_2$ but $\bar{x}_1 > \tilde{x}_1$, then x_1^e is given by (5.2.6) but $x_2^e = \bar{x}_2$.

Clower (1965) proposed a construction of the effective demand for commodity i that is based on respecting the budget constraint and the quantity constraints for all other commodities but on neglecting the quantity constraint on commodity i itself. Whereas the solution of the optimization problem for the Drèze demands yields the effective demand vector valid for all commodities, in the case of Clower demands the consumer is supposed to solve n separate optimization problems that differ from one another by which quantity constraint is omitted. The overall effective demand vector is then composed by forming an effective demand vector, the ith element of which is the ith component of the solution vector for the ith optimization problem. Formally the difference can be shown as follows. Let x be the n-vector of commodities, $U(x)$ the utility function, p the price vector, and m_0 an initial endowment of (nominal) money. Then the Drèze demand vector solves

$$\text{maximize}_{x} \quad U(x)$$
$$\text{subject to} \quad p'x = m_0$$
$$x \leqq \bar{x}$$

The derivation of Clower demands first requires the solution of the n problems

$$\text{maximize} \quad U(x)$$
$$\text{subject to} \quad p'x = m_0$$
$$x_j \leqq \bar{x}_j \qquad \text{for all } j \neq i$$
$$i = 1, \ldots, n$$

Let the solution vector of the ith problem be denoted by $x^i = (x^i_1, \ldots, x^i_n)$. The Clower demand vector then is $(x^1_1, x^2_2, \ldots, x^i_i, \ldots, x^n_n)$.

Svensson (1980) has criticized these approaches and finds the behavioral theory underlying the Clower demand concept unsatisfactory. It is clear, for example, that if the Drèze demand concept is applied there can be no discrepancy between effective demands and actual trades, which may appear to be counterintuitive. At the same time, the Clower demands may violate the budget constraint (see exercise 5.1).

The behaviorally more satisfactory procedure may be to cast the problem as one of expected utility maximization. Even in this case one may make various choices about model specification. In the general case such derivations are likely to be difficult and expected utility maximization has not led to simple, econometrically tractable formulations of effective demands and supplies.

In the simplest case, expected utility maximization may just lead to the Walrasian demands. Consider the case of two goods x_1, x_2, utility function $U(x_1, x_2)$, and budget constraint $Y - p_1x_1 - p_2x_2 = 0$. Assume that only x_1 is subject to rationing and that the ration $\bar{x}_1$ has density $f(\bar{x}_1)$.

If $\bar{x}_1 < \tilde{x}_1$ (the Walrasian demand), the consumer chooses $\bar{x}_1$ and his utility is $U[\bar{x}_1, (Y - p_1 \bar{x}_1)/p_2]$. If $\bar{x}_1 \geqq \tilde{x}_1$, he chooses $\tilde{x}_1$ and his utility is $U[\tilde{x}_1, (Y - p_1 \tilde{x}_1)/p_2]$. His expected utility is

$$
E(U) = \int_0^{\tilde{x}_1} U[\bar{x}_1, (Y - p_1\bar{x}_1)/p_2] f(\bar{x}_1 | \bar{x}_1 \leqq \tilde{x}_1) \mathrm{d}\bar{x}_1 \, \Pr\{\bar{x}_1 \leqq \tilde{x}_1\}
$$
$$
+ U[\tilde{x}_1, (Y - p_1 \tilde{x}_1)/p_2] \, \Pr\{\bar{x}_1 > \tilde{x}_1\}
$$

Differentiating with respect to $\tilde{x}_1$ yields

$$
\frac{\mathrm{d}E(U)}{\mathrm{d}\tilde{x}_1} = U[\tilde{x}_1, (Y - p_1 \tilde{x}_1/p_2] f(\tilde{x}_1)
$$
$$
- \frac{\partial}{\partial \tilde{x}_1} U[\tilde{x}_1, (Y - p_1 \tilde{x}_1)/p_2] \, \Pr\{\bar{x}_1 > \tilde{x}\}
$$
$$
- U[\tilde{x}_1, (Y - p_1 \tilde{x}_1)/p_2] f(\tilde{x}_1) = 0
$$

which holds if and only if $\partial U[\tilde{x}_1, (Y - p_1 \tilde{x}_1)/p_2]/\partial \tilde{x}_1 = 0$, i.e. if $\tilde{x}_1$ is the Walrasian demand.

From the point of view of the econometrician, the average demand is different. To simplify matters further, assume that $U = x_1 x_2$, from which $\tilde{x}_1 = Y/2p_1$. In the sample, quantities consumed are $\bar{x}_1$ when $\bar{x}_1 < \tilde{x}_1$ and are $\tilde{x}_1$ otherwise. Hence if individual rations have density $f(\bar{x}_1)$ the average demand observed is

$$
E(x_1) = \int_0^{\tilde{x}_1} \bar{x}_1 f(\bar{x}_1 | \bar{x}_1 \leqq \tilde{x}_1) \mathrm{d}\bar{x}_1 \, \Pr\{\bar{x}_1 \leqq \tilde{x}_1\} + \tilde{x}_1 \, \Pr\{\bar{x}_1 > \tilde{x}_1\}
$$

If $f(\bar{x}_1)$ is, say, exponential with density $a e^{-a\bar{x}_1}$,

$$
E(x_1) = \int_0^{\tilde{x}_1} x_1 a e^{-a\bar{x}_1} \mathrm{d}\bar{x}_1 + \tilde{x}_1 \, e^{-a\tilde{x}_1} = [1 - e^{-a(Y/2p_1)}]/a
$$

For example, if there is a 0.5 probability that the Walrasian demand will be rationed, $a = 0.138\,63$. If, further, $Y = 10$, $p_1 = 1$, then $\tilde{x}_1 = 5$, but $E(x_1) = 3.606\,72$.

In practice, the Clower demand concept has predominated. This is the case for macroeconomic models such as those by Barro and Grossman (1971), Malinvaud (1976), and others, as well as for econometric formulations such as those of Ito (1980) and Gourieroux, Laffont and Monfort (1980a, 1980b). We now turn to some specific alternative formulations.

Systems of Effective Demands and Supplies

Numerous theoretical studies have analyzed a stylized economy in which there are only two markets, namely a market for commodities and a market for labor.[1] Some of the key differences among models pertain to the manner in which effective demands and supplies are formulated. Some of the leading candidate formulations that have the mathematical virtue of being at least piecewise linear are reviewed in some detail by Portes (1977) and we outline these below. We concentrate on two-market models. The demands and supplies of the two goods are denoted by D_1, S_1, D_2, S_2. As before, we denote the notional or Walrasian quantities by $\sim$ and the effective quantities by the appropriate symbol without the $\sim$; realized transactions will be denoted by Q_1 and Q_2.

The first formulation we consider is due to Ito (1980) and it posits the following demand and supply functions:

$$D_1 = \widetilde{D}_1 + \alpha_1(Q_2 - \widetilde{S}_2)$$
$$S_1 = \widetilde{S}_1 + \alpha_2(Q_2 - \widetilde{D}_2)$$
$$Q_1 = \min(D_1, S_1)$$
$$D_2 = \widetilde{D}_2 + \alpha_3(Q_1 - \widetilde{S}_1) \tag{5.2.13}$$
$$S_2 = \widetilde{S}_2 + \alpha_4(Q_1 - \widetilde{D}_1)$$
$$Q_2 = \min(D_2, S_2)$$

Thus, for example, the effective demand for commodities, D_1, is equal to the Walrasian demand plus a spillover term, which is zero if $Q_2 = \widetilde{S}_2$ (the transacted amount of labor equals the Walrasian supply; i.e. laborers are unconstrained in their labor supply) and is negative otherwise. Formulating the model as (5.2.13) shows that α_i must be positive for it to make economic sense.

Model (5.2.13) is very similar to the formulation due to Barro and Grossman (1971, 1976), Muellbauer and Portes (1978), and Gourieroux, Laffont and Monfort (1980a), according to which

$$D_1 = \begin{cases} \widetilde{D}_1 & \text{if } S_2 \leq D_2 \\ \widetilde{D}_1 + \alpha_1(Q_2 - \widetilde{S}_2) & \text{otherwise} \end{cases}$$

$$S_1 = \begin{cases} \widetilde{S}_1 & \text{if } D_2 \leq S_2 \\ \widetilde{S}_1 + \alpha_2(Q_2 - \widetilde{D}_2) & \text{otherwise} \end{cases}$$

$$Q_1 = \min(D_1, S_1)$$

---

[1] For a review see Drazen (1980). See also Malinvaud (1976, 1980, 1982), Portes (1981), Barro and Grossman (1971), and many others.

(5.2.14)

$$D_2 = \begin{cases} \tilde{D}_2 & \text{if } S_1 \leq D_1 \\ \tilde{D}_2 + \alpha_3(Q_1 - \tilde{S}_1) & \text{otherwise} \end{cases}$$

$$S_2 = \begin{cases} \tilde{S}_2 & \text{if } D_1 \leq S_1 \\ \tilde{S}_2 + \alpha_4(Q_1 - \tilde{D}_1) & \text{otherwise} \end{cases}$$

$$Q_2 = \min(D_2, S_2)$$

A slightly different system is suggested by Benassy (1975):

$$D_1 = \tilde{D}_1 + \alpha_1(Q_2 - S_2)$$
$$S_1 = \tilde{S}_1 + \alpha_2(Q_2 - D_2)$$
$$Q_1 = \min(D_1, S_1)$$
$$D_2 = \tilde{D}_2 + \alpha_3(Q_1 - S_1)$$
$$S_2 = \tilde{S}_2 + \alpha_4(Q_1 - D_1)$$
$$Q_2 = \min(D_2, S_2)$$

(5.2.15)

whereby the spillovers are measured as discrepancies between realized transactions and effective demands and supplies rather than the notional ones.

Each of these systems is capable of being in one of four regimes:

1 $D_1 < S_1, \quad D_2 < S_2$
2 $D_1 < S_1, \quad D_2 > S_2$
3 $D_1 > S_1, \quad D_2 < S_2$
4 $D_1 > S_1, \quad D_2 > S_2$

which, remembering that subscript 1 refers to commodities and 2 to labor, are usually identified as Keynesian unemployment (1), underconsumption (2), classical unemployment (3), and repressed inflation (4).

Consider the solution of system (5.2.13) in each of the regimes. In this simple model prices are given exogenously (thus the model is an analog to model A in chapter 2) and hence $\tilde{D}_1, \tilde{S}_1, \tilde{D}_2, \tilde{S}_2$ are given exogenously. Defining $y' = (D_1, S_1, D_2, S_2)$ and $b' = (\tilde{D}_1 - \alpha_1\tilde{S}_2, \tilde{S}_1 - \alpha_2\tilde{D}_2, \tilde{D}_2 - \alpha_3\tilde{S}_1, \tilde{S}_2 - \alpha_4\tilde{D}_1)$, the solutions are those of the simultaneous equations models

$$A_i y = b \qquad i = 1, \ldots, 4 \tag{5.2.16}$$

where

$$A_1 = \begin{bmatrix} 1 & 0 & -\alpha_1 & 0 \\ 0 & 1 & -\alpha_2 & 0 \\ -\alpha_3 & 0 & 1 & 0 \\ -\alpha_4 & 0 & 0 & 1 \end{bmatrix}, \qquad A_2 = \begin{bmatrix} 1 & 0 & 0 & -\alpha_1 \\ 0 & 1 & 0 & -\alpha_2 \\ -\alpha_3 & 0 & 1 & 0 \\ -\alpha_4 & 0 & 0 & 1 \end{bmatrix}$$

$$A_3 = \begin{bmatrix} 1 & 0 & -\alpha_1 & 0 \\ 0 & 1 & -\alpha_2 & 0 \\ 0 & -\alpha_3 & 1 & 0 \\ 0 & -\alpha_4 & 0 & 1 \end{bmatrix}, \qquad A_4 = \begin{bmatrix} 1 & 0 & 0 & -\alpha_1 \\ 0 & 1 & 0 & -\alpha_2 \\ 0 & -\alpha_3 & 1 & 0 \\ 0 & -\alpha_4 & 0 & 1 \end{bmatrix}$$

A minimal requirement for the existence of a solution is that each of the A_i matrices have nonvanishing determinant. These are easily seen to be $1 - \alpha_1\alpha_3,\, 1 - \alpha_1\alpha_4,\, 1 - \alpha_2\alpha_3,\, 1 - \alpha_2\alpha_4$; hence the product of the spillover coefficient $\alpha_i\alpha_j$ ($i = 1,2;\ j = 3,4$) must not equal unity.

Although (5.2.13), (5.2.14), and (5.2.15) appear to be different, their solutions for the *observable, transacted* quantities are the same. Consider regime 1, the case of Keynesian unemployment. Then $D_1 = Q_1$ and $D_2 = Q_2$, and thus the first and fourth equations of (5.2.13) become

$$\begin{aligned} Q_1 - \alpha_1 Q_2 &= \tilde{D}_1 - \alpha_1 \tilde{S}_2 \\ -\alpha_3 Q_1 + Q_2 &= \tilde{D}_2 - \alpha_3 \tilde{S}_1 \end{aligned} \qquad (5.2.17)$$

For regime 1 the first, second, fourth, and fifth equations of (5.2.15) become

$$Q_1 = \tilde{D}_1 + \alpha_1(Q_2 - S_2)$$
$$S_1 = \tilde{S}_1$$
$$Q_2 = \tilde{D}_2 + \alpha_3(Q_1 - S_1)$$
$$S_2 = \tilde{S}_2$$

which further reduces to (5.2.17). Finally, the reader may verify that (5.2.14) yields the same answer. It is easy to check that the two formulations yield identical solutions for the other regimes (see exercise 5.3).

Since observed quantities are equally compatible with any of these formulations, data cannot distinguish between them. However, the solution values of the three systems (5.2.13), (5.2.14), (5.2.15) are not the same for the effective demands and supplies. Thus if the models were enlarged by the addition of price adjustment equations which depend on excess demands, as in $p_{1t} = p_{1t-1} + \gamma_1(D_1 - S_1)$ and $p_{2t} = p_{2t-1} + \gamma_2(D_2 - S_2)$, the models would cease to be observationally equivalent (Portes 1977).

Is the Debate About Effective Demand Concepts Necessary?

Lee (1986) has proposed an interesting interpretation of a fixed-price equilibrium which makes it unnecessary to settle the argument of which type of effective demand formulation is behaviorally most reasonable. We start out with a framework for the consumer not unlike that of (5.2.1) and (5.2.2). The utility function is written as

$$U(x_1, x_2, x_m) \qquad (5.2.18)$$

where x_m denotes money, the market for which is always in equilibrium, and the budget constraint as

$$p_1x_1 - p_2x_2 + x_m = x_m^0 \tag{5.2.19}$$

where x_m^0 denotes initial money balances, with the price of money normalized to unity. The minus sign indicates that x_2 represents labor services sold by the consumer. Solving the usual utility maximization problem yields the Walrasian demands and supplies

$$\tilde{x}_i = \tilde{x}_i(p_1, p_2, x_m^0) \qquad i = 1, 2, m$$

If quantity constraints $x_1 \leq \bar{x}_1$, $x_2 \leq \bar{x}_2$ exist, the appropriate Lagrangian is $V = U(x_1, x_2, x_m) + \lambda(x_m^0 - p_1x_1 + p_2x_2 - x_m) + \mu_1(\bar{x}_1 - x_1) + \mu_2(\bar{x}_2 - x_2)$ and the Kuhn-Tucker conditions for the optimal solution are

$$U_1 - \lambda p_1 - \mu_1 \leq 0$$

$$x_1(U_1 - \lambda p_1 - \mu_1) = 0$$

$$U_2 + \lambda p_2 - \mu_2 \leq 0$$

$$x_2(U_2 + \lambda p_2 - \mu_2) = 0$$

$$U_m - \lambda \leq 0$$

$$x_m(U_m - \lambda) = 0$$

$$x_m^0 - p_1x_1 + p_2x_2 - x_m \geq 0$$

$$\lambda(x_m^0 - p_1x_1 + p_2x_2 - x_m) = 0$$

$$\bar{x}_1 - x_1 \geq 0$$

$$\mu_1(\bar{x}_1 - x_1) = 0$$

$$\bar{x}_2 - x_2 \geq 0$$

$$\mu_2(\bar{x}_2 - x_2) = 0$$

On the assumption that the solution is interior, i.e. that x_1, x_2, x_m are positive, the above system can be reduced to

$$U_1 - \lambda p_1 - \mu_1 = 0$$

$$U_2 + \lambda p_2 - \mu_2 = 0 \tag{5.2.20}$$

$$U_m - \lambda = 0$$

$$\mu_1, \mu_2, \lambda \geq 0$$

and, moreover, $\lambda > 0$ in the absence of satiation. Now define

$$r_1 = U_1(\bar{x})/U_m(\bar{x})$$

$$r_2 = -U_2(\bar{x})/U_m(\bar{x}) \tag{5.2.21}$$

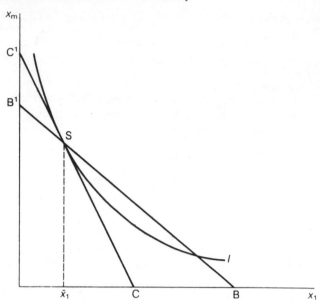

Figure 5.1

to be the marginal rates of substitution evaluated at the quantity constraint vector $\bar{x}$, and ask what budget constraint would bring about a Walrasian demand (supply) for $\bar{x}$. To make a diagrammatic treatment possible (figure 5.1), omit x_2 for a moment and plot x_1 on the horizontal and x_m on the vertical axis. If the budget constraint BB' is the actual budget constraint and $\bar{x}_1$ the quantity constraint on good 1, the constrained optimum is at point S. This point will be a quantity-unconstrained optimum if the budget constraint is given by CC'. Since at S the new budget constraint is tangent to I at S, the prices implicit in this hypothetical budget constraint are r_1 and r_2, and it can be written as

$$r_1 \bar{x}_1 - r_2 \bar{x}_2 + x_m = \bar{x}_m^0 \qquad (5.2.22)$$

where the hypothetical money endowment $\bar{x}_m^0$ is related to the actual one, x_m^0, by

$$x_m^0 - \bar{x}_m^0 = (p_1 - r_1)\bar{x}_1 + (r_2 - p_2)\bar{x}_2 \qquad (5.2.23)$$

It follows from (5.2.20) and (5.2.21) that

$$p_1 \leqq r_1$$
$$p_2 \geqq r_2 \qquad (5.2.24)$$

and (5.2.24) characterizes a quantity constrained optimum.

A similar development holds for the firm whose objective is to maximize profit $p_1x_1 - p_2x_2 + x_m$ subject to the implicit production function $f(x) = 0$ and the quantity constraints $x_1 \leq \bar{x}_1$, $x_2 \leq \bar{x}_2$. Defining the marginal rates of substitution for the firm by $s_1 = f_1(\bar{x})/f_m(\bar{x})$ and $s_2 = -f_2(\bar{x})/f_m(\bar{x})$, we obtain the characterization of the constrained solution given by

$$s_1 \leq p_1$$

$$s_2 \geq p_2$$ (5.2.25)

Hence if a vector $\bar{x}$ is to be optimal for both consumers and producers, we must have

$$s_1 \leq p_1 \leq r_1$$

$$s_2 \geq p_2 \geq r_2$$ (5.2.26)

Lee (1986) assumes that the consumer and producer will not both be rationed simultaneously in a given market. It follows from (5.2.20) that if, say, $p_2 > r_2$, then μ_2 is positive and hence, by complementary slackness, $x_2 = \bar{x}_2$. Conversely, if $p_2 = r_2$, the quantity constraint is not effective. Hence, the assumption implies that we will never encounter $s_1 < p_1 < r_1$ or $s_2 > p_2 > r_2$. Thus if $s_1 < p_1$ then $p_1 = r_1$, and similarly for the other possible cases.

Lee proves four important theorems, two for the consumer and two corresponding ones for the producer. We state those applicable to the consumer.

Let V denote the indirect utility function and write the marginal rates of substitution r_i and the hypothetical budget C as functions of the constraint quantities as in $r_i(\bar{x})$, $C(\bar{x})$. Let V_i denote $\partial V/\partial x_i$, $V_C = \partial V/\partial C$ and $r = (r_1, r_2)$. Then

$$V_1[r(\bar{x}), C(\bar{x})] = V_C[r(\bar{x}), C(\bar{x})][r_1(\bar{x}) - p_1]$$

$$V_2[r(\bar{x}), C(\bar{x})] = V_C[r(\bar{x}), C(\bar{x})][p_2 - r_2(\bar{x})]$$ (5.2.27)

which follows easily from Roy's identity and (5.2.23).

Let the Clower demands be denoted by $x_i^c(p, M | x_j)$, $j \neq i$. Then

$$V_i \leq 0 \quad \text{if and only if } x_i^c(p, M | \bar{x}_j) \leq \bar{x}_i$$

$$V_i \geq 0 \quad \text{if and only if } x_i^c(p, M | \bar{x}_j) \geq \bar{x}_i$$ (5.2.28)

Together (5.2.26), (5.2.27) and (5.2.28) (and the corresponding theorems for the producer) show that all Clower demands and supplies are at least as great as the ration quantities $\bar{x}$. It also follows from the theorems that $p_i = r_i$ implies that the consumer's Clower demands and supplies equal $\bar{x}_i$, and $p_i = s_i$ implies similar equalities for firms. It immediately follows that the transacted quantity in market i, which is the amount actually traded, is the minimum of the amounts Clower-demanded and Clower-supplied.

Consider, for example, market 1, and assume that $s_1 < p_1 = r_1$. Then the firm's Clower supply of good 1 exceeds $\bar{x}_1$ and we can write

$$\bar{x}_1 = \min (\text{consumer's demand for 1, firm's supply of 1})$$

Thus, the min condition that is specified in econometric disequilibrium models and is applied to effective demand and supply functions of the Clower type is a consequence of a fixed price equilibrium, without the need for a behavioral justification. A similar argument is made by Lee for the Gourieroux, Laffont and Monfort (1980a) version of the effective demand structure. It is still true, however, that with endogenous price adjustment the situation is more complicated in that behavioral assumptions may well have observable consequences. This is because different behavioral assumptions lead to different excess demands; if price changes are proportional to excess demand then the specification of the latter obviously matters, while in the simple case it does not.

5.3   Introduction to the Problem of Coherency: Some Examples

On several occasions we have alluded to the property of coherency in disequilibrium models. This is a property that ensures that disequilibrium (and other latent variable) models are internally consistent in a manner to be described. In the present section we give some simple examples of the problem and illustrate why coherency is an essential prerequisite to estimation. We go into more detail in subsequent sections.

In any latent variable model we are given some exogenous variables x and "nature" draws some errors u from its "urn"; these determine some unobserved variables y^* from a set of structural relations $h(y^*,x,u) = 0$. The investigator characteristically observes some variables $y = g(y^*)$; the mapping from y^* to y is usually expressed in terms of certain subsets (regimes) in the space of y^*. Such a model is coherent if there exists a well-defined reduced form $y^* = f(x,u)$. We illustrate this idea with several examples below.

Harvest Model

As a first illustration we consider the harvest model introduced in chapter 1 in simplified form (Goldfeld and Quandt 1975). We achieve the simplification by lumping all nonessential exogenous variables and coefficients into the error terms of the equations:

$$q_t = u_{1t} \tag{5.3.1}$$

$$h_t = \alpha_1 p_t + u_{2t} \tag{5.3.2}$$

$$p_t = \alpha_2 y_t + u_{3t} \tag{5.3.3}$$

$$y_t = \min(q_t, h_t) \tag{5.3.4}$$

In these equations, q_t is the crop and depends only on exogenous variables and the error term (all lumped into u_{1t}); harvest intentions h_t depend on the price (and u_{2t}); and price depends on the quantity actually harvested, y_t, which in turn is the lesser of the crop and harvest intentions.

Consider the two possible cases:

Case 1: $h_t < q_t$. In this case $y_t = h_t$, and solving (5.3.2) and (5.3.3) for h_t gives

$$h_t = \frac{\alpha_1 u_{3t} + u_{2t}}{1 - \alpha_1 \alpha_2}$$

Provided that $1 - \alpha_1 \alpha_2 > 0$, the condition $h_t < q_t$ implies

$$(1 - \alpha_1 \alpha_2) q_t > \alpha_1 u_{3t} + u_{2t}$$

or

$$u_{1t} > \alpha_1 \alpha_2 u_{1t} + \alpha_1 u_{3t} + u_{2t} \tag{5.3.5}$$

Case 2: $h_t > q_t$. Then $y_t = q_t$ and

$$h_t = \alpha_1(\alpha_2 q_t + u_{3t}) + u_{2t} = \alpha_1 \alpha_2 u_{1t} + \alpha_1 u_{3t} + u_{2t}$$

and

$$u_{1t} < \alpha_1 \alpha_2 u_{1t} + \alpha_1 u_{3t} + u_{2t} \tag{5.3.6}$$

The two inequalities (5.3.5) and (5.3.6) contradict each other. The significance of this is that given the values of all the exogenous variables and error terms, *one and only one regime* may be observed. Figure 5.2 is drawn on the assumption that $\alpha_1 > 0$, $\alpha_2 < 0$ and hence $1 - \alpha_1 \alpha_2 > 0$. If $h < q$, then the solution for h (and y) is given by the intersection of the two lines and q must have been as shown by q_1. In the converse case, q must be as shown by q_2. The price is then p_2, but at this price there is an unsatisfied "harvest desire" of AB. In figure 5.3 both functions are negatively sloped with demand being less steep. Positing $q < h$, say with a value of q_2, price is obtained from the demand function and is p_2. At that price, however, $h < q$, contradicting the original assumption that $q < h$. What happens in this case is that if we work out the solution values for the endogenous variables on the assumption that these values have relative magnitudes defining one type of regime, we actually obtain values that fall in the other regime. Hence the model is inconsistent. Notice that the relative slopes of the two lines are such that $\alpha_1 < 1/\alpha_2$; hence the condition $1 - \alpha_1 \alpha_2 > 0$ is violated (see exercise 5.6).

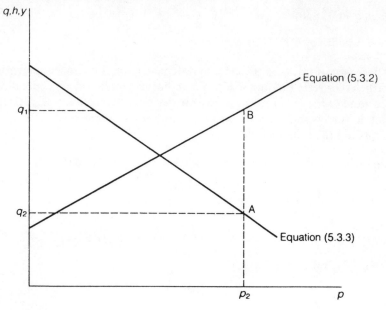

Figure 5.2

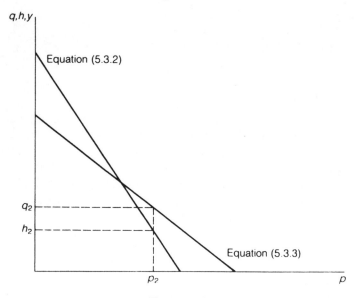

Figure 5.3

Planned Economy Model

Consider the following simple aggregate model of a planned economy (Charemza and Quandt 1982):

$$D_t = \beta_1' x_{1t} + \alpha_1 Q_t^* + u_{1t} \tag{5.3.7}$$

$$S_t = \beta_2' x_{2t} + \alpha_2 Q_t^* + u_{2t} \tag{5.3.8}$$

$$\overset{\cdot}{Q_t} = \min(D_t, S_t) \tag{5.3.9}$$

$$Q_t^* = Q_t + \gamma(D_t - S_t) + u_{3t} \tag{5.3.10}$$

where Q_t^* is the planned level of output. Equations (5.3.7) and (5.3.8) thus assume that both demand and supply depend on the planned level of output which, by (5.3.10), is set by reference to actual realizations, exceeding it if excess demand is positive and falling short of it in the converse case.[2]

Now write (5.3.7), (5.3.8), and (5.3.10) of the model as

$$\begin{aligned} A_1 y_t &= v_t \quad \text{if } D_t < S_t \\ A_2 y_t &= v_t \quad \text{otherwise} \end{aligned} \tag{5.3.11}$$

where $y_t' = (D_t, S_t, Q_t^*)$, $v_t' = (\beta_1' x_{1t} + u_{1t}, \beta_2' x_{2t} + u_{2t}, u_{3t})$,

$$A_1 = \begin{bmatrix} 1 & 0 & -\alpha_1 \\ 0 & 1 & -\alpha_2 \\ -(1+\gamma) & \gamma & 1 \end{bmatrix}$$

$$A_2 = \begin{bmatrix} 1 & 0 & -\alpha_1 \\ 0 & 1 & -\alpha_2 \\ -\gamma & -(1-\gamma) & 1 \end{bmatrix}$$

and where we have used the facts that $Q_t = D_t$ when $D_t < S_t$ and conversely. The determinants of A_1 and A_2 are $\Delta_1 = 1 + \gamma(\alpha_2 - \alpha_1) - \alpha_1$ and $\Delta_2 = 1 + \gamma(\alpha_2 - \alpha_1) - \alpha_2$. Solving the two equation systems in (5.3.11) gives

$$\begin{aligned} D_t &= (1/\Delta_1) \{(1 + \gamma\alpha_2) v_{1t} - \alpha_1 \gamma v_{2t} + \alpha_1 v_{3t}\} \\ S_t &= (1/\Delta_1) \{\alpha_2(1+\gamma) v_{1t} + [1 - \alpha_1(1+\gamma)] v_{2t} + \alpha_2 v_{3t}\} \end{aligned} \tag{5.3.12}$$

if $D_t < S_t$ and

$$\begin{aligned} D_t &= (1/\Delta_2) \{[1 - \alpha_2(1-\gamma)] v_{1t} + \alpha_1(1-\gamma) v_{2t} + \alpha_1 v_{3t}\} \\ S_t &= (1/\Delta_2) \{\alpha_2\gamma v_{1t} + (1 - \alpha_1\gamma) v_{2t} + \alpha_2 v_{3t}\} \end{aligned} \tag{5.3.13}$$

---

[2] Equation (5.3.10) assumes perfect foresight by planners and is not very plausible. More realistic plan adjustment equations are to be found in Portes, Quandt, Winter and Yeo (1984, 1985, 1987).

in the converse case. For internal consistency, the solution values must stand in the same relation to one another as in the condition that defines the regime in question; thus the D_t, S_t in (5.3.12) must obey $D_t < S_t$ and the D_t, S_t in (5.3.13) must obey $D_t > S_t$. Imposing these requirements yields

$$v_{1t}(1 - \alpha_2) + v_{2t}(\alpha_1 - 1) + v_{3t}(\alpha_1 - \alpha_2) < 0 \qquad (5.3.14)$$

for the first regime, and

$$v_{1t}(1 - \alpha_2) + v_{2t}(\alpha_1 - 1) + v_{3t}(\alpha_1 - \alpha_2) > 0 \qquad (5.3.15)$$

in the second, *provided that both determinants are positive*. If both determinants were negative, each of the inequality signs in (5.3.14) and (5.3.15) would be reversed. In both of these situations the two inequalities contradict one another and hence only one of them can hold: thus, a particular set of exogenous variable values and error term realizations can map into only one regime. If the determinants Δ_1 and Δ_2 had opposite signs, the inequalities in (5.3.14) and (5.3.15) would point in the same direction and both inequalities could hold simultaneously; hence a given vector v_t would simultaneously be compatible with both excess demand and supply. The model would thus be seriously internally inconsistent. In other words, "nature" must be able to solve the structural equations in a unique and consistent fashion for the jointly determined variables, otherwise the model does not make sense.

Illustration Based on Transforming Random Variables

We have been arguing that internal consistency requires that the reduced form of the model be unique; for when it is, it is not possible for demand to be simultaneously greater as well as smaller than supply. The equations of the model define the transformation from the error terms, which are random variables, to the endogenous variables of the model. In the present subsection we consider an extremely simple case in which we are given a random variable x with p.d.f. $f(x)$ and a transformation $x = g(y)$, and in which we seek to construct the p.d.f. of the random variable y. Figure 5.4 exhibits the "normal" case when $g(y)$ is one-to-one. Transforming from $f(x)$ to $h(y)$ requires that the probability associated with any Δx (the hatched area in the first quadrant) be equal to the probability associated with the Δy into which this Δx is transformed (the hatched area in the third quadrant). Since the probability in x-space is $f(x)\,dx$, when $x = g(y)$ the probability in y-space is $h(y)\,dy = f[g(y)]g'(y)\,dy$.[3]

In figure 5.5 the function $g(y)$ is many-to-one (or its inverse is one-to-

---

[3] Since $g'(y)$ could be negative, we actually need to take the absolute value $|g'(y)|$. It is plausible geometrically why this Jacobian is needed to obtain $h(y)$: if $g(y)$ is steep, then $g'(y)$ is small, hence a narrow x-interval maps into a wide y-interval; thus to preserve areas, $h(y)$ must be relatively low above the y-axis.

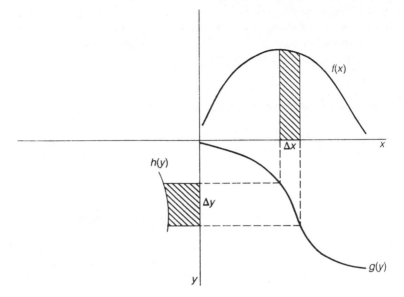

Figure 5.4

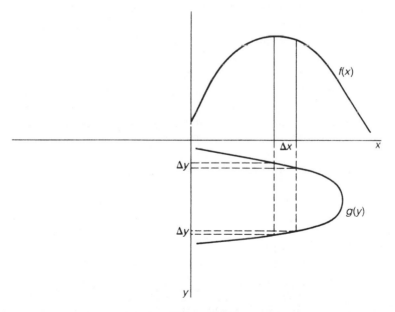

Figure 5.5

many). A given x-interval maps into two y-intervals. There is nothing specified in the model that would tell us how the given probability (area above Δx)
is to be distributed into two subareas over the two Δy intervals; hence there is
no way of constructing $h(y)$.

5.4   Coherency Continued: Simultaneous Models

We now consider some examples in which there is more than one endogenous
variable.

Probit and Tobit Models

The simplest such model is the following (condensed) probit model:

$$y_1^* = \alpha_1 y_2 + u_1 \qquad\qquad (5.4.1)$$

$$y_2 = \alpha_2 y_1 + u_2 \qquad\qquad (5.4.2)$$

$$y_1 = \begin{cases} 1 & \text{if } y^* > 0 \\ 0 & \text{otherwise} \end{cases} \qquad\qquad (5.4.3)$$

If y_1 is interpreted as representing the existence of fair employment laws, y_1^*
the (unobservable) sentiment for labor, and y_2 wages, (5.4.1)–(5.4.3) is a
model of the type introduced by Heckman (1978) and discussed by Schmidt
(1978) and Maddala (1983b). Solving for y_1^* yields

$$y_1^* = \alpha_1 \alpha_2 y_1 + \alpha_1 u_2 + u_1 \qquad\qquad (5.4.4)$$

and internal consistency requires a one-to-one correspondence between y_1
and y_1^*. Thus $y_1 = 1$ requires $\alpha_1 \alpha_2 + \alpha_1 u_2 + u_1 > 0$ and $y_1 = 0$ requires
$\alpha_1 u_2 + u_1 \leq 0$. We can guarantee that these two conditions do not hold
simultaneously if and only if $\alpha_1 \alpha_2 = 0$, which is the appropriate coherency
condition in this case.

   A generalization of the above is a tobit-type model (Amemiya 1974b) in
which

$$y_1^* = \alpha_1 y_2 + u_1 \qquad\qquad (5.4.5)$$

$$y_2 = \alpha_2 y_1 + u_2 \qquad\qquad (5.4.6)$$

$$y_1 = \begin{cases} y_1^* & \text{if } y_1^* > 0 \\ 0 & \text{otherwise} \end{cases} \qquad\qquad (5.4.7)$$

When $y_1 = y_1^* > 0$, we have as a solution

$$y_1^* = \frac{1}{1 - \alpha_1 \alpha_2} (u_1 + \alpha_1 u_2) > 0 \qquad\qquad (5.4.8)$$

and when $y_1^* \leqq 0$ (i.e. $y_1 = 0$),

$$y_1^* = u_1 + \alpha_2 u_2 \leqq 0 \tag{5.4.9}$$

Equations (5.4.8) and (5.4.9) must never hold simultaneously; hence we must require for coherency $1 - \alpha_1\alpha_2 > 0$.

Two-Market Disequilibrium Model

As an illustration, we rewrite the model of (5.2.13) in the following condensed form (see Amemiya 1977 or Gourieroux, Laffont and Monfort 1980b for more details):

$$D_1 = \alpha_1 Q_2 + u_1 \tag{5.4.10}$$

$$S_1 = \alpha_2 Q_2 + u_2 \tag{5.4.11}$$

$$Q_1 = \min(D_1, S_1) \tag{5.4.12}$$

$$D_2 = \beta_1 Q_1 + u_3 \tag{5.4.13}$$

$$S_2 = \beta_2 Q_1 + u_4 \tag{5.4.14}$$

$$Q_2 = \min(D_2, S_2) \tag{5.4.15}$$

In this model we distinguish four cases:

1   $Q_1 = D_1 < S_1$, $Q_2 = D_2 < S_2$
2   $Q_1 = D_1 < S_1$, $Q_2 = S_2 \leqq D_2$
3   $Q_1 = S_1 \leqq D_1$, $Q_2 = D_2 < S_2$
4   $Q_1 = S_1 \leqq D_1$, $Q_2 = S_2 \leqq D_2$

We must make sure that the reduced form is unique; i.e. that the mapping from (D_1, S_1, D_2, S_2) to (u_1, u_2, u_3, u_4) is one-to-one. Consider first case 1. From (5.4.10) and (5.4.13) we have

$$D_1 = \alpha_1 D_2 + u_1$$
$$D_2 = \beta_1 D_1 + u_3$$

whence

$$D_1 = \frac{\alpha_1 u_3 + u_1}{1 - \alpha_1\beta_1} \tag{5.4.16}$$

$$D_2 = \frac{\beta_1 u_1 + u_3}{1 - \alpha_1\beta_1} \tag{5.4.17}$$

Moreover, by the definition of this case, it must be true that $D_1 < S_1$, $D_2 < S_2$, and hence

$$\frac{\alpha_1 u_3 + u_1}{1 - \alpha_1 \beta_1} < \alpha_2 D_2 + u_2 = \alpha_2 \left(\frac{\beta_1 u_1 + u_3}{1 - \alpha_1 \beta_1} \right) + u_2 \qquad (5.4.18)$$

by substituting (5.4.17), and also

$$\frac{\beta_1 u_1 + u_3}{1 - \alpha_1 \beta_1} < \beta_2 D_1 + u_4 = \beta_2 \left(\frac{\alpha_1 u_3 + u_1}{1 - \alpha_1 \beta_1} \right) + u_4 \qquad (5.4.19)$$

The coherency conditions will turn out to be the requirement that $1 - \alpha_i \beta_j$ $(i = 1, 2; j = 1, 2)$ all have the same sign. Let us therefore assume that all $1 - \alpha_i \beta_j$ are positive; an equivalent argument has to be completed for the case that they are all negative. Rearranging (5.4.18) and (5.4.19) we obtain for case 1:

$$\frac{(1 - \alpha_2 \beta_1) u_1}{1 - \alpha_1 \beta_1} + \frac{(\alpha_1 - \alpha_2) u_3}{1 - \alpha_1 \beta_1} < u_2 \qquad (5.4.20)$$

$$\frac{(\beta_1 - \beta_2) u_1}{1 - \alpha_1 \beta_1} + \frac{(1 - \alpha_1 \beta_2) u_3}{1 - \alpha_1 \beta_1} < u_4 \qquad (5.4.21)$$

We now obtain the equivalent results for case 2. In this case

$$D_1 = \alpha_1 S_2 + u_1$$
$$S_2 = \beta_2 D_1 + u_4$$

Solving for D_1, S_2 and substituting in the inequality conditions that define this case, we obtain

$$\frac{(1 - \alpha_2 \beta_2) u_1}{1 - \alpha_1 \beta_2} + \frac{(\alpha_1 - \alpha_2) u_4}{1 - \alpha_1 \beta_2} < u_2 \qquad (5.4.22)$$

and

$$\frac{(1 - \alpha_1 \beta_1) u_4}{1 - \alpha_1 \beta_2} < \frac{(\beta_1 - \beta_2) u_1}{1 - \alpha_1 \beta_2} + u_3$$

which can be rewritten, if $(1 - \alpha_1 \beta_1)/(1 - \alpha_1 \beta_2) > 0$, as

$$\frac{(\beta_1 - \beta_2) u_1}{1 - \alpha_1 \beta_1} + \frac{(1 - \alpha_1 \beta_2) u_3}{1 - \alpha_1 \beta_1} > u_4 \qquad (5.4.23)$$

Obviously $(1 - \alpha_1 \beta_1)/(1 - \alpha_1 \beta_2)$ is positive whether all $1 - \alpha_i \beta_j$ are positive or all are negative. From the result it is clear that (5.4.22) does not contradict (5.4.20) or (5.4.21) since it involves different sets of us. However, (5.4.23) is a direct contradiction of (5.4.21); hence cases 1 and 2 cannot occur simultaneously as required.

A complete treatment of this particular model requires that we examine all four cases and ascertain that the coherency conditions, namely that all $1 - \alpha_i \beta_j$ have the same sign, ensure that no two cases can coexist and that one case will always occur; moreover, that these conditions are necessary as well (see exercise 5.7). This can easily become an arduous task and we shall state general theorems due to Gourieroux, Laffont and Monfort in the next section; this will ease considerably the burden of verifying coherency. For a somewhat different treatment, see Ito (1980).

Bivariate Tobit Model

Consider now the following tobit model in which y_1^*, y_2^* are the latent variables and y_1, y_2 the observed variables, and in which w_1, w_2 represent the composite effect of exogenous variables and error terms. We have

$$y_1^* = \gamma_1 y_2 + w_1$$

$$y_1 = \begin{cases} y_1^* & \text{if } y_1^* > 0 \\ 0 & \text{otherwise} \end{cases}$$

$$y_2^* = \gamma_2 y_1 + w_2$$
$$\qquad\qquad (5.4.24)$$

$$y_2 = \begin{cases} y_2^* & \text{if } y_2^* > 0 \\ 0 & \text{otherwise} \end{cases}$$

There are obviously four cases to distinguish, and these together with the solutions to the endogenous variables are as follows:

Case 1: $y_1 > 0$, $y_2 > 0$

$$\begin{bmatrix} y_1^* \\ y_2^* \end{bmatrix} = \begin{bmatrix} y_1 \\ y_2 \end{bmatrix} = \frac{1}{1 - \gamma_1 \gamma_2} \begin{bmatrix} w_1 + \gamma_1 w_2 \\ \gamma_2 w_1 + w_2 \end{bmatrix} > \begin{bmatrix} 0 \\ 0 \end{bmatrix} \qquad (5.4.25)$$

Case 2: $y_1 > 0$, $y_2 = 0$

$$\begin{aligned} y_1^* &= w_1 & > 0 \\ y_2^* &= \gamma_2 w_1 + w_2 & \leq 0 \end{aligned} \qquad (5.4.26)$$

Case 3: $y_1 = 0$, $y_2 > 0$

$$\begin{aligned} y_1^* &= \gamma_1 w_2 + w_1 & \leq 0 \\ y_2^* &= w_2 & > 0 \end{aligned} \qquad (5.4.27)$$

Case 4: $y_1 = 0$, $y_2 = 0$

$$\begin{aligned} y_1^* &= w_1 & \leq 0 \\ y_2^* &= w_2 & \leq 0 \end{aligned} \qquad (5.4.28)$$

In order to represent the possible solutions geometrically, assume that $\gamma_1 > 0$, $\gamma_2 > 0$, and $1 - \gamma_1 \gamma_2 > 0$. Then the set of w_1, w_2 values corresponding to the four regimes is shown in figure 5.6. Since $1 - \gamma_1 \gamma_2 > 0$, the line $w_2 = -w_1 / \gamma_1$ is steeper than the line $w_2 = -\gamma_2 w_1$.

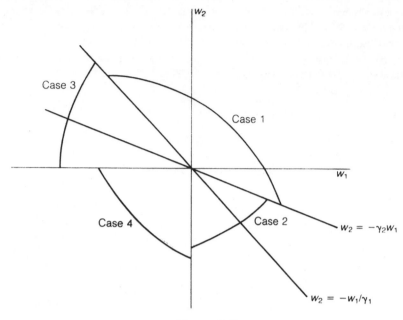

Figure 5.6

The entire space of w_1, w_2 values is partitioned into four nonoverlapping and mutually exhaustive sets. In figure 5.7, on the other hand, we assume that $1 - \gamma_1\gamma_2 < 0$. The relative steepness of the two lines is reversed and the inequalities implied by (5.4.25) are also reversed; hence case 1 overlaps cases 2, 3, and 4, and w_1, w_2 combinations in this region are compatible with two regimes at once, while some w_1, w_2 combinations correspond to no regime at all.

Returning to figure 5.6, we note that the regimes correspond to cones with the four spanning vectors

$$\begin{bmatrix} 1 \\ -\gamma_2 \end{bmatrix}, \begin{bmatrix} -\gamma_1 \\ 1 \end{bmatrix}, \begin{bmatrix} -1 \\ 0 \end{bmatrix}, \begin{bmatrix} 0 \\ -1 \end{bmatrix}$$

arranged in the following particular fashion. Collect the first two vectors in a matrix A,

$$A = \begin{bmatrix} 1 & -\gamma_1 \\ -\gamma_2 & 1 \end{bmatrix}$$

and the last two in a matrix B,

$$B = \begin{bmatrix} -1 & 0 \\ 0 & -1 \end{bmatrix}$$

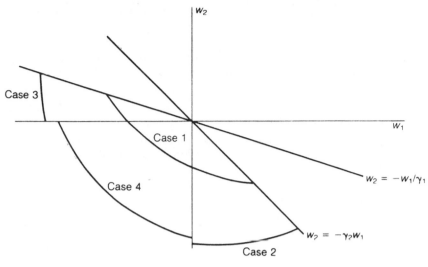

Figure 5.7

The spanning vectors for any particular regime are obtained by choosing exactly two vectors, of which each may be selected from either A or B. Thus there are four spanning matrices, which are

$$
\begin{bmatrix} 1 & -\gamma_1 \\ -\gamma_2 & 1 \end{bmatrix}, \begin{bmatrix} 1 & 0 \\ -\gamma_2 & -1 \end{bmatrix}, \begin{bmatrix} -1 & -\gamma_1 \\ 0 & 1 \end{bmatrix}, \begin{bmatrix} -1 & 0 \\ 0 & -1 \end{bmatrix}
$$

The question is when do the cones given by matrices defined in this fashion provide a partition, i.e. divide up the space into nonoverlapping and mutually exhaustive cones. Samelson, Thrall and Wesler (1958) prove the following theorem. Let the column vectors of two $n \times n$ matrices be represented by $\xi_1, \ldots, \xi_n$ and $\eta_1, \ldots, \eta_n$ respectively. Form the $n \times n$ matrix consisting of columns $\alpha_1, \ldots, \alpha_n$, where α_i is either ξ_i or η_i, and assume every such choice of αs is linearly independent. Then we have the following:

Theorem   The 2^n cones $(\alpha_1, \ldots, \alpha_n)$ partition n-space if and only if the sign of the determinant of the matrix $(\alpha_1, \ldots, \alpha_n)$ is $(-1)^s$, where s is the number of ηs among the αs.[4]

In the present context, the following interpretation is relevant. If P is a nonsingular matrix, then if matrices A and B give a partition, so do PA and PB. (This is obvious if $\det(P) > 0$, for then, if A is partitioned (A_1, A_2) and B is partitioned (B_1, B_2), the sign of $\det(PA_1, PB_2)$ is the same as that of

---

[4] An alternative necessary and sufficient condition is that for every choice of $n-1$ αs the ξ- and η-vectors corresponding to the omitted index are on opposite sides of the hyperplane defined by the $n-1$ αs in question.

$\det(A_1, B_2)$. If $\det(P) < 0$, the signs change, but a partition still occurs.) If A and B give a partition (and the vectors of B play the role of the ηs of the theorem), then $(-1)^n \det(B) > 0$, $\det(-B) > 0$ and $\det(-B^{-1}) > 0$. Defining $P = -B^{-1}$ and $C = -B^{-1}A$, it follows that C and $-I$ give a partition. Now construct the matrix D by replacing h of the columns of C by the corresponding column of $-I$. If C_h is the principal submatrix of C, obtained by striking out from C those h columns and corresponding rows, $\det(D) = (-1)^h \det(C_h)$; but by the theorem, the sign of $\det(D)$ is $(-1)^h$. Hence $\det(C_h)$ must be positive. It follows that A and B give a partition if and only if all the principal minors of C are positive. In the present case,

$$-B^{-1}A = \begin{bmatrix} 1 & -\gamma_1 \\ -\gamma_2 & 1 \end{bmatrix}$$

and the requirement boils down to $1 - \gamma_1\gamma_2 > 0$.

5.5   Uniqueness of the Solution and Ito's Contraction Mapping

An alternative way of looking at these questions is to ask how one would compute the observed transacted quantities if one were given a particular disequilibrium or simultaneous probit or tobit model. Assume, for example, that one wishes to conduct Monte Carlo experiments. We might be given (5.4.10)–(5.4.15), and we know how to generate normally distributed errors $u_1, \ldots, u_4$; but how do we determine Q_1 and Q_2? The natural suggestion would be to iterate on these equations: assume some arbitrary starting values for Q_1 and Q_2; use the equations to compute new Q_1 and Q_2 values; substitute these on the right hand side of the equations and compute new Q_1, Q_2 values; and generally proceed likewise until convergence occurs. The key question, of course, is under what circumstances convergence will occur. In figure 5.8 we show the equations (5.4.5) and (5.4.6). We start iterating by using assumed values $y_1 = y_2 = 0$. Then $y_1^* = u_1$ and $y_2 = u_2$ at the end of this iteration; the lines have been drawn on the assumption $u_1 < 0$ and $u_2 > 0$. Under the regime definitions, $y_1 = 0$, $y_2 = u_2$ and the first iteration carries us to point A. Substituting the corresponding y_1, y_2 values carries us to point B, and repeating the procedure takes us ultimately to C. It is easy to see that the relative position of the two lines gives $\alpha_2 < 1/\alpha_1$, which we previously found to be the appropriate coherency condition. In figure 5.9 we depict the disequilibrium model (5.4.10)–(5.4.15). The four lines are identified by their slopes; thus the line marked by $1/\beta_1$ identifies (5.4.13) and so on. Again assuming starting values of zero (for Q_1 and Q_2), we start at the origin and iteration carries us to point A, then to point B, and ultimately to the solution C. The lines are drawn on the assumption that $1/\beta_2 > 1/\beta_1 > \alpha_1 > \alpha_2$, which clearly implies the coherency conditions discussed earlier. It is straight-

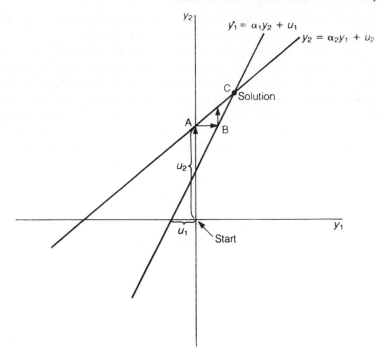

Figure 5.8

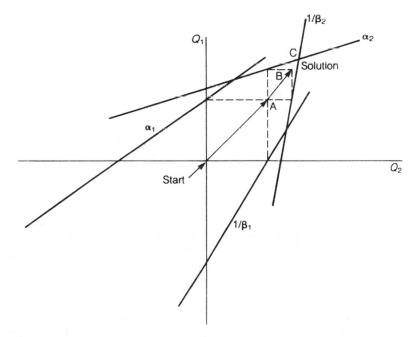

Figure 5.9

forward to verify that violations of coherency conditions lead to divergence in the hypothetical iterations (see exercises 5.8 and 5.9).

Ito (1980) provides a general theorem for the convergence of such a process; the conditions are stronger than those for the general coherency conditions discussed so far and stronger than those required for the theorems of the next section. The Ito theorem is of interest, however, for it speaks directly to the iterative process discussed above and is applied by Ito to a general model with $n + 1$ markets, where one may think of the first n as commodity markets and the last one as a labor market. The model is

$$D_i = \tilde{D}_i + \sum_{j=1}^{n} \gamma_{ij}^{d}(Q_j - \tilde{D}_j) + \alpha_i^{d}(Q_{n+1} - \tilde{S}_{n+1}) \qquad i = 1, \ldots, n$$

$$(5.5.1)$$

$$S_i = \tilde{S}_i + \sum_{j=1}^{n} \gamma_{ij}^{s}(Q_j - \tilde{S}_j) + \alpha_i^{s}(Q_{n+1} - \tilde{D}_{n+1}) \qquad i = 1, \ldots, n$$

$$(5.5.2)$$

$$Q_i = \min(D_i, S_i) \qquad\qquad\qquad\qquad\qquad i = 1, \ldots, n$$

$$(5.5.3)$$

$$D_{n+1} = \tilde{D}_{n+1} + \sum_{j=1}^{n} \beta_j^{d}(Q_j - \tilde{S}_j) \qquad\qquad (5.5.4)$$

$$S_{n+1} = \tilde{S}_{n+1} + \sum_{j=1}^{n} \beta_j^{s}(Q_j - \tilde{D}_j) \qquad\qquad (5.5.5)$$

$$Q_{n+1} = \min(D_{n+1}, S_{n+1}) \qquad\qquad (5.5.6)$$

Commodity markets experience spillovers from other commodity markets (hence $\gamma_{ii}^{d} = \gamma_{ii}^{s} = 0$) and from the labor market; the latter, in turn, experiences spillovers from all the commodity markets. In general, γ_{ij}^{d} is negative if i and j are substitutes. If good j and leisure are substitutes, β_j^{s} and α_j^{d} are positive. Finally, β_j^{d} and α_i^{s} are positive, and if marginal costs are increasing, the γ_{ij}^{s} are negative. Ito further assumes that

$$-\sum_{i=1}^{n} \gamma_{ij}^{d} + \beta_j^{s} < 1 \qquad j = 1, \ldots, n$$

$$-\sum_{i=1}^{n} \gamma_{ij}^{s} + \beta_j^{d} < 1 \qquad j = 1, \ldots, n$$

$$(5.5.7)$$

$$\sum_{i=1}^{n} \alpha_i^{d} < 1$$

$$\sum_{i=1}^{n} \alpha_i^{s} < 1$$

which says, in effect, that the sum of the effects of a given "frustration" should not exceed the value of that frustration. In order to prove uniqueness, however, Ito assumes the stronger conditions

$$0 \leq \sum_{i=1}^{n} \max(|\gamma_{ij}^{d}|, |\gamma_{ij}^{s}|) + \max(|\beta_{j}^{d}|, |\beta_{j}^{s}|) < 1 \qquad \text{for all } j$$

(5.5.8)

$$0 \leq \sum_{i=1}^{n} \max(|\alpha_{i}^{d}|, |\alpha_{i}^{s}|) < 1$$

Ito's proof is based on the following proposition (Luenberger 1969). First, for any two elements x and $y \in R^n$, define the distance function $d(x,y)$ by the properties (a) $d(x,y) \geq 0$; (b) $d(x,y) = d(y,x)$; (c) $d(x,y) = 0$ if and only if $x = y$, and (d) for any three elements x, y, z, $d(x,y) \leq d(x,z) + d(z,y)$. A function $f:R^n \rightarrow R^n$, with the property that for any two elements x, y it is true that $d[f(x), f(y)] < d(x,y)$, is called a contraction mapping. Then we have:

Proposition   Let f be a contraction mapping on R^n. Then there exists a unique fixed point x^0, i.e. $x^0 = f(x^0)$, with the property that $x^0 = \lim_{t \to \infty} x_t$, where $x_t = f(x_{t-1})$.

We now apply this proposition to (5.5.1)–(5.5.6). Define

$$Q = (Q_1, Q_2, \ldots, Q_n, Q_{n+1})$$

and the mapping f by

$$f(Q) = [f_1(Q), f_2(Q), \ldots, f_n(Q), f_{n+1}(Q)]$$

where

$$f_i(Q) = \min[D_i(Q), S_i(Q)] \qquad i = 1, \ldots, n+1 \tag{5.5.9}$$

and consider the metric $d(Q, Q^*)$ given by

$$d(Q, Q^*) = \sum_{i=1}^{n+1} |Q_i - Q_i^*|$$

We note that for any four numbers x_1, x_2, y_1, y_2 it is true that $|\min(x_1, x_2) - \min(y_1, y_2)| \leq \max(|x_1 - y_1|, |x_2 - y_2|)$ (see exercise 5.10). Then we can write the distance between $f(Q)$ and $f(Q^*)$ as follows:

$$d[f(Q), f(Q^*)] = \sum_{i=1}^{n+1} |f_i(Q) - f_i(Q^*)|$$

$$= \sum_{i=1}^{n+1} |\min[D_i(Q), S_i(Q)] - \min[D_i(Q^*), S_i(Q^*)]|$$

$$\leq \sum_{i=1}^{n+1} \max[\,|D_i(Q) - D_i(Q^*)|, |S_i(Q) - S_i(Q^*)|\,]$$

$$(5.5.10)$$

by applying the result of exercise 5.10. We now substitute in (5.5.10) from the appropriate equations in (5.5.1)–(5.5.6). This yields

$$d[f(Q), f(Q^*)]$$

$$\leq \sum_{i=1}^{n} \max\left[\left|\sum_{j=1}^{n} \gamma_{ij}^{d}(Q_j - Q_j^*) + \alpha_i^{d}(Q_{n+1} - Q_{n+1}^*)\right|, \right.$$

$$\left.\left|\sum_{j=1}^{n} \gamma_{ij}^{s}(Q_j - Q_j^*) + \alpha_i^{s}(Q_{n+1} - Q_{n+1}^*)\right|\right]$$

$$+ \max\left[\left|\sum_{j=1}^{n} \beta_j^{d}(Q_j - Q_j^*)\right|, \left|\sum_{j=1}^{n} \beta_j^{s}(Q_j - Q_j^*)\right|\right]$$

$$\leq \sum_{i=1}^{n} \max\left[\left|\sum_{j=1}^{n} \gamma_{ij}^{d}\right| |Q_j - Q_j^*| + |\alpha_i^{d}| |Q_{n+1} - Q_{n+1}^*|, \right.$$

$$\left.\left|\sum_{j=1}^{n} \gamma_{ij}^{s}\right| |Q_j - Q_j^*| + |\alpha_i^{s}| |Q_{n+1} - Q_{n+1}^*|\right]$$

$$+ \max\left[\left|\sum_{j=1}^{n} \beta_j^{d}\right| |Q_j - Q_j^*|, \left|\sum_{j=1}^{n} \beta_j^{s}\right| |Q_j - Q_j^*|\right]$$

$$\leq \sum_{i=1}^{n} \sum_{j=1}^{n} \max(|\gamma_{ij}^{d}|, |\gamma_{ij}^{s}|)|Q_j - Q_j^*|$$

$$+ \sum_{i=1}^{n} \max(|\alpha_i^{d}|, |\alpha_i^{s}|)|Q_{n+1} - Q_{n+1}^*|$$

$$+ \sum_{j=1}^{n} \max(|\beta_j^{d}|, |\beta_j^{s}|)|Q_j - Q_j^*|$$

$$= \sum_{j=1}^{n} \left\{\sum_{i=1}^{n} \max(|\gamma_{ij}^{d}|, |\gamma_{ij}^{s}|) + \max(|\beta_j^{d}|, |\beta_j^{s}|)\right\} |Q_j - Q_j^*|$$

$$+ \sum_{j=1}^{n} \max(|\alpha_i^{d}|, |\alpha_i^{s}|)|Q_{n+1} - Q_{n+1}^*|$$

$$< \sum_{j=1}^{n+1} |Q_j - Q_j^*|$$

$$(5.5.11)$$

where the last inequality follows from condition (5.5.8). Expression (5.5.11) proves that f is a contraction mapping; hence a unique fixed point exists.

Applying the Ito conditions to the simple two-market model consisting of (5.4.10)–(5.4.15) yields the requirements $0 \leq \alpha_1 < 1, 0 \leq \alpha_2 < 1, 0 \leq \beta_1 < 1, 0 \leq \beta_2 < 1$, which are clearly sufficient for coherency but are not necessary.

5.6   Necessary and Sufficient Conditions for Coherency

In order to state necessary and sufficient conditions in compact form, we return once again to the model given by (5.4.10)–(5.4.15). Four cases are distinguished, and for each of the four there is a mapping from the latent dependent variable vector $y'_t = (D_{1t}, S_{1t}, D_{2t}, S_{2t})$ to the vector of disturbances $u'_t = (u_{1t}, u_{2t}, u_{3t}, u_{4t})$ (where we recall that the present convention is to include the effect of exogenous variables in the us). If A_i denotes the matrix of coefficients, we can write the ith regime, as in (5.2.16), as

$$A_i y_t = u_t \qquad i = 1, \ldots, 4 \tag{5.6.1}$$

and the mapping over the union of regimes can be written as

$$f = \sum_{i=1}^{4} A_i I(i)$$

where $I(i)$ is the indicator function, which has a value of unity if y_t falls into the cone associated with the ith regime and zero otherwise. We require for coherency that the mapping f be (a) one-to-one and (b) onto. The first condition implies that distinct y_ts map into distinct u_ts. The second implies that there are no u_ts that are not the image of some y_t. The mapping is then invertible. Gourieroux, Laffont and Monfort (1980b) prove the following theorems:

Theorem 1   If $f = \Sigma_i A_i I(i)$, where the A_i are each invertible, is continuous, a necessary and sufficient condition for invertibility is that the determinants of all A_i matrices have the same sign.

Consider again a two-market case and let the appropriate cones be given by $C_1 = \{D_1 > S_1, D_2 > S_2\}$, $C_2 = \{D_1 > S_1, D_2 < S_2\}$, $C_3 = \{D_1 < S_1, D_2 < S_2\}$, $C_4 = \{D_1 < S_1, D_2 > S_2\}$. Denote the closures of the cones by $\overline{C}_i$. Then we have:

Theorem 2   If (a) $A_i = A_{i+1}$ on $\{D_1 = S_1, D_2 = S_2\}$ for $i = 1, \ldots, 4$ and (b) $A_i(\overline{C}_i \cap \overline{C}_{i+1}) = A_{i+1}(\overline{C}_i \cap \overline{C}_{i+1})$ for $i = 1, \ldots, 4$, then f is invertible if and only if the determinants of all A_i matrices have the same sign.

The second theorem requires that all A_i coincide on the subspace $\{D_1 = S_1,$

$D_2 = S_2$} and that on the common boundary between two cones the mappings applicable to those cones coincide.

An example of the applicability of theorem 1 is given by the disequilibrium model with a nonstochastic price adjustment equation but different speeds of adjustment γ_1, γ_2 for cases of excess demand and excess supply (Laffont and Monfort 1976; Gourieroux, Laffont and Monfort 1980b). Thus

$$D_t = \alpha_1 p_t + \beta_1' x_{1t} + u_{1t}$$

$$S_t = \alpha_2 p_t + \beta_2' x_{2t} + u_{2t}$$

$$p_t = p_{t-1} + \gamma_1(D_t - S_t) \qquad \text{if } D_t \geq S_t$$

$$p_t = p_{t-1} + \gamma_2(D_t - S_t) \qquad \text{otherwise}$$

$$Q_t = \min(D_t, S_t)$$

Substituting from the two adjustment equations in demand and supply, we obtain the two systems

$$\begin{bmatrix} 1-\alpha_1\gamma_1 & \alpha_1\gamma_1 \\ -\alpha_2\gamma_1 & 1+\alpha_2\gamma_1 \end{bmatrix} \begin{bmatrix} D_t \\ S_t \end{bmatrix} = \begin{bmatrix} \alpha_1 p_{t-1}+\beta_1' x_{1t}+u_{1t} \\ \alpha_2 p_{t-1}+\beta_2' x_{2t}+u_{2t} \end{bmatrix} \tag{5.6.2}$$

and

$$\begin{bmatrix} 1-\alpha_1\gamma_2 & \alpha_1\gamma_2 \\ -\alpha_2\gamma_2 & 1+\alpha_2\gamma_2 \end{bmatrix} \begin{bmatrix} D_t \\ S_t \end{bmatrix} = \begin{bmatrix} \alpha_1 p_{t-1}+\beta_1' x_{1t}+u_{1t} \\ \alpha_2 p_{t-1}+\beta_2' x_{2t}+u_{2t} \end{bmatrix} \tag{5.6.3}$$

Denoting the matrices on the left in (5.6.2) and (5.6.3) by A_1 and A_2, it is clear that the mappings under A_1 and A_2 on the boundary $D_t = S_t$ coincide. If $\gamma_1 \gamma_2 > 0$, $\alpha_1 < 0$, $\alpha_2 > 0$, as would be normally expected, the matrices A_1, A_2 are invertible and the mapping $A_1 I(1) + A_2 I(2)$ is continuous; hence the model is coherent if the determinants $1 + \gamma_1(\alpha_2 - \alpha_1)$ and $1 + \gamma_2(\alpha_2 - \alpha_1)$ have the same sign, as will be the case under the sign restrictions above.

Models that fall under theorem 1 are the two-market disequilibrium model given by (5.4.10)–(5.4.15), the harvest model given by (5.3.1)–(5.3.4), and the tobit model of (5.4.24) (see exercise 5.11).

An application of theorem 2 is the case of the model due to Gourieroux, Laffont and Monfort (1980a). They posit that the demand (supply) of an agent in market i is the unconstrained (Walrasian) demand (supply) if the agent is not constrained in market j. The effective demands and supplies are given by (5.4.10), (5.4.11), (5.4.13), and (5.4.14). Recall that if the constraint in market i is set at the level of the Walrasian solution, we obtain the Walrasian demand (supply) for market j. Hence the Walrasian demands and supplies satisfy the system, and we have

$$\tilde{D}_1 = \alpha_1 \tilde{S}_2 + u_1$$

$$\tilde{S}_1 = \alpha_2 \tilde{D}_2 + u_2$$

$$(5.6.4)$$

$$\tilde{D}_2 = \beta_1 \tilde{S}_1 + u_3$$

$$\tilde{S}_2 = \beta_2 \tilde{D}_1 + u_4$$

from which we can easily obtain the solutions for the Walrasian quantities. Now consider the four regimes:

Case 1: $D_1 < S_1$, $D_2 < S_2$. Then consumers are not constrained in product markets and firms are not constrained in labor markets. Hence consumers' labor supply and firms' product supply is Walrasian (i.e. the solution from (5.6.4)) and the remaining demand and supply are the effective demand and supply. Thus

$$D_1 = \alpha_1 D_2 + u_1$$

$$S_1 = (u_2 + \alpha_2 u_3)/(1 - \alpha_2 \beta_1)$$

$$D_2 = \beta_1 D_1 + u_3$$ $$(5.6.5)$$

$$S_2 = (u_4 + \beta_2 u_1)/(1 - \alpha_1 \beta_2)$$

To write this in more standard form, we define $y_t = (D_{1t}, S_{1t}, D_{2t}, S_{2t})$, $u_t = (u_{1t}, u_{2t}, u_{3t}, u_{4t})$. We wish to write (5.6.5) as $A_1 y_t = u_t$, where

$$A_1 = \begin{bmatrix} 1 & 0 & -\alpha_1 & 0 \\ \alpha_2 \beta_1 & 1 - \alpha_2 \beta_1 & -\alpha_2 & 0 \\ -\beta_1 & 0 & 1 & 0 \\ -\beta_2 & 0 & \alpha_1 \beta_2 & 1 - \alpha_1 \beta_2 \end{bmatrix}$$

which has a determinant of $(1 - \alpha_1 \beta_2)(1 - \alpha_2 \beta_1)(1 - \alpha_1 \beta_1)$.

Case 2: $D_1 < S_1$ and $S_2 < D_2$. Proceeding likewise, we find that A_2 is

$$A_2 = \begin{bmatrix} 1 & 0 & 0 & -\alpha_1 \\ 0 & 1 & 0 & -\alpha_2 \\ -\beta_1 & 0 & 1 & 0 \\ -\beta_2 & 0 & 0 & 1 \end{bmatrix}$$

with determinant $1 - \alpha_1 \beta_2$.

Case 3: $S_1 < D_1$ and $D_2 < S_2$. Then

$$A_3 = \begin{bmatrix} 1 & 0 & -\alpha_1 & 0 \\ 0 & 1 & -\alpha_2 & 0 \\ 0 & -\beta_1 & 1 & 0 \\ 0 & -\beta_2 & 0 & 1 \end{bmatrix}$$

and the determinant is $1 - \alpha_2 \beta_1$.

Case 4: $S_1 < D_1$, $S_2 < D_2$. We have

$$
A_4 = \begin{bmatrix}
1 - \alpha_1\beta_2 & \alpha_1\beta_2 & 0 & -\alpha_1 \\
0 & 1 & 0 & -\alpha_2 \\
0 & -\beta_1 & 1 - \alpha_2\beta_1 & \alpha_2\beta_1 \\
0 & -\beta_2 & 0 & 1
\end{bmatrix}
$$

with determinant $(1 - \alpha_1\beta_2)(1 - \alpha_2\beta_1)(1 - \alpha_2\beta_2)$.

All four determinants will have the same sign if and only if $1 - \alpha_1\beta_1$, $1 - \alpha_1\beta_2$, $1 - \alpha_2\beta_1$, $1 - \alpha_2\beta_2$ all have the same sign. To insure that the mappings coincide on the relevant facets of the cones, it is required that $1 - \alpha_1\beta_2$ and $1 - \alpha_2\beta_1$ be positive.

Interpretation of the Coherency Conditions

Dynamics can be introduced into disequilibrium models by stipulating some appropriate quantity adjustment mechanism. Since in the two-market case there are, in general, four regimes, the quantity adjustment will have one of four different forms. Consider regime 1, the case of Keynesian unemployment. In this case we could write

$$
\begin{aligned}
\dot{Q}_1 &= f_1(S_1 - Q_1) \\
\dot{Q}_2 &= f_2(S_2 - Q_2)
\end{aligned}
\tag{5.6.6}
$$

where f_1 and f_2 are two monotone increasing functions and where $f_1(0) = f_2(0) = 0$. The rationale for (5.6.6) is that the more the effective supply in each market exceeds the transacted quantity, the more prices will tend to fall in that market and the more the transacted quantity in that market will rise. Substituting for S_1 and S_2 from (5.4.11) and (5.4.13),

$$
\begin{aligned}
\dot{Q}_1 &= f_1(\alpha_2 Q_2 + u_2 - Q_1) \\
\dot{Q}_2 &= f_2(\beta_2 Q_1 + u_4 - Q_2)
\end{aligned}
\tag{5.6.7}
$$

Linearizing (5.6.7) about some point (Q_1^0, Q_2^0) yields

$$
\begin{bmatrix} \dot{Q}_1 \\ \dot{Q}_2 \end{bmatrix} = \begin{bmatrix} f_1(\alpha_2 Q_2^0 + u_2 - Q_1^0) \\ f_2(\beta_2 Q_1^0 + u_4 - Q_2^0) \end{bmatrix} + \begin{bmatrix} -f_1' & f_1'\alpha_2 \\ f_2'\beta_2 & -f_2' \end{bmatrix} \begin{bmatrix} Q_1 - Q_1^0 \\ Q_2 - Q_2^0 \end{bmatrix}
\tag{5.6.8}
$$

System (5.6.8) will be locally stable if the eigenvalues of the matrix on the right hand side have negative real parts. The eigenvalues are the solutions to

$$
(-f_1' - \lambda)(-f_2' - \lambda) - f_1'f_2'\alpha_2\beta_2 = 0
$$

or

$$
\lambda^2 + (f_1' + f_2')\lambda + f_1'f_2'(1 - \alpha_2\beta_2) = 0
$$

If α_2, β_2 are positive, the roots are real. Since f_1', f_2' are positive by the assumptions about the dynamic process, the sum of the roots, $-f_1' - f_2'$, is negative. Both roots are negative if their product, $f_1'f_2'(1 - \alpha_2\beta_2)$, is positive, as is the case if $1 > \alpha_2\beta_2$. Similar inequalities ensure the stability of the process in the other regimes; hence coherency implies local stability and conversely. (See also exercise 5.12.)

Coherency in Nonlinear Models

In models in which there are nonlinearities beyond those due to the min condition, there are no simple theorems with which the presence of coherency can be established. But not only is it generally much harder to analyze the question of coherency in these cases, but coherency is not likely to be present in most of these. We consider a simple example (Quandt 1982a) that illustrates the point.

We consider a single market in which consumers are subject to "discouragement" in the sense that greater proportionate rationing reduces their effective supply. (However, the particular model is suggested not for its verisimilitude but to illustrate a point). We posit

$$D = \gamma(D-Q)/Q + u_1$$
$$S = u_2 \qquad\qquad (5.6.9)$$
$$Q = \min(D,S)$$

where, as in earlier examples, u_1 and u_2 are shorthand for the effect of all exogenous variables and error terms. There are two cases to distinguish:

Case 1: $D \leq S$. In this case $D = u_1$ and $S = u_2$, and thus case 1 is obtained if $u_1 \leqq u_2$.

Case 2: $D > S$. Then

$$D = \gamma(D-S)/S + u_1$$
$$S = u_2 \qquad\qquad (5.6.10)$$

We can write the first equation of (5.6.10) as

$$Du_2 - \gamma D + \gamma u_2 = u_1 u_2$$

or

$$D = \frac{u_1 u_2 - \gamma u_2}{u_2 - \gamma} \qquad\qquad (5.6.11)$$

which is how the random variable D is generated (since u_2 may be very close to γ, D will be very large numerically with some probability). Coherency requires that one and only one regime be implied, and hence that

$$u_1 \leq u_2 \qquad \text{if and only if } \frac{u_1 u_2 - \gamma u_2}{u_2 - \gamma} \leq u_2$$

(For if $u_1 \leq u_2$, we would infer by case 1 that $D \leq S$ and if, at the same time, $(u_1 u_2 - \gamma u_2)/(u_2 - \gamma) > u_2$, we would infer from case 2 that $D > S$.) Now, there are two subcases:

Case 2(a): $u_2 - \gamma > 0$. Then the required inequality is $u_1 u_2 - \gamma u_2 \leq u_2(u_2 - \gamma)$, or $u_1 u_2 \leq u_2^2$. If further $u_2 > 0$, then the required inequality holds. However, if $u_2 < 0$, it does not. (The economically plausible case is $\gamma < 0$; hence $u_2 - \gamma > 0$ does not allow us to infer the sign of u_2.)

Case 2(b): $u_2 - \gamma < 0$. Then $u_1 u_2 - \gamma u_2 > u_2(u_2 - \gamma)$, $u_1 u_2 > u_2^2$. Since γ is plausibly negative, in this case u_2 must be negative and $u_1 < u_2$. Hence in this case the required inequality holds.

Overall, coherency does not obtain in this model because of case 2(a). The only way one could eliminate case 2(a) is by imposing a fairly unattractive restriction on the distribution of the random variable u_2.

Consider, finally, a nonlinear tobit model as follows:

$$y_1^* = \alpha_1 y_2 + u_1 \tag{5.6.12}$$

$$y_2 = e^{\alpha_2 y_1} + u_2 \tag{5.6.13}$$

$$y_1 = \begin{cases} y_1^* & \text{if } y_1^* > 0 \\ 0 & \text{otherwise} \end{cases} \tag{5.6.14}$$

which is the same as (5.4.4) to (5.4.6) except for the second equation. Assume that $\alpha_1 > 0$ and $\alpha_2 < 0$. We then have the following two cases:

Case 1: $y_1 = y_1^* > 0$. Then

$$y_1^* = \alpha_1 e^{\alpha_2 y_1^*} + \alpha_1 u_2 + u_1$$

This has a positive solution for y_1^* if and only if $\alpha_1 + \alpha_1 u_2 + u_1 > 0$.

Case 2: $y_1 = 0$ and $y_1^* < 0$. Then

$$y_1^* = \alpha_1 + \alpha_1 u_2 + u_1 < 0.$$

Hence, the sign of $\alpha_1 + \alpha_1 u_2 + u_1$ uniquely determines which regime is at hand. However, the situation is quite different if α_2 is positive or if the term $e^{\alpha_2 y_1}$ is replaced by different functions of y_1 (see exercise 5.13).

Exercises

5.1   Construct a simple case for a consumer in which the Clower demands violate his budget constraint.

5.2   Express (5.2.9) approximately with a linear spillover term.

5.3   Verify that (5.2.13), (5.2.14), and (5.2.15) yield pairwise identical solutions in all regimes.

5.4   Derive from (5.2.13), (5.2.14), and (5.2.15) the values of the (effective) excess demands.

5.5   Prove (5.2.23).

5.6   Show diagrammatically that if (5.3.2) and (5.3.3) are both negatively sloped but the demand equation is steeper than the harvest equation, no contradiction arises.

5.7   Complete the coherency argument for the model given by (5.4.10)–(5.4.15).

5.8   Construct diagrams analogous to figures 5.8 and 5.9 in which the coherency conditions are violated.

5.9   Construct diagrams analogous to figures 5.8 and 5.9 for the probit model given by (5.4.1)–(5.4.3) for the cases in which the coherency condition is and is not satisfied respectively. Show, in particular, that divergence occurs if it is not satisfied.

5.10 Prove that for any four numbers x_1, x_2, y_1, y_2 it is true that $|\min(x_1,x_2) - \min(y_1,y_2)| \leq \max(|x_1-y_1|, |x_2-y_2|)$.

5.11 Prove that theorem 1 of section 5.6 is applicable to the models given by (a) (5.4.10)–(5.4.15); (b) (5.3.1)–(5.3.4); (c) (5.4.24).

5.12 What is the dynamic process the stability of which implies the coherency of the model given in (5.3.1)–(5.3.4)?

5.13 Analyze the coherency of the model in (5.6.12)–(5.6.14) when the term $e^{\alpha_2 y_1}$ in (5.6.13) is replaced by (a) $\alpha_2 y_1^2$; (b) α_2/y_1.

6

Estimation in Multimarket Models

6.1 Introduction

In the present chapter we examine maximum likelihood estimation in latent variable models in which there is more than one latent variable. In the previous chapter we examined the question of coherency for probit, tobit, and disequilibrium models; we now take the same types of models and derive their likelihood functions. These will generally be more complicated than the corresponding functions for univariate models and computation of the estimates will generally be harder and costlier. The principal reason for these difficulties will be seen to be the fact that the likelihood function for many of the models contains multiple integrals of density functions.

In section 6.2 we discuss estimation in the discrete choice model and in the standard probit, tobit, and logit models. Disequilibrium models are considered in section 6.3. The likelihood functions of most of these models require multiple integration of density functions and for this reason we develop some of the fundamental principles of numerical integration in section 6.4. Section 6.5 is devoted to the analysis of disequilibrium models in the case of a particular nonnormal error density. Section 6.6 deals with the anticipatory pricing model of Green and Laffont (1981) which is an interesting extension of more standard multimarket models.

6.2 Discrete Choice, Probit, Logit, and Tobit Models

Consider a situation in which utility maximizing consumers choose among m discrete alternatives. We assume that the utility that the ith consumer derives from the jth alternative depends on some observable variables x_{ij} characterizing the ith individual and jth alternative, on some unknown parameters and on some additive errors. We can thus write

$$U_{ij} = V(x_{ij}, \beta) + \epsilon_{ij} \qquad (6.2.1)$$

or, denoting $V(x_{ij}, \beta)$ for brevity by V_{ij}, $U_{ij} = V_{ij} + \epsilon_{ij}$. The probability that the kth alternative is chosen can be written as

$$P_{ik} = \Pr\{V_{ij} + \epsilon_{ij} \leq V_{ik} + \epsilon_{ik} \quad \forall\, j \neq k\}$$

$$= \Pr\{\epsilon_{ij} \leq V_{ik} - V_{ij} + \epsilon_{ik} \quad \forall\, j \neq k\}$$

$$= \int_{-\infty}^{\infty} \left[\int_{-\infty}^{V_{ik}-V_{i1}+\epsilon_{ik}} \cdots \int_{-\infty}^{V_{ik}-V_{im}+\epsilon_{ik}} g(\epsilon_{i1}, \ldots, \epsilon_{im}) d\epsilon_{im} \cdots d\epsilon_{i1} \right] d\epsilon_{ik}$$

$$(6.2.2)$$

where $g(\epsilon_{i1}, \ldots, \epsilon_{im})$ is the joint p.d.f. of the ϵ_{ij} disturbances. Alternatively, defining the $m-1$ random variables $\delta_{ijk} = \epsilon_{ij} - \epsilon_{ik}, j \neq k$, letting δ denote the vector $(\delta_{ij1}, \ldots, \delta_{ijm})$, and letting $h(\delta)$ be the joint density of the δs, we also have

$$P_{ik} = \Pr\{V_{ik} - V_{ij} \geq \epsilon_{ij} - \epsilon_{ik} \quad \forall\, j \neq k\}$$

$$= \int_{-\infty}^{V_{ik}-V_{i1}} \cdots \int_{-\infty}^{V_{ik}-V_{im}} h(\delta) d\delta_{ijm} \cdots d\delta_{ij1} \qquad (6.2.3)$$

In the particular case in which the nonrandom part of utility is linear, as in

$$U_{ij} = \beta' x_{ij} + \epsilon_{ij} \qquad (6.2.4)$$

we may replace V_{ij} in the above formulas by $\beta' x_{ij}$.

The joint probability that n individuals each choose a particular alternative is the likelihood, which is easily seen to be

$$L = \prod_{i=1}^{n} P_{i1}^{y_{i1}} \cdots P_{im}^{y_{im}} \qquad (6.2.5)$$

where $y_{ij} = 1$ if the ith individual chooses alternative j and $= 0$ otherwise.

In general, the evaluation of the probabilities in (6.2.5) is difficult, since the multiple integral in (6.2.4) may well have to be evaluated numerically. This is the case if, for example, $h(\delta)$ is a joint normal density.[1] In this particular case, the model is known as the multinomial probit model.

An enormous simplification due to McFadden (1973; see also Domencich and McFadden 1975 for an interesting application) is the conditional logit model, in which it is assumed that the errors ϵ are identically and independently distributed with extreme value (Weibull) distribution. Accordingly, suppressing the index i that indexes individuals,

---

[1] If there are 1000 individuals in the sample and four alternatives, every evaluation of the likelihood function requires the evaluation of 1000 triple integrals. If an iterative algorithm requires as many as 1000 evaluations of the likelihood function, the number of integral evaluations may be already very costly. If a Newton-type algorithm is used in which both first and second partial derivatives with respect to β are required and if these are obtained by numerical differencing, the computational burden may become prohibitive. See, for example, Hausman and Wise (1978), Maddala (1983b).

$$\Pr\{\epsilon_j < \epsilon\} = F(\epsilon) = \exp(-e^{-\epsilon}) \tag{6.2.6}$$

which has p.d.f.

$$f(\epsilon_j) = \exp\{-\epsilon_j - e^{-\epsilon_j}\} \tag{6.2.7}$$

Rewriting (6.2.3) only slightly, the probability that the kth alternative is selected is, by the i.i.d. assumption,

$$P_k = \Pr\{\epsilon_j < \epsilon_k + \beta'x_k - \beta'x_j\} \qquad \text{for all } j \neq k$$

which can be written

$$P_k = \int_{-\infty}^{\infty} \prod_{j \neq k} F(\epsilon_k + \beta'x_k - \beta'x_j) f(\epsilon_k) d\epsilon_k$$

The integrand then is

$$\prod_{j \neq k} [\exp\{-e^{-\epsilon_k - \beta'x_k + \beta'x_j}\} \exp\{-\epsilon_k - e^{-\epsilon_k}\}]$$

$$= \exp\left\{-\epsilon_k - e^{-\epsilon_k}\left(1 + \sum_{j \neq k} e^{\beta'x_j}/e^{\beta'x_k}\right)\right\} \tag{6.2.8}$$

Now let

$$\log\left(1 + \sum_{j \neq k} e^{\beta'x_j}/e^{\beta'x_k}\right) = \log\left(\sum_{j=1}^{m} e^{\beta'x_j}/e^{\beta'x_k}\right) = \alpha_k$$

The integrand then is $\exp\{-\epsilon_k - e^{-\epsilon_k + \alpha_k}\}$. Letting $\epsilon_k^* = \epsilon_k - \alpha_k$, the integral becomes

$$P_k = \int_{-\infty}^{\infty} \exp\{-\epsilon_k^* - \alpha_k - e^{-\epsilon_k^*}\} d\epsilon_k^*$$

$$= e^{-\alpha_k} \int_{-\infty}^{\infty} \exp\{-\epsilon_k^* - e^{-\epsilon_k^*}\} d\epsilon_k^* = e^{-\alpha_k} = \frac{e^{\beta'x_k}}{\sum_{j=1}^{m} e^{\beta'x_j}} \tag{6.2.9}$$

since the last integral equals unity. This then is the probability of choosing the kth alternative in the conditional logit model. The computational simplicity of (6.2.9) in contrast with the multinomial probit model may argue in favor of the former. However, the logit model possesses the property of independence of irrelevant alternatives, namely that the odds-ratio of any pair of alternatives k and i, P_k/P_i, does not depend on the characteristics of any of the remaining alternatives. This may well be deemed an unreasonable property in certain contexts and the probit model may therefore be preferred.[2]

As a particular illustration of discrete choice, consider the model of Plant (1984) dealing with overtime participation in the Seattle-Denver income maintenance experiment. Let y_t denote household income earned in period t, G the "guarantee level", and τ the tax rate. A household that participates in the program receives payments of $G - y_t\tau$ if $G - y_t\tau > 0$. Thus, if we ignore the possibility that the household maximizes utility, it would participate if $y_t < G/\tau$. If the household maximizes utility, it turns out to be the case that the household participates in the program if $\log y_t \leq \log(G/\tau) + \eta\tau/2$, where η is the compensated elasticity of labor supply and is an unknown parameter from the econometrician's point of view. Given the joint density of the log(incomes) in various periods, we can formulate the probability of any particular participation pattern. Thus, for the participation pattern "no, yes, no" (NYN) in a three-year period, we obtain the probability as

$$
P_{\text{NYN}} = \int_{\log\left(\frac{G}{\tau}\right) + \frac{\eta\tau}{2}}^{\infty} \int_{-\infty}^{\log\left(\frac{G}{\tau}\right) + \frac{\eta\tau}{2}} \int_{\log\left(\frac{G}{\tau}\right) + \frac{\eta\tau}{2}}^{\infty} f(\log y_1, \log y_2, \log y_3) \, d\log y_1 \, d\log y_2 \, d\log y_3 \tag{6.2.10}
$$

and the likelihood is the product over households of terms such as (6.2.10). This presents the same computational problem as before if the log(incomes) are normally distributed.

We finally consider the simultaneous tobit model (Maddala 1983b) which is essentially the same as (5.4.24). Let

$$
y_{1t}^* = \gamma_1 y_{2t} + \beta_1' x_{1t} + u_{1t}
$$

$$
y_{2t}^* = \gamma_2 y_{1t} + \beta_2' x_{2t} + u_{2t} \tag{6.2.11}
$$

$$
y_{1t} = \begin{cases} y_{1t}^* & \text{if } y_{1t}^* > 0 \\ 0 & \text{otherwise} \end{cases}
$$

$$
y_{2t} = \begin{cases} y_{2t}^* & \text{if } y_{2t}^* > 0 \\ 0 & \text{otherwise} \end{cases}
$$

Let $f(u_{1t}, u_{2t})$ be the joint p.d.f. of the error terms and assume that the coherency condition $1 - \gamma_1\gamma_2 > 0$ holds. Clearly four regimes exist:

1   $y_{1t} > 0$, $y_{2t} > 0$

---

[2] Modifications of the logit model, such as the nested logit model, may also lack the property of independence of irrelevant alternatives. See, for example, Maddala (1983b).

2   $y_{1t} > 0$, $y_{2t} = 0$
3   $y_{1t} = 0$, $y_{2t} > 0$
4   $y_{1t} = y_{2t} = 0$

In regime 1, the density of y_{1t}, y_{2t} is obtained from the first two equations of (6.2.11) by substituting in $f(u_{1t}, u_{2t})$ and multiplying by the Jacobian of the transformation $1 - \gamma_1\gamma_2$; hence the part of the likelihood corresponding to the subsample of points in regime 1 is

$$L_1 = \prod_{\text{regime 1}} (1 - \gamma_1\gamma_2) f(y_{1t} - \gamma_1 y_{2t} - \beta_1 x_{1t}, \; y_{2t} - \gamma_2 y_{1t} - \beta_2 x_{2t})$$

For regime 2, $y_2 = 0$ and substitution from the first equation of (6.2.11) first yields $f(y_{1t} - \beta_1' x_{1t}, u_{2t})$. All values of $u_{2t} \leq -\gamma_2 y_{1t} - \beta_2' x_{2t}$ yield $y_{2t} = 0$ and so we must integrate out u_{2t} over the relevant range, yielding the corresponding piece of the likelihood

$$L_2 = \prod_{\text{regime 2}} \int_{-\infty}^{-\gamma_2 y_{1t} - \beta_2' x_{2t}} f(y_{1t} - \beta_1' x_{1t}, u_{2t}) du_{2t}$$

Proceeding similarly,

$$L_3 = \prod_{\text{regime 3}} \int_{-\infty}^{-\gamma_1 y_{2t} - \beta_1' x_{1t}} f(u_{1t}, y_{2t} - \beta_2' x_{2t}) du_{1t}$$

and

$$L_4 = \prod_{\text{regime 4}} \int_{-\infty}^{-\beta_2' x_{2t}} \int_{-\infty}^{-\beta_1' x_{1t}} f(u_{1t}, u_{2t}) du_{1t} du_{2t}$$

The likelihood we seek is

$$L = L_1 L_2 L_3 L_4 \tag{6.2.12}$$

It is noteworthy that once again multiple integration is required for the evaluation of the likelihood. It is also easy to see that as the number of tobit-type variables increases, the multiplicity of the integrals in (6.2.12) increases as well.

6.3   Disequilibrium Models

The derivation of the likelihood functions for multimarket models follow logically from the corresponding derivations for a single market with disequilibrium. As in that case, one may distinguish models with or without endogenous price adjustment, and if a price adjustment equation is present, it may or may not include an error term. These cases correspond to models A, C, and D in chapter 2. To simplify the notation, we omit the observation index t in most of this section.

Model A

We begin with the simplest possible model, given by (5.4.10) to (5.4.15), which we repeat here for convenience:

$$D_1 = \alpha_1 Q_2 + \mu_1 + u_1 \tag{6.3.1}$$

$$S_1 = \alpha_2 Q_2 + \mu_2 + u_2 \tag{6.3.2}$$

$$Q_1 = \min(D_1, S_1) \tag{6.3.3}$$

$$D_2 = \beta_1 Q_1 + \mu_3 + u_3 \tag{6.3.4}$$

$$S_2 = \beta_2 Q_1 + \mu_4 + u_4 \tag{6.3.5}$$

$$Q_2 = \min(D_2, S_2) \tag{6.3.6}$$

The notation abstracts from economic detail and lumps all exogenous variables into the terms μ_1 to μ_4. Assume for simplicity that u_1, u_2, u_3, u_4 are distributed normally and independently of one another and that u_i has mean 0 and variance σ_i^2. As we discussed in chapter 5, for each regime there is a unique mapping from the vector $u' = (u_1, u_2, u_3, u_4)$ to the vector $y' = (D_1, S_1, D_2, S_2)$, given by

$$A_i y = u + \mu \qquad i = 1, \ldots, 4 \tag{6.3.7}$$

where A_i corresponds to regimes as follows:

Regime 1: $D_1 < S_1, D_2 < S_2$. Then

$$A_1 = \begin{bmatrix} 1 & 0 & -\alpha_1 & 0 \\ 0 & 1 & -\alpha_2 & 0 \\ -\beta_1 & 0 & 1 & 0 \\ -\beta_2 & 0 & 0 & 1 \end{bmatrix}$$

Regime 2: $D_1 < S_1, D_2 > S_2$. Then

$$A_2 = \begin{bmatrix} 1 & 0 & 0 & -\alpha_1 \\ 0 & 1 & 0 & -\alpha_2 \\ -\beta_1 & 0 & 1 & 0 \\ -\beta_2 & 0 & 0 & 1 \end{bmatrix}$$

Regime 3: $D_1 > S_1$, $D_2 < S_2$. Then

$$A_3 = \begin{bmatrix} 1 & 0 & -\alpha_1 & 0 \\ 0 & 1 & -\alpha_2 & 0 \\ 0 & -\beta_1 & 1 & 0 \\ 0 & -\beta_2 & 0 & 1 \end{bmatrix}$$

Regime 4: $D_1 > S_1$, $D_2 > S_2$. Then

$$A_4 = \begin{bmatrix} 1 & 0 & 0 & -\alpha_1 \\ 0 & 1 & 0 & -\alpha_2 \\ 0 & -\beta_1 & 1 & 0 \\ 0 & -\beta_2 & 0 & 1 \end{bmatrix}$$

Thus, given the joint density of *us*, which in our case is simply

$$f(u) = \frac{1}{(2\pi)^2 \sigma_1 \sigma_2 \sigma_3 \sigma_4} \exp\left\{ -\frac{1}{2} \sum_{i=1}^{4} \frac{u_i^2}{\sigma_i^2} \right\} \tag{6.3.8}$$

we can easily obtain the density of the vector y in each of the four regimes as

$$f_i(y) = \frac{|\det(A_i)|}{(2\pi)^2 \sigma_1 \sigma_2 \sigma_3 \sigma_4} \exp\left\{ -\frac{1}{2} \sum_{j=1}^{4} (A_{ji} y - \mu_j)^2 / \sigma_j^2 \right\} \tag{6.3.9}$$

where A_{ji} denotes the *j*th row of the matrix A_i. In analogy with (2.3.5) and (2.3.6) we can write the density of Q_1, Q_2 as

$$\begin{aligned} h(Q_1, Q_2) = \; & g(Q_1, Q_2 | D_1 < S_1, D_2 < S_2)\Pr\{D_1 < S_1, D_2 < S_2\} \\ & + g(Q_1, Q_2 | D_1 < S_1, D_2 \geq S_2)\Pr\{D_1 < S_1, D_2 \geq S_2\} \\ & + g(Q_1, Q_2 | D_1 \geq S_1, D_2 < S_2)\Pr\{D_1 \geq S_1, D_2 < S_2\} \\ & + g(Q_1, Q_2 | D_1 \geq S_1, D_2 \geq S_2)\Pr\{D_1 \geq S_1, D_2 \geq S_2\} \end{aligned}$$

and

$$g(Q_1, Q_2 | D_1 < S_1, D_2 < S_2)$$

$$= \int_{Q_1}^{\infty} \int_{Q_2}^{\infty} f_1(Q_1, S_1, Q_2, S_2)\, dS_2\, dS_1 / \Pr\{D_1 < S_1, D_2 < S_2\}$$

$$g(Q_1, Q_2 | D_1 < S_1, D_2 \geq S_2)$$

$$= \int_{Q_1}^{\infty} \int_{Q_2}^{\infty} f_2(Q_1, S_1, D_2, Q_2)\, dD_2\, dS_1 / \Pr\{D_1 < S_1, D_2 \geq S_2\}$$

$$g(Q_1, Q_2 | D_1 \geq S_1, D_2 < S_2)$$

$$= \int_{Q_1}^{\infty} \int_{Q_2}^{\infty} f_3(D_1, Q_1, Q_2, S_2)\, dS_2\, dD_1 / \Pr\{D_1 \geq S_1, D_2 < S_2\}$$

$$g(Q_1, Q_2 | D_1 \geq S_1, D_2 \geq S_2)$$

$$= \int_{Q_1}^{\infty} \int_{Q_2}^{\infty} f_4(D_1, Q_1, D_2, Q_2) \, dD_2 \, dD_1 / \Pr\{D_1 \geq S_1, D_2 \geq S_2\}$$

The final form of the density is then similar to (2.3.7):

$$h(Q_1, Q_2) = \int_{Q_1}^{\infty} \int_{Q_2}^{\infty} f_1(Q_1, S_1, Q_2, S_2) \, dS_2 \, dS_1 + \int_{Q_1}^{\infty} \int_{Q_2}^{\infty} f_2(Q_1, S_1, D_2, Q_2) \, dD_2 \, dS_1$$

$$+ \int_{Q_1}^{\infty} \int_{Q_2}^{\infty} f_3(D_1, Q_1, Q_2, S_2) \, dS_2 \, dD_1 + \int_{Q_1}^{\infty} \int_{Q_2}^{\infty} f_4(D_1, Q_1, D_2, Q_2) \, dD_2 \, dD_1$$

$$(6.3.10)$$

The likelihood is $L = \prod_t h(Q_{1t}, Q_{2t})$. Although the density function appears to be somewhat forbidding because of the four double integrals in (6.3.10), the difficulties are mostly illusory in the present case. Substituting Q_1 and Q_2 in the appropriate places in $f_1, f_2, f_3,$ and f_4 yields for the exponent parts of these densities the quantities E_1, E_2, E_3, E_4:

$$E_1 = -\frac{1}{2} \left[\frac{(Q_1 - \alpha_1 Q_2 - \mu_1)^2}{\sigma_1^2} + \frac{(S_1 - \alpha_2 Q_2 - \mu_2)^2}{\sigma_2^2} \right.$$
$$\left. + \frac{(-\beta_1 Q_1 + Q_2 - \mu_3)^2}{\sigma_3^2} + \frac{(-\beta_2 Q_1 + S_2 - \mu_4)^2}{\sigma_4^2} \right]$$

$$E_2 = -\frac{1}{2} \left[\frac{(Q_1 - \alpha_1 Q_2 - \mu_1)^2}{\sigma_1^2} + \frac{(S_1 - \alpha_2 Q_2 - \mu_2)^2}{\sigma_2^2} \right.$$
$$\left. + \frac{(-\beta_1 Q_1 + D_2 - \mu_3)^2}{\sigma_3^2} + \frac{(-\beta_2 Q_1 + Q_2 - \mu_4)^2}{\sigma_4^2} \right]$$

$$E_3 = -\frac{1}{2} \left[\frac{(D_1 - \alpha_1 Q_2 - \mu_1)^2}{\sigma_1^2} + \frac{(Q_1 - \alpha_2 Q_2 - \mu_2)^2}{\sigma_2^2} \right.$$
$$\left. + \frac{(-\beta_1 Q_1 + Q_2 - \mu_3)^2}{\sigma_3^2} + \frac{(-\beta_2 Q_1 + S_2 - \mu_4)^2}{\sigma_4^2} \right]$$

$$E_4 = -\frac{1}{2} \left[\frac{(D_1 - \alpha_1 Q_2 - \mu_1)^2}{\sigma_1^2} + \frac{(Q_1 - \alpha_2 Q_2 - \mu_2)^2}{\sigma_2^2} \right.$$
$$\left. + \frac{(-\beta_1 Q_1 + D_2 - \mu_3)^2}{\sigma_3^2} + \frac{(-\beta_2 Q_1 + Q_2 - \mu_4)^2}{\sigma_4^2} \right]$$

When we integrate with respect to S_1 and S_2 in f_1, to D_2 and S_1 in f_2, etc., the integrands factor. The first integral in (6.3.10) becomes

$$(1/\sigma_1)\phi\left(\frac{Q_1-\alpha_1 Q_2-\mu_1}{\sigma_1}\right)\ (1/\sigma_3)\phi\left(\frac{-\beta_1 Q_1+Q_2-\mu_3}{\sigma_3}\right)$$

$$\times\left[1-\Phi\left(\frac{Q_1-\alpha_2 Q_2-\mu_2}{\sigma_2}\right)\right]\left[1-\Phi\left(\frac{-\beta_2 Q_1+Q_2-\mu_4}{\sigma_4}\right)\right]$$

where ϕ is the standard normal density and Φ the standard normal distribution. Similarly, the second term becomes

$$(1/\sigma_1)\phi\left(\frac{Q_1-\alpha_1 Q_2-\mu_1}{\sigma_1}\right)\ (1/\sigma_4)\phi\left(\frac{-\beta_2 Q_1+Q_2-\mu_4}{\sigma_4}\right)$$

$$\times\left[1-\Phi\left(\frac{Q_1-\alpha_2 Q_2-\mu_2}{\sigma_2}\right)\right]\left[1-\Phi\left(\frac{-\beta_1 Q_1+Q_2-\mu_3}{\sigma_3}\right)\right]$$

the third one is

$$(1/\sigma_2)\phi\left(\frac{Q_1-\alpha_2 Q_2-\mu_2}{\sigma_2}\right)\ (1/\sigma_3)\phi\left(\frac{-\beta_1 Q_1+Q_2-\mu_3}{\sigma_3}\right)$$

$$\times\left[1-\Phi\left(\frac{Q_1-\alpha_2 Q_2-\mu_1}{\sigma_1}\right)\right]\left[1-\Phi\left(\frac{-\beta_2 Q_1+Q_2-\mu_4}{\sigma_4}\right)\right]$$

and the last one is

$$(1/\sigma_2)\phi\left(\frac{Q_1-\alpha_2 Q_2-\mu_2}{\sigma_2}\right)\ (1/\sigma_4)\phi\left(\frac{-\beta_2 Q_1+Q_2-\mu_4}{\sigma_4}\right)$$

$$\times\left[1-\Phi\left(\frac{Q_1-\alpha_1 Q_2-\mu_1}{\sigma_1}\right)\right]\left[1-\Phi\left(\frac{-\beta_1 Q_1+Q_2-\mu_3}{\sigma_3}\right)\right]$$

Hence in this particular model no new computational difficulties arise since the double integral decomposes into the product of two single integrals which are easily and efficiently evaluated in FORTRAN by using the ERF or (in double precision) the DERF functions. However, the situation becomes more complicated with what may superficially appear to be a minor change of the model.

A variant of model A is the Ito (1980) model given by (5.2.13). Assume that the Walrasian demands and supplies are linear functions of exogenous variables and error terms, e.g.

$$\begin{aligned}
\widetilde{D}_1 &= \beta_1' x_1 + u_1 \\
\widetilde{S}_1 &= \beta_2' x_2 + u_2 \\
\widetilde{D}_2 &= \beta_3' x_3 + u_3 \\
\widetilde{S}_2 &= \beta_4' x_4 + u_4
\end{aligned}$$
$$(6.3.11)$$

(Note that in this model the spillovers are denoted by $\alpha_1, \ldots, \alpha_4$.) The mappings from the error terms to the effective demands and supplies are obtained by first eliminating Q_1 and Q_2 from the equations for each regime. Thus, in regime 1, $D_1 < S_1$ and $D_2 < S_2$; hence using the min conditions,

$$
\begin{aligned}
D_1 &= \tilde{D}_1 + \alpha_1(D_2 - \tilde{S}_2) \\
S_1 &= \tilde{S}_1 + \alpha_2(D_2 - \tilde{D}_2) \\
D_2 &= \tilde{D}_2 + \alpha_3(D_1 - \tilde{S}_1) \\
S_2 &= \tilde{S}_2 + \alpha_4(D_1 - \tilde{D}_1)
\end{aligned}
\tag{6.3.12}
$$

In regime 2, $D_1 < S_1$ and $S_2 < D_2$. We therefore write the first and fourth equations as

$$
\begin{aligned}
Q_1 &= \tilde{D}_1 + \alpha_1(Q_2 - \tilde{S}_2) \\
Q_2 &= \tilde{S}_2 + \alpha_4(Q_1 - \tilde{D}_1)
\end{aligned}
$$

which yields $Q_1 = \tilde{D}_1$, $Q_2 = \tilde{S}_2$. All four equations of the regime can be written as

$$
\begin{aligned}
D_1 &= \tilde{D}_1 \\
S_1 &= \tilde{S}_1 + \alpha_2(S_2 - \tilde{D}_2) \\
D_2 &= \tilde{D}_2 + \alpha_3(D_1 - \tilde{S}_1) \\
S_2 &= \tilde{S}_2
\end{aligned}
\tag{6.3.13}
$$

Similarly, we have in regime 3

$$
\begin{aligned}
D_1 &= \tilde{D}_1 + \alpha_1(D_2 - \tilde{S}_2) \\
S_1 &= \tilde{S}_1 \\
D_2 &= \tilde{D}_2 \\
S_2 &= \tilde{S}_2 + \alpha_4(S_1 - \tilde{D}_1)
\end{aligned}
\tag{6.3.14}
$$

and finally in regime 4

$$
\begin{aligned}
D_1 &= \tilde{D}_1 + \alpha_1(S_2 - \tilde{S}_2) \\
S_1 &= \tilde{S}_1 + \alpha_2(S_2 - \tilde{D}_2) \\
D_2 &= \tilde{D}_2 + \alpha_3(S_1 - \tilde{S}_1) \\
S_2 &= \tilde{S}_2 + \alpha_4(S_1 - \tilde{D}_1)
\end{aligned}
\tag{6.3.15}
$$

As before, we denote (D_1, S_1, D_2, S_2) as y'. In addition, using $\tilde{y}' = (\tilde{D}_1, \tilde{S}_1, \tilde{D}_2, \tilde{S}_2)$, the four regimes can now be written compactly as

$$
A_i y = B_i \tilde{y}
\tag{6.3.16}
$$

where

$$
A_1 = \begin{bmatrix} 1 & 0 & -\alpha_1 & 0 \\ 0 & 1 & -\alpha_2 & 0 \\ -\alpha_3 & 0 & 1 & 0 \\ -\alpha_4 & 0 & 0 & 1 \end{bmatrix}, \quad
A_2 = \begin{bmatrix} 1 & 0 & 0 & 0 \\ 0 & 1 & 0 & -\alpha_2 \\ -\alpha_3 & 0 & 1 & 0 \\ 0 & 0 & 0 & 1 \end{bmatrix}
$$

$$A_3 = \begin{bmatrix} 1 & 0 & -\alpha_1 & 0 \\ 0 & 1 & 0 & 0 \\ 0 & 0 & 1 & 0 \\ 0 & -\alpha_4 & 0 & 1 \end{bmatrix}, \quad A_4 = \begin{bmatrix} 1 & 0 & 0 & -\alpha_1 \\ 0 & 1 & 0 & -\alpha_2 \\ 0 & -\alpha_3 & 1 & 0 \\ 0 & -\alpha_4 & 0 & 1 \end{bmatrix}$$

$$B_1 = \begin{bmatrix} 1 & 0 & 0 & -\alpha_1 \\ 0 & 1 & -\alpha_2 & 0 \\ 0 & -\alpha_3 & 1 & 0 \\ -\alpha_4 & 0 & 0 & 1 \end{bmatrix}, \quad B_2 = \begin{bmatrix} 1 & 0 & 0 & 0 \\ 0 & 1 & -\alpha_2 & 0 \\ 0 & -\alpha_3 & 1 & 0 \\ 0 & 0 & 0 & 1 \end{bmatrix}$$

$$B_3 = \begin{bmatrix} 1 & 0 & 0 & -\alpha_1 \\ 0 & 1 & 0 & 0 \\ 0 & 0 & 1 & 0 \\ -\alpha_4 & 0 & 0 & 1 \end{bmatrix}, \quad B_4 = \begin{bmatrix} 1 & 0 & 0 & -\alpha_1 \\ 0 & 1 & -\alpha_2 & 0 \\ 0 & -\alpha_3 & 1 & 0 \\ -\alpha_4 & 0 & 0 & 1 \end{bmatrix}$$

Since $\tilde{y}$ can be written as $z + u$, where $z' = (\beta_1' x_1, \beta_2' x_2, \beta_3' x_3, \beta_4' x_4)$, we finally obtain the mapping

$$u = -z + B_i^{-1} A_i y \tag{6.3.17}$$

Substitution from (6.3.17) into (6.3.8) will no longer result in the factoring of the integrand. An intuitive way of looking at this is to note that the manner in which the spillovers enter (5.2.13) causes some of the equations to contain two error terms; hence even if these error terms are independent, the aggregate disturbances of the equations will not be. The density functions f_1 to f_4 are obtained by substituting from (6.3.17) in the normal density of us as before (and multiplying by the Jacobian of the transformation), but now integration of a bivariate normal density with nonzero correlation will be required. As before, the likelihood is the product of the densities.

Some Numerical Results for model A

To examine the magnitude of the biases due to not estimating such a model correctly, Goldfeld and Quandt (1979) employed sampling experiments in which Walrasian quantities were given by

$$\begin{aligned} \tilde{D}_1 &= \beta_{10} + \beta_{11} x_1 + u_1 \\ \tilde{S}_1 &= \beta_{20} + \beta_{21} x_2 + u_2 \\ \tilde{D}_2 &= \beta_{30} + \beta_{31} x_3 + u_3 \\ \tilde{S}_2 &= \beta_{40} + \beta_{41} x_4 + u_4 \end{aligned} \tag{6.3.18}$$

and "true" data were generated from (5.2.13), using (6.3.18). Three methods of estimation were considered:

1   A method based on ignoring the existence of spillovers, in which the

model collapses for estimating purposes to two single-market models.

2   A method based on recognizing the presence of the spillovers, but (incorrectly) pretending that they are exogenous.

3   The correct maximum likelihood method.

Root mean square errors of the four slope parameters are displayed in table 6.1 for a sample size of 30 (50 replications) and a sample size of 60 (25 replications). The superiority of maximum likelihood method is marked and is also confirmed by other measures not reported here.

Model C

The development of the appropriate likelihood function follows directly from (2.3.18). Assume that two price adjustment equations are given:[3]

$$\Delta p_1 = \gamma_1(D_1 - S_1) \tag{6.3.19}$$

$$\Delta p_2 = \gamma_2(D_2 - S_2) \tag{6.3.20}$$

Analogously to the single-market case, the following relations hold:

$$\begin{aligned} D_i &= Q_i + \frac{1}{\gamma_i}\Delta p_i \\ S_i &= Q_i \end{aligned} \qquad \text{if } \Delta p_i > 0 \tag{6.3.21}$$

and

$$\begin{aligned} D_i &= Q_i \\ S_i &= Q_i - \frac{1}{\gamma_i}\Delta p_i \end{aligned} \qquad \text{if } \Delta p_i < 0 \tag{6.3.22}$$

for $i = 1, 2$. Since Δp_i is observed in model C, we can identify which of the four regimes was obtained for each observation. Thus, for example, if $\Delta p_1 > 0$ and $\Delta p_2 > 0$,

Table 6.1   Root mean square errors

	Sample size					
	30			60		
	Method			Method		
Coefficient	1	2	3	1	2	3
β_{11}	0.682	0.464	0.262	0.208	0.287	0.124
β_{21}	0.339	0.307	0.159	0.336	0.342	0.115
β_{31}	0.254	0.202	0.202	0.256	0.153	0.136
β_{41}	0.327	0.352	0.126	0.233	0.263	0.096

[3] The price adjustment equations may have asymmetric adjustments; e.g. $\Delta p_1 = \gamma_{11}(D_1 - S_1)$ if $D_1 - S_1 > 0$ and $\Delta p_1 = \gamma_{12}(D_1 - S_1)$ otherwise. For details, see Ito (1980).

$$
\begin{bmatrix} D_1 \\ S_1 \\ D_2 \\ S_2 \end{bmatrix} = \begin{bmatrix} 1 & 0 & 1/\gamma_1 & 0 \\ 1 & 0 & 0 & 0 \\ 0 & 1 & 0 & 1/\gamma_2 \\ 0 & 1 & 0 & 0 \end{bmatrix} \begin{bmatrix} Q_1 \\ Q_2 \\ \Delta p_1 \\ \Delta p_2 \end{bmatrix}
\tag{6.3.23}
$$

or $y = C_i w$, where $w' = (Q_1, Q_2, \Delta p_1, \Delta p_2)$. Equation (6.3.23) defines C_4; C_1, C_2, and C_3 are given by

$$
C_1 = \begin{bmatrix} 1 & 0 & 0 & 0 \\ 1 & 0 & -1/\gamma_1 & 0 \\ 0 & 1 & 0 & 0 \\ 0 & 1 & 0 & -1/\gamma_2 \end{bmatrix}, \quad C_2 = \begin{bmatrix} 1 & 0 & 0 & 0 \\ 1 & 0 & -1/\gamma_1 & 0 \\ 0 & 1 & 0 & 1/\gamma_2 \\ 0 & 1 & 0 & 0 \end{bmatrix},
$$

$$
C_3 = \begin{bmatrix} 1 & 0 & 1/\gamma_1 & 0 \\ 1 & 0 & 0 & 0 \\ 0 & 1 & 0 & 0 \\ 0 & 1 & 0 & -1/\gamma_2 \end{bmatrix}
$$

Then, when $f_1(y), \ldots, f_4(y)$ are obtained from substituting (6.3.17) into (6.3.8), we need to transform once more from $f_i(y)$ to $\det(C_i) f_i(C_i w)$. The likelihood function then is

$$
L = \prod_{i=1}^{4} \prod_{R_i} |\det(C_i)| f_i(C_i w)
\tag{6.3.24}
$$

A somewhat more complicated case arises if (6.3.1), (6.3.2), (6.3.4), (6.3.5) contain p_1 and p_2 on the right hand side as in[4]

$$
\begin{aligned}
D_1 &= \alpha_1 Q_2 + \delta_1 p_1 + \mu_1 + u_1 \\
S_1 &= \alpha_2 Q_2 + \delta_2 p_1 + \mu_2 + u_2 \\
D_2 &= \alpha_3 Q_1 + \delta_3 p_2 + \mu_3 + u_3 \\
S_2 &= \alpha_4 Q_1 + \delta_4 p_2 + \mu_4 + u_4
\end{aligned}
\tag{6.3.25}
$$

Clearly, the price in period $t-1$ is taken to be predetermined in period t. Equations (6.3.21) and (6.3.22) still hold, but it may be more convenient to write them as

$$
\begin{aligned}
D_i &= Q_i + \frac{1}{\gamma_i} p_i - \frac{1}{\gamma_i} p_{i,-1} \\
S_i &= Q_i
\end{aligned}
\qquad \text{if } \Delta p_i > 0
\tag{6.3.26}
$$

---

[4] The reader may wish to analyze the case in which each equation in (6.3.25) contains both p_1 and p_2.

and

$$D_i = Q_i$$

$$S_i = Q_i - \frac{1}{\gamma_i} p_i + \frac{1}{\gamma_i} p_{i,-1}$$

$$\text{if } \Delta p_i < 0 \qquad\qquad (6.3.27)$$

for $i = 1, 2$.

Substituting the Ds and Ss from (6.3.25) into (6.3.26) and (6.3.27) we obtain the structural equations for the observable endogenous variables Q_1, Q_2, p_1, p_2 from which the likelihood may be obtained analogously to (6.3.24).

Model D

The price adjustment equations (6.3.19) and (6.3.20) are now replaced by

$$\Delta p_1 = \gamma_1 (D_1 - S_1) + u_5 \qquad\qquad (6.3.28)$$

$$\Delta p_2 = \gamma_2 (D_2 - S_2) + u_6 \qquad\qquad (6.3.29)$$

and the joint p.d.f. of disturbances (6.3.8) must now be replaced by the six-variate normal density

$$f(u) = \frac{1}{(2\pi)^3 \prod\limits_{i=1}^{6} \sigma_i} \exp\left\{ -\frac{1}{2} \sum_{i=1}^{6} \frac{u_i^2}{\sigma_i^2} \right\} \qquad\qquad (6.3.30)$$

It now becomes necessary to show explicitly where the prices occur in the demand and supply equations. Thus, (6.3.11) may be written as

$$
\begin{aligned}
\tilde{D}_1 &= \delta_1 p_1 + \beta_1' x_1 + u_1 \\
\tilde{S}_1 &= \delta_2 p_1 + \beta_2' x_2 + u_2 \\
\tilde{D}_2 &= \delta_3 p_2 + \beta_3' x_3 + u_3 \\
\tilde{S}_2 &= \delta_4 p_2 + \beta_4' x_4 + u_4
\end{aligned}
\qquad\qquad (6.3.31)
$$

(obviously, other specifications are also possible). The A and B matrices of (6.3.16) can be derived in corresponding fashion. For example, for regime 2 we have

$$
A_2 = \begin{bmatrix}
1 & 0 & 0 & 0 & -\delta_1 & 0 \\
0 & 1 & 0 & -\alpha_2 & -\delta_2 & \alpha_2\delta_3 \\
-\alpha_3 & 0 & 1 & 0 & \alpha_3\delta_2 & -\delta_3 \\
0 & 0 & 0 & 1 & 0 & -\delta_4 \\
-\gamma_1 & \gamma_1 & 0 & 0 & 1 & 0 \\
0 & 0 & -\gamma_2 & \gamma_2 & 0 & 1
\end{bmatrix}
$$

$$
B_2 = \begin{bmatrix}
1 & 0 & 0 & 0 & 0 & 0 \\
0 & 1 & -\alpha_2 & 0 & 0 & 0 \\
0 & -\alpha_3 & 1 & 0 & 0 & 0 \\
0 & 0 & 0 & 1 & 0 & 0 \\
0 & 0 & 0 & 0 & 1 & 0 \\
0 & 0 & 0 & 0 & 0 & 1
\end{bmatrix}
$$

where y is now defined as $y' = (D_1, S_1, D_2, S_2, p_1, p_2)$ and where $z' = (z_1, z_2, z_3, z_4, p_{1,-1}, p_{2,-1})$, the last two elements being the lagged values of p_1 and p_2, and the first four representing $\beta_1' x_1$, $\beta_2' x_2$, etc. (see exercise 6.1). Since $u = -z + B_i^{-1} A_i y$ as in (6.3.17), we can obtain the densities $f_i(y)$; the density of the observable random variables is then

$$
h(Q_1, Q_2, p_1, p_2) = \int_{Q_1}^{\infty} \int_{Q_2}^{\infty} f_1(y)\,\mathrm{d}S_2\,\mathrm{d}S_1 + \int_{Q_1}^{\infty} \int_{Q_2}^{\infty} f_2(y)\,\mathrm{d}D_2\,\mathrm{d}S_1
$$

$$
+ \int_{Q_1}^{\infty} \int_{Q_2}^{\infty} f_3(y)\,\mathrm{d}S_2\,\mathrm{d}D_1 + \int_{Q_1}^{\infty} \int_{Q_2}^{\infty} f_4(y)\,\mathrm{d}D_2\,\mathrm{d}D_1
$$

from which the likelihood is obtained as usual.

6.4   Integration

Substantial numerical problems arise in disequilibrium and related models, because the joint density of the observable variables requires multiple integrals of density functions. In the two-market case, the p.d.f. consists of the sum of four two-dimensional integrals; in the three-market case, it consists of the sum of eight three-dimensional integrals; and so on. Since the integral of the normal density does not exist in closed form, it must be approximated by numerical integration; this can create a substantial computational burden. In the present section we explore some unidimensional and multidimensional integration formulas.

We consider the integral

$$
\int_a^b w(x) f(x)\,\mathrm{d}x
$$

where $f(x)$ is the function we are interested in and where $w(x)$ is a weight function – possibly a constant. We wish to approximate the integral, which we assume throughout to exist, with a weighted sum of integrand values; thus

$$\int_a^b w(x) f(x) \, dx = \sum_{j=1}^n \alpha_j f(x_j) + \epsilon \qquad (6.4.1)$$

where the x_j are some particular values, the α_j are some coefficients, and ϵ is the error in the approximation. We obtain such formulas if we select n points between a and b, interpolate $f(x)$ by a polynomial, and use the integral of the interpolating polynomial as our approximation.

Newton-Cotes Integration

A simple choice of the n x_js is to choose them to be equally spaced in the interval (a, b), including the end points. Then $x_1 = a$, $x_2 = a + h$, $x_3 = a + 2h, \ldots, x_n = b$, where $h = (b-a)/(n-1)$. We first note the following basic lemma:

Lemma   If $x_1, \ldots, x_n$ are distinct, there exist $\alpha_1, \ldots, \alpha_n$ so that

$$\int_a^b w(x) f(x) \, dx = \sum_{j=1}^n \alpha_j f(x_j) \qquad (6.4.2)$$

if $f(x)$ is a polynomial of degree less than or equal to $n-1$.

Proof It is sufficient to show the claim for the powers of x, x^0, $x^1, \ldots, x^{n-1}$, since by the linearity of the operation of integration it will then also hold for the polynomial $\sum_{k=0}^{n-1} \beta_k x^k$. Requiring (6.4.2) to hold for the powers of x, x^0, $x^1, \ldots, x^{n-1}$ implies

$$\int_a^b w(x) \, dx = \sum_{j=1}^n \alpha_j$$

$$\int_a^b w(x) x \, dx = \sum_{j=1}^n \alpha_j x_j \qquad (6.4.3)$$

$$\int_a^b w(x) x^{n-1} \, dx = \sum_{j=1}^n \alpha_j x_j^{n-1}$$

Equation (6.4.3) is a system of simultaneous equations in the unknowns α_j, with Vandermonde coefficient matrix

$$\begin{bmatrix} 1 & 1 & \cdots & 1 \\ x_1 & x_2 & \cdots & x_n \\ \cdots & \cdots & \cdots & \cdots \\ x_1^{n-1} & x_2^{n-1} & \cdots & x_n^{n-1} \end{bmatrix} \qquad (6.4.4)$$

which is nonsingular (see exercise 6.3). Hence a unique solution exists for the α_j which make the approximation exact. □

Now consider the case when the weight function $w(x) = 1$. The two-point Newton-Cotes formula is obtained by solving the following two-equation analogue of (6.4.3.):

$$\int_a^b dx = b - a = \alpha_1 + \alpha_2$$

$$\int_a^b x dx = \frac{b^2 - a^2}{2} = \alpha_1 a + \alpha_2 b$$

Solving for α_1, α_2 yields $\alpha_1 = \alpha_2 = (b-a)/2$.
   Thus the two-point Newton-Cotes formula is

$$\int_a^b f(x)dx \approx \frac{b-a}{2} f(a) + \frac{b-a}{2} f(b)$$

which is called the trapezoidal rule. Analogously one can obtain Simpson's rule as the three-point formula (Zellner 1971 provides a FORTRAN program for the iterated version of this):

$$\int_a^b f(x)dx \approx \frac{b-a}{6} f(a) + \frac{4(b-a)}{6} f\left(\frac{a+b}{2}\right) + \frac{b-a}{6} f(b)$$

Denote by f_j the value of the integrand corresponding to x_j and let $h = (b-a)/(n-1)$. Then the Newton-Cotes formulas have α_j values as given in table 6.2 (Hildebrand 1956; Stroud 1974).
   A disadvantage of Newton-Cotes formulas is that taking more points in the integration formula does not necessarily improve the estimate. In fact, there are functions for which, as $n \to \infty$, the Newton-Cotes formula does not converge to the correct value of the integral (Stroud 1974). What is true, however, is that convergence can be obtained by the following device: first divide up the original interval into m subintervals and then apply an n-point Newton-Cotes formula to each subinterval; then let m (not n) become arbitrarily large. Thus, for $n = 2$ and $h = (b-a)/m$ we obtain the repeated trapezoidal formula as

$$\int_a^b f(x)dx \approx \frac{h}{2} f(a) + h \sum_{i=2}^m f[a+(i-1)h] + \frac{h}{2} f(b)$$

Table 6.2   Newton-Cotes formulas

n	α_1	α_2	α_3	α_4	α_5	α_6	α_7	α_8
2	$\dfrac{h}{2}$	$\dfrac{h}{2}$						
3	$\dfrac{h}{3}$	$\dfrac{4h}{3}$	$\dfrac{h}{3}$					
4	$\dfrac{3h}{8}$	$\dfrac{9h}{8}$	$\dfrac{9h}{8}$	$\dfrac{3h}{8}$				
5	$\dfrac{14h}{45}$	$\dfrac{64h}{45}$	$\dfrac{24h}{45}$	$\dfrac{64h}{45}$	$\dfrac{14h}{45}$			
6	$\dfrac{95h}{288}$	$\dfrac{375h}{288}$	$\dfrac{250h}{288}$	$\dfrac{250h}{288}$	$\dfrac{375h}{288}$	$\dfrac{95h}{288}$		
7	$\dfrac{41h}{140}$	$\dfrac{216h}{140}$	$\dfrac{27h}{140}$	$\dfrac{272h}{140}$	$\dfrac{27h}{140}$	$\dfrac{216h}{140}$	$\dfrac{41h}{140}$	
8	$\dfrac{5257h}{17280}$	$\dfrac{25039h}{17280}$	$\dfrac{9261h}{17280}$	$\dfrac{20923h}{17280}$	$\dfrac{20923h}{17280}$	$\dfrac{9261h}{17280}$	$\dfrac{25039h}{17280}$	$\dfrac{5257h}{17280}$

A FORTRAN subroutine NEWCT1 for evaluating ordinary Newton-Cotes formulas is given in appendix 6.A.

Gaussian Integration

The Newton-Cotes formulas have two unattractive features: (1) as $n \to \infty$ they do not necessarily converge to the true value of the integral; and (2) some of the coefficients (for values of $n > 8$) are negative, which is counterintuitive if one thinks of them as generalizations of trapezoidal formulas in which integrand values have positive weights, and is prone to propagate roundoff error. These difficulties are not present in Gaussian formulas, which have the additional virtue that an n-point formula is exact for polynomials up to degree $2n - 1$.

It is convenient to take again $w(x) = 1$ and to consider the integral

$$\int_{-1}^{1} f(x)\,dx$$

(for cases with other weight functions see Stroud 1974; Hildebrand 1956). The restriction of the limits of integration to $(-1,1)$ loses no generality, for we can always transform from the range $-1 \leq x \leq 1$ to the range $a \leq y \leq b$. Thus, if we seek

$$\int_a^b f(y)\,dy$$

we set $y = [(b-a)x + b+a]/2$ and our objective becomes

$$\frac{b-a}{2} \int_{-1}^{1} f\{[(b-a)x + b+a]/2\}\,dx$$

Hence, if the appropriate weights are α_j for integrating over $(-1,1)$, they are $\alpha_j (b-a)/2$ for the range (a,b).

Gaussian formulas make use of orthogonal polynomials. An nth degree polynomial $P_n(x)$ is orthogonal in the interval $(-1,1)$ (or, in more general cases, in the interval (a,b)) to all polynomials $Q_{n-1}(x)$ of degree less than or equal to $n-1$ if for all such polynomials

$$\int_{-1}^{1} P_n(x)Q_{n-1}(x)\,dx = 0 \tag{6.4.5}$$

For the unit weight function the appropriate polynomials are the Legendre polynomials which are (Hildebrand 1956)

$$P_0(x) = 1$$
$$P_1(x) = x$$
$$P_2(x) = (3x^2 - 1)/2$$
$$P_3(x) = (5x^3 - 3x)/2$$
$$P_4(x) = (35x^4 - 30x^2 + 3)/8$$
$$P_5(x) = (63x^5 - 70x^3 + 15x)/8$$

and they satisfy the difference equation

$$(n+1)P_{n+1}(x) - (2n+1)xP_n(x) + nP_{n-1}(x) = 0$$

In particular, they have the properties that

$$\int_{-1}^{1} P_n(x)P_m(x)\,dx = \begin{cases} 0 & \text{if } n \neq m \\ 2/(2n+1) & \text{if } n = m \end{cases}$$

It is noteworthy that the polynomial $P_n(x)$ that satisfies (6.4.5) is unique[5] and that it has distinct roots in the $(-1,1)$ interval.

---

[5] If other weight functions $w(x)$ are used, the orthogonality condition is defined relative to that $w(x)$ as $\int w(x)P_n(x)Q_{n-1}(x)\,dx = 0$ and the uniqueness relative to that weight function still holds.

We now express the integral as a weighted sum of the integrand at $n+1$ points:

$$\int_{-1}^{1} f(x)\,dx = \sum_{j=1}^{n+1} \alpha_j f(x_j) \tag{6.4.6}$$

The issue is to determine the α_j and the x_j so that (6.4.6), which in general is only an approximation, becomes exact if f is a polynomial of degree $2n+1$. The points x_j will turn out to be the roots of the Legendre polynomial $P_{n+1}(x)$. To show this, consider an arbitrary nth degree polynomial $Q_n(x)$, which by suitable rearrangement can always be written in terms of the Legendre polynomials as

$$Q_n(x) = \sum_{i=0}^{n} \gamma_i P_i(x) \tag{6.4.7}$$

Multiplying $Q_n(x)$ by $P_{n+1}(x)$ and integrating yields

$$\int_{-1}^{1} Q_n(x)P_{n+1}(x)\,dx = 0 \tag{6.4.8}$$

since $P_{n+1}(x)$ is orthogonal to each $P_i(x)$, $i = 0, \ldots, n$.

The integrand in (6.4.8) is of degree $2n+1$ and we require (6.4.6) to be exact up to this degree. Thus, if the function to be integrated is a polynomial of degree $2n+1$, it follows from (6.4.8) that its "approximation" (the right hand side of (6.4.6)) must also be zero; hence

$$\sum_{j=1}^{n+1} \alpha_j Q_n(x_j)P_{n+1}(x_j) = 0$$

But since $Q_n(x_j)$ is arbitrary, $P_{n+1}(x_j)$ must be zero; hence the x_j $(j=1, \ldots, n+1)$ must be zeros of the Legendre polynomial of degree $n+1$.

Finally, we can determine the weighting coefficients α_j. If $L_j(x)$ is the Lagrange polynomial

$$L_j(x) = \frac{\displaystyle\prod_{\substack{i=1 \\ i\neq j}}^{n+1} (x-x_i)}{\displaystyle\prod_{\substack{i=1 \\ i\neq j}}^{n+1} (x_j-x_i)}$$

any nth degree polynomial $Q_n(x)$ can be expressed exactly at the points x_j as

$$Q_n(x) = \sum_{j=1}^{n+1} Q_n(x_j) L_j(x)$$

Integrating, we obtain

$$\int_{-1}^{1} Q_n(x)\,dx = \sum_{j=1}^{n+1} Q_n(x_j) \int_{-1}^{1} L_j(x)\,dx \qquad (6.4.9)$$

and hence $\alpha_j = \int_{-1}^{1} L_j(x)\,dx$. It is not difficult to show (see Kuo 1965) that if the x_j are the zeros of the Legendre polynomial of order $n+1$, then $L_j(x)$ can be written as $P_{n+1}(x)/[(x-x_j)P'_{n+1}(x_j)]$. (See exercises 6.4, 6.5).

Unlike the Newton-Cotes formulas, the Gaussian integration formulas converge to the integral as $n \to \infty$ for continuous integrands. Appendix 6.A also contains a FORTRAN subroutine GAULG1 for Gauss-Legendre integration for values of $n = 2, \ldots, 11$, and another subroutine GAUS for an n-fold repeated two-point Gauss-Legendre quadrature in which first the interval of integration is divided into n subintervals and then two-point Gauss-Legendre integration is applied to each. Many other integration formulas exist; for the interval $(-\infty,\infty)$ with weight function e^{-x^2} the relevant polynomials are the Hermite polynomials, and for the interval $(0,\infty)$ with weight function e^{-x} the appropriate polynomials are the Laguerre polynomials (see Hildebrand 1956; Stroud 1974). Tables of points x_j and weights α_j are in Stroud and Secrest (1966).

Monte Carlo Integration

Monte Carlo procedures employ randomness either to simulate another process involving probabilities or to provide an analog to a deterministic calculation. The latter procedure is employed in integrating by Monte Carlo techniques. An interesting application to a disequilibrium model is in Kooiman, van Dijk and Thurik (1985).

There are at least two ways of Monte Carlo integrating

$$I = \int_{a}^{b} f(x)\,dx \qquad (6.4.10)$$

First consider the "hit-or-miss" method (Rubinstein 1981). If it is known that $f(x) < M$, for some M, in the interval (a,b), we generate successive pairs of uniformly distributed numbers (Quandt 1983b), call them (x_i, y_i), $i = 1, \ldots, n$, such that $a \le x_i \le b$, $0 \le y_i \le M$. Let n_s be the number of cases in which $y_i \le f(x_i)$. Then (see figure 6.1) the integral is approximated by the fraction n_s/n times the area of the rectangle with sides ab and $0M$, i.e. $\hat{I} = (n_s/n)(b-a)M$. Let p be the (true) probability that $y_i \le f(x_i)$, that is to say it is the ratio of the area under $f(x)$ in figure 6.1 to the total area

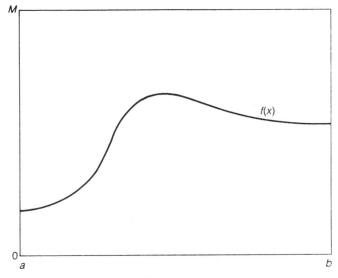

Figure 6.1

of the rectangle (which is estimated by $\hat{p} = n_s/n$). Then $I = p(b-a)M$. Clearly $E(\hat{I}) = I$ and $\text{var}(\hat{I}) = \sigma_1^2 = (b-a)^2 M^2 p(1-p)/n$ by virtue of the fact that the hit-or-miss method is a sequence of Bernoulli trials. Since $(\hat{p}-p)/[p(1-p)/n]^{1/2}$ is asymptotically distributed as $N(0,1)$, the error in the approximation behaves as $1/\sqrt{n}$. (See exercise 6.7.)

The alternative sample-mean method starts out with the definition of the expected values of $f(x)$. If $g(x)$ is any density function over the interval (a,b), we have by definition

$$E[f(x)] = \int_a^b f(x)g(x)\,dx \tag{6.4.11}$$

If, for example, $g(x)$ is chosen to be the uniform density $g(x) = 1/(b-a)$, then

$$E[f(x)] = \frac{1}{b-a} \int_a^b f(x)\,dx = \frac{I}{b-a} \tag{6.4.12}$$

Now if we draw a sample of n xs, $x_1, \ldots, x_n$, uniformly (because $g(x)$ was assumed to be uniform) from the (a,b) interval, then, by the Kolmogorov theorem, the sequence $f(x_i)$ obeys the strong law of large number and $\sum_i f(x_i)/n$ converges almost surely to $E[f(x)]$. Hence, I can be approximated as a sample mean with arbitrary accuracy as

$$I \approx \frac{b-a}{n} \sum_{i=1}^{n} f(x_i) \equiv \hat{I} \qquad (6.4.13)$$

Since $\hat{I}$ is the sum of i.i.d. random variables with variance $E(\hat{I}^2) - [E(\hat{I})]^2$,

$$\mathrm{var}(\hat{I}) = \sigma_2^2 = \frac{1}{n} \left[(b-a)^2 \int_a^b f(x)^2/(b-a)\,dx - I^2 \right]$$

and $(\hat{I} - I)/\sigma_2$ is asymptotically distributed as $N(0,1)$. The error in the approximation, $|\hat{I} - I|$, then behaves as $1/\sqrt{n}$, which is the same as for the hit-and-miss method and shows a not particularly rapid rate of convergence. Anticipating some of our later discussion of integrating in several dimensions, it is worth noting that the rate of convergence or the amount of work performed to reach given accuracy does not depend on the dimensionality of the integral.

The variance of the hit-or-miss method can be rewritten as $\sigma_1^2 = [(b-a)M - I]I/n$. The difference is given by

$$\sigma_1^2 - \sigma_2^2 = \frac{b-a}{n} \left[MI - \int_a^b f(x)^2\,dx \right]$$

Since $M \geqq f(x)$ by definition, $Mf(x) \geqq f(x)^2$, and integrating, $MI \geqq \int_a^b f(x)^2\,dx$. Hence the hit-or-miss method has variance at least as large as the sample-mean method (Rubinstein 1981).

The efficiency of Monte Carlo integration can be substantially enhanced by selecting many of the x values in a range where $f(x)$ is large and few x values where it is small. This is called *importance sampling* and requires the choice of a density $g(x)$ that has a lot of mass where $f(x)$ is large, e.g. a density with the property that $\mathrm{var}[f(x)/g(x)]$ is small; that is to say, as x varies we want $f(x)/g(x)$ not to vary a great deal. Then

$$I = \int_a^b [f(x)/g(x)]g(x)\,dx = E[f(x)/g(x)]$$

and the integral can be approximated as $[\sum_{i=1}^{n} f(x_i)/g(x_i)]/n$. Knowledge of a suitable $g(x)$ is useful, but using the $g(x)$ that actually minimizes the variance of $f(x)/g(x)$ is not practical because it requires knowledge of the integral we seek (see exercise 6.6.). Other variance reduction techniques are the use of antithetic and control variates (Hendry 1984; Hammersley and Handscomb 1964). In general, Monte Carlo integration is difficult to apply if the boundaries of the region of integration (in several dimensions) are irregular and complicated, and is likely to be very inefficient (except in the case of importance sampling) if the values of the integrand show large variation. Under the best of circumstances it is likely to be an expensive method if the integrals are required with high precision, as is the case when they are needed as input in a numerical optimization problem.[6]

Multivariate Integration

Immediate multidimensional integration formulas may be obtained by generalizing formulas such as (6.4.1). Thus if $f(x,y)$ is a function of two variables, the integral in the x-direction, for any specified value of y, is approximated by $\Sigma_{j=1}^{n} \alpha_j f(x_j,y)$. Then the integral we seek is obtained by applying a similar integration formula for the y-direction, yielding

$$\sum_{i=1}^{m} \beta_i \sum_{j=1}^{n} \alpha_j f(x_j,y_i) = \sum_{i=1}^{m} \sum_{j=1}^{n} \alpha_j \beta_i f(x_j,y_i)$$

Bivariate integration routines are given in appendix 6.B, which contains a bivariate version of Gauss-Legendre integration (GAULG2) for general functions. Particularly powerful and ingenious approximations are available when the integrand is the multivariate normal density, and appendix 6.B also contains BIV2D, which is a subroutine that integrates the bivariate normal density based on the method of Owen (1956) (see also the next subsection). Appendix 6.C contains integration routines for three dimensions. GAULG3 provides Gauss-Legendre integration. DUTT3 is a trivariate integrator based on the tetrachoric series the terms of which involve Gaussian quadrature with Hermite polynomials (Dutt 1976). Finally, TRINT provides trivariate integration over a rectangular region using repeated two-point Gauss-Legendre integration.

The computer intensiveness of multidimensional integration is avoided by the so-called Clark approximation (Clark 1961) if the density function is multivariate normal. It is most easily motivated with reference to the discrete choice problem with choice probabilities given by (6.2.3).[7] We suppress the index that indexes individuals and write it as

$$P_k = \Pr\{\eta_1 \leq \mu_1, \ldots, \eta_m \leq \mu_m\} \tag{6.4.14}$$

where there are $m - 1$ inequalities on the right hand side, $\mu_j = V_k - V_j$, which further equals $\beta'(x_k - x_j)$ in the linear utility case, and where the $\epsilon_j - \epsilon_k = \eta_j$ are distributed as $N(0,\Sigma)$. Clearly, by defining new random variables $v_j = \eta_j - \mu_j$, (6.4.14) can also be written as

$$P_k = \Pr\{v_1 \leq 0, \ldots, v_m \leq 0\}$$

---

[6]Manski and Lerman (1981) compare multivariate Monte Carlo integration with Clark integration (see below) and find the former expensive.

[7]For extensive details see Daganzo (1979).

$$= \Pr\left\{\max_{j \neq k} v_j \leq 0\right\} \tag{6.4.15}$$

where the v_j are distributed as $N(\bar{v}, \Sigma)$, where $\bar{v} = -\mu$. If the density of max v_j had a particularly simple form, the evaluation of (6.4.15) would cause no great difficulties.

Consider the trivariate normal density of v_1, v_2, v_3 with means $\bar{v}_1, \bar{v}_2, \bar{v}_3$ and covariance matrix

$$\Sigma = \begin{bmatrix} \sigma_{11} & \sigma_{12} & \sigma_{13} \\ \sigma_{21} & \sigma_{22} & \sigma_{23} \\ \sigma_{31} & \sigma_{32} & \sigma_{33} \end{bmatrix}$$

Let $\sigma = (\sigma_{11} + \sigma_{22} - 2\sigma_{12}^2)^{1/2}$. Then the random variable $v_{12} = \max(v_1, v_2)$ has

$$E(v_{12}) = \bar{v}_1 \Phi\left(\frac{\bar{v}_1 - \bar{v}_2}{\sigma}\right) + \bar{v}_2\left[1 - \Phi\left(\frac{\bar{v}_1 - \bar{v}_2}{\sigma}\right)\right] + \sigma\phi\left(\frac{\bar{v}_1 - \bar{v}_2}{\sigma}\right)$$

$$E(v_{12}^2) = (\bar{v}_1^2 + \sigma_{11})\Phi\left(\frac{\bar{v}_1 - \bar{v}_2}{\sigma}\right) + (\bar{v}_2 + \sigma_{22})$$

$$\times\left[1 - \Phi\left(\frac{\bar{v}_1 - \bar{v}_2}{\sigma}\right)\right] + (\bar{v}_1 + \bar{v}_2)\sigma\phi\left(\frac{\bar{v}_1 - \bar{v}_2}{\sigma}\right)$$

$$\mathrm{var}(v_{12}) = E(v_{12}^2) - E(v_{12})^2$$

$$\sigma_{(12)3} = E\{[v_{12} - E(v_{12})](v_3 - \bar{v}_3)\} = \sigma_{13}\Phi\left(\frac{\bar{v}_1 - \bar{v}_2}{\sigma}\right) +$$

$$\sigma_{23}\left[1 - \Phi\left(\frac{\bar{v}_1 - \bar{v}_2}{\sigma}\right)\right]$$

If one were to assume, *as is patently false*, that the maximum of two normally distributed variables is itself normally distributed, the above formulas could be applied recursively: we would now be dealing, in effect, with random variables v_{12}, v_3, v_4 with means $E(v_{12})$, $\bar{v}_3$, $\bar{v}_4$ and covariance matrix

$$\begin{bmatrix} \mathrm{var}(v_{12}) & \sigma_{(12)3} & \sigma_{(12)4} \\ \sigma_{(12)3} & \sigma_{33} & \sigma_{34} \\ \sigma_{(12)4} & \sigma_{34} & \sigma_{44} \end{bmatrix}$$

from which we can obtain the moments of $\max(v_{12}, v_3)$, and so on. After $m - 2$ applications of the procedure we obtain the mean $E(v_{12,\ldots,m})$ and variance $\mathrm{var}(v_{12,\ldots,m})$ of $m - 1$ v_js; hence the required probability is $\Phi\{-E(v_{12,\ldots,m})/[\mathrm{var}(v_{12,\ldots,m})]^{1/2}\}$. The accuracy of the approximation is reported to be satisfactory in a variety of tests except when the variances are substantially unequal and when the correlations are high (Daganzo 1979). Subroutines CLARK2 in appendix 6.B and CLARK3 in appendix 6.C evaluate the integral for the bivariate and trivariate case respectively.

Special Cases of Multivariate Normal Integration

The first and simplest special case is that of the bivariate normal. Hausman and Wise (1978) have provided a modification of a method due to Owen (1956) which is designed to obtain the upper-tail integral for the normal with unit variances, which is thus written in the following form:

$$I(h,k;\rho) = \frac{1}{2\pi(1 - \rho^2)^{1/2}} \times$$

$$\int_{-\infty}^{h} \int_{-\infty}^{k} \exp\left\{ -\frac{1}{2} (x^2 - 2\rho xy + y^2)/(1-\rho^2) \right\} dx\,dy$$

We can differentiate this with respect to ρ and then the result can be integrated with respect to x and y. Integrating then with respect to ρ yields the result:

$$I(h,k;\rho) = \frac{1}{2} \Phi(h) + \frac{1}{2} \Phi(k) - T\left[h, \frac{k - \rho h}{h(1 - \rho^2)^{1/2}}\right]$$

$$- T\left[k, \frac{h - \rho k}{k(1 - \rho^2)^{1/2}}\right]$$

if $hk > 0$ or if $hk = 0$ and h or $k \geq 0$;

$$I(h,k;\rho) = \frac{1}{2} \Phi(h) + \frac{1}{2} \Phi(k) - T\left[h, \frac{k - \rho h}{h(1 - \rho^2)^{1/2}}\right]$$

$$- T\left[k, \frac{h - \rho k}{k(1 - \rho^2)^{1/2}}\right] - \frac{1}{2}$$

if $hk < 0$ or if $hk = 0$ and h or $k < 0$,
where

$$T(u, v) = -\frac{\tan^{-1} v}{2\pi} - \frac{1}{2\pi} \sum_{j=0}^{\infty} c_j v^{2j+1}$$

and

$$c_j = (-1)^j \frac{1}{2j + 1}\left[1 - \exp\left(-\frac{1}{2} u^2\right) \sum_{i=0}^{j} \frac{u^{2i}}{2^i i!}\right]$$

The FORTRAN routine BIV2D in appendix 6.B performs the integration according to this method.

A considerable simplification occurs in the multivariate integral (6.2.2) if the ϵ_{ij} are i.i.d. normal with mean zero and unit variance. In that case (6.2.2) becomes

$$P_{ik} = \int_{-\infty}^{\infty} \frac{1}{\sqrt{(2\pi)}} e^{-\epsilon_{ik}^2/2} \prod_{j \neq k} \Phi(V_{ik} - V_{ij} + \epsilon_{ik}) d\epsilon_{ik}$$

Since $\Phi(\ )$ is evaluated on a computer very rapidly and accurately by the ERF (or DERF) function, in effect only a one-dimensional numerical integration has to be performed by the user's computer program.

The last case we consider is due to Hausman (1980) and is based on the assumption that V_{ij} in (6.2.2) is linear in the unknown parameters, i.e. that (6.2.4) is in effect. The vector β is assumed to have p components and we assume (for this simplification to be useful) that p is small relative to the number of alternatives m. We further assume that (a) β is itself normally distributed with mean μ_β and covariance matrix Σ_β, (b) Σ_β is diagonal, and (c) Σ_ϵ, the covariance matrix of the ϵs, is also diagonal. Then

$$P_{ik} = \Pr\{(x_{ik} - x_{ij})'\beta \geq \delta_{ijk} \quad \forall j \neq k\}$$
$$= \Pr\{(x_{ik} - x_{ij})'\mu_\beta \geq \delta_{ijk} + (x_{ij} - x_{ik})'(\beta - \mu_\beta) \quad \forall j \neq k\} \quad (6.4.16)$$

Define the right hand side in the second probability in (6.4.16) as ξ_{ijk}. The random vector $\xi_{ik}' = (\xi_{i1k}, \ldots, \xi_{imk})$ is normal with mean zero and covariance matrix $\Sigma_\xi = A\Sigma_\epsilon A' + X\Sigma_\beta X'$, where A is an $(m-1) \times m$ matrix given by

$$A = \begin{bmatrix} 1 & & & & -1 & & & & \\ & \cdot & & & \vdots & & & & \\ & & \cdot & & -1 & & & & \\ & & & 1 & -1 & & & & \\ & & & & -1 & 1 & & & \\ & & & & \vdots & & \cdot & & \\ & & & & -1 & & & \cdot & \\ & & & & & & & & 1 \end{bmatrix}$$

with zeros in all other positions and where

$$X = \begin{bmatrix} (x_{i1} - x_{ik})' \\ \vdots \\ (x_{im} - x_{ik})' \end{bmatrix}$$

and is $(m-1) \times p$. From assumptions (b) and (c) it follows that Σ_ξ can be written as

$$\Sigma_\xi = QQ' + \Sigma_{\epsilon(k)} \quad (6.4.17)$$

where $\Sigma_{\epsilon(k)}$ is the matrix Σ_ϵ from which its kth row and column have been deleted, and where Q is the partitioned matrix $Q = (X\Sigma_\beta^{1/2}, \sigma_{\epsilon_k}i)$, with i being a vector of all ones, $i' = (1, 1, \ldots, 1)$.

It is now convenient to define an $m+p$ vector of random variables distributed i.i.d. as $N(0,1)$. Let this vector be denoted by $(v, w)' = (v_1, \ldots, v_{k-1}, v_{k+1}, \ldots, v_m, w_1, \ldots, w_{p+1})$. We can then write

$$\xi_{ik} = \Sigma_{\epsilon(k)}^{1/2} v - Qw \qquad (6.4.18)$$

because it follows from (6.4.18) that ξ_{ik} is normal with mean zero and variance given by (6.4.17). Substituting this on the right in (6.4.16),

$$P_{ik} = \Pr\{(x_{ik} - x_{ij})' \mu_\beta \geq \xi_{ijk} \quad \forall j \neq k\}$$

$$= \Pr\left\{v_j \leq \left[(x_{ik} - x_{ij})' \mu_\beta + \sum_{\ell=1}^{p+1} q_{j\ell} w_\ell\right] \middle/ \sigma_{\epsilon_j} \quad \forall j \neq k\right\} \qquad (6.4.19)$$

If F and G are the distribution functions of scalars v and w, respectively, the following convolution formula holds (Marsaglia 1963):

$$\Pr\{v < c - w\} = \int \Pr\{v < c - w | w\} dG = E[F(c - w)]$$

where c is a constant vector and the expectation is taken with respect to G. We can then write (6.4.19) as

$$P_{ik} = \frac{1}{(2\pi)^{(p+1)/2}}$$

$$\times \int_{-\infty}^{\infty} \cdots \int_{-\infty}^{\infty} \prod_{j \neq k} \Phi\left[\left\{(x_{ik} - x_{ij})' \mu_\beta + \sum_{\ell=1}^{p+1} q_{j\ell} w_\ell\right\} \middle/ \sigma_{\epsilon_j}\right]$$

$$\times \exp\left\{\frac{-t't}{2}\right\} dt_1 \ldots dt_{p+1}$$

If, as we have assumed, p is small relative to m, we have transformed the multiple integration into one of lower dimension, which represents a considerable cost saving.

6.5 A Non Normal Density

The cost and the problems of accuracy in numerical integration promise a positive payoff to replacing the normal density with some other density whose integrals can be written in closed form. Such a density is the Sargan density, introduced by Goldfeld and Quandt (1981a) and given by

$$f(u) = K e^{-\alpha|u|} \left(1 + \sum_{j=1}^{P} \gamma_j \alpha^j |u|^j\right) \qquad (6.5.1)$$

where $\alpha > 0$, $\gamma_j \geq 0$, $j = 1, \ldots, P$, and K is a function of α and the γs. In the present section we briefly consider the properties of this density and its applicability to disequilibrium and other latent variable models.

Basic Properties

Since distributions of error terms should be specified as parsimoniously as possible, values of P of 1 or 2 are the only ones that are likely to be useful ($P = 0$ yields the Laplace density). The first- and second-order densities then are

$$f_1(u) = \frac{\alpha e^{-\alpha|u|}}{2(1+\gamma_1)} (1 + \alpha\gamma_1 |u|) \tag{6.5.2}$$

and

$$f_2(u) = \frac{\alpha e^{-\alpha|u|}}{2(1+\gamma_1+2\gamma_2)} (1 + \alpha\gamma_1 |u| + \alpha^2\gamma_2 u^2) \tag{6.5.3}$$

It is easy to show (Tse 1987) that the moment generating function for (6.5.3) is

$$\mu(\theta) = \left[\frac{\alpha}{\alpha+\theta} + \frac{\alpha}{\alpha-\theta} + \frac{\gamma_1\alpha^2}{(\alpha+\theta)^2} + \frac{\gamma_1\alpha^2}{(\alpha-\theta)^2} + \frac{2\gamma_2^3\alpha}{(\alpha+\theta)^3} + \frac{2\gamma_2^3\alpha}{(\alpha-\theta)^3} \right] \bigg/ $$
$$2(1 + \gamma_1 + 2\gamma_2) \tag{6.5.4}$$

The mean is obviously zero and the variance is[8]

$$\sigma^2 = \frac{2+6\gamma_1+24\gamma_2}{\alpha^2(1+\gamma_1+2\gamma_2)}$$

It is easy to show that (a) for all P values greater than or equal to 1, $f'(u)$ is continuous if and only if $\gamma_1 = 1$; (b) for all P values greater than or equal to 1 and $\gamma_1 = 1$, $f''(u)$ is continuous at $u = 0$; (c) the second-order density is unimodal if $\gamma_2 < 0.5$ (see exercise 6.8). For a sample of n independent u_is, the log-likelihood for the first-order density with $\gamma_1 = 1$ is

$$\log L = n \log\alpha - n \log 4 - \alpha \sum_{i=1}^{n} |u_i| + \sum_{i=1}^{n} \log(1 + \alpha|u_i|) \tag{6.5.5}$$

Setting the derivative with respect to α equal to zero yields

$$\frac{n}{\alpha} = \sum_{i=1}^{n} |u_i| - \sum_{i=1}^{n} \frac{|u_i|}{1+\alpha|u_i|} \tag{6.5.6}$$

which has a unique positive solution for α, since

---

[8] The moment generating function in general is

$$\mu(\theta) = (K/2) \sum_{j=0}^{P} j! \, [\alpha^{j+1}\gamma_j/(\alpha+\theta)^{j+1} + \alpha^{j+1}\gamma_j/(\alpha-\theta)^{j+1}]$$

with the moments $\mu_r = 0$ if r is odd and $\mu_r = (K/\alpha^r) \sum_{j=0}^{P} \gamma_j (j+r)!$ if r is even. See Tse (1983).

$$\frac{\partial^2 \log L}{\partial \alpha^2} = -\frac{n}{\alpha^2} - \sum_{i=1}^{n} \frac{u_i^2}{(1+\alpha|u_i|)^2} \tag{6.5.7}$$

is negative everywhere. To obtain the Cramer-Rao bound we require the expected value of the second term of (6.5.7):

$$E\left\{\frac{u^2}{(1+\alpha|u|)^2}\right\} = \int_{-\infty}^{\infty} \frac{u^2}{(1+\alpha|u|)^2} \left[\frac{\alpha}{4} e^{-\alpha|u|} (1+\alpha|u|)\right] du$$

$$= \frac{\alpha}{2} \int_{0}^{\infty} \frac{u^2 e^{-\alpha u}}{1+\alpha u} du \tag{6.5.8}$$

Letting $y = \alpha u$ and writing $y^2 = (y+1)^2 - 2y - 1$, (6.5.8) becomes

$$E\left\{\frac{u^2}{(1+\alpha|u|)^2}\right\} = \frac{1}{\alpha^2} \{I_1 + I_2 + I_3\} = \frac{3}{\alpha^2} \tag{6.5.9}$$

where $I_1 = 2$, $I_2 = 1 - 0.219\ 383e$, $I_3 = 0.219\ 383e$. Hence the Cramer-Rao bound is

$$E\left(-\frac{\partial^2 \log L}{\partial \alpha^2}\right)^{-1} = \frac{\alpha^2}{4n}$$

Standard Regression Model

In the model

$$Y = X\beta + U \tag{6.5.10}$$

where Y is $n \times 1$, X is $n \times k$, we now posit that elements of U are independently distributed according to first order Sargan densities with $\gamma_1 = 1$. The likelihood function is obtained immediately from (6.5.5). Denoting the regression equation for the ith observation as $y_i = \beta'x_i + u_i$ and by Σ_+ and Σ_- summation over positive and negative terms of $y_i - \beta'x_i$, we can write

$$\frac{\partial^2 \log L}{\partial \alpha^2} = -\frac{n}{\alpha^2} - \sum_{+} \frac{(y_i - \beta'x_i)^2}{[1+\alpha(y_i - \beta'x_i)]^2} - \sum_{-} \frac{(y_i - \beta'x_i)^2}{[1-\alpha(y_i - \beta'x_i)]^2}$$

$$\frac{\partial^2 \log L}{\partial \beta_j^2} = -\sum_{+} \frac{\alpha^2 x_{ij}^2}{[1+\alpha(y_i - \beta'x_i)]^2} - \sum_{-} \frac{\alpha^2 x_{ij}^2}{[1-\alpha(y_i - \beta'x_i)]^2}$$

$$\frac{\partial^2 \log L}{\partial \alpha \partial \beta_j} = \sum_{+} x_{ij} - \sum_{-} x_{ij} - \sum_{+} \frac{x_{ij}}{[1+\alpha(y_i - \beta'x_i)]^2} + \sum_{-} \frac{x_{ij}}{[1-\alpha(y_i - \beta'x_i)]^2}$$

$$\frac{\partial^2 \log L}{\partial \beta_j \partial \beta_k} = \sum_{+} \frac{\alpha^2 x_{ij} x_{ik}}{[1+\alpha(y_i - \beta'x_i)]^2} + \sum_{-} \frac{\alpha^2 x_{ij} x_{ik}}{[1-\alpha(y_i - \beta'x_i)]^2}$$

It is easy to show that $E(\partial^2 \log L/\partial \alpha \partial \beta') = 0$. To obtain

$$E\left(-\frac{1}{n}\ \frac{\partial^2 \log L}{\partial \beta \partial \beta'}\right)^{-1}$$

we first note that it will contain a term $X'X/n$. In addition, it will contain the $E\{\alpha^2/(1+\alpha|u|)^2\}$ which can be shown to be (approximately) $0.109\alpha^2 e$. Hence

$$E\left(-\frac{1}{n}\ \frac{\partial^2 \log L}{\partial \beta \partial \beta'}\right)^{-1} = \frac{(X'X/n)^{-1}}{0.109\alpha^2 e}$$

It follows that the asymptotic distribution of $\sqrt{n}(\hat{\beta} - \beta)$ is $N(0, (3.375/\alpha^2) (X'X/n)^{-1})$. Since the asymptotic distribution of $\sqrt{n}(\hat{\beta}_{\text{OLS}} - \beta)$ is $N(0, \sigma^2(X'X/n)^{-1})$ and $\sigma^2 = 4/\alpha^2$, the efficiency of OLS when the errors actually have Sargan distribution is approximately 0.84.

Cost of Misspecification

An interesting question is how serious a misspecification it might be if the error terms are actually normally distributed, but the investigator mistakenly assumes that they have Sargan distribution. (The reverse case, while interesting in principle, is likely to be of lesser importance.) This question and similar ones have been investigated by Goldfeld and Quandt (1981a), Arabmazar and Schmidt (1982), Missiakoulis (1983), Kafei and Schmidt (1985), and Tse (1987). Goldfeld and Quandt (1981a) performed Monte Carlo experiments with a simple disequilibrium model in which the true errors were normal but the likelihood function to be maximized was derived on the assumption of first-order Sargan distributed errors. The root mean square errors of the estimates were greater than with the correctly specified likelihood but only slightly so and the misspecification did not appear to be too serious. Missiakoulis (1983) examines first- and second-order Sargan error distributions in the probit model

$$y_t^* = \mu + u_t$$
$$y_t = 1 \quad \text{if } y_t^* > 0$$
$$y_t = 0 \quad \text{otherwise}$$

for six alternative assumptions about the distribution of u_t. This error term is alternately assumed to have as its true distribution the normal, Laplace, logistic, and t with 5, 10, and 20 degrees of freedom. Overwhelmingly, the asymptotic bias of $\hat{\mu}$ from the first-order Sargan was smaller than for the second-order Sargan. Kafei and Schmidt (1985) examine the tobit and the truncated regression model with the true errors being normally distributed. They find that the asymptotic bias is greater in the truncated than in the censored case but is relatively small (particularly in the tobit case) when the amount of censoring (truncation) is less than 50 per cent. They also find by comparing this case with its obverse that it is costlier to assume normality when the truth is Sargan than the reverse – a finding somewhat at variance with Goldfeld and Quandt (1981a). Kafei and Schmidt also find that the second-order Sargan does better than the first-order one. Finally, Tse (1987) compares the normal with various Sargan densities and finds that the second-order Sargan density provides a reasonable approximation.

Disequilibrium Model with Sargan Densities

Consider the simple model A and let the error terms have independent first-order Sargan densities with parameters α_1, α_2 (with $\gamma_1 = \gamma_2 = 1$). The joint density of demand and supply is

$$g(D,S) = \left[\frac{\alpha_1}{4} \exp\{-\alpha_1|D-\beta_1'x_1|\} \,(1 + \alpha_1|D-\beta_1'x_1|) \right]$$

$$\times \left[\frac{\alpha_2}{4} \exp\{-\alpha_2|S-\beta_2'x_2|\} \,(1 + \alpha_2|S-\beta_2'x_2|) \right] \quad (6.5.11)$$

The p.d.f. of Q is obtained by performing the integrations as in (2.3.7). Since the integrals depend on the signs of $Q - \beta_i'x_i$, it is convenient to define

$$\xi(Q,\alpha_i,\beta_i,x_i) = \frac{\alpha_i}{4} \exp\{-\alpha_i|Q-\beta_i'x_i|\}\,(1+\alpha_i|Q-\beta_i'x_i|)$$

$$\psi_{\mathrm{I}}(Q,\alpha_i,\beta_i,x_i) = \frac{1}{2} \exp\{-\alpha_i(Q-\beta_i'x_i)\}$$

$$+ \frac{1}{4} \alpha_i(Q-\beta_i'x_i)\exp\{-\alpha_i(Q-\beta_i'x_i)\}$$

$$\psi_{\mathrm{II}}(Q,\alpha_i,\beta_i,x_i) = 1 - \frac{1}{2} \exp\{\alpha_i(Q-\beta_i'x_i)\}$$

$$+ \frac{1}{4} \alpha_i(Q-\beta_i'x_i)\exp\{\alpha_i(Q-\beta_i'x_i)\}$$

It can be shown easily that

$$h(Q) = \begin{cases} \xi(Q,\alpha_1,\beta_1,x_1)\psi_{\mathrm{I}}(Q,\alpha_2,\beta_2,x_2) + \xi(Q,\alpha_2,\beta_2,x_2)\psi_{\mathrm{I}}(Q,\alpha_1,\beta_1,x_1) \\ \quad \text{if } Q \geqq \beta_1'x_1,\ Q \geqq \beta_2'x_2 \\[4pt] \xi(Q,\alpha_1,\beta_1,x_1)\psi_{\mathrm{I}}(Q,\alpha_2,\beta_2,x_2) + \xi(Q,\alpha_2,\beta_2,x_2)\psi_{\mathrm{II}}(Q,\alpha_1,\beta_1,x_1) \\ \quad \text{if } Q < \beta_1'x_1,\ Q \geqq \beta_2'x_2 \\[4pt] \xi(Q,\alpha_1,\beta_1,x_1)\psi_{\mathrm{II}}(Q,\alpha_2,\beta_2,x_2) + \xi(Q,\alpha_2,\beta_2,x_2)\psi_{\mathrm{I}}(Q,\alpha_1,\beta_1,x_1) \\ \quad \text{if } Q \geqq \beta_1'x_1,\ Q < \beta_2'x_2 \\[4pt] \xi(Q,\alpha_1,\beta_1,x_1)\psi_{\mathrm{II}}(Q,\alpha_2,\beta_2,x_2) + \xi(Q,\alpha_2,\beta_2,x_2)\psi_{\mathrm{II}}(Q,\alpha_1,\beta_1,x_1) \\ \quad \text{if } Q < \beta_1'x_1,\ Q < \beta_2'x_2 \end{cases} \quad (6.5.12)$$

The likelihood is obviously the product of terms given by (6.5.12). Goldfeld and Quandt (1981a) show that the likelihood function based on (6.5.12) is continuous and has continuous first partial derivatives (exercise 6.10).

A significant but perhaps discouraging result is that employing the Sargan density still permits the likelihood function to be unbounded in parameter space. Define the sets T_1, T_2, T_3, T_4 as follows:

$$T_1 = \{t \,|\, Q_t \geq \beta_1' x_{1t}, \ Q_t \geq \beta_2' x_{2t}\}$$

$$T_2 = \{t \,|\, Q_t < \beta_1' x_{1t}, \ Q_t \geq \beta_2' x_{2t}\}$$

$$T_3 = \{t \,|\, Q_t \geq \beta_1' x_{1t}, \ Q_t < \beta_2' x_{2t}\}$$

$$T_4 = \{t \,|\, Q_t < \beta_1' x_{1t}, \ Q_t < \beta_2' x_{2t}\}$$

and abbreviate $\xi(Q_t, \alpha_i, \beta_i, x_{it})$ as ξ_{it}, $\psi_{\mathrm{I}}(Q_t, \alpha_i, \beta_i, x_{it})$ as $\psi_{\mathrm{I}it}$, and similarly for ψ_{II}. The likelihood is

$$L = \prod_{t \epsilon T_1} (\xi_{1t}\psi_{\mathrm{I}2t} + \xi_{2t}\psi_{\mathrm{I}1t}) \prod_{t \epsilon T_2} (\xi_{1t}\psi_{\mathrm{I}2t} + \xi_{2t}\psi_{\mathrm{II}1t})$$

$$\times \prod_{t \epsilon T_3} (\xi_{1t}\psi_{\mathrm{II}2t} + \xi_{2t}\psi_{\mathrm{I}1t}) \prod_{t \epsilon T_4} (\xi_{1t}\psi_{\mathrm{II}2t} + \xi_{2t}\psi_{\mathrm{II}1t}) \qquad (6.5.13)$$

Assume that β_1 has k_1 elements and that the number of members in T_1 and T_3 together is less than or equal to k_1. We can then choose β_1 so that $Q_t = \beta_1' x_{1t}$ for all $t \epsilon T_1 \cup T_3$. Choose α_2, β_2 to be some finite numbers and let $\alpha_1 \to \infty$. Then (a) $\xi_{1t} \to \infty$ for $t \epsilon T_1 \cup T_3$, (b) $\psi_{\mathrm{I}2t} \neq 0$ and $\psi_{\mathrm{II}2t} \neq 0$ for $t \epsilon T_1 \cup T_3$, (c) $\xi_{2t} \neq 0$ for $t \epsilon T_2 \cup T_4$, and (d) $\psi_{\mathrm{II}1t} \to 1$ for $t \epsilon T_2 \cup T_4$. It follows immediately that $L \to \infty$. It is also clear immediately that if $T_1 \cup T_3$ contained more than k_1 elements, we could not find a β_1 such that all $\xi_{1t} \to \infty$; with probability 1 at least one ξ_{1t} would approach zero and would have order strictly less than $0(\alpha_1^{-2})$, whereas the unbounded terms are only of order $0(\alpha_1^2)$. Hence the likelihood would not become unbounded.

To consider a two-market model, rewrite (6.3.1) to (6.3.6) in slightly more general form as follows:

$$D_1 = \gamma_1 Q_2 + \beta_1' x_1 + u_1$$

$$S_1 = \gamma_2 Q_2 + \beta_2' x_2 + u_2$$

$$Q_1 = \min(D_1, S_1)$$

$$D_2 = \gamma_3 Q_1 + \beta_3' x_3 + u_3$$

$$S_2 = \gamma_4 Q_1 + \beta_4' x_4 + u_4$$

$$Q_2 = \min(D_2, S_2)$$

If we now assume that the u_i have independent Sargan densities $f(u_i) = (\alpha_i/4)\exp\{-\alpha_i|u_i|\}(1 + \alpha_i|u_i|)$, the density of u_1, u_2, u_3, u_4 is

$$f(u_1, u_2, u_3, u_4) = \frac{\alpha_1 \alpha_2 \alpha_3 \alpha_4}{256} \exp\left\{ -\sum_{i=1}^{4} \alpha_i |u_i| \right\} \prod_{i=1}^{4} (1 + \alpha_i |u_i|)$$

$$(6.5.14)$$

Just as before we have four regimes with matrices A_i (see (6.3.7) and thereafter).

Corresponding to (6.3.9) we have for regime 1

$$f_1(y) = |\det(A_i)| \frac{\alpha_1 \alpha_2 \alpha_3 \alpha_4}{256}$$

$$\times \exp\{ -\alpha_1 |D_1 - \gamma_1 D_2 - \beta_1' x_1| - \alpha_2 |S_1 - \gamma_2 D_2 - \beta_2' x_2|$$
$$- \alpha_3 |D_2 - \gamma_3 D_1 - \beta_3' x_3| - \alpha_4 |S_2 - \gamma_4 D_1 - \beta_4' x_4| \}$$
$$\times (1 + \alpha_1 |D_1 - \gamma_1 D_2 - \beta_1' x_1|)(1 + \alpha_2 |S_1 - \gamma_2 D_2 - \beta_2' x_2|)$$
$$\times (1 + \alpha_3 |D_2 - \gamma_3 D_1 - \beta_3' x_3|)(1 + \alpha_4 |S_2 - \gamma_4 D_1 - \beta_4' x_4|) \quad (6.5.15)$$

This is the term in which D_1, D_2 will be replaced by Q_1 and Q_2 and in which S_1 and S_2 are integrated out. Because this is the simple case in which the integrals factor, we have

$$\int_{Q_1}^{\infty} \int_{Q_2}^{\infty} f_1(y) \, dS_2 \, dS_1 = |\det(A_i)| \frac{\alpha_1 \alpha_3}{16}$$

$$\times \exp\{ -\alpha_1 |Q_1 - \gamma_1 Q_2 - \beta_1' x_1| - \alpha_3 |Q_2 - \gamma_3 Q_1 - \beta_3' x_3| \}$$
$$\times (1 + \alpha_1 |Q_1 - \gamma_1 Q_2 - \beta_1' x_1|)(1 + \alpha_3 |Q_2 - \gamma_3 Q_1 - \beta_3' x_3|)$$

$$\times \int_{Q_1}^{\infty} \frac{\alpha_4}{4} \exp\{ -\alpha_4 |S_2 - \gamma_4 Q_1 - \beta_4' x_4| \}$$

$$\times (1 + \alpha_4 |S_2 - \gamma_4 Q_1 - \beta_4' x_4|) \, dS_2$$

$$\times \int_{Q_1}^{\infty} \frac{\alpha_2}{4} \exp\{ -\alpha_2 |S_1 - \gamma_2 Q_2 - \beta_2' x_2| \}$$

$$\times (1 + \alpha_2 |S_1 - \gamma_2 Q_2 - \beta_2' x_2|) \, dS_1 \quad (6.5.16)$$

Each of the integrals in (6.5.16) is of exactly the same form as in the single-market disequilibrium model.

6.6 Models with Anticipatory Pricing

Green and Laffont (1981) and Ducos, Green and Laffont (1982) have explored a model in which prices are determined quite differently from the ordinary disequilibrium models. In the standard models, prices are either completely rigid (model A) or are adjusted according to some price adjustment equation (e.g. model D). The basic postulate of the anticipatory price setting model is that in period t that price is observed which would equate expected demand and supply in that period, i.e. the demand and the supply that would materialize with zero error terms. Although the market's anticipation of such values of demand and supply is correct on the average, disequilibrium arises because in any concrete period there occur nonzero errors. In a single-market model we have

$$D_t = \alpha_1 p_t^* + \beta_1' x_{1t} + u_{1t}$$
$$S_t = \alpha_2 p_t^* + \beta_2' x_{2t} + u_{2t} \qquad (6.6.1)$$
$$Q_t = \min(D_t, S_t)$$

where

$$p_t^* = (\beta_2' x_{2t} - \beta_1' x_{1t})/(\alpha_1 - \alpha_2) \qquad (6.6.2)$$

It is obvious that the price change from the previous period contains no information concerning whether excess demand or supply occurs. Estimation of (6.6.1) is as usual if (6.6.2) is disregarded as a set of restrictions. If (6.6.2) is taken into account, the first two equations of (6.6.1) become

$$D_t = -\frac{\alpha_1 \beta_1'}{\alpha_1 - \alpha_2} x_{1t} + \frac{\alpha_1 \beta_2'}{\alpha_1 - \alpha_2} x_{2t} + u_{1t}$$

$$S_t = -\frac{\alpha_1 \beta_1'}{\alpha_1 - \alpha_2} x_{1t} + \frac{\alpha_1 \beta_2'}{\alpha_1 - \alpha_2} x_{2t} + u_{2t}$$

and the parameters are not identified. Hence this model is not of interest.

A more interesting model is the multimarket model introduced by Green and Laffont (1981), which is distinguished not only by the anticipatory price setting mechanism, but also by the fact that inventories play a crucial role in the model. In this respect it is an attempt to answer Blinder's (1980) criticism of disequilibrium models. The model has a commodity market and a labor market. We have

$$D_{1t} = \alpha_{11} p_t + \alpha_{12} w_t \qquad\qquad\quad + \gamma_1(Q_{2t} - S_{2t}) + u_{1t} \qquad (6.6.3)$$

$$S_{1t} = \beta_1 p_t - \beta_1 w_t + \delta_1(s_t - s_t^*) + \gamma_2(Q_{2t} - D_{2t}) + u_{2t} \qquad (6.6.4)$$

$$D_{2t} = \alpha_2 p_t - \alpha_2 w_t + \delta_2(s_t - s_t^*) + \gamma_3(Q_{1t} - S_{1t}) + u_{3t} \qquad (6.6.5)$$

$$S_{2t} = \beta_{21} p_t + \beta_{22} w_t \qquad\qquad\quad + \gamma_4(Q_{1t} - D_{1t}) + u_{4t} \qquad (6.6.6)$$

$$Q_{1t} = \min(D_{1t}, S_{1t}) \qquad (6.6.7)$$

$$Q_{2t} = \min(D_{2t}, S_{2t}) \qquad (6.6.8)$$

where D_{1t}, S_{1t} refer to the commodity market and D_{2t}, S_{2t} to the labor market, s_t is the beginning of period inventories, s_t^* is desired inventories, and p_t, w_t are the logarithms of prices and wages respectively.[9] All demand and supply functions depend on the commodity price and on the wage. All equations contain spillover terms with positive spillover coefficients from the other market (see, for example, (5.2.15)). The commodity supply and labor demand equations also contain the further restriction that they depend on the real wage. These equations also contain the discrepancy between beginning-of-period inventories and desired inventories; if this discrepancy is positive, we would expect commodity supply to be greater and labor demand to be less. Hence $\delta_1 > 0$ and $\delta_2 < 0$.

The "anticipatory" prices and wages that clear the markets when error terms are zero are obtained by equating demand and supply in each market when the error terms and spillover terms are zero. Hence

$$\delta_1(s_t - s_t^*) + \beta_1(p_t^* - w_t^*) = \alpha_{11}p_t^* + \alpha_{12}w_t^* \equiv Q_{1t}^a \tag{6.6.9}$$

$$\delta_2(s_t - s_t^*) + \alpha_2(p_t^* - w_t^*) = \beta_{21}p_t^* + \beta_{22}w_t^* \equiv Q_{2t}^a \tag{6.6.10}$$

which define Q_1^a and Q_2^a, quantities that will turn out to be useful below. We further obtain

$$p_t^* = (s_t - s_t^*)[\delta_1(\beta_{22} + \alpha_2) - \delta_2(\alpha_{12} + \beta_1)]/\Delta \tag{6.6.11}$$

$$w_t^* = (s_t - s_t^*)[\delta_2(\alpha_{11} - \beta_1) - \delta_1(\beta_{21} - \alpha_2)]/\Delta \tag{6.6.12}$$

where $\Delta = (\alpha_{11} - \beta_1)(\beta_{22} + \alpha_2) - (\beta_{21} - \alpha_2)(\alpha_{12} + \beta_1)$ (see exercise 6.11).

As is usual in models of this type, four regimes may be identified, corresponding to Keynesian unemployment ($D_{1t} < S_{1t}$, $D_{2t} < S_{2t}$), under-consumption ($D_{1t} < S_{1t}$, $D_{2t} > S_{2t}$), classical unemployment ($D_{1t} > S_{1t}$, $D_{2t} < S_{2t}$), and repressed inflation ($D_{1t} > S_{1t}$, $D_{2t} > S_{2t}$). Denoting by v_t' the vector ($Q_{1t}^a + u_{1t}$, $Q_{1t}^a + u_{2t}$, $Q_{2t}^a + u_{3t}$, $Q_{2t}^a + u_{4t}$), and by y_t' the vector (D_{1t}, S_{1t}, D_{2t}, S_{2t}), we can write the four regimes as

$$A_i y_t = v_t \qquad i = 1, \ldots, 4 \tag{6.6.13}$$

where

$$A_1 = \begin{bmatrix} 1 & 0 & -\gamma_1 & \gamma_1 \\ 0 & 1 & 0 & 0 \\ -\gamma_3 & \gamma_3 & 1 & 0 \\ 0 & 0 & 0 & 1 \end{bmatrix}, \qquad A_2 = \begin{bmatrix} 1 & 0 & 0 & 0 \\ 0 & 1 & \gamma_2 & -\gamma_2 \\ -\gamma_3 & \gamma_3 & 1 & 0 \\ 0 & 0 & 0 & 1 \end{bmatrix}$$

[9] For the microtheoretic discussion of the various restrictions on the parameters see Green and Laffont (1981) and Blinder and Fischer (1979). In any concrete application, desired inventories themselves would normally have to be modelled; here we simply represent them by s_t^*.

$$A_3 = \begin{bmatrix} 1 & 0 & -\gamma_1 & \gamma_1 \\ 0 & 1 & 0 & 0 \\ 0 & 0 & 1 & 0 \\ \gamma_4 & -\gamma_4 & 0 & 1 \end{bmatrix}, \qquad A_4 = \begin{bmatrix} 1 & 0 & 0 & 0 \\ 0 & 1 & \gamma_2 & -\gamma_2 \\ 0 & 0 & 1 & 0 \\ \gamma_4 & -\gamma_4 & 0 & 1 \end{bmatrix}$$

Equation (6.6.13) can be solved for each regime as $y_t = A_i^{-1} v_t$. For example,

$$A_1^{-1} = \frac{1}{1-\gamma_1\gamma_3} \begin{bmatrix} 1 & -\gamma_1\gamma_3 & \gamma_1 & -\gamma_1 \\ 0 & 1-\gamma_1\gamma_3 & 0 & 0 \\ \gamma_3 & -\gamma_3 & 1 & -\gamma_1\gamma_3 \\ 0 & 0 & 0 & 1-\gamma_1\gamma_3 \end{bmatrix}$$

Since each regime is defined by a particular relationship between demands and supplies, the solutions impose corresponding relationships upon the error terms. Thus, in regime 1 the solution is

$$D_{1t} = Q_{1t}^a + \frac{u_{1t} - \gamma_1\gamma_3 u_{2t} + \gamma_1(u_{3t} - u_{4t})}{1 - \gamma_1\gamma_3}$$

$$S_{1t} = Q_{1t}^a + u_{2t}$$

$$D_{2t} = Q_{2t}^a + \frac{\gamma_{3t}(u_{1t} - u_{2t}) + u_{3t} - \gamma_1\gamma_3 u_{4t}}{1 - \gamma_1\gamma_3} \qquad (6.6.14)$$

$$S_{2t} = Q_{2t}^a + u_{4t}$$

We now impose the coherency conditions $1-\gamma_1\gamma_3 > 0$, $1-\gamma_2\gamma_3 > 0$, $1-\gamma_1\gamma_4 > 0$, $1-\gamma_2\gamma_4 > 0$. Since this regime corresponds to $D_{1t} < S_{1t}$, $D_{2t} < S_{2t}$, we obtain from (6.6.14) the restrictions

$$u_{2t} - u_{1t} - \gamma_1(u_{3t} - u_{4t}) > 0, \qquad \gamma_3(u_{2t} - u_{1t}) - (u_{3t} - u_{4t}) > 0 \quad (6.6.15)$$

Similar constraints are obtained for the other regimes. We have for regime 2:

$$u_{2t} - u_{1t} - \gamma_2(u_{3t} - u_{4t}) > 0, \qquad \gamma_3(u_{2t} - u_{1t}) - (u_{3t} - u_{4t}) < 0 \quad (6.6.16)$$

for regime 3:

$$u_{2t} - u_{1t} - \gamma_1(u_{3t} - u_{4t}) < 0, \qquad \gamma_4(u_{2t} - u_{1t}) - (u_{3t} - u_{4t}) > 0 \quad (6.6.17)$$

and for regime 4:

$$u_{2t} - u_{1t} - \gamma_2(u_{3t} - u_{4t}) < 0, \qquad \gamma_4(u_{2t} - u_{1t}) - (u_{3t} - u_{4t}) < 0 \quad (6.6.18)$$

These four inequalities partition the space of possible error terms.

Estimation and Testing

The test of the hypothesis of equilibrium versus disequilibrium is based on the properties of the composite error term in the dynamic relationship that governs the evolution of inventories over time. The change in inventories is simply the difference between production and consumption; thus

$$s_{t+1} - s_t = gQ_{2t} - Q_{1t} \qquad (6.6.19)$$

where g is the marginal (and average) product of labor and is assumed to be constant. Depending on which regime is operating, we must substitute for Q_{1t} either D_{1t} or S_{1t} and for Q_{2t} either D_{2t} or S_{2t}; then, whichever of these substitutions occurred, we further substitute for D_{1t} or S_{1t} and D_{2t} or S_{2t} from the appropriate $y_t = A_i^{-1}v_t$. This leads to (6.6.19) being replaced by

$$s_{t+1}-s_t=gQ_{2t}^a-Q_{1t}^a+ \begin{cases} \dfrac{u_{1t}(g\gamma_3-1)+u_{2t}\gamma_3(\gamma_1-g)+u_{3t}(g-\gamma_1)+u_{4t}\gamma_1(1-g\gamma_3)}{1-\gamma_1\gamma_3} \\ \qquad\qquad\qquad\qquad\qquad\qquad\qquad\qquad \text{for regime 1} \\[4pt] -u_{1t}+gu_{4t} \qquad\qquad\qquad\qquad\qquad \text{for regime 2} \\[4pt] -u_{2t}+gu_{3t} \qquad\qquad\qquad\qquad\qquad \text{for regime 3} \\[4pt] \dfrac{u_{1t}\gamma_4(\gamma_2-g)+u_{2t}(g\gamma_4-1)+u_{3t}\gamma_2(1-g\gamma_4)+u_{4t}(g-\gamma_2)}{1-\gamma_2\gamma_4} \\ \qquad\qquad\qquad\qquad\qquad\qquad\qquad\qquad \text{for regime 4} \\ \qquad\qquad\qquad\qquad\qquad\qquad\qquad\qquad\qquad (6.6.20) \end{cases}$$

The composite error term is different in the four regimes and the expectation of the composite error term conditional on the regime will not be equal to zero. Equation (6.6.20) can be rewritten still further. Substitute (6.6.11) and (6.6.12) into the left hand sides of (6.6.9) and (6.6.10); then substitute these expressions for Q_{1t}^a and Q_{2t}^a into the expression $gQ_{2t}^a - Q_{1t}^a$ that occurs in (6.6.20). Both Q_{2t}^a and Q_{1t}^a are proportional to $s_t - s_t^*$, with the factor of proportionality being

$$K = \{(g\beta_{21}-\alpha_{11})[\delta_1(\beta_{22}+\alpha_2)-\delta_2(\alpha_{12}+\beta_1)]$$
$$\qquad + (g\beta_{22}-\alpha_{12})[\delta_2(\alpha_{11}-\beta_1)-\delta_1(\beta_4-\alpha_2)]\}/\Delta$$

Thus (6.6.20) can be summarized as

$$s_{t+1} = (1+K)s_t - Ks_t^* + \phi_i(u_t) \qquad i=1,\ldots,4 \qquad (6.6.21)$$

where $\phi_i(u_t)$ represents the composite error term in the ith regime.

A similar equation can be derived on the assumption that all markets clear. We set the spillovers equal to zero in (6.6.3) to (6.6.6) and set demands equal to corresponding supplies. Thus we obtain p^*, w^*, and the values of commodity and labor transactions in equilibrium. These can then be substituted for Q_{1t} and Q_{2t} in (6.6.19). The key difference between the result here and (6.6.20) is that with market clearing there are no "regimes" in the equation describing the time path of equilibrium. Hence, the composite error term of this equation, which is linear in the u_ts, has an expected value of zero.

The underlying idea of the test of the equilibrium hypothesis proposed by Green and Laffont (1981) and Ducos, Green and Laffont (1982) is the following. If we partitioned the data by regimes and estimated (6.6.20) separately for each, we would expect to find different constant terms in the equations for the various regimes if the equilibrium hypothesis were false, since then (and only then) does the expected value of the error term conditional on a data partitioning give a nonzero value and one which is different from regime to regime. Of course, we do not know *a priori* which regime is in effect in each period. To test whether there is a single constant, we would have to estimate the model for each of the 4^T possible partitions and compare the overall likelihood of these partitions with the likelihood of the single-constant case. Since this is hardly practical, Ducos, Green and Laffont simplify the problem by assuming that $u_{2t} = u_{3t} = u_{4t} = 0$ for all t. Then it follows from (6.6.15) to (6.6.18) and the positiveness of the γ_i coefficients that only regime 1 (Keynesian unemployment) and regime 4 (repressed inflation) are possible. The remaining two incarnations of (6.6.21) are

$$s_{t+1} = (1+K)s_t - Ks_t^* + \begin{cases} \psi_1 u_{1t} & \text{if } u_{1t} < 0 \\ \psi_2 u_{1t} & \text{if } u_{1t} > 0 \end{cases} \qquad (6.6.22)$$

where $\psi_1 = (g\gamma_3 - 1)/(1 - \gamma_1\gamma_3)$, $\psi_2 = (\gamma_2 - g)\gamma_4/(1 - \gamma_2\gamma_4)$. If, as is possible, the rationing of labor demand reduces sales by less than output, $\gamma_2 < g$; and if rationing of sales by one unit reduces output by less than a unit, then $g\gamma_3 < 1$. Hence ψ_1 and ψ_2 are both negative. This model may be estimated by maximum likelihood, since the density function of s_{t+1} is

$$f(s_{t+1}) = \begin{cases} f_1(s_{t+1}) = \dfrac{1}{\sqrt{(2\pi)}\sigma_1|\psi_1|} \exp\left\{ -\dfrac{1}{2\sigma_1^2\psi_1^2} [s_{t+1} - (1+K)s_t + Ks_t^*]^2 \right\} \\ \qquad\qquad\qquad \text{if } \dfrac{s_{t+1} - (1+K)s_t + Ks_t^*}{\psi_1} < 0 \\ f_2(s_{t+1}) = \dfrac{1}{\sqrt{(2\pi)}\sigma_2|\psi_2|} \exp\left\{ -\dfrac{1}{2\sigma_2^2\psi_2^2} [s_{t+1} - (1+K)s_t + Ks_t^*]^2 \right\} \\ \qquad\qquad\qquad\qquad\qquad\qquad\qquad\qquad\qquad \text{otherwise} \end{cases}$$

Let T_1 and T_2 denote the index sets over which $[s_{t+1} - (1+K)s_t + Ks_t^*] > 0$ and < 0 respectively. These index sets then correspond to the partitioning of the model according to the sign of the error term, and are "observable" for any particular set of values being assigned to the unknown coefficients. Then the likelihood is

$$L = \prod_{T_1} f_1(s_{t+1}) \prod_{T_2} f_2(s_{t+1}) \qquad (6.6.23)$$

which may be maximized by numerical techniques. The null hypothesis of equilibrium is then tested by testing whether $\psi_1 = \psi_2$, which may be accomplished by a likelihood ratio test.

In an empirical application, Ducos, Green and Laffont reject the equilibrium hypothesis quite unambiguously. Nevertheless, the procedure has to be treated with some caution. It rests on very strong assumptions about structural coefficients and particularly strong assumptions about the error terms ($u_{2t} = u_{3t} = u_{4t} = 0$) that are not plausible. The likelihood function also has a structure where a sorting of terms is involved that depends on the values of the parameters; functions of this type are likely to have numerous local optima. If that is the case, only a local optimum may be found when the model is estimated under the alternative hypothesis of disequilibrium. Thus the test may, in practice, unduly favor the equilibrium hypothesis.

Exercises

6.1   Derive matrices A_1, A_3, A_4 and B_1, B_3, B_4 for model D.

6.2   Consider the probit model in which y_1^*, y_2^* are the latent and y_1, y_2 the observed random variables:

$$y_1^* = \alpha_1 y_2 + u_1$$

$$y_2^* = \alpha_2 y_1 + u_2$$

$$y_1 = \begin{cases} 1 & \text{if } y_1^* > 0 \\ 0 & \text{otherwise} \end{cases}$$

$$y_2 = \begin{cases} 1 & \text{if } y_2^* > 0 \\ 0 & \text{otherwise} \end{cases}$$

where u_1, u_2 are jointly normal.
(a) Under what circumstances is this model coherent? (b) When the model is coherent, what is the joint probability of y_1, y_2?

6.3   Prove that the matrix (6.4.4) is nonsingular if $x_i \neq x_j$ for all i,j.

6.4   Show that the weighting coefficients α_1, α_2, α_3 for the three-point Gauss-Legendre integration formula are 5/9, 8/9, 5/9.

6.5   Prove that $L_j(x) = P_{n+1}(x)/[(x - x_j)P'_{n+1}(x_j)]$ if x_j is a root of $P_{n+1}(x) = 0$.

6.6   Show that the variance of $f(x)/g(x)$ can be minimized for $f(x) > 0$ by choosing $g(x) = f(x)\int_b^a f(x)\,dx$.

6.7   Use Chebyshev's inequality to determine the number of trials n so that the error in the estimate $\hat{I}$ does not exceed ϵ.

6.8   Show for the Sargan densities given in general by (6.5.1) that (a) for all $P \geq 1$, $f(u)$ is continuous if and only if $\gamma_1 = 1$; (b) for all $P \geq 1$ and $\gamma_1 = 1$, $f''(u)$ is continuous at $u = 0$; (c) the second-order density $f_2(u)$ is unimodal if $\gamma_2 < 0.5$.

6.9   Derive the cumulative distribution function for the first- and second-order Sargan densities.

6.10 Show that the likelihood function based on (6.5.12) is continuous and has continuous first partial derivatives with respect to the parameters.

6.11 Derive (6.6.11) and (6.6.12).

6.12 Consider the linear systems (6.6.13) and the dynamic adjustment processes $\dot{Q}_{1t} = k_1[\min(D_{1t}, S_{1t}) - Q_{1t}]$, $\dot{Q}_{2t} = k_2[\min(D_{2t}, S_{2t}) - Q_{2t}]$, where k_1, k_2 are positive constants. Prove that the adjustment process is locally stable if $1 - \gamma_1\gamma_3 > 0$, $1 - \gamma_1\gamma_4 > 0$, $1 - \gamma_2\gamma_3 > 0$, $1 - \gamma_2\gamma_4 > 0$.

Appendix 6.A
FORTRAN Subroutines for Univariate Integration: NEWCT1,
GAULG1, GAUS

```
      SUBROUTINE GAUS(A,B,N,FUNCT,GA,IER)
      IMPLICIT REAL*8 (A-H,O-Z)
C
C     A AND B ARE LIMITS OF INTEGRATION, A<B
C     N MUST BE EVEN AND REPRESENTS NUMBER OF POINTS
C     GA IS THE INTEGRAL
C
      DATA SQ3R/0.577350269/
      IER=0
      IF(MOD(N,2).NE.0.OR.A.GE.B) GOTO 900
      IF(A.GE.B) GOTO 900
      H=(B-A)/N
      M=0
      GA=0.
      BET=A+H*(1.+SQ3R)
      ALF=A+H*(1.-SQ3R)
1     GA=GA+FUNCT(ALF)+FUNCT(BET)
      IF(M.LT.(N/2-1)) GOTO 2
      GA=GA*H
      RETURN
2     ALF=ALF+2.*H
      BET=BET+2.*H
      M=M+1
      GOTO 1
900   IER=-3
      RETURN
      END
      SUBROUTINE NEWCT1(A,B,N,FUNC,ANS,IER)
      IMPLICIT REAL*8 (A-H,O-Z)
C
C     NEWTON-COTES FORMULAS
C     VERY INACCURATE ON NORMAL DENSITY WITH N<7
C
C     A=LOWER LIMIT,B=UPPER LIMIT, REQUIRED A<B
C     N=NUMBER OF POINTS,2<=N<=9
C     FUNC=NAME OF FUNCTION, REQUIRES EXTERNAL FUNC STATEMENT IN
C         CALLING ROUTINE
C     ANS=ANSWER
C     IER=-3 INPUT ERROR
C
      DIMENSION FF(9),D(8)
      DIMENSION C(8,9),CC(8,10)
      DATA D/1.0,1.0,3.0,2.0,5.0,1.0,7.0,4.0/
      DATA CC/1.,1.,1.,7.,19.,41.,751.,969.,1.,4.,3.,32.,75.,216.,3577.,
     1 5888.,0.,1.,3.,12.,50.,27.,1323.,-928.,0.,0.,1.,32.,50.,272.,
     2 2989.,10496.,0.,0.,0.,7.,75.,27.,2989.,-4540.,0.,0.,0.,0.,19.,
     3 216.,1323.,10496.,0.,0.,0.,0.,0.,41.,3577.,-928.,0.,0.,0.,0.,0.,
     4 0.,751.,5888.,0.,0.,0.,0.,0.,0.,989.,2.,3.,8.,45.,288.,140.,
     5 17280.,14175./
      IER=0
      DO 20 I=1,8
      DO 10 J=1,9
10    C(I,J)=CC(I,J)/CC(I,10)
20    CONTINUE
      IF(N.LT.2.OR.N.GT.9) GOTO 900
      IF(A.GE.B) GOTO 900
      NM1=N-1
      XINT=(B-A)/NM1
      FF(1)=FUNC(A)
      ARG=A+XINT
      DO 100 I=1,NM1
      FF(I+1)=FUNC(ARG)
```

```
100     ARG=ARG+XINT
        ANS=0.
        DO 120 I=1,N
120     ANS=ANS+C(NM1,I)*FF(I)
        ANS=ANS*D(NM1)*XINT
890     RETURN
900     IER=-3
        GOTO 890
        END
        SUBROUTINE GAULG1(A,B,N,FUNC,ANS,IER)
        IMPLICIT REAL*8 (A-H,O-Z)
C
C       GAUSS-LEGENDRE INTEGRATION
C
C       A=LOWER LIMIT, B=UPPER LIMIT; REQUIRE A<B
C       N=NUMBER OF POINTS; 2<=N<=11
C       FUNC=NAME OF FUNCTION TO BE INTEGRATED;MUST BE DECLARED IN
C            EXTERNAL STATEMENT IN CALLING ROUTINE
C       ANS=ANSWER
C       IER=-3 INPUT ERROR
C
        DIMENSION FF(11),X(11),W(10,6),Z(10,6)
        DATA W/1.0,0.5555555555,0.3478548451,0.2369268851,0.1713244924,
     $  0.1294849662,0.1012285363,0.08127438836,0.0666713443,0.0556685671
     $,0.0,0.8888888889,0.6521451549,0.4786286705,0.3607615730,
     $  0.2797053915,0.2223810345,0.1806481606,0.1494513492,0.1255803695,
     $  0.0,0.0,0.0,0.5688888889,0.4679139346,0.3818300505,0.3137066459,
     $  0.2606106964,0.2190863625,0.1862902109,0.0,0.0,0.0,0.0,0.0,
     $  0.4179591837,0.3626837834,0.3123470770,0.2692667193,0.2331937645,
     $  0.0,0.0,0.0,0.0,0.0,0.0,0.0,0.0,0.3302393550,0.2955242247,0.262804544
     $5,0.0,0.0,0.0,0.0,0.0,0.0,0.0,0.0,0.0,0.0,0.2729250868/
        DATA Z/0.5773502692,0.7745966692,0.8611363116,0.9061798459,
     $  0.9324695142,0.9491079123,0.9602898565,0.9681602395,0.9739065285,
     $  0.9782286581,0.0,0.0,0.3399810436,0.5384693101,0.6612093865,
     $  0.7415311856,0.7966664774,0.8360311073,0.8650633667,0.8870625998,
     $  0.0,0.0,0.0,0.0,0.2386191861,0.4058451514,0.5255324099,0.61337143
     $27,0.6794095683,0.7301520056,0.0,0.0,0.0,0.0,0.0,0.0,0.1834346425,
     $0.3242534234,0.4333953941,0.5190961292,0.0,0.0,0.0,0.0,0.0,0.0,0.0,0.0
     $,0.0,0.1488743390,0.2695431559,0.0,0.0,0.0,0.0,0.0,0.0,0.0,0.0,0.0,0.0
     $,0.0/
        IER=0
        IF(N.LT.2.OR.N.GT.11) GOTO 900
        IF(A.GE.B) GOTO 900
        IEV=MOD(N,2)
        IROW=N-1
        ICOL=(N+1)/2
        ICOLE=ICOL-IEV
        DO 50 I=1,ICOL
50      X(I)=((B-A)*Z(IROW,I)+B+A)/2.
        DO 60 I=1,ICOLE
60      X(ICOL+I)=((A-B)*Z(IROW,I)+B+A)/2.
        DO 70 I=1,N
70      FF(I)=FUNC(X(I))
        SUM=0.
        DO 80 I=1,ICOL
80      SUM=SUM+W(IROW,I)*FF(I)
        DO 90 I=1,ICOLE
90      SUM=SUM+W(IROW,I)*FF(ICOL+I)
        ANS=SUM*(B-A)/2.
890     RETURN
900     IER=-3
        GOTO 890
        END
```

Appendix 6.B
FORTRAN Subroutines for Bivariate Integration: GAULG2,
BIV2D, CLARK2

```
      FUNCTION BIV2(Z1,Z2,R,IER)
      IMPLICIT REAL*8 (A-H,O-Z)
C         USING OWEN-CADWELL-DALEY EVALUATION--ACCURATE TO ABOUT 4 DEC.
C         WITH PERMISSION OF JERRY HAUSMAN
      TCAD(THETA,X2A,A)=THETA*.15915494*DEXP(-.5*X2A*A/THETA)
C
C         CLOSER APPROX BY DALEY--MAY WANT TO USE
      TCAD2(T,X,A)=T*(1.+.00868*(X*A)**4)
C
C      UNIVARIATE LOWER TAIL AREA
      GAUSS(XX)=(1.+DERF(XX*.7071067800))*.5
C
      IER=0
      X1=Z1
      X2=Z2
      FF1=0.
      FF2=0.
      G1=GAUSS(X1)
      G2=GAUSS(X2)
      BIV2=0.
      SUM=X1+X2
      S2=G1+G2
      IF(R .EQ. 0)GO TO 30
      RR=1.-R*R
      IF(RR)20,40,100
   20 IER=-3
      RETURN
C         INDEPENDENCE
   30 BIV2=G1*G2
      GO TO 99
   40 IF(R .EQ. 1.)GO TO 70
      IF(SUM .LE. 0.)GO TO 99
      BIV2=.5*S2-1.
      GO TO 99
   70 IF((X2-X1) .LT. 0.)GO TO 80
      BIV2=G1
      GO TO 99
   80 BIV2=G2
      GO TO 99
  100 RSQR=1./DSQRT(RR)
      DELTA=.5
      P1=X1*X2
      IF(P1)51,52,53
   52 IF(SUM .LT. 0.)GO TO 51
   53 DELTA=0.
   51 F1=1.
      F2=1.
      IF(X1 .NE. 0.)GO TO 71
      IF(X2 .NE. 0.)GO TO 72
      BIV2=DATAN(R*RSQR)*.15915494+.25
      GO TO 99
   72 T1=.5-.5*G1
      IF(X2 .LT. 0.)T1=-T1
      GO TO 61
   71 T1=0.
      A1=(X2/X1-R)*RSQR
      IF(A1)75,61,54
   75 A1=-A1
      F1=-1.
   54 IF(A1 .LE. 1.)GO TO 82
      X1=DABS(X1)
      GG1=GAUSS(X1)
      X1=A1*X1
```

```
      A1=1./A1
      GG2=GAUSS(X1)
      FF1=.5*(GG1+GG2)-GG1*GG2
      FF1=FF1*F1
      F1=-F1
  82  THETA=DATAN(A1)
      X2A=X1*X1
      IF(X2A .GT. 150.)GO TO 61
      T1=TCAD(THETA,X2A,A1)*F1
      T1=TCAD2(T1,X1,A1)
C         RESTORE X1 TO ORIGINAL VALUE
  61  X1=Z1
      IF(X2 .NE. 0.)GO TO 73
      T2=.5-.5*G2
      IF(X1 .LT. 0.)T2=-T2
      GO TO 62
  73  T2=0.
      A2=(X1/X2-R)*RSQR
      IF(A2)74,62,55
  74  A2=-A2
      F2=-1.
  55  IF(A2 .LE. 1.)GO TO 81
      X2=DABS(X2)
      GG3=GAUSS(X2)
      X2=A2*X2
      A2=1./A2
      GG4=GAUSS(X2)
      FF2=.5*(GG3+GG4)-GG3*GG4
      FF2=FF2*F2
      F2=-F2
  81  THETA=DATAN(A2)
      X2A=X2*X2
      IF(X2A .GT. 150.)GO TO 62
      T2=TCAD(THETA,X2A,A2)*F2
      T2=TCAD2(T2,X2,A2)
  62  BIV2=.5*(G1+G2)-T1-T2-DELTA-FF1-FF2
  99  IF(BIV2 .GT. 1.)BIV2=1.
      IF(BIV2 .LT. 0.)BIV2=0.
      RETURN
      END
      SUBROUTINE GAULG2(AX,BX,AY,BY,NX,NY,FUNC,ANS,IER)
      IMPLICIT REAL*8 (A-H,O-Z)
      DIMENSION FF(11,11),X(11),W(10,6),Z(10,6),Y(11)
      DATA W/1.0,0.5555555555,0.3478548451,0.2369268851,0.1713244924,
     $ 0.1294849662,0.1012285363,0.08127438836,0.066713443,0.0556685671
     $,0.0,0.8888888889,0.6521451549,0.4786286705,0.3607615730,
     $ 0.2797053915,0.2223810345,0.1806481606,0.1494513492,0.1255803695,
     $ 0.0,0.0,0.0,0.5688888889,0.4679139346,0.3818300505,0.3137066459,
     $ 0.2606106964,0.2190863625,0.1862902109,0.0,0.0,0.0,0.0,0.0,
     $ 0.4179591837,0.3626837834,0.3123470770,0.2692667193,0.2331937645,
     $ 0.0,0.0,0.0,0.0,0.0,0.0,0.0,0.3302393550,0.2955242247,0.262804544
     $5,0.0,0.0,0.0,0.0,0.0,0.0,0.0,0.0,0.0,0.0,0.0,0.2729250868/
      DATA Z/0.5773502692,0.7745966692,0.8611363116,0.9061798459,
     $ 0.9324695142,0.9491079123,0.9602898565,0.9681602395,0.9739065285,
     $ 0.9782286581,0.0,0.0,0.3399810436,0.5384693101,0.6612093865,
     $ 0.7415311856,0.7966664774,0.8360311073,0.8650633667,0.8870625998,
     $ 0.0,0.0,0.0,0.0,0.0,0.2386191861,0.4058451514,0.5255324099,0.61337143
     $27,0.6794095683,0.7301520056,0.0,0.0,0.0,0.0,0.0,0.0,0.1834346425,
     $0.3242534234,0.4333953941,0.5190961292,0.0,0.0,0.0,0.0,0.0,0.0,0.0,0.0
     $,0.0,0.1488743390,0.2695431559,0.0,0.0,0.0,0.0,0.0,0.0,0.0,0.0,0.0,0.0
     $,0.0/
      IER=0
      IF(NX.LT.2.OR.NX.GT.11.OR.NY.LT.2.OR.NY.GT.11) GOTO 900
      IF(AX.GE.BX)GOTO 900
      IEVX=MOD(NX,2)
      IROWX=NX-1
      ICOLX=(NX+1)/2
      ICOLEX=ICOLX-IEVX
      IF(AY.GE.BY) GOTO 900
      IEVY=MOD(NY,2)
```

```
      IROWY=NY-1
      ICOLY=(NY+1)/2
      ICOLEY=ICOLY-IEVY
      DO 50 I=1,ICOLX
50    X(I)=((BX-AX)*Z(IROWX,I)+BX+AX)/2.
      DO 60 I=1,ICOLEX
60    X(ICOLX+I)=((AX-BX)*Z(IROWX,I)+BX+AX)/2.
      DO 65 I=1,ICOLY
65    Y(I)=((BY-AY)*Z(IROWY,I)+BY+AY)/2.
      DO 68 I=1,ICOLEY
68    Y(ICOLY+I)=((AY-BY)*Z(IROWY,I)+BY+AY)/2.
      DO 70 I=1,NX
      DO 70 J=1,NY
70    FF(I,J)=FUNC(X(I),Y(J))
      SUM=0.
      DO 80 I=1,ICOLX
      DO 80 J=1,ICOLY
80    SUM=SUM+W(IROWX,I)*W(IROWY,J)*FF(I,J)
      DO 85 I=1,ICOLEX
      DO 85 J=1,ICOLY
85    SUM=SUM+W(IROWX,I)*W(IROWY,J)*FF(ICOLX+I,J)
      DO 90 I=1,ICOLX
      DO 90 J=1,ICOLEY
90    SUM=SUM+W(IROWX,I)*W(IROWY,J)*FF(I,ICOLY+J)
      DO 95 I=1,ICOLEX
      DO 95 J=1,ICOLY
95    SUM=SUM+W(IROWX,I)*W(IROWY,J)*FF(ICOLX+I,ICOLY+J)
      ANS=SUM*(BX-AX)*(BY-AY)/4.
890   RETURN
900   IER=-3
      GOTO 890
      END
      FUNCTION CLARK2(X1,X2,R12)
C THIS FUNCTION EVALUATES THE INTEGRAL OF A BIVARIATE
C NORMAL DENSITY FUNCTION WITH ZERO MEANS AND UNIT VARIANCES
C FROM X1 TO INFINITY, X2 TO INFINITY, USING
C THE CLARK APPROXIMATION.
C
C REFERENCE: DAGANZO, ET AL., TRANSPORTATION SCIENCE, NOV. 1977, P.338.
C
C REPRODUCED WITH PERMISSION FROM MARK PLANT
C
      IMPLICIT REAL*8 (A-H,O-Z)
      COMMON/CONST/RT2PI,RT2
      COMMON/CDATA/PHI,PHIN
      RT2=DSQRT(2.0D0)
      RT2PI=DSQRT(2.0*3.141592653897900)
C TO SAVE COMPUTATION TIME THE TWO CONSTANTS COMPUTED ABOVE CAN
C  BE COMPUTED OUTSIDE THE SUBROUTINE.
C
C THE STATEMENTS BELOW CHECK THAT THE CORRELATION MATRIX IS POSITIVE
C DEFINITE.  IF NOT, AN ERROR MESSAGE IS PRINTED AND A VALUE OF -999.0
C IS RETURNED.
C
      DET=1.0D0-R12*R12
      IF(DET.GT.0.0D0)GO TO 1
      WRITE(6,2)
    2 FORMAT(' ERROR IN FUNCTION CLARK:COVARIANCE MATRIX NOT POSITIVE DE
     &FINITE. CLARK=-999.0.')
      CLARK2=-999.0
      RETURN
1     CALL AMAX(X1,X2,1.0,1.0,R12,F1,F2)
      CLARK2=0.5-0.5*DERF(F1/DSQRT(F2)/RT2)
      RETURN
      END
      SUBROUTINE AMAX(A1,A2,S1,S2,R,F1,F2)
C COMPUTES MEAN AND VARIANCE (F1,F2) OF THE MAX OF TWO
C NORMAL VARIABLES DISTRIBUTED N(A1,A2,S1,S2,R)
      IMPLICIT REAL*8(A-H,O-Z)
      COMMON/CONST/RT2PI,RT2
```

```
COMMON/CDATA/PHI,PHIN
RTS1=DSQRT(S1)
RTS2=DSQRT(S2)
Q=DSQRT(S1+S2-2.0*RTS1*RTS2*R)
ALPHA=(A1-A2)/Q
PHI=0.5+0.5*DERF(ALPHA/RT2)
PHIN=1.0-PHI
EPS=1.0/RT2PI*DEXP(ALPHA**2*(-0.5))
F1=A1*PHI+A2*PHIN+Q*EPS
V2=(A1**2+S1)*PHI+(A2**2+S2)*PHIN+(A1+A2)*EPS*Q
F2=V2-(F1*F1)
RETURN
END
```

Appendix 6.C
FORTRAN Subroutines for Trivariate Integration: GAULG3,
DUTT3, TRINT, CLARK3

```
      FUNCTION CLARK3(X1,X2,X3,R12,R13,R23)
C THIS FUNCTION EVALUATES THE INTEGRAL OF A TRIVARIATE
C NORMAL DENSITY FUNCTION WITH ZERO MEANS AND UNIT VARIANCES
C FROM X1 TO INFINITY, X2 TO INFINITY, X3 TO INFINITY USING
C THE CLARK APPROXIMATION.DOES NOT CHECK CORRELATION MATRIX FOR
C POSITIVE DEFINITENESS.
C REFERENCE: DAGANZO, ET AL., TRANSPORTATION SCIENCE, NOV. 1977, P.338.
C
C REPRODUCED WITH PERMISSION FROM MARK PLANT
C
      IMPLICIT REAL*8 (A-H,O-Z)
      COMMON/CONST/RT2PI,RT2
      COMMON/CDATA/PHI,PHIN
      RT2=DSQRT(2.000)
      RT2PI=DSQRT(2.0*3.141592653897900)
C TO SAVE COMPUTATION TIME THE TWO CONSTANTS COMPUTED ABOVE CAN
C  BE COMPUTED OUTSIDE THE SUBROUTINE.
      CALL AMAX(X1,X2,1.0,1.0,R12,F1,F2)
      RNEW=((R13*PHI)+(R23*PHIN))/DSQRT(F2)
      CALL AMAX(X3,F1,1.0,F2,RNEW,G1,G2)
      CLARK3=0.5-0.5*DERF(G1/DSQRT(G2)/RT2)
      RETURN
      END
      SUBROUTINE AMAX(A1,A2,S1,S2,R,F1,F2)
C COMPUTES MEAN AND VARIANCE (F1,F2) OF THE MAX OF TWO
C NORMAL VARIABLES DISTRIBUTED N(A1,A2,S1,S2,R)
      IMPLICIT REAL*8(A-H,O-Z)
      COMMON/CONST/RT2PI,RT2
      COMMON/CDATA/PHI,PHIN
      RTS1=DSQRT(S1)
      RTS2=DSQRT(S2)
      Q=DSQRT(S1+S2-2.0*RTS1*RTS2*R)
      ALPHA=(A1-A2)/Q
      PHI=0.5+0.5*DERF(ALPHA/RT2)
      PHIN=1.0-PHI
      EPS=1.0/RT2PI*DEXP(ALPHA**2*(-0.5))
      F1=A1*PHI+A2*PHIN+Q*EPS
      V2=(A1**2+S1)*PHI+(A2**2+S2)*PHIN+(A1+A2)*EPS*Q
      F2=V2-(F1*F1)
      RETURN
      END
```

```
      SUBROUTINE GAULG3(AX,BX,AY,BY,AZ,BZ,NX,NY,NZ,FUNC,ANS,IER)
      IMPLICIT REAL*8 (A-H,O-Z)
      DIMENSION FF(11,11,11),X(11),W(10,6),P(10,6),Y(11),Z(11)
      DATA W/1.0,0.5555555555,0.3478548451,0.2369268851,0.1713244924,
     $ 0.1294849662,0.1012285363,0.08127438836,0.06667134.3,0.0556685671
     $,0.0,0.8888888889,0.6521451549,0.4786286705,0.3607615730,
     $ 0.2797053915,0.2223810345,0.1806481606,0.1494513492,0.1255803695,
     $ 0.0,0.0,0.0,0.5688888889,0.4679139346,0.3818300505,0.3137066459,
     $ 0.2606106964,0.2190863625,0.1862902109,0.0,0.0,0.0,0.0,0.0,
     $ 0.4179591837,0.3626837834,0.3123470770,0.2692667193,0.2331937645,
     $ 0.0,0.0,0.0,0.0,0.0,0.0,0.0,0.0,0.0,0.3302393550,0.2955242247,0.262804544
     $5,0.0,0.0,0.0,0.0,0.0,0.0,0.0,0.0,0.0,0.2729250868/
      DATA P/0.5773502692,0.7745966692,0.8611363116,0.9061798459,
     $ 0.9324695142,0.9491079123,0.9602898565,0.9681602395,0.9739065285,
     $ 0.9782286581,0.0,0.0,0.3399810436,0.5384693101,0.6612093865,
     $ 0.7415311856,0.7966664774,0.8360311073,0.8650633667,0.8870625998,
     $ 0.0,0.0,0.0,0.0,0.2386191861,0.4058451514,0.5255324099,0.61337143
     $27,0.6794095683,0.7301520056,0.0,0.0,0.0,0.0,0.0,0.0,0.0,0.1834346425,
     $0.3242534234,0.4333953941,0.5190961292,0.0,0.0,0.0,0.0,0.0,0.0,0.0,0.0
     $,0.0,0.1488743390,0.2695431559,0.0,0.0,0.0,0.0,0.0,0.0,0.0,0.0,0.0,0.0
     $,0.0/
      IER=0
      IF(NX.LT.2.OR.NX.GT.11.OR.NY.LT.2.OR.NY.GT.11.OR.NZ.LT.2.OR.NZ
     1 .GT.11) GOTO 900
      IF(AX.GE.BX.OR.AY.GE.BY.OR.AZ.GE.BZ) GOTO 900
      IEVX=MOD(NX,2)
      IROWX=NX-1
      ICOLX=(NX+1)/2
      ICOLEX=ICOLX-IEVX
      IEVY=MOD(NY,2)
      IROWY=NY-1
      ICOLY=(NY+1)/2
      ICOLEY=ICOLY-IEVY
      IEVZ=MOD(NZ,2)
      IROWZ=NZ-1
      ICOLZ=(NZ+1)/2
      ICOLEZ=ICOLZ-IEVZ
      DO 50 I=1,ICOLX
50    X(I)=((BX-AX)*P(IROWX,I)+BX+AX)/2.
      DO 60 I=1,ICOLEX
60    X(ICOLX+I)=((AX-BX)*P(IROWX,I)+BX+AX)/2.
      DO 65 I=1,ICOLY
65    Y(I)=((BY-AY)*P(IROWY,I)+BY+AY)/2.
      DO 68 I=1,ICOLEY
68    Y(ICOLY+I)=((AY-BY)*P(IROWY,I)+BY+AY)/2.
      DO 69 I=1,ICOLZ
69    Z(I)=((BZ-AZ)*P(IROWZ,I)+BZ+AZ)/2.
      DO 70 I=1,ICOLEZ
70    Z(ICOLZ+I)=((AZ-BZ)*P(IROWZ,I)+BZ+AZ)/2.
      DO 78 I=1,NX
      DO 78 J=1,NY
      DO 78 K=1,NZ
78    FF(I,J,K)=FUNC(X(I),Y(J),Z(K))
      SUM=0.
      DO 80 I=1,ICOLX
      DO 80 J=1,ICOLY
      DO 80 K=1,ICOLZ
80    SUM=SUM+W(IROWX,I)*W(IROWY,J)*W(IROWZ,K)*FF(I,J,K)
      DO 85 I=1,ICOLEX
      DO 85 J=1,ICOLY
      DO 85 K=1,ICOLZ
85    SUM=SUM+W(IROWX,I)*W(IROWY,J)*W(IROWZ,K)*FF(ICOLX+I,J,K)
      DO 90 I=1,ICOLX
      DO 90 J=1,ICOLEY
      DO 90 K=1,ICOLZ
90    SUM=SUM+W(IROWX,I)*W(IROWY,J)*W(IROWZ,K)*FF(I,ICOLY+J,K)
      DO 95 I=1,ICOLEX
      DO 95 J=1,ICOLEY
      DO 95 K=1,ICOLZ
95    SUM=SUM+W(IROWX,I)*W(IROWY,J)*W(IROWZ,K)*FF(ICOLX+I,ICOLY+J,K)
```

```
        DO 100 I=1,ICOLX
        DO 100 J=1,ICOLY
        DO 100 K=1,ICOLEZ
100      SUM=SUM+W(IROWX,I)*W(IROWY,J)*W(IROWZ,K)*FF(I,J,ICOLZ+K)
        DO 105 I=1,ICOLEX
        DO 105 J=1,ICOLY
        DO 105 K=1,ICOLEZ
105      SUM=SUM+W(IROWX,I)*W(IROWY,J)*W(IROWZ,K)*FF(ICOLX+I,J,ICOLZ+K)
        DO 110 I=1,ICOLX
        DO 110 J=1,ICOLEY
        DO 110 K=1,ICOLEZ
110      SUM=SUM+W(IROWX,I)*W(IROWY,J)*W(IROWZ,K)*FF(I,ICOLY+J,ICOLZ+K)
        DO 115 I=1,ICOLEX
        DO 115 J=1,ICOLEY
        DO 115 K=1,ICOLEZ
115     SUM=SUM+W(IROWX,I)*W(IROWY,J)*W(IROWZ,K)*FF(ICOLX+I,ICOLY+J,ICOLZ+
       1K)
        ANS=SUM*(BX-AX)*(BY-AY)*(BZ-AZ)/8.
890     RETURN
900     IER=-3
        GOTO 890
        END
```

```
       SUBROUTINE TRINT(AX,BX,AY,BY,AZ,BZ,N,FUNCT,GA,IER)
       IMPLICIT REAL*8 (A-H,O-Z)
C      N MUST BE EVEN
C      ITERATED GAUSS-LEGENDRE INTEGRATION IN 3 DIMENSIONS
       DATA SQ3R/0.577350269D0/
C      AX,BX,AY,BY,AZ,BZ ARE LOWER AND UPPER LIMITS OF INTEGRATION
C       ALONG THE X,Y,Z AXES.NX,NY,NZ ARE THE NUMBER OF POINTS OF
C       INTEGRATION WHICH MUST BE EVEN.X,Y,Z ARE WORK ARRAYS OF SIZE
C       AT LEAST NX,NY,NZ. THE ANSWER IS RETURNED IN V. FUNCT IS THE
C       NAME OF THE FUNCTION SUBPROGRAM THAT EVALUATES THE INTEGRAND
C       AND MAY BE PASSED TO THE SUBROUTINE.  INPUT ERROR CAUSES
C       NONSTANDARD RETURN.
       IER=0
       IF(MOD(NX,2).NE.0) GOTO 900
       IF(MOD(NY,2).NE.0) GOTO 900
       IF(MOD(NZ,2).NE.0) GOTO 900
       IF(AX.GE.BX.OR.AY.GE.BY.OR.AZ.GE.BZ) GOTO 900
       HX=(BX-AX)/N
       HY=(BY-AY)/N
       HZ=(BZ-AZ)/N
       M1=0
       M2=0
       M3=0
       GA=0.
       BETX=AX+HX*(1.+SQ3R)
       ALFX=AX+HX*(1.-SQ3R)
       BETY=AY+HY*(1.+SQ3R)
       ALFY=AY+HY*(1.-SQ3R)
       BETZ=AZ+HZ*(1.+SQ3R)
       ALFZ=AZ+HZ*(1.-SQ3R)
1      GA=GA+FUNCT(ALFX,ALFY,ALFZ)+FUNCT(ALFX,BETY,ALFZ)+FUNCT(BETX,ALFY,
      1ALFZ)+FUNCT(ALFX,ALFY,BETZ)+FUNCT(ALFX,BETY,BETZ)
      2+FUNCT(BETX,ALFY,BETZ)+FUNCT(BETX,BETY,ALFZ)+FUNCT(BETX,BETY,BETZ)
       IF(M1.LT.(N/2-1)) GOTO 2
       IF(M2.LT.(N/2-1)) GOTO 3
       IF(M3.LT.(N/2-1)) GOTO 4
       GA=GA*HX*HY*HZ
       RETURN
2      ALFX=ALFX+2.*HX
       BETX=BETX+2.*HX
       M1=M1+1
       GOTO 1
3      ALFY=ALFY+2.*HY
       BETY=BETY+2.*HY
       ALFX=AX+HX*(1.-SQ3R)
       BETX=AX+HX*(1.+SQ3R)
       M2=M2+1
       M1=0
       GOTO 1
4      ALFZ=ALFZ+2.*HZ
       BETZ=BETZ+2.*HZ
       BETX=AX+HX*(1.+SQ3R)
       ALFX=AX+HX*(1.-SQ3R)
       BETY=AY+HY*(1.+SQ3R)
       ALFY=AY+HY*(1.-SQ3R)
       M3=M3+1
       M1=0
       M2=0
       GOTO 1
900    IER=-3
       RETURN
       END
       FUNCTION DUTT3(X1,X2,X3,R12,R13,R23)
       IMPLICIT REAL*8(A-H,O-Z)
       IF(.FALSE.) CALL BDUMMY
       COMMON/ROOT/RT2
       RT2=DSQRT(2.0D0)
C
```

```
C  FOR THIS FORMULA SEE DUTT, P. 554
C
       DUTT3=0.125-0.25*((0.5*DERF(X1/RT2))+(0.5*DERF(X2/RT2))+
      1 (0.5*DERF(X3/RT2)))+0.5*(D2(X1,X2,R12)+D2(X1,X3,R13)+D2(X2,X3,R23
      1 ))+D3(X1,X2,X3,R12,R13,R23)
       IF(DUTT3 .GE. 0.0) GO TO 10
       TRIV=0.0
   10 RETURN
       END
       FUNCTION D2(X1,X2,R)
C
C  SEE DUTT, P. 554-- HIS SUBSCRIPTING IS INCORRECT. FOR
C  CORRECTION SEE P. 550.
C
       IMPLICIT REAL*8(A-H,O-Z)
       COMMON/HERMIT/Q(12),Y(12)
       PI=3.14159265358979932384626433
       D2=0
       DO 10 I=1,12
       DO 20 J=1,12
       RIJ=DEXP(R*Q(I)*Q(J))
       X1Q=X1*Q(I)
       X2Q=X2*Q(J)
       DSTAR=(RIJ*DCOS(X1Q-X2Q))-(1.0/RIJ*DCOS(X1Q+X2Q))
       D2=D2+(Y(I)*Y(J)*DSTAR)
   20 CONTINUE
   10 CONTINUE
       D2=1.0/(PI**2)*D2
       RETURN
       END
       FUNCTION D3(X1,X2,X3,R12,R13,R23)
C
C  SEE DUTT P. 554
C
       IMPLICIT REAL*8 (A-H,O-Z)
       COMMON/HERMIT/Q(12),Y(12)
       COMMON/ROOT/RT2
       D3=0
       PI=3.14159265358979324626433
       DO 20 L=1,12
       DO 20 M=1,12
       DO 20 N=1,12
       QLM=Q(L)*Q(M)*R12
       QLN=Q(L)*Q(N)*R13
       QMN=Q(M)*Q(N)*R23
       QX1=Q(L)*X1
       QX2=Q(M)*X2
       QX3=Q(N)*X3
       DSTAR=DEXP(-1.0*(QLM+QLN+QMN))*DSIN(QX1+QX2+QX3)
      & -DEXP(QLM+QLN-QMN)*DSIN(QX2-QX1+QX3)
      & -DEXP(QLM-QLN+QMN)*DSIN(QX1-QX2+QX3)
      & -DEXP(QLN-QLM+QMN)*DSIN(QX1+QX2-QX3)
   20 D3=D3+(Y(L)*Y(M)*Y(N)*DSTAR)
       D3=1.0/(((PI**3)*RT2)*D3
       RETURN
       END
       BLOCK DATA
       IMPLICIT REAL*8(A-H,O-Z)
       COMMON/BDUMMY/I
       COMMON/HERMIT/Q(12),Y(12)
       DATA Q(1),Q(2),Q(3),Q(4),Q(5),Q(6),Q(7),Q(8),Q(9),Q(10),Q(11),Q(12
      &)/8.5078035191942      ,  7.4364764524592      ,  6.5416750050975      ,
      &  5.7327471752510      ,  4.9780413746384      ,  4.2603836050191      ,
      &  3.5693067640730      ,  2.8977286432223      ,  2.2404678516908      ,
```

```
&   1.5934804298161      , 0.95342192293209      , 0.31737009662943/
 DATA  Y(1),Y(2),Y(3),Y(4),Y(5),Y(6),Y(7),Y(8),Y(9),Y(10),Y(11),Y(12
&)/0.19562845953530D-16,0.88544894684639D-13, 0.46566884897419D-10,
&  0.70105501814059D-08, 0.43355318738362D-06, 0.13352533865031D-04,
&  0.23076819593631D-03, 0.24323726193472D-02, 0.16713237137043D-01,
&  0.80163910013783D-01, 0.30016043103593      ,  1.3452154705271  /
 END
```

7

Empirical Models of Disequilibrium

7.1 Introduction

In this last chapter we review some empirical models of disequilibrium. This review is not intended to be exhaustive or even thorough; rather, we only illustrate certain classes of models with brief examples. In particular we omit empirical models that are straightforward applications of the standard models A through D.

Section 7.2 deals with a model of the labor market, and section 7.3 elaborates the case of planned economies which was first introduced in chapter 2. Section 7.4 is devoted to a microeconomic application which permits rationing to occur as a result of optimal marketing strategies. Section 7.5 covers a two-market macroeconometric model, and section 7.6 deals with the market for investment goods.

7.2 Labor Market Models

In this section we examine a particular class of labor market models. We omit from consideration approaches that are based on partial adjustment (Sarantis 1981; Briguglio 1984) as well as those that explicitly consider the aggregation of micromarkets (Lambert 1984; Hajivassiliou 1986b).[1] We thus deal here with models that are in the tradition of the canonical model with the simple min condition.

One of the earliest models of this type is due to Rosen and Quandt (1978). It posits the existence of an aggregate production function

$$Q_t = f(L_t, K_t, t) \tag{7.2.1}$$

where Q_t is aggregate output, L_t is the quantity (hours) of labor, K_t is the quantity of capital services, and t is a time trend proxying technological

---

[1] See section 4.5 for a discussion of the former and section 4.4 for a discussion of the latter.

progress. Profit maximization yields the equality of the marginal product of labor and the real wage:

$$\frac{w_t}{p_t} = \frac{\partial f(L_t, K_t, t)}{\partial L_t} \tag{7.2.2}$$

Using (7.2.1) to eliminate K_t from (7.2.2) yields an expression for the demand for labor which contains the endogenous variable Q_t and is thus not a reduced form equation. Rosen and Quandt write it for purposes of estimation as

$$\ln D_t = \alpha_0 + \alpha_1 \ln(w_t/p_t) + \alpha_2 \ln Q_t + \alpha_3 t + u_{1t} \tag{7.2.3}$$

where u_{1t} is the usual normally distributed error term and where Q_t is treated as if it were exogenous.[2]

The supply curve is based on utility maximization by workers and is written as

$$\ln S_t = \beta_0 + \beta_1 \ln(w_{nt}/p_t) + \beta_2 A_{nt} + \beta_3 \ln H_t + u_{2t} \tag{7.2.4}$$

where w_{nt}, the net wage, is $(1 - \theta_t) w_t$ (with θ_t representing the marginal tax rate), A_{nt} is net nonlabor income, and H_t is a measure of the potential labor force, which is a scale variable intended to account for the growth of population.

It is then posited that the econometrician observes the quantity of labor transacted

$$\ln L_t = \min(\ln D_t, \ln S_t) \tag{7.2.5}$$

If the model consisted only of (7.2.2), (7.2.4), and (7.2.5), the wage would have to be taken to be exogenous. This is avoided by specifying an adjustment equation governing the behavior of real wages as

$$\ln(w_t/p_t) - \ln(w_{t-1}/p_{t-1}) = \gamma_1 (\ln D_t - \ln S_t) + \gamma_2 Z_t + u_{3t} \tag{7.2.6}$$

where Z_t is alternately considered to be a constant, or the level of unionization, or the rate of change of unionization. The last case represents the hypothesis that unions have an impact only in the periods in which they change in relative size and that their monopoly power dissipates after the current period.

The model consisting of (7.2.3) through (7.2.6) is a standard model D and can be estimated by maximizing the likelihood function. For this purpose, Rosen and Quandt (1978) employed annual US data for the years 1930 through 1973. The parameter estimates were on the whole reasonable, with α_1

---

[2] It is interesting to note that if (7.2.1) is specified as a CES production function, the following relations hold between the αs and the parameters of the CES production function: σ (elasticity of substitution), h (returns to scale), and λ (rate of Hicks neutral technological change): $\alpha_1 = -\sigma$, $\alpha_2 = (\sigma h + 1 - \sigma)/h$, $\alpha_3 = -\lambda(1 - \sigma)/h$.

negative, α_2 positive, and both close to unity in absolute value. α_3 was negative but insignificant, while β_1 varied in sign across different versions of the model and was also insignificant. β_2 turned out positive, which is counterintuitive, but similar results had been noted in implementations of the equilibrium paradigm (Lucas and Rapping 1970). The coefficient γ_1 is positive and $1/\gamma_1$ is significantly different from zero in one version but not significant in another version of the model; the case for rejecting the null hypothesis of equilibrium is thus somewhat ambiguous (see section 3.4). The coefficient γ_2 is positive for every definition of the variable Z_t but the likelihood is highest when Z_t is defined as the unionization rate.

The worst feature of the model was the predicted values of excess demand, $\ln \hat{D}_t - \ln \hat{S}_t$, obtained by substituting in the equations for each period the values of the predetermined variables and solving for the jointly dependent variables. These predictions indicated positive excess demands throughout the Depression of the 1930s. It remained for Romer (1981) to show that the culprit was almost certainly the inclusion of the nonlabor income variable in the model, which in reality is almost certainly endogenous, although it is treated as being exogenous. The inclusion of this variable has yielded some anomalous results in other work as well (Lucas and Rapping 1970) and Romer showed, by reestimating the model without this variable, that the resulting predictions of unemployment track the historical measured unemployment series quite closely.

In more recent work, Quandt and Rosen (1986a) have extended this work in several important ways:

1   The demand function now includes lagged output to account for the possibility of slow adjustment. It thus becomes

$$\ln D_t = \alpha_0 + \alpha_1 \ln(w_t/p_t) + \alpha_2 \ln Q_t + \alpha_3 t + \alpha_4 \ln Q_{t-1} + u_{1t}$$
$$(7.2.7)$$

2   The supply function now also includes the lagged real wage which is the implication of some simple expectational models:

$$\ln S_t = \beta_0 + \beta_1 \ln(w_{nt}/p_t) + \beta_2 \ln H_t + \beta_3 \ln(w_{nt-1}/p_{t-1}) + u_{2t}$$
$$(7.2.8)$$

3   Wage adjustment is now assumed to occur in the nominal wage and be influenced not only by wages and price changes of various lags, but also by the measured unemployment rate U_t instead of by the logarithmic excess demand as in (7.2.6). Accordingly

$$\ln w_t = \gamma_0 + \gamma_1 \ln w_{t-1} + \gamma_2 U_t + \gamma_3 (\ln p_t - \ln p_{t-1})$$
$$+ \gamma_4 (\ln p_{t-1} - \ln p_{t-2}) + \gamma_5 \ln w_{t-2} + u_{3t} \qquad (7.2.9)$$

The use of U_t rather than $\ln D_t - \ln S_t$ rests on the observation that the economic agents responsible for changing wages observe the former but do not observe the latter.

4   The model makes p_t explicitly endogenous and the equation determining prices is

$$\ln p_t = \delta_0 + \delta_1 \ln p_{t-1} + \delta_2(\ln w_t - \ln w_{t-1})$$
$$+ \delta_3(\ln w_{t-1} - \ln w_{t-2}) + \delta_4(\ln n_t - \ln n_{t-1}) + \delta_5 t + u_{4t}$$

$$(7.2.10)$$

where n_t is the price of energy.

5   It is not reasonable to take U_t to be exogenous in a model of this kind and an equation is needed to explain its determination. If V_t denotes the vacancy rate and if we ignore the fact that the measured unemployment rate does not measure exactly the difference between D_t and S_t, then $D_t = L_t(1 + V_t)$, $S_t = L_t(1 + U_t)$, and $D_t/S_t = (1 + V_t)/(1 + U_t)$. Taking logarithms yields to an approximation

$$\ln D_t - \ln S_t = V_t - U_t$$

Since data for V_t are not available in the US, V_t is approximated as λ_1/U_t. The last estimating equation is then written as

$$\ln D_t - \ln S_t = \lambda_1/U_t - U_t + \lambda_2 B_t + u_{5t}$$

$$(7.2.11)$$

where B_t measures unemployment benefits and where the inclusion of the term $\lambda_2 B_t$ is intended to account for the possibility that the vacancy–unemployment relationship is not constant over time.

The likelihood function is derived in appendix 7.A. The model is estimated from annual US data for the years 1929 through 1979. Two subcases are considered:

Model 1 The model is as stated in (7.2.7)–(7.2.11), plus the min condition given by (7.2.5), with the error terms normally distributed and independent of one another and over time.

Model 2 The error terms in (7.2.9) and (7.2.10) are allowed to have first-order serial correlation (for the modification of the likelihood function in this case see Quandt and Rosen 1986a).

The coefficient estimates for the two subcases are contained in table 7.1. The likelihood ratio test rejects model 1 in favor of model 2. All the parameters have the *a priori* signs and most of them have reasonable magnitudes. Most of the parameters of interest are also more significant in model 2 than in model 1.

Quandt and Rosen (1986a) examine the excess demands implied by the estimated model by several methods:

(a)   In each period the system of equations is solved, using the estimated values of the coefficients, for the endogenous variables, and $\widehat{\ln D}_t - \widehat{\ln S}_t$ is computed.

(b)   Stochastic simulations are performed in which simulated normal error

Table 7.1   Estimates of labor market models
(*t* values in parentheses)

	Model 1	Model 2
α_0	−2.8604	−2.9994
	(−7.79)	(−7.87)
α_1	−0.6424	−0.6670
	(−16.23)	(−16.34)
α_2	0.7120	0.7156
	(14.78)	(14.38)
α_3	0.0020	0.0027
	(1.39)	(1.90)
α_4	0.0884	0.0882
	(2.35)	(2.31)
β_0	2.2511	2.3445
	(3.12)	(3.25)
β_1	−0.4152	−0.4103
	(−1.98)	(−1.98)
β_2	0.5698	0.5571
	(5.02)	(4.92)
β_3	0.4989	0.5003
	(2.33)	(2.36)
γ_0	0.0672	0.2710
	(4.40)	(1.24)
γ_1	0.9668	0.3185
	(6.31)	(2.26)
γ_2	−0.3601	−1.6373
	(−3.17)	(−5.49)
γ_3	0.9676	0.4256
	(4.91)	(2.10)
γ_4	0.0376	0.6137
	(0.161)	(3.12)
γ_5	0.0106	0.4747
	(0.070)	(3.51)
δ_0	0.3052	0.3090
	(1.74)	(1.49)
δ_1	0.9101	0.9069
	(18.66)	(15.38)
δ_2	0.0173	0.1834
	(0.0945)	(1.87)
δ_3	0.2500	0.1513
	(2.54)	(2.28)
δ_4	0.2811	0.1773
	(4.13)	(3.53)
δ_5	0.0032	0.0036
	(2.13)	(1.83)
λ_1	0.0017	0.0015
	(5.95)	(5.54)
λ_2	0.0085	0.0074
	(1.74)	(1.54)

Table 7.1　*Continued*

	Model 1	Model 2
ρ_3	–	0.3080
		(1.93)
ρ_4	–	0.9894
		(53.37)
σ_1^2	2.17×10^{-4}	2.20×10^{-4}
	(4.43)	(4.40)
σ_2^2	1.77×10^{-3}	1.74×10^{-3}
	(4.15)	(4.10)
σ_3^2	8.62×10^{-4}	1.16×10^{-3}
	(4.59)	(3.82)
σ_4^2	6.03×10^{-4}	4.05×10^{-4}
	(2.41)	(4.01)
σ_5^2	4.52×10^{-4}	4.21×10^{-4}
	(1.35)	(1.23)
$\log L$	462.53	475.96

       terms (with variance equal to the estimated variance) are added to each equation and the system is then solved for the endogenous variables; the average of $\widehat{\ln D_t} - \widehat{\ln S_t}$ is computed over 100 repetitions of this procedure.

(c)   In the simulations as in (b), the fraction of the replications of the experiment in which predicted demand exceeds predicted supply is determined.

(d)   The conditional probability $\Pr\{D_t > S_t | L_t\}$ is computed from the estimated coefficient values (see section 2.8).

In general, the various measures show very similar qualitative patterns; however, the two excess demand measures, (a) and (b), and the simulated fraction of times that demand exceeds supply, (c), agree better with one another than any of those agrees with $\Pr(D_t > S_t | L_t)$, which is the only one of the four measures that is conditional on L_t and appears for this reason to give somewhat sharper discrimination between excess demand and excess supply periods.

    The dynamic system of estimated equations is locally stable (see exercise 7.2) and also permits the computation of a natural rate of unemployment, i.e. a rate that is implied by a constant rate of growth in wages and prices. This natural rate is the solution of the equation

$$AU_t^2 + B_t U_t + C = 0 \tag{7.2.12}$$

where

$$\overline{W}_t = [\gamma_0 + G(-\gamma_1 + \gamma_3 + \gamma_4 - 2\gamma_5]/(1 - \gamma_1 - \gamma_5)$$

$$\bar{P}_t = [\delta_0 + (\delta_2 + \delta_3 - \delta_1)G + \delta_4(\ln n_t - \ln n_{t-1}) + \delta_5 t]/(1 - \delta_1)$$

$$A = \gamma_2(\alpha_1 - \beta_1 - \beta_3)/(1 - \gamma_1 - \gamma_5) + 1 \qquad (7.2.13)$$

$$B_t = (\alpha_1 - \beta_1 - \beta_3)(\bar{W}_t - \bar{P}_t) - \lambda_2 B_t + z_{1t} - z_{2t}$$

$$C = -\lambda_1$$

and where G is the assumed rate of growth of prices and wages (e.g. $\ln w_t - \ln w_{t-1} = G$) and z_{1t}, z_{2t} are defined in appendix 7.A (see exercise 7.3). Finally, the model is also used to investigate the short-run tradeoff between unemployment and inflation. To find this tradeoff, the output level is repeatedly perturbed for a particular period and then the system is solved for U_t and $\ln w_t$ (and hence, implicitly, for $\ln w_t - \ln w_{t-1}$, because in any period t, $\ln w_{t-1}$ is already known). This produces a "Phillips curve," a locus of points in the U_t, $\ln w_t - \ln w_{t-1}$ plane for that year, with the approximate equation in recent years of $\Delta w/w = -0.2 - 2U$.

Since the estimation of a disequilibrium model allows the estimation of excess demand and of the probability that excess demand has occurred, it empirically "sorts" data points between excess demand and supply. This raises the interesting question of whether the results are compatible with the view that, in reality, all data points correspond to excess demand (supply). Thus, one might conjecture that free-market economies always exhibit excess supply of labor, whereas centrally planned economies always exhibit excess demand for goods (and labor).

To test this type of hypothesis, Quandt and Rosen (1985) apply the Rogers test based on R_1 (see section 3.6) to a variant of this model; the null hypothesis is that excess supply of labor was always the case during the sample period. This requires the computation of $\Pr\{D_t - S_t < 0\}$. This is accomplished as follows. Define $F_t = \ln D_t - \ln S_t$, and solve (7.2.9) and (7.2.10) for $\ln w_t$, $\ln p_t$, yielding

$$\ln w_t = c_{11} U_t + c_{12t} + c_{13} u_{3t} + c_{14} u_{4t}$$

$$\ln p_t = c_{21} U_t + c_{22t} + c_{23} u_{3t} + c_{24} u_{4t}$$

where the cs depend on the coefficients of the model and some of them depend on predetermined variables as well. Substituting these solutions in (7.2.7) and (7.2.8), we can express

$$F_t = A_1 U_t + A_{2t} + A_3 u_{3t} + A_4 u_{4t} + u_{1t} - u_{2t} \qquad (7.2.14)$$

where the As further depend on coefficients and predetermined variables. Equations (7.2.11) and (7.2.14) can be written in compact form as

$$F_t - \lambda_1/U_t + U_t - \lambda_2 B_t = v_{1t}$$
$$F_t - A_1 U_t - A_{2t} \qquad\qquad = v_{2t} \qquad (7.2.15)$$

where $v_{1t} = u_{5t}$, $v_{2t} = A_3 u_{3t} + A_4 u_{4t} + u_{1t} - u_{2t}$ and represent a transformation from the normal variables v_{1t}, v_{2t} to F_t, U_t. From this it is easy to derive the joint p.d.f. $f(F_t, U_t)$, from which the required probability is

$$\Pr\{F_t < 0\} = \int_0^\infty \int_{-\infty}^0 f(F_t, U_t) \mathrm{d}F_t \mathrm{d}U_t \qquad (7.2.16)$$

Application of the Rogers test leads to rejection of the hypothesis of chronic excess supply for values of c (see (3.6.3)) greater than 0.8.

The model consisting of (7.2.5) and (7.2.7)–(7.2.11) does not have a "natural" equilibrium counterpart. Thus, setting $D_t = S_t = Q_t$ in this model yields a system of five stochastic equations in only four endogenous variables. Instead, to estimate a comparable equilibrium model, Quandt and Rosen (1988) formulate a generalization of the Lucas and Rapping (1970) model and estimate it by standard full information maximum likelihood. Expectations play an important role in such a model and they employ alternately adaptive as well as rational expectations mechanisms. The adaptive expectations version is conclusively rejected. The comparison of the rational expectations version with the disequilibrium model yields less clearcut discrimination. The two models' forecasting abilities are comparable, although the parameter estimates for the disequilibrium model are slightly more sensible from the economic point of view. The disequilibrium model is cautiously favored.

7.3   Models of Planned Economies

Consider the case of certain planned economies in which prices are set exogenously by a central planning authority. If we were to model the market for, say, consumer goods, we could specify a more or less conventional demand function; a supply function that would have to depend, *inter alia*, on the amount of goods that the central planning authority *plans* to have available; and a min condition, since prices are institutionally unable to adjust so as to clear markets. However, in general it is not correct to treat the central plan for consumption as an exogenous variable, and in chapter 2 it was suggested that the central planning authority attempts to minimize a quadratic loss function which contains as its arguments (a) the departure in the plan from a steady growth objective, (b) the extent of plan over- or underfulfillment, and (c) the extent of current and future disequilibrium. These considerations lead to the class of models that are the focus of the present section.

The initial empirical work in this area was done by Portes and Winter (1977, 1980) and in the second of their papers they estimated a simple disequilibrium model for consumption in several planned economies (i.e. without a plan adjustment equation). Charemza and Quandt (1982) introduced the notion of a plan adjustment equation. Finally, Portes, Quandt, Winter and Yeo (1984, 1985, 1987) and Portes, Quandt and Yeo (1985) have applied models of this type to the consumption sector in Poland.

We introduce the following notation:

$C_t^d(C_t^s)$ = demand for (supply of) consumption goods

C_t = realized consumption

Q_t = net material product (output)

Y_t = disposable income

A_t = net financial assets

I_t = investment expenditure

D_t = defense expenditure

An asterisk (*) denotes planned quantities and a tilde ($\sim$) denotes "surprise" variables. Thus we define

$$\widetilde{Q}_t = (Q_t - Q_t^*)/Q_t^*$$
$$\widetilde{I}_t = (I_t/Q_t - I_t^*/Q_t^*)Q_t$$
$$\widetilde{D}_t = (D_t/Q_t - D_t^*/Q_t^*)Q_t$$

$\widetilde{A}_t$ = deviation of A_t from a second-order exponential time trend fitted to the A_t series

Several models were specified by Portes, Quandt, Winter and Yeo. All the models share the same demand and supply equations and the min condition:

$$C_t^d = \alpha_1 \Delta A_{t-1} + \alpha_2 \Delta Y_t + \alpha_3 Y_{t-1} + u_{1t} \qquad (7.3.1)$$

$$C_t^s = \beta_1 C_t^* + \beta_2 C_t^* \widetilde{Q}_t + \beta_3 \widetilde{A}_t + \beta_4 \widetilde{D}_t + \beta_5 \widetilde{I}_t + u_{2t} \qquad (7.3.2)$$

$$C_t = \min(C_t^d, C_t^s) \qquad (7.3.3)$$

The demand function is a standard Houthakker-Taylor demand function for which we expect *a priori* that $\alpha_1 < 0$, $\alpha_2, \alpha_3 > 0$. In the supply function it is ultimately assumed that $\beta_1 = 1$ (and this is not rejected by the data). Hence consumption goods supply is equal to the plan except in as much as there are surprises in the evolution of net liquid assets, of net material product, in defense expenditures or in investment expenditures. The models differ with respect to the manner in which the plan adjustment equation is specified.

Model 1   This is the "basic" model with adjustment equation

$$C_t^* = \delta_1 C_{t-1}^* + \delta_2 C_{t-1} + \delta_3 C_{t-2} + \delta_4 \widetilde{A}_{t-2} + \gamma(C_t^d - C_t^s) + u_{4t}$$
$$(7.3.4a)$$

Model 2   On the grounds that planners are unlikely to know $C_t^d - C_t^s$ at the time that C_t^* is being set, it may be reasonable to replace the excess demand appearing in the adjustment equation by its expectation at time $t - 1$. It is convenient at this point to simplify notation by defining

$$z_{1t} = \alpha_1 \Delta A_{t-1} + \alpha_2 \Delta Y_t + \alpha_3 Y_{t-1}$$
$$z_{2t} = \beta_3 \widetilde{A}_{t-1} + \beta_4 \widetilde{D}_t + \beta_5 \widetilde{I}_t$$
$$z_{3t} = \delta_1 C^*_{t-1} + \delta_2 C_{t-1} + \delta_3 C_{t-2} + \delta_4 \widetilde{A}_{t-2}$$
$$z_{4t} = \widetilde{Q}_t$$

Then, if it is assumed that expectations of zs can be approximated by realized values, with $E(z_{4t} u_{4t}) = 0$, we have (see exercise 7.5)

$$E_{t-1}(C^d_t - C^s_t) = \frac{z_{1t} - z_{2t} - (\beta_1 + \beta_2 z_{4t}) z_{3t}}{1 + \gamma(\beta_1 + \beta_2 z_{4t})} \qquad (7.3.5)$$

This term then replaces $C^d_t - C^s_t$ in the adjustment equation.

Model 3 If it is assumed that surprise variables have expectation zero, that $E(z_{1t}) = z_{1t}$, $E(z_{3t}) = z_{3t}$, $E(z_{4t} z_{3t}) = 0$, and $E(z_{4t} u_{4t}) = 0$, then (7.2.5) is replaced by (see exercise 7.5)

$$E_{t-1}(C^d_t - C^s_t) = \frac{z_{1t} - \beta_1 z_{3t}}{1 + \beta_1 \gamma} \qquad (7.3.6)$$

Model 4 In this model we treat C^*_{t+1} as the endogenous plan variable rather than C^*_t, since we cannot reasonably assume that planners know C^d_t and C^s_t at the time that C^*_t is set. This leads to a change in the timing of the adjustment equation, which now becomes

$$C^*_{t+1} = \delta_1 C^*_t + \delta_2 C_t + \delta_3 C_{t-1} + \gamma(C^d_t - C^s_t) + \delta_4 \widetilde{A}_{t-1} + u_{4t}$$
$$(7.3.4b)$$

The likelihood functions for these models are derived in appendix 7.B.[3]

These models were estimated by maximizing the appropriate likelihood function with Polish data from the period 1955–80. In estimation, the reasonable restriction $\beta_1 = 1$ was imposed, which implies that supply equals the plan except for surprises. Coefficient estimates and their asymptotic standard errors for models 1 and 4 are displayed in table 7.2. On the whole the coefficient estimates are very reasonable. An apparent exception is the coefficient β_5, since *a priori* we would expect positive investment and defense surprises to occur at the expense of consumption. The results appear to say that positive investment surprises have not so much a crowding-out effect but a multiplier effect. We can also calculate that the constant growth rate of C_t that is compatible with exact plan realization is 5.7 per cent (in model 4) which is tolerably close to the actual growth rate of 6.3 per cent. Using the

---

[3] In the concrete application γ was allowed to take on different values γ_1 and γ_2 depending on the sign of excess demand.

Table 7.2   Estimates of disequilibrium models for Poland
(*t* values in parentheses)

	Model 1	Model 4
α_1	−0.222	−0.201
	(−2.289)	(−2.209)
α_2	0.899	0.898
	(20.432)	(6.603)
α_3	0.989	0.988
	(494.500)	(329.333)
σ_1^2	2.685	2.742
	(1.613)	(1.872)
β_2	0.026	−0.023
	(0.122)	(−0.090)
β_3	−0.272	−0.190
	(−1.838)	(−1.118)
β_4	−5.171	−5.637
	(−2.310)	(−13.264)
β_5	0.304	0.352
	(2.394)	(2.667)
σ_2^2	47.676	52.949
	(2.676)	(2.484)
δ_1	−1.029	−0.445
	(3.701)	(−2.317)
δ_2	2.033	1.477
	(11.170)	(8.392)
δ_3	0.069	0.026
	(0.250)	(0.159)
δ_4	1.943	1.385
	(4.347)	(6.960)
γ_1	0.619	1.055
	(2.301)	(3.689)
γ_2	$-\gamma_1$	0.282
		(1.679)
σ_4^2	123.5	39.072
	(2.368)	(2.976)
log L	−144.6	−137.8

same techniques as in section 7.2, we can also classify periods between excess demand and excess supply. The various models largely agree on the classification and with the prior judgments about the course of the Polish economy, except for the year 1978 for which all models predicted excess supply which an *a priori* judgment would consider unreasonable. In Portes, Quandt,

Winter and Yeo (1984) this finding was rationalized by noting that the plan figure for 1978 was excessively and atypically optimistic; hence the mechanics of the model could not help but generate a large supply prediction for that year (see (7.3.2)). Considering the datum C^*_{1978} to be the aberration, Portes, Quandt, Winter and Yeo (1985) reformulated model 4 by treating that one datum as an unknown parameter. Writing the likelihood function for model 4 in general as

$$L = \prod_{t=1}^{T} f(C_t, C^*_{t+1}) \tag{7.3.7}$$

the modifications necessary to enable C^*_{1978} to be treated as a parameter are in two steps:

1   When $t = 1978$, C^*_t is predetermined. Since we want to estimate it, we replace C^*_t in the appropriate term of (7.3.7) by the parameter ϵ.

2   When $t = 1977$, C^*_{t+1} is jointly determined. When we replace C^*_{t+1} by ϵ (in the term of (7.3.7) with $t = 1977$), we are removing a jointly dependent variable and replacing it by a constant. We must then assume that $u_{4t} \equiv 0$ for that observation, or else u_{4t} would be an exact linear function of u_{1t} and u_{2t}. The adjustment equation for that observation becomes

$$C^*_{1977} = \frac{1}{\delta_1} [\epsilon - \delta_2 C_{1977} - \delta_3 C_{1976} - \delta_4 \widetilde{A}_{1976} - \gamma(C^d_{1977} - C^s_{1977})]$$

where γ is again γ_1 or γ_2, depending on the sign of excess demand. When C^*_{1977} is substituted in the supply function, the following two-regime simple disequilibrium model emerges:

$$\begin{bmatrix} 1 & 0 \\ (\beta_1 + \beta_2 z_{4t})\left(\dfrac{\gamma_2 + \delta_2}{\delta_1}\right) & 1 - (\beta_1 + \beta_2 z_{4t})\dfrac{\gamma_2}{\delta_1} \end{bmatrix} \begin{bmatrix} C^d_t \\ C^s_t \end{bmatrix} = \begin{bmatrix} z_{1t} + u_{1t} \\ z_{9t} + u_{2t} \end{bmatrix}$$

$$\text{if } C^d_t < C^s_t$$

$$\begin{bmatrix} 1 & 0 \\ (\beta_1 + \beta_2 z_{4t})\dfrac{\gamma_1}{\delta_1} & 1 - (\beta_1 + \beta_2 z_{4t})\left(\dfrac{\gamma_1 - \delta_2}{\delta_1}\right) \end{bmatrix} \begin{bmatrix} C^d_t \\ C^s_t \end{bmatrix} = \begin{bmatrix} z_{1t} + u_{1t} \\ z_{9t} + u_{2t} \end{bmatrix}$$

$$\text{if } C^d_t \geq C^s_t$$

where

$$z_{9t} = (\beta_1 + \beta_2 z_{4t})[\epsilon - \delta_3 C_{t-1} - \delta_4 \widetilde{A}_{t-1}]/\delta_1 + z_{2t}$$

and

$$C_t = \min(C^d_t, C^s_t)$$

The corresponding term of the likelihood is obtained by defining

$$p_{21t} = (\beta_1 + \beta_2 z_{4t}) \left(\frac{\gamma_1 + \delta_2}{\delta_1} \right)$$

$$p_{22t} = 1 - (\beta_1 + \beta_2 z_{4t}) \frac{\gamma_2}{\delta_1}$$

$$q_{21t} = (\beta_1 + \beta_2 z_{4t}) \frac{\gamma_1}{\delta_1}$$

$$q_{22t} = 1 - (\beta_1 + \beta_2 z_{4t}) \left(\frac{\gamma_1 - \delta_2}{\delta_1} \right)$$

$$H_t = \frac{q_{21} \sigma_1^2 (q_{22t} C_t - z_{9t}) - z_{1t} \sigma_2^2}{\sigma_2^2 + q_{21t}^2 \sigma_1^2}$$

$$L_t = \frac{z_{1t}^2 \sigma_2^2 + (q_{22t} C_t - z_{9t})^2 \sigma_1^2}{\sigma_2^2 + q_{21t}^2 \sigma_1^2}$$

The appropriate likelihood function term then is

$$h(C_t) = \frac{1}{\sqrt{(2\pi)} \sigma_1} \exp\left\{ -\frac{1}{2\sigma_1^2} (C_t - z_{1t})^2 \right\}$$

$$\times \left[1 - \Phi\left(\frac{(p_{21t} + p_{22t}) C_t - z_{9t}}{\sigma_2} \right) \right]$$

$$+ \frac{|q_{22t}|}{\sqrt{(2\pi)} (\sigma_2^2 + q_{21t}^2 \sigma_1^2)^{1/2}} \exp\left\{ -\frac{H_t - L_t^2}{2\sigma_1^2 \sigma_2^2 / (\sigma_2^2 + q_{21t}^2 \sigma_1^2)} \right\}$$

$$\times \left[1 - \Phi\left(\frac{C_t + H_t}{\sigma_1 \sigma_2 / (\sigma_2^2 + q_{21t}^2 \sigma_1^2)^{1/2}} \right) \right]$$

Estimation with this amended likelihood was also successful. Portes, Quandt, Winter and Yeo (1985) then reestimate the amended model a large number of times, each time treating the planned consumption figure of a different year as a parameter. On the whole, the estimate for ϵ when it replaces C_t^* tends to be very close to the actual value of the C_t^* that it is estimating. However, the most noteworthy thing is that in the last few years, but in particular in 1978, the estimated asymptotic standard error of ϵ is very large; this suggests doubt in these later years about the compatibility of the planners' plan determination mechanism with the earlier years and with the model in general. It does not appear to be a coincidence that this happens in the years in which the Polish economy was beset by near catastrophic difficulties.

Finally, in Portes, Quandt and Yeo (1985) the Rogers test is performed to test the null hypothesis that only excess demand has occurred. The null hypothesis is rejected for all values of $C \geq 0.8$ for each of the models considered.

7.4   A Microeconomic Model of Marketing

An interesting microeconomic application is discussed in Kooiman, van Dijk and Thurik (1985). Consider the problem of a retail food store that has to apportion its total floor space T between the amount of space allocated for sales activities S and the amount allocated to other activities $T - S$ (such as administration, storage, etc.). The actual quantity of sales Q is constrained by a "sales possibility frontier" and by a demand function. Thus

$$Q \leq Q^s(S, T - S, X) \tag{7.4.1}$$

$$Q \leq Q^d(S, X) \tag{7.4.2}$$

where X is a vector of exogenous variables. The firm wishes to maximize Q subject to (7.4.1), (7.4.2), and $0 \leq S \leq T$. The X-vector includes a proxy for price P, the occupancy cost per unit area C, and the relative shares in sales of fresh products F. Kooiman, van Dijk and Thurik make the specific assumptions that

$$Q^s = \beta(X)(S - \gamma)^{\pi\epsilon}(T - S)^{(1 - \pi)\epsilon} \tag{7.4.3}$$

where $0 \leq \gamma \leq S$, $0 \leq \pi \leq 1$, $\epsilon > 0$ and

$$\beta(X) = e^{\beta_0}(1 + P)C^{\beta_1}$$

and that

$$Q^d = \delta(X)(S - \gamma)^\nu \tag{7.4.4}$$

where $\nu > 0$, and

$$\delta(X) = e^{\delta_0 + \delta_1 F}(1 + P)^{1 + \delta_2}$$

They further impose the requirement that $\nu \geq \pi\epsilon$, which guarantees that in the region $\gamma < S \leq T$ the demand function (7.4.4) and "supply" function (7.4.3) intersect only once (see exercise 7.9) in Q–S space.

Now it is clear that $Q^s = 0$ if S is either γ or T and that Q^s reaches a maximum when

$$S = \gamma + \pi(T - \gamma) \tag{7.4.5}$$

Denote this value of S and the corresponding value of Q^s by S_1 and Q_1^s respectively. Also denote the S and Q^s values where $Q^d = Q^s$ by S_2 and Q_2^s. Then, if at S_1 the value of $Q^d > Q_1^s$, the solution to the optimization problem is $Q = Q_1^s$, $S = S_1 \geq S_2$ by the unique intersection property and the fact that $\partial Q^d/\partial S > 0$ (by 7.4.4)). Alternatively, if at S_1 we have $Q_1^s > Q_2^s$, the solution is $Q = Q_2^s$, $S = S_2 > S_1$. The optimization problem can then be rewritten as follows:

$$Q = Q^s(S; T, X)$$
$$S = \max(S_1, S_2)$$
$$\frac{\partial Q^s(S_1; T, X)}{\partial S_1} = 0 \tag{7.4.6}$$
$$Q^s(S_2; T, X) = Q^d(S_2; X)$$

In order to obtain the likelihood function, one must introduce suitable error terms. It is natural to specify that the demand and supply functions have multiplicative errors e^{u_1} and e^{u_2}, where u_1 and u_2 are independent normals with zero means and variances σ_1^2, σ_2^2. A third error term is needed in the model, for we wish to end up with a joint density of S and Q after a third variable (S_1 or S_2) has been integrated out. Kooiman, van Dijk and Thurik find it convenient to write $(S_1 - \gamma)/(T - \gamma) = e^{-\phi}$, where ϕ has an independent gamma distribution with scale parameter ψ; i.e. the density of ϕ is $\psi^{-\alpha} \phi^{\alpha-1} \exp(-\phi/\psi)/\Gamma(\alpha)$. They further require (a) $\alpha > 1$ to ensure a density of zero at $S = \gamma$, and (b) $E(e^{-\phi}) = \pi$, which implies $\alpha \log(1 + \psi) = -\log\pi$. This latter requirement is natural, since from the maximizing solution for S_1 we have $(S_1 - \gamma)/(T - \gamma) = \pi$; hence the stochastic assumption is such that this equation is satisfied "on the average." The implication follows from the moment generating function of the gamma density, which is $M(\theta) = (1 - \theta\psi)^{-\alpha}$. If $f(S_1, S_2, Q)$ is the joint density for S_1, S_2, and Q, the required density of S and Q is

$$h(S, Q) = \int_\gamma^S f(S, S_2, Q) dS_2 + \int_\gamma^S f(S_1, S, Q) dS_1 \tag{7.4.7}$$

and the likelihood is the usual product of such terms. The actual derivation of (7.4.7) is somewhat involved and the reader is referred to Kooiman, van Dijk and Thurik (1985). Maximum likelihood estimates are obtained and are found to be illuminating.[4] All coefficients except δ_2 are significant at the 0.05 level. The supply elasticity with respect to occupancy cost C is positive and is 0.749. The parameter γ, which measures the threshold of the amount of selling space at (or below) which sales supply is zero, moved to zero in estimation and was deleted from the model. The coefficient ϵ measures the returns to

---

[4] The authors also show that, as one may expect, the likelihood function is unbounded in parameter space. Since unboundedness occurs when all observations are assigned to the $Q \leq Q^s$ regime with equality for at least one observation, they maximize the likelihood by constraining it (via a penalty function) to avoid the region in parameter space where such a regime assignment occurs.

scale (see (7.4.3)) and is 0.865. At the same time, π measures the proportion of sales area to total area when supply is maximized: for $\gamma = 0$, (7.4.5) gives $S/T = \pi$. Its value is estimated at 0.642. The coefficient δ_1 measures the effect on demand of the percentage space devoted to fresh products, and is 1.390. The coefficient δ_2 is not significant, which the authors attribute to their using an unsatisfactory proxy for selling prices. The selling-space elasticity of demand γ is 0.910 and is not significantly different from 1. One may conclude that the estimates are quite reasonable.

7.5   A Two-Market Macromodel

Simultaneous markets models as discussed in general terms in chapters 5 and 6 get their primary impetus from simple macromodels in which there is an aggregate labor market and an aggregate goods market. Several empirical models of this general type have been formulated and we shall review only one of these. For other applications see Kooiman and Kloek (1980, 1985), Sneessens (1981a, 1983), Vilares (1982) and the excellent review by Laffont (1983).

We concentrate on the model introduced by Artus, Laroque and Michel (1984) and further elaborated by Borglin, Karlsson and Petersson (1986).[5] Their economy consists of a producing sector and a household sector; aggregate demands and supplies are derived as if each sector contained a single agent.

In the producing sector there is a single output Q with price p and a single variable input L (labor) with wage w. The agent's profit function is

$$\pi(Q, L, u_1, u_2) = pQ(1 + u_1) - wL(1 + u_2) - c_1 wL_{-1}\left(\frac{L}{L_{-1}} - 1\right)^2$$

$$- c_2 pG(L)\left\{\max\left[\left(\frac{Q}{G(L)} - 1\right), 0\right]\right\}^2 \qquad (7.5.1)$$

where u_1 and u_2 are error terms > -1, c_1 and c_2 are positive coefficients, and $G(L)$ is a Cobb-Douglas function, $G(L) = AL^\alpha K^\beta$, and represents a capacity function. The error terms may be interpreted as the errors that entrepreneurs make in observing prices and wages and are needed to make estimation possible.

The first and second terms of (7.5.1) are the standard revenue and cost terms, modified by the introduction of random errors. The third term is an obvious "cost of adjustment" term. The last term expresses the notion that no additional penalty is incurred only if an output level less than capacity out-

---

[5] For further elaborations in the same vein see also Artus and Avouy-Dovi (1984), Artus, Avouy-Dovi and Laroque (1985) and Karlsson (1987).

put is produced. The representative firm maximizes profit subject to quantity constraints on Q and L given by $Q \leq \overline{Q}$, $L \leq \overline{L}$. If neither constraint is effective, the solution is just the solution of $\partial\pi/\partial Q = 0$ and $\partial\pi/\partial L = 0$. If the output is rationed, the firm solves the program

maximize $\pi(Q,L,u_1,u_2)$
subject to $Q \leq \overline{Q}$

which yields the labor demand function $L^d(\overline{Q})$. In this case, $\partial\pi/\partial Q > 0$ but $\partial\pi/\partial L = 0$. If the input is rationed, it solves the program

maximize $\pi(Q,L,u_1,u_2)$
subject to $L \leq \overline{L}$

which yields the output supply function $Q^s(\overline{L})$.[6] Here $\partial\pi/\partial L > 0$ but $\partial\pi/\partial Q = 0$.

In the household sector, labor supply is assumed to be given exogenously, so that

$$L^s = \overline{S} + u_3 \tag{7.5.2}$$

and demand[7] depends on the actually transacted amount of labor L, as in

$$Q^d(L,u_4) = \gamma + \delta L + u_4 \tag{7.5.3}$$

Labor supply is thus given by (7.5.2), and product demand from (7.5.3) is $\gamma + \delta\min(L^s,\overline{L}) + u_4$, where $\overline{L}$ is the perceived amount to which labor supply is rationed. Given these relations, Q^* and L^* represent a fixed-price equilibrium if they are the solutions to one of the four possible regimes:

Keynesian unemployment

$$L^* < \overline{S} + u_3$$
$$\frac{\partial\pi(Q^*,L^*,u_1,u_2)}{\partial L} = 0$$
$$Q^* = Q^d(L^*,u_4) \tag{7.5.4}$$
$$\frac{\partial\pi(Q^*,L^*,u_1,u_2)}{\partial Q} > 0$$

Labor supply is assumed to be unaffected.

---

[6] The firm cannot be simultaneously constrained in both markets.

[7] We abstract here from the further complication, present in both Artus, Laroque and Michel (1984) and in Borglin, Karlsson and Petersson (1986), that total goods demand is actually domestic demand plus export demand minus imports plus an autonomous demand term. With this complication it is necessary to introduce a rationing scheme which allocates a shortage of goods among domestic consumption, exports and imports. The ration scheme chosen reduces domestic consumption and exports and increases imports by amounts proportional to total excess demand with the proportions adding to unity.

Classical unemployment

$$L^* < \bar{S} + u_3$$

$$\frac{\partial \pi(Q^*, L^*, u_1, u_2)}{\partial L} = 0$$

$$Q^* \lesseqgtr Q^d(L^*, u_4) \tag{7.5.5}$$

$$\frac{\partial \pi(Q^*, L^*, u_1, u_2)}{\partial Q} = 0$$

Underconsumption

$$L^* = \bar{S} + u_3$$

$$\frac{\partial \pi(Q^*, L^*, u_1, u_2)}{\partial L} \geqq 0$$

$$Q^* = Q^d(L^*, u_4) \tag{7.5.6}$$

$$\frac{\partial \pi(Q^*, L^*, u_1, u_2)}{\partial Q} > 0$$

Repressed inflation

$$L^* = \bar{S} + u_3$$

$$\frac{\partial \pi(Q^*, L^*, u_1, u_2)}{\partial L} \geqq 0$$

$$Q^* \lesseqgtr Q^d(L^*, u_4) \tag{7.5.7}$$

$$\frac{\partial \pi(Q^*, L^*, u_1, u_2)}{\partial Q} = 0$$

In order to derive the likelihood function, it is important that unique solutions exist in each regime. This is not strictly the case in the present model, and Artus, Laroque and Michel show that the Keynesian unemployment regime may, in general, have several solutions. However, they have experimented with large numbers of possible parameter values, including the set of values obtained in estimation, and found that predominantly a unique solution existed, thus justifying the form of the likelihood, at least pragmatically.

The four sets of conditions (7.5.4) to (7.5.7) define a partition of the four-dimensional space of us, with each partition corresponding to one of the regimes. These conditions also establish a mapping $F: \{u_1, u_2, u_3, u_4\} \rightarrow \{Q, L\}$. The probability that (Q, L) lies in some particular rectangle B in Q–L space is the sum of the probabilities of the intersections of $F^{-1}(B)$ with each of the four partitions in u-space. The density of (Q, L) is correspondingly the sum of four terms which can be obtained from (7.5.4) to (7.5.7). Consider the case of Keynesian unemployment. The second equation of (7.5.4) can be written as follows:

$$\frac{\partial \pi(Q,L,u_1,u_2)}{\partial L} = -w\left[1 + u_2 - 2c_1\left(\frac{L}{L_{-1}} - 1\right)\right]$$

$$+ c_2 pG'(L)\left[\frac{Q^2}{G(L)^2} - 1\right] I_{Q \leqq G} = 0 \qquad (7.5.8)$$

where $I_{Q \leqq G} = 0$ if $Q \leqq G$ and is 1 otherwise.

Equation (7.5.8) in turn yields

$$\frac{\partial \pi(Q,L,u_1,u_2)}{\partial L} = -wu_2 + \frac{\partial \pi(Q,L,0,0)}{\partial L} = 0 \qquad (7.5.9)$$

The third equation of (7.5.4) is

$$Q = \gamma + \delta L + u_4 \qquad (7.5.10)$$

We also have from the first and fourth equations

$$L < \bar{S} + u_3 \qquad (7.5.11)$$

and

$$\frac{\partial \pi(Q,L,u_1,u_2)}{\partial Q} = p(1 + u_1) + 2c_2 p\left[\frac{Q}{G(L)} - 1\right]$$

$$= pu_1 + \frac{\partial \pi(Q,L,0,0)}{\partial Q} > 0 \qquad (7.5.12)$$

If the us are independent normals, (7.5.9) to (7.5.12) yield the density term

$$f_K(Q,L) = J_K \phi\left[\frac{\partial \pi(Q,L,0,0)}{\partial L} \frac{1}{w\sigma_2}\right] \phi\left(\frac{Q - \gamma - \delta L}{\sigma_4}\right)$$

$$\times \left[1 - \Phi\left(\frac{L - \bar{S}}{\sigma_3}\right)\right]\left\{1 - \Phi\left[-\frac{\partial \pi(Q,L,0,0)}{\partial Q} \frac{1}{p\sigma_1}\right]\right\}$$

$$(7.5.13)$$

where, as usual, ϕ and Φ are the standard normal density and distribution, where J_K (K: Keynesian) is the Jacobian of the mapping from u_2, u_4 to Q and L, and where σ_i^2 is the variance of u_i.

In the practical implementation of this model, Artus, Laroque and Michel (1984) assumed $\bar{S}$ to be a linear function of the sum of employment L and unemployment. They also assumed domestic goods demand to depend on permanent wage income and permanent other income, exports to depend on competitors' real export prices, and the import share to depend on the same variables and a time trend. The model was estimated for France with quarterly data from 1963/II to 1978/IV and yielded coefficient estimates that agreed with *a priori* expectations, which is gratifying in the light of the relative sparseness of the overall specification. The estimates were used to calculate the probability of the four regimes and this exercise confirms the pervasiveness of the rationing of supply (although there are a few brief periods of repressed inflation). The calculated endogenous variables track reality well; for example, the predicted excess supply of labor and measured unemployment are highly correlated, as are the excess demand for goods and the degree of capacity utilization. Finally, one may compute the coefficient estimates in a corresponding equilibrium model in which prices and wages are allowed to adjust so as to clear the market. The competitive-equilibrium real wage may then be compared with the actual real wage; the discrepancies between the two series tend to be well related to the state of excess demand in the two markets. Thus, for example, the equilibrium real wage exceeds the observed real wage from 1963 to 1966; this corresponds to excess demand for labor in most quarters of that period. Borglin, Karlsson and Petersson (1986) carry this type of analysis further and, in particular, compare their results for Sweden with those for France and the US obtained by Artus and Avouy-Dovi (1984).

7.6   A Model of Investment Goods

According to the standard equilibrium model, the price of a good and the quantity of transactions are jointly determined in the marketplace through the interplay of the forces of demand and supply. In spite of this, most studies of investment goods concentrate on the demand side, and the supply side is either absent or rudimentary. The supply side *is* considered, either implicitly or explicitly, by Maddala and Kadane (1966) and Berndt (1976) who treat the price of capital (services) as endogenous, and by Engle and Foley (1974) who posit a supply function that is linear in potential GNP, the difference between potential and actual GNP, and the price of capital.

Nishimizu, Quandt and Rosen (1982) construct a model of the market for investment goods that explicitly takes into account both the demand and the supply functions. On the demand side they adopt Jorgenson's (1967, 1971) investment theory (see also Hall and Jorgenson 1967; Bischoff 1971; Hall 1977) which rests on the following principal assumptions: (1) output and input markets are perfectly competitive; (2) the production function is of the Cobb-Douglas type with constant returns to scale; (3) capital is fully malleable. Letting Q_t denote output, p_t its price, and c_t the price of the capital-input flow, it can be shown that the optimal or desired stock of capital is given by

$$K_t^* = \rho Q_t(p_t/c_t) \qquad (7.6.1)$$

where ρ is the capital-elasticity of output. It is posited that changes in the desired stock of capital are translated into investment only with lags; thus

$$K_t - K_{t-1} = \sum_{j=0}^{\infty} w_j (K_{t-j}^* - K_{t-j-1}^*) \qquad (7.6.2)$$

where the w_js are parameters. If we assume that replacement investment is proportional to the capital stock, and if we include a constant and an error term and rearrange the equation, we obtain investment demand as

$$I_t^D = \alpha_c + \sum_{j=0}^{\infty} \alpha_j K_{t-j}^* + \delta K_{t-1} + u_{1t} \qquad (7.6.3)$$

Using (7.6.1) to replace K_{t-j}^* places output Q_t on the right hand side of (7.6.3), and it is then treated as an exogenous variable. This is a specification error, made for the sake of simplifying the model, which is analogous to the treatment of output in the labor market model of section 7.2.

Obviously, for tractability (7.6.3) must also have the infinite lag replaced by a finite one. Nishimizu, Quandt and Rosen (1982) choose a finite lag of at most 15 quarters and constrain the α_j to be generated by an Almon distributed lag of at most third degree with one or both endpoints constrained to zero; thus $\alpha_j = \theta_1 + \theta_2(j-1) + \theta_3(j-1)^2 + \theta_4(j-1)^3$. The parameters to be estimated in the demand function thus consist of α_c, θ_2, θ_3, θ_4 and the variance of u_{1t} (the parameter δ was previously calculated by the algorithm used to generate the investment series).

Now let q_t denote the purchase price of a unit of capital.[8] Then assuming profit maximization and specifying desired supply to be linear, we can write

$$I_t^{S*} = \beta_0 + \beta_1(q_t/p_t) + \beta_2 t + \beta_3(w_t/p_t) + \beta_4(c_t/p_t) + u_{2t} \qquad (7.6.4)$$

where w_t represents wages. Nishimizu, Quandt and Rosen further assume that I_t^{S*} may not be instantaneously achievable because it takes time to change production levels; thus they write

$$I_t^S - I_{t-1} - \gamma(I_t^{S*} - I_{t-1}) \qquad (7.6.5)$$

where $0 < \gamma < 1$ and where

$$I_t = \min(I_t^D, I_t^S) \qquad (7.6.6)$$

Substituting (7.6.4) in (7.6.5) gives

$$\begin{aligned} I_t^S = &\gamma\beta_0 + \gamma\beta_1(q_t/p_t) + \gamma\beta_2 t + \gamma\beta_3(w_t/p_t) + \gamma\beta_4(c_t/p_t) \\ &+ (1-\gamma)I_{t-1} + \gamma u_{2t} \end{aligned} \qquad (7.6.7)$$

which is the effective supply function to be estimated.[9] Finally, a price adjustment equation is specified:

---

[8] The relation between c_t and q_t is given by $c_t = q_t(r_t + \delta)(1 - A_t)/(1 - u_t)$, where r_t is the real rate of return, u_t is the profit tax rate, and A_t is the present value of tax savings which arise from a unit of investment.

[9] Nishimizu, Quandt and Rosen omit the term $\gamma\beta_4(c_t/p_t)$ in practice since the variable c_t/p_t was highly correlated with q_t/p_t and its inclusion led to counterintuitive results.

$$\frac{q_t}{p_t} - \frac{q_{t-1}}{p_{t-1}} = \xi\,(I_t^D - I_t^S) + u_{3t} \tag{7.6.8}$$

The model consisting of (7.6.3), (7.6.7), (7.6.6), and (7.6.8) is a standard model D disequilibrium model with two minor exceptions: (1) the Almon distributed lag in the demand equation, and (2) the fact that the demand equation is nonlinear in q_t and hence the Jacobian of the transformation from the errors to the endogenous variables is not a constant.

The model was estimated from quarterly Japanese data for the period 1952/I to 1976/IV. The supply parameters are as expected; thus the asset price and the time trend have a positive and real wages a negative effect on supply. The supply elasticities (evaluated at the mean values of the variables) are large, and the elasticity with respect to asset price is large enough (i.e. 26.6 to 28.4, depending on the particular version of the model) to support the assumption made in some previous studies that the supply function is horizontal. The Almon lag structures estimated a mean lag of 7.5 quarters when a quadratic lag structure is assumed and 22.2 quarters for the cubic lag structure; both are well within the range of other investigators (Jorgensen 1971), but suggest that the data do not pin down the demand function with very much precision. The parameter γ is approximately 0.46 and indicates that nearly one-half of the discrepancy between desired and lagged actual supply represents actual adjustment. The coefficient in the price adjustment equation is positive but its reciprocal is not significantly different from zero; hence the hypothesis of equilibrium cannot be rejected in the present model. This is further underscored by the fact that the maximized likelihood values for the disequilibrium model and the corresponding equilibrium model are nearly identical. This conclusion provides an interesting contrast to the fact that in the estimation of labor market models the hypothesis of equilibrium is generally rejected.

Exercises

7.1 Prove the assertions in footnote 2 of this chapter.

7.2 Consider (7.2.7)–(7.2.11). Linearize (7.2.11) by a Taylor series expansion about a value U_0 of U. Now eliminate $\ln D_t$, $\ln S_t$ and U_t to obtain a simultaneous difference equation system in $\ln w_t$, $\ln p_t$. Show that the roots of the characteristic polynomial of the system are the values of x that satisfy

$$M_{11}M_{22} - M_{12}M_{21} = 0$$

where

$$M_{11} = \frac{1 + \gamma_2(\alpha_1 - \beta_1)}{1 + \lambda_1/U_0^2}\,x^2 + \left[-\gamma_1 - \frac{\gamma_2\beta_3}{1 + \lambda_1/U_0^2} \right] x - \gamma_5$$

$$M_{12} = \left[-\gamma_3 - \frac{\gamma_2(\alpha_1 - \beta_1)}{1 + \lambda_1/U_0^2} \right] x^2 + \left[\frac{\gamma_2\beta_3}{1 + \lambda_1/U_0^2} + \gamma_3 - \gamma_4 \right] x + \gamma_4$$

$$M_{21} = -\delta_2 x^2 + (\delta_2 - \delta_3) x + \delta_3$$

$$M_{22} = x^2 - \delta_1 x$$

7.3   Derive the results stated in (7.2.12) and (7.2.13).

7.4   Derive a detailed expression for (7.2.16). How would you evaluate the integral in the expression?

7.5   Prove (7.3.5) and (7.3.6).

7.6   Why would one obtain inefficient estimates if one estimated the planned economy models 2 or 3 of section 7.3 by independently estimating (a) the simple disequilibrum model corresponding to (7.3.1)–(7.3.3) and (b) the plan adjustment equation?

7.7   Show that the two-regime model given by (7.B.3) and (7.B.4) is coherent.

7.8   Find expressions for $\Pr\{C_t^d > C_t^s\}$ for each of the models in section 7.3.

7.9   Prove that the functions (7.4.3) and (7.4.4) have a unique intersection in the region $\gamma < S \leq T$ if $\nu \geq \pi\epsilon$.

7.10 Derive the other three parts of the density analogous to (7.5.13). Obtain the Jacobians for each case.

Appendix 7.A
Derivation of the Labor Market Likelihood Function

To simplify the notation, D_t, S_t, w_t, p_t will denote here the natural logarithm of demand, supply, nominal wage, and price, respectively. U_t denotes the measured unemployment rate, and z_{1t}, z_{2t}, z_{3t}, z_{4t}, z_{5t} are linear functions of predetermined variables and coefficients. The model can then be written as

$$D_t = \alpha_1 w_t - \alpha_1 p_t + z_{1t} + u_{1t} \tag{7.A.1}$$

$$S_t = \beta_1 w_t - \beta_1 p_t + z_{2t} + u_{2t} \tag{7.A.2}$$

$$L_t = \min(D_t, S_t) \tag{7.A.3}$$

$$w_t = \gamma_2 U_t + \gamma_3 p_t + z_{3t} + u_{3t} \tag{7.A.4}$$

$$p_t = \delta_2 w_t + z_{4t} + u_{4t} \tag{7.A.5}$$

$$D_t - S_t = \lambda_1/U_t - U_t + z_{5t} + u_{5t} \tag{7.A.6}$$

where

$$z_{1t} = \alpha_0 + \alpha_2 \ln Q_t + \alpha_3 t + \alpha_4 \ln Q_{t-1}$$

$$z_{2t} = \beta_0 + \beta_1 \ln(1 - \theta_t) + \beta_2 \ln H_t + \beta_3 \ln(1 - \theta_{t-1}) + \beta_3 w_{t-1} - \beta_3 p_{t-1}$$

$$z_{3t} = \gamma_0 + \gamma_1 w_{t-1} - \gamma_3 p_{t-1} + \gamma_4(p_{t-1} - p_{t-2}) + \gamma_5 w_{t-2}$$

$$z_{4t} = \delta_0 + \delta_1 p_{t-1} - (\delta_2 - \delta_3) w_{t-1} - \delta_3 w_{t-2} + \delta_4(\ln n_t - \ln n_{t-1}) + \delta_5 t$$

$$z_{5t} = \lambda_2 B_t$$

Assuming that $u_{1t}, \ldots, u_{5t}$ are jointly normal with mean vector zero and diagonal covariance matrix, the joint probability density function of $(D_t, S_t, w_t, p_t, U_t)$ is

$$
f(D_t, S_t, w_t, p_t, U_t)
$$

$$
= \frac{|\Delta_t|}{(2\pi)^{5/2}\sigma_1\sigma_2\sigma_3\sigma_4\sigma_5} \exp\left\{ -\frac{1}{2}\left[\frac{(D_t - \alpha_1 w_t + \alpha_1 p_t - z_{1t})}{\sigma_1^2} \right.\right.
$$

$$
+ \frac{(S_t - \beta_1 w_t + \beta_1 p_t - z_{2t})^2}{\sigma_2^2} + \frac{(w_t - \gamma_2 U_t - \gamma_3 p_t - z_{3t})^2}{\sigma_3^2}
$$

$$
\left.\left. + \frac{(p_t - \delta_2 w_t - z_{4t})^2}{\sigma_4^2} + \frac{(D_t - S_t - \lambda_1/U_t + U_t - z_{5t})^2}{\sigma_5^2} \right]\right\} \qquad (7.\text{A}.7)
$$

where Δ_t is the Jacobian of the transformation $(\lambda_1/U_t + 1)(1 - \delta_2\gamma_3) - \alpha_1\gamma_2\delta_2 + \alpha_1\gamma_2 + \beta_1\gamma_2\delta_2 - \beta_1\gamma_2$. The required density is

$$
h(L_t, w_t, p_t, U_t) = \int_{L_t}^{\infty} f(D_t, L_t, w_t, p_t, U_t)\,\mathrm{d}D_t + \int_{L_t}^{\infty} f(L_t, S_t, w_t, p_t, U_t)\,\mathrm{d}S_t
$$

$$(7.\text{A}.8)$$

Define further

$$z_{6t} = L_t - \lambda_1/U_t + U_t$$

$$z_{7t} = \alpha_1 w_t - \alpha_1 p_t + z_{1t}$$

$$z_{8t} = L_t + \lambda_1/U_t - U_t$$

$$z_{9t} = \beta_1 w_t - \beta_1 p_t + z_{2t}$$

$$\phi_1^2 = \frac{\sigma_2^2\sigma_5^2}{\sigma_2^2 + \sigma_5^2}$$

$$\phi_2^2 = \frac{\sigma_1^2\sigma_5^2}{\sigma_1^2 + \sigma_5^2}$$

$$A_t = \frac{\sigma_5^2 z_{9t} + \sigma_2^2 z_{6t}}{\sigma_5^2 + \sigma_2^2}$$

$$B_t = \frac{\sigma_5^2 z_{9t}^2 + \sigma_2^2 z_{6t}^2}{\sigma_5^2 + \sigma_2^2}$$

$$C_t = \frac{\sigma_5^2 z_{7t} + \sigma_1^2 z_{8t}}{\sigma_5^2 + \sigma_1^2}$$

$$F_t = \frac{\sigma_5^2 z_{7t}^2 + \sigma_1^2 z_{8t}^2}{\sigma_5^2 + \sigma_1^2}$$

Performing the integrations indicated in (7.A.8) yields

$$h(L_t, w_t, p_t, U_t) = G_{1t}(G_{2t}G_{3t} + G_{4t}G_{5t}) \tag{7.A.9}$$

where

$$G_{1t} = \frac{|\Delta_t|}{2\pi\sigma_3\sigma_4} \exp\left\{ -\frac{1}{2}\left[\frac{(w_t - \gamma_2 U_t - \gamma_3 p_t - z_{3t})^2}{\sigma_3^2} + \frac{(p_t - \delta_2 w_t - z_{4t})^2}{\sigma_4^2} \right] \right\}$$

$$G_{2t} = \frac{1}{(2\pi)^{1/2}\sigma_1} \exp\left\{ -\frac{1}{2}\left[\frac{(L_t - z_{7t})^2}{\sigma_1^2} \right] \right\}$$

$$G_{3t} = \frac{1}{(2\pi)^{1/2}(\sigma_2^2 + \sigma_5^2)^{1/2}} \exp\left\{ -\frac{1}{2\phi_1^2}(B - A_t^2) \right\} \left[1 - \Phi\left(\frac{L_t - A_t}{\phi_1}\right) \right]$$

$$G_{4t} = \frac{1}{(2\pi)^{1/2}\sigma_2} \exp\left\{ -\frac{1}{2}\left[\frac{(L_t - z_{9t})^2}{\sigma_2^2} \right] \right\}$$

$$G_{5t} = \frac{1}{(2\pi)^{1/2}(\sigma_1^2 + \sigma_5^2)^{1/2}} \exp\left\{ -\frac{1}{2\phi_2^2}(B - C_t^2) \right\} \left[1 - \Phi\left(\frac{L_t - A_t}{\phi_2}\right) \right]$$

$$\Phi(\omega) = \int_{-\infty}^{\omega} \frac{1}{\sqrt{(2\pi)}} e^{-x^2/2} dx$$

The log-likelihood then is

$$L = \sum_t \log h(L_t, w_t, p_t, U_t) \tag{7.A.10}$$

Appendix 7.B
Derivation of the Planned Economy Models' Likelihood Functions

Assume that u_{1t}, u_{2t}, and u_{4t} are serially independent normal variates with a diagonal covariance matrix.

Model 1

The p.d.f. of C_t^d, C_t^s, C_t^* is

$$f(C_t^d, C_t^s, C_t^*) = \frac{|1 + \gamma(\beta_1 + \beta_2 z_{4t})|}{(2\pi)^{3/2}\sigma_1\sigma_2\sigma_4}$$

$$\times \exp\left\{ -\frac{1}{2}\left[\frac{(C_t^d - z_{1t})^2}{\sigma_1^2} + \frac{[C_t^s - (\beta_1 + \beta_2 z_{4t})C_t^* - z_{2t}]^2}{\sigma_2^2} \right.\right.$$

$$\left.\left. + \frac{(-\gamma C_t^d + \gamma C_t^s + C_t^* - z_{3t})^2}{\sigma_4^2} \right]\right\} \tag{7.B.1}$$

The p.d.f. of the observable random variables C_t, C_t^* is

$$h(C_t, C_t^*) = \int_{C_t}^{\infty} f(C_t, C_t^s, C_t^*) dC_t^s + \int_{C_t}^{\infty} f(C_t^d, C_t, C_t^*) dC_t^d \tag{7.B.2}$$

Completing the square, the integrals in (7.B.2) can be obtained as

$$\int_{C_t}^{\infty} f(C_t, C_t^s, C_t^*) dC_t^s = \frac{|1 + \gamma(\beta_1 + \beta_2 z_{4t})|}{2\pi\sigma_1(\sigma_4^2 + \gamma^2\sigma_2^2)^{1/2}}$$

$$\times \exp\left\{ -\frac{1}{2}\left[\frac{(C_t - z_{1t})^2}{\sigma_1^2} + \frac{A_{2t} - A_{1t}^2}{\omega_1^2} \right]\right\}$$

$$\times \left[1 - \Phi\left(\frac{C_t - A_{1t}}{\omega_1}\right) \right]$$

$$\int_{C_t}^{\infty} f(C_t^d, C_t, C_t^*) dC_t^d = \frac{|1 + \gamma(\beta_1 + \beta_2 z_{4t})|}{2\pi\sigma_1(\sigma_4^2 + \gamma^2\sigma_1^2)^{1/2}}$$

$$\times \exp\left\{ -\frac{1}{2}\left[\frac{(C_t - z_{5t})^2}{\sigma_2^2} + \frac{A_{4t} - A_{3t}^2}{\omega_2^2} \right]\right\}$$

$$\times \left[1 - \Phi\left(\frac{C_t - A_{3t}}{\omega_2}\right) \right]$$

where

$$z_{5t} = z_{2t} + (\beta_1 + \beta_2 z_{4t})C_t^*$$

$$z_{6t} = C_t^* - \gamma C_t - z_{3t}$$

$$z_{7t} = C_t^* + \gamma C_t - z_{3t}$$

$$A_{1t} = \frac{\sigma_4^2 z_{5t} - \sigma_2^2 \gamma z_{6t}}{\sigma_4^2 + \gamma^2\sigma_2^2}$$

$$A_{2t} = \frac{\sigma_4^2 z_{5t}^2 + \sigma_2^2 z_{6t}^2}{\sigma_4^2 + \gamma^2\sigma_2^2}$$

$$A_{3t} = \frac{\sigma_4^2 z_{1t} + \sigma_1^2 \gamma z_{7t}}{\sigma_4^2 + \gamma^2 \sigma_1^2}$$

$$A_{4t} = \frac{\sigma_4^2 z_{1t}^2 + \sigma_1^2 z_{7t}^2}{\sigma_4^2 + \gamma^2 \sigma_1^2}$$

$$\omega_1^2 = \frac{\sigma_2^2 \sigma_4^2}{\sigma_4^2 + \gamma^2 \sigma_2^2}$$

$$\omega_2^2 = \frac{\sigma_1^2 \sigma_4^2}{\sigma_4^2 + \gamma^2 \sigma_1^2}$$

Models 2 and 3

Since the expected excess demand in the adjustment equation depends only on predetermined variables, the density function for C_t, C_t^* is the product of the density of C_t from the simple disequilibrium model corresponding to (7.3.1)–(7.3.3) and the density of C_t^* from the adjustment equation. (See exercise 7.6.)

Model 4

Because the current value of C_t appears on the right hand side of (7.3.4b), the system of equations has two "regimes":

(a) $C_t^d < C_t^s$

$$\begin{bmatrix} 1 & 0 & 0 \\ 0 & 1 & 0 \\ -\delta_2 - \gamma & \gamma & 1 \end{bmatrix} \begin{bmatrix} C_t^d \\ C_t^s \\ C_{t+1}^* \end{bmatrix} = \begin{bmatrix} z_{1t} + u_{1t} \\ (\beta_1 + \beta_2 z_{4t}) C_t^* + z_{2t} + u_{2t} \\ z_{8t} + u_{4t} \end{bmatrix} \qquad (7.B.3)$$

(b) $C_t^d \geq C_t^s$

$$\begin{bmatrix} 1 & 0 & 0 \\ 0 & 1 & 0 \\ -\gamma & \gamma - \delta_2 & 1 \end{bmatrix} \begin{bmatrix} C_t^d \\ C_t^s \\ C_{t+1}^* \end{bmatrix} = \begin{bmatrix} z_{1t} + u_{1t} \\ (\beta_1 + \beta_2 z_{4t}) C_t^* + z_{2t} + u_{2t} \\ z_{8t} + u_{4t} \end{bmatrix} \qquad (7.B.4)$$

where z_{8t} is defined as $z_{8t} = \delta_1 C^* + \delta_3 C_{t-1} + \delta_4 \tilde{A}_{t-1}$. From (7.B.3) and (7.B.4) we can obtain the p.d.f.s of C_t^d, C_t^s, and C_{t+1}^*. Completing the square, integrating out C_t^s for (a) and C_t^d for (b), and adding we obtain the p.d.f. of C_t, C_{t+1}^* as

$$f(C_t, C_{t+1}^*) = \frac{1}{2\pi\sigma_1(\sigma_4^2 + \gamma^2 \sigma_2^2)^{1/2}} \exp\left\{ -\frac{1}{2} \left[\frac{(C_t - z_{1t})^2}{\sigma_1^2} + \frac{A_{2t} - A_{1t}^2}{\omega_1^2} \right] \right\}$$
$$\times \left[1 - \Phi\left(\frac{C_t - A_{1t}}{\omega_1} \right) \right]$$

$$+ \frac{1}{2\pi\sigma_2(\sigma_4^2 + \gamma^2\sigma_1^2)^{1/2}} \exp\left\{ -\frac{1}{2}\left[\frac{(C_t - z_{5t})^2}{\sigma_2^2} + \frac{A_{4t} - A_{3t}^2}{\omega_2^2} \right] \right\}$$

$$\times \left[1 - \Phi\left(\frac{C_t - A_{3t}}{\omega_2} \right) \right]$$

where A_{1t}, A_{2t}, A_{3t}, A_{4t}, ω_1, ω_2, and z_{5t} are as before and the previously defined z_{6t} and z_{7t} are now given by:

$$z_{6t} = C_{t+1}^* - (\delta_2 + \gamma)C_t - z_{3t}$$

$$z_{7t} = C_{t+1}^* - (\delta_2 - \gamma)C_t - z_{3t}$$

In the model as actually estimated separate γ-parameters are estimated for the excess demand and excess supply regimes; thus $\gamma = \gamma_1$ if $C_t^d > C_t^s$ and $\gamma = \gamma_2$ otherwise. In this case the appropriate terms (corresponding to the two regimes) contain γ_1 and γ_2 respectively.

References

Acton, F. (1970) *Numerical Methods That Work*, Harper and Row.

Amemiya, T. (1974a) "A note on a Fair and Jaffee model," *Econometrica*, 42, 759–62.

Amemiya, T. (1974b) "Multivariate regression and simultaneous equation models when the dependent variables are truncated normal," *Econometrica*, 42, 999–1012.

Amemiya, T. (1974c) "The nonlinear two-stage least-squares estimator," *Journal of Econometrics*, 2, 105–10.

Amemiya, T. (1977) "The solvability of a two-market disequilibrium model," working paper no. 82, Institute for Mathematical Studies in the Social Sciences, Stanford University.

Amemiya, T. (1985) *Advanced Econometrics*, Oxford: Basil Blackwell.

Amemiya, T. and G. Sen. (1977) "The consistency of the maximum likelihood estimator in a disequilibrium model," technical report no. 238, Institute for Mathematical Studies in the Social Sciences, Stanford University.

Arabmazar, A. and P. Schmidt (1982) "An investigation of the robustness of the tobit estimator to non-normality," *Econometrica*, 50, 1055–64.

Arad Wiener, R. (1975) "The implications of a long-tailed distribution structure to portfolio selection and capital asset pricing," PhD dissertation, Dept of Statistics, Princeton University.

Artus, P., G. Laroque and G. Michel (1984) "Estimation of a quarterly econometric model with quantity rationing," *Econometrica*, 52, 1387–1414.

Artus, P. and S. Avouy-Dovi (1984) "Une estimation comparative de modèles avec rationnements quantitatifs pour la France et les Etats-Unis," working paper no. 8405, INSEE, Paris.

Artus, P., S. Avouy-Dovi and G. Laroque (1985) "Estimation d'une maquette macroéconomique trimestrielle avec rationnements quantitatifs," *Annales de l'INSEE*, 57, 3–25.

Artus, P. and P.-A. Muet (1983) "Investment, output and labor constraints, and financial constraints: the estimation of a model with several regimes," paper no. 83–03 bis, O.F.C.E., Paris.

Ashenfelter, O. (1980) "Unemployment as disequilibrium in a model of aggregate labor supply," *Econometrica*, 48, 547–64.

Aurikko, E. (1985) "Testing disequilibrium adjustment models for Finnish exports of goods," *Oxford Bulletin of Economics and Statistics*, 47, 33–50.

Barro, R.J. and H.I. Grossman (1971) "A general disequilibrium model of income and employment," *American Economic Review*, 61, 82–93.

Barro, R.J. and H.I. Grossman (1976) *Money Employment and Inflation*, Cambridge University Press.

Batchelor, R.A. (1977) "A variable-parameter model of exporting behavior," *Review of Economic Studies*, XLIV, 43–58.

Benassy, J.P. (1975) "Neo-Keynesian disequilibrium theory in a monetary economy," *Review of Economic Studies*, XLII, 503–24.

Benassy, J.P. (1977) "On quantity signals and the foundations of effective demand theory," *Scandinavian Journal of Economics*, 79, 147–68.

Berndt, E.R. (1976) "Reconciling alternative estimates of the elasticity of substitution," *Review of Economics and Statistics*, 58, 59–68.

Bischoff, C. (1971) "Business investment in the 1970s: a comparison of models," *Brookings Paper on Economic Activity*, 1, 13–58.

Blinder, A.S. (1980) "Inventories in the Keynesian macromodels," *Kyklos*, 33, 585–614.

Blinder, A.S. and S. Fischer (1979) "Inventories, rational expectations and the business cycle," working paper no. 381, NBER.

Boender, C.G.E., A.H.G. Rinnooy Kan, G.T. Timmer and L. Stougie (1982) "A stochastic method for global optimization," *Mathematical Programming*, 22, 125–40.

Borglin, A., T. Karlsson and E. Petersson (1986) "A disequilibrium model for Sweden," Dept of Economics, University of Lund, paper presented at the Econometric Society European Meetings, Budapest, Sept. 2–5.

Bowden, Roger J. (1978a) *The Econometrics of Disequilibrium*, Amsterdam: North-Holland.

Bowden, Roger J. (1978b) "Specification, estimation and inference for models of markets in disequilibrium," *International Economic Review*, 19, 711–26.

Bowden, Roger J. (1979) "On the probability structure of pure and fuzzy switches in a simple disequilibrium model," University of Western Australia.

Bowden, Roger, J. (1980) "On the use of slack and dual variables for markets in disequilibrium and other models with economic constraints," Universities of Western Australia and California, Berkeley.

Briguglio, P.L. (1984) "The specification and estimation of a disequilibrium labour market model," *Applied Economics*, 16, 539–54.

Broadberry, S.N. (1983) "Unemployment in interwar Britian: a disequilibrium approach," *Oxford Economic Papers*, 35, 463–85.

Broer, D.P. and J.C. Siebrand (1985) "A macroeconomic disequilibrium model of product market and labour market for The Netherlands," *Applied Economics*, 17, 633–46.

Brown, R.L., J. Durbin and J.M. Evans (1975) "Techniques for testing the constancy of regression relations over time," *Journal of the Royal Statistical Society*, series B, 37, 149–92.

Burkett, J.P. (1981) "Marginal and conditional probabilities of excess demand," *Economics Letters*, 8, 159–62.

Chanda, A. and G.S. Maddala (1983a) "Methods of estimation for models of markets with bounded price variation under rational expectations," *Economics Letters*, 13, 181–4.

Chanda, A. and G.S. Maddala (1983b) "Estimation of disequilibrium models with inventories under rational expectations," paper presented at the Econometric Society Meetings, Pisa, August 28 to September 3.

Charemza, W. (1979) "Some spectral definitions for disequilibrium analysis," *Economics Letters*, 2, 33–5.

Charemza, W. and J. Domsta (1981) "Estimation of demand and supply functions from univariate sample with known separation," *Economics Letters*, 8, 163–8.

Charemza, W., M. Gronicki and R.E. Quandt (1985) "Modelling parallel markets in centrally planned economies: the case of the automobile market in Poland," Princeton University, mimeo.

Charemza, W. and R.E. Quandt (1982) "Models and estimation of disequilibrium for centrally planned economies," *Review of Economic Studies*, XLIX, 109–16.

Chow, G.C. (1977) "A reformulation of simultaneous equation models of markets in disquilibrium," research memo. no. 5, Econometric Research Program, Princeton University.

Chow, G.C. (1983) *Econometrics*, New York: McGraw-Hill.

Clark, C.E. (1961) "The greatest of a finite set of random variables," *Operations Research*, 9, 145–62.

Clower, R.W. (1965) "The Keynesian counter-revolution: a theoretical appraisal," in *The Theory of Interest Rates*, Hahn, F.M. and F.P.R. Brechling (eds), London: Macmillan.

Cosslett, S.R. and L.-F. Lee (1985) "Serial correlation in discrete variable models," *Journal of Econometrics*, 27, 79–98.

Daganzo, C. (1979) *Multinomial Probit*, New York: Academic Press.

Dagenais, M.G. (1980) "Specification and estimation of a dynamic disequilibrium model," *Economics Letters*, 5, 323–8.

Dempster, A.P., N.M. Laird and D.B. Rubin (1977) "Maximum likelihood from incomplete data via the E-M algorithm," *Journal of the Royal Statistical Society*, series B, 39, 1–22.

Deville, H. (1982) "On the estimation of mixed disequilibrium-equilibrium models," discussion paper no. 8216, Centre d'Econométrie, Université Libre de Bruxelles.

Domencich, T. and D. McFadden (1975) *Urban Travel Demand*, Amsterdam: North Holland.

Drazen, Allan (1980) "Recent developments in macroeconomic disequilibrium theory," *Econometrica*, 48, 283–306.

Drèze, J.H. (1975) "Existence of an exchange equilibrium under price rigidities," *International Economic Review*, 16, 301–20.

Ducos, G., J. Green and J.-J. Laffont (1982) "A test of the equilibrium hypothesis based on inventories," *European Economic Review*, 18, (1969) 209–19.

Durbin, J. (1969) "Tests for serial correlation in regression analysis based on the periodogram of least-squares residuals," *Biometrika*, 56, (1976) 1–15.

Dutt, J.E., (1976) "Numerical aspects of multivariate normal probabilities in econometric models," *Annals of Economic and Social Measurement*, 5, 547–61.

Eaton, J. and R.E. Quandt (1983) "A model of rationing and labor supply: theory and estimation," *Economica*, 50, 221–34.

Engle, R.F. and D.K. Foley (1974) "An asset price model of aggregate investment," *International Economic Review*, 16, 625–47.

Fair, R.C. (1977) "A note on the computation of the tobit estimator," *Econometrica*, 45, 1723–7.

Fair, R.C. and D.M. Jaffee (1972) "Methods of estimation for markets in disequilibrium,' *Econometrica*, 40, 497–514.

Fair, R.C. and H.H. Kelejian (1974) "Methods of estimation for markets in disequilibrium: a further study," *Econometrica*, 42, 177–90.

Frei, G. (1984) "Methoden zur Schaetzung des Kanonischen Ungleichewichtsmodells," Forschungsstelle fur empirische Wirtschaftsforschung, Hochschule, St Gallen, mimeo.

Garbade, K. (1977) "Two methods for examining the stability of regression coefficients," *Journal of the American Statistical Association*, 72, 54–63.

Gersovitz, M. (1980) "On classification probabilities for the disequilibrium model," *Journal of Econometrics*, 14, 239–46.

Gersovitz, M. (1982) "Estimation of the two-gap model," *Journal of International Economics*, 12, 111–24.

Ginsburgh, V., A. Tishler and I. Zang (1980) "Alternative estimation methods for two-regime models," *European Economic Review*, 13, 207–28.

Ginsburgh, V. and I. Zang (1978) "Price taking or price making behavior in export pricing," discussion paper no. 7805, CORE, Université Catholique de Louvain.

Goldfeld, S.M., D.M. Jaffee and R.E. Quandt (1978) "A rationing model of FHLBB advances," research memo. no. 26, Financial Research Center, Princeton University, November.

Goldfeld, S.M., D.M. Jaffee and R.E. Quandt (1980) "A model of FHLBB advances: rationing or market clearing?," *Review of Economics and Statistics*, LXII, 339–47.

Goldfeld, S.M. and R.E. Quandt (1972) *Nonlinear Methods in Econometrics*, Amsterdam: North Holland.

Goldfeld, S.M. and R.E. Quandt (1973) "A Markov model for switching regressions," *Journal of Econometrics*, 1, 3–16.

Goldfeld, S.M. and R.E. Quandt (1975) "Estimation in a disequilibrium model and the value of information," *Journal of Econometrics*, 3, 325–48.

Goldfeld, S.M. and R.E. Quandt (1976) "Techniques for estimating switching regressions," in *Studies in Nonlinear Estimation*, Goldfeld, S.M. and R.E. Quandt (eds), Ballinger.

Goldfeld, S.M. and R.E. Quandt (1978) "Some properties of the simple disequilibrium model with covariance," *Economics Letters*, 1, 343–6.

Goldfeld, S.M. and R.E. Quandt (1979) "Estimation in multimarket disequilibrium models," *Economics Letters*, 4, 341–7.

Goldfeld, S.M. and R.E. Quandt (1981a) "Econometric modelling with nonnormal disturbances," *Journal of Econometrics*, 17, 141–55.

Goldfeld, S.M. and R.E. Quandt (1981b) "Single market disequilibrium models: estimation and testing," *The Economic Studies Quarterly*, XXXII, 12–28.

Goldfeld, S.M. and R.E. Quandt (1986a) "The econometrics of rationing models," Econometric Research Program, research memo. no. 322, Princeton University.

Goldfeld, S.M. and R.E. Quandt (1986b) "The effects of multiple uncertainty on rationing," *Economics Letters* 22, 127–32.

Gourieroux, C. (1984) *Econométrie des Variables Qualitatives*, Paris: Economica.

Gourieroux, C., A. Holly and A. Monfort (1982) "Likelihood ratio, Wald test and Kuhn-Tucker test in linear models with inequality constraints on regression parameters," *Econometrica*, 50, 63–80.

Gourieroux, C., J.-J. Laffont and A. Monfort (1980a) "Disequilibrium econometrics in simultaneous equation systems," *Econometrica*, 48, 75–96.

Gourieroux, C., J.-J. Laffont and A. Monfort (1980b) "Coherency conditions in simultaneous linear equation models with endogenous switching regimes," *Econometrica*, 48, 675–96.

Gourieroux, C., J.-J. Laffont and A. Monfort (1980c) "Tests of the equilibrium vs. disequilibrium hypotheses: a comment," *International Economic Review*, 21, 245–7.

Gourieroux, C., J.-J. Laffont and A. Monfort (1984) "Econométrie des modèles d'équilibres avec rationnement: une mise à jour," *Annales de l'INSEE*, 55/56, 5–38.

Gourieroux, C. and A. Monfort (1980) "Estimation methods for markets with controlled prices," working paper no. 8012, INSEE.

Gourieroux, C., A. Monfort and A. Trognon (1983) "Une approche générale de l'autocorrélation," INSEE working paper no. 8317.

Gourieroux, C., A. Monfort and A. Trognon (1985) "A general approach of serial correlation," CEPREMAP, working paper no. 8424, 1983; also *Econometric Theory*, 1, 315–40.

Green, J. and J.-J. Laffont (1981) "Disequilibrium dynamics with inventories and anticipatory price-setting," *European Economic Review*, 16, 199–223.

Hajivassiliou, V.A. (1983) "Estimating and testing an aggregative disequilibrium model of the US labor market," Massachusetts Institute of Technology, mimeo.

Hajivassiliou, V.A. (1984) "Analysing the determinants of the external debt repayments problem of LDCs: estimation using a panel set of data," Massachusetts Institute of Technology, mimeo.

Hajivassiliou, V.A. (1986a) "Two misspecification tests for the simple switching regressions disequilibrium model," *Economics Letters*, 22, 343–8.

Hajivassiliou, V.A. (1986b) "An aggregative disequilibrium model of the US labor market," Yale University.

Hall, R.E. (1977) "Investment, interest rates, and the effects of stabilization policies," Massachusetts Institute of Technology, mimeo.

Hall, R.E. and D.W. Jorgensen (1967) "Tax policy and investment behavior," *American Economic Review*, 57, 391–414.

Hall, S.G., S.G.B. Henry, A. Markandya and M. Pemberton (1985) "A disequilibrium model of the UK labour market: some estimates using rational expectations," paper presented at the World Congress of the Econometric Society, Cambridge, MA.

Hammersley, J.M. and D.C. Handscomb (1964) *Monte Carlo Methods*, London: Methuen.

Hartley, M.J. (1976) "The estimation of markets in disequilibrium: the fixed supply case," *International Economic Review*, 17, 687–700.

Hartley, M.J. (1977) "On the calculation of the maximum likelihood estimator for a model of markets in disequilibrium," discussion paper no. 409, Economic Research Group, State University of New York at Buffalo.

Hartley, M.J. and P. Mallela (1977) "The asymptotic properties of a maximum likelihood estimator for a model of markets in disequilibrium," *Econometrica*, 45, 1205–20.

Hartley, M.J. and S.T. Mennemeyer (1974) "The estimation of markets in excess demand with incomplete data: the market for physicians' services," discussion paper no. 317, Dept of Economics, State University of New York at Buffalo.

Harvey, A.C. (1975) "Comment," *Journal of the Royal Statistical Society*, Series B, 37, 179–80.

Hausman, J.A. (1980) "Les modèles probit de choix qualitatifs," *Cahiers du Seminaire d'Econometrie*, 21, 11–31.

Hausman, J.A. and D.A. Wise (1978) "A conditional probit model for qualitative choice: discrete decisions recognizing interdependence and heterogeneous preferences," *Econometrica*, 46, 403–26.

Heckman, J. (1978) "Dummy exogenous variables in simultaneous equations systems," *Econometrica*, 46, 931–59.

Hendry, D.F. (1984) "Monte Carlo experimentation in econometrics," *Handbook of Econometrics*, vol. II, Amsterdam: North Holland.

Hildebrand, F.B. (1956) *Introduction to Numerical Analysis*, New York: McGraw-Hill.

Howard, D.H. (1976) "The disequilibrium model in controlled economy: an empirical test of the Barro-Grossman model," *American Economic Review*, 66, 871–9.

Howard, D.H. (1979) *The Disequilibrium Model in a Controlled Economy*, Lexington Books, D.C. Heath & Co.

Hwang, H.-S. (1980) "A test of a disequilibrium model," *Journal of Econometrics*, 12, 319–34.

Ito, T. (1980) "Methods of estimation for multi-market disequilibrium models," *Econometrica*, 48, 97–126.

Ito, T. and K. Ueda (1981) "Tests of equilibrium hypothesis in disequilibrium econometrics: an international comparison of credit rationing," *International Economic Review*, 22, 691–708.

Johnston, J. (1984) *Econometric Methods*, 3rd edn, McGraw-Hill.

Jorgenson, D.W. (1967) "The theory of investment behaviour," in *Determinants of Investment Behaviour*, R. Ferber (ed.), New York: Columbia University Press.

Jorgenson, D.W. (1971) "Econometric studies of investment behavior: a survey," *The Journal of Economic Literature*, 9, 1111–47.

Kåfei, M.-A. and P. Schmidt (1985) "On the adequacy of the 'Sargan distribution' as an approximation to the normal," *Communications in Statistics Theory and Methods*, 14, 509–26.

Karlsson, T. (1987) *A Macroeconomic Disequilibrium Model*, Lund Economic Studies No. 42.

Katz, B.G. (1979) "The disequilibrium model in a controlled economy: comment," *American Economic Review*, 69, 721–5.

Katz, B.G. and J. Owen (1984) "Disequilibrium theory, waiting costs, and saving behavior in centrally planned economies," *Journal of Comparative Economics*, 8, 404–17.

Kelejian, H. (1971) "Two-stage least squares and econometric systems linear in parameters but nonlinear in endogenous variables," *Journal of the American Statistical Association*, 66, 373–4.

Kiefer, N.M. (1977) "Models of switching, disequilibrium and endogenous structural change and the value of information," report 7757, Center for Mathematical Studies in Business and Economics, University of Chicago, November.

Kiefer, N.M. (1978a) "Comment on 'Estimating mixtures of normal distributions and switching regressions'," *Journal of the American Statistical Association*, 73, 744–5.

Kiefer, N.M. (1978b) "Discrete parameter variation: efficient estimation of a switching disequilibrium model," *Econometrica*, 46, 427–34.

Kiefer, N.M. (1978c) "Comment," *Journal of the American Statistical Association*, 73, 744–5.

Kiefer, N.M. (1980a) "A note on regime classification in disequilibrium models," *Review of Economic Studies*, 47, 637–9.

Kiefer, N.M. (1980b) "A note on switching regressions and logistic discrimination," *Econometrica*, 48, 1065–9.

Kooiman, P. (1984) "Smoothing the aggregate fixed-price model and the use of business survey data," *Economic Journal*, 94, 899–913.

Kooiman, P. (1986) *Some Empirical Models for Markets in Disequilibrium*, PhD dissertation, Erasmus University, Rotterdam.

Kooiman, P., H.K. van Dijk and A.R. Thurik (1985) "Likelihood diagnostics and Bayesian analysis of a micro-economic disequilibrium model for retail services," *Journal of Econometrics*, 29, 121–48.

Kooiman, P. and T.Kloek (1980) "An aggregate two market disequilibrium model with foreign trade," working paper, Erasmus University, Rotterdam.

Kooiman, P. and T. Kloek (1985) "An empirical two market disequilibrium model for Dutch manufacturing," *European Economic Review*, 29, 323–54.

Kornai, J. (1979) "Resource-constrained versus demand-constrained systems," *Econometrica*, 47, 801–20.

Kornai, J. (1980a) *Economics of Shortage*, Amsterdam: North-Holland.

Kornai, J. (1980b) " 'Hard' and 'Soft' budget constraint," *Acta Economica*, 24, 231–47.

Kuo, S.S. (1965) *Numerical Methods and Computers*, Reading, MA: Addison-Wesley.

Laffont, J.-J. (1983) "Fixed-price models: a survey of recent empirical work," paper no. 8305, Groupe de Recherche en Economie Mathématique et Quantitative, University of Toulouse.

Laffont, J.-J. and R. Garcia (1977) "Disequilibrium econometrics for business loans," *Econometrica*, 45, 1187–204.

Laffont, J.-J. and A. Monfort (1976) "Econométrie des modèles d'équilibre avec rationnement," *Annales de l'INSEE*, 24, 3–40.

Laffont, J.-J. and A. Monfort (1979) "Disequilibrium econometrics in dynamic models," *Journal of Econometrics*, 11, 353–61.

Lambert, J.-P. (1984) *Disequilibrium Macro Models based on Business Survey Data: theory and estimation for the Belgian manufacturing sector*, CORE, Louvain-la-Neuve.

Lee, L.-F. (1982) "Test for normality in the econometric disequilibrium markets model," *Journal of Econometrics*, 19, 109–23.

Lee, L.-F. (1983) "Tests for serial correlation for the disequilibrium market model, switching regression model and related models," paper no. 95, Center for Econometrics and Decision Sciences, University of Florida.

Lee, L.-F. (1984a) "Regime classifications in the disequilibrium market models," *Economics Letters*, 14, 187–93.

Lee, L.-F. (1984b) "The likelihood function and a test for serial correlation in a disequilibrium market model," *Economics Letters*, 14, 195–200.

Lee, L.-F. and R.H. Porter (1984) "Switching regression models with imperfect sample separation information – with an application to cartel stability," *Econometrica*, 52, 391–418.

Lee, L.-F. (1986) "The specification of multi-market disequilibrium econometric models," *Journal of Econometrics*, 32, 297–332.

Lenderink, R.S.G. and J.C. Siebrand (1976) *A Disequilibrium Model of the Labour Market*, Rotterdam University Press.

Lewis, P.E.T. (1983) "Disequilibrium in the Australian aggregate labour market," *Economics Letters*, 11, 185–9.

Lindsay, C.M. and B. Feigenbaum (1984) "Rationing by waiting lists," *American Economic Review*, 74, 404–17.

Lucas, R. and L. Rapping (1970) "Real wages, employment and inflation," in *Microeconomic Foundations of Employment and Inflation Theory*, Phelps, E. (ed), New York: W.W. Norton.

Luenberger, D.G. (1969) *Optimization by Vector Space Methods*, Wiley.

Mackinnon, J.G. (1978) "Modelling a market which is sometimes in disequilibrium," discussion paper no. 287, Department of Economics, Queen's University, Kingston, Ontario, Canada, April.

Mackinnon, J.G. and N.D. Olewiler (1980) "Disequilibrium estimation of the demand for copper," *The Bell Journal of Economics*, 11, 197–211.

Maddala, G.S. (1980) "Disequilibrium, self-selection and switching models," social science working paper 303, California Institute of Technology.

Maddala, G.S. (1983a) "Methods of estimation for models of markets with bounded price variation," *International Economic Review*, 24, 361–78.

Maddala, G.S. (1983b) *Limited-Dependent and Qualitative Variables in Econometrics*, Cambridge University Press.

Maddala, G.S. (1986) "Disequilibrium, self-selection and switching models," in *Handbook of Econometrics*, vol. III, Amsterdam: North-Holland.

Maddala, G.S. and J.B. Kadane (1966) "Some notes on the estimation of the constant elasticity of substitution production functions," *Review of Economics and Statistics*, 48, 340–4.

Maddala, G.S. and F.D. Nelson (1973) "Limited dependent variable methods for the estimation of markets in disequilibrium," working paper 73-7, Department of Economics, University of Rochester.

Maddala, G.S. and F.D. Nelson (1974) "Maximum likelihood methods for models of markets in disequilibrium," *Econometrica*, 42, 1013–30.

Malinvaud, E. (1976) *The Theory of Unemployment Reconsidered*, Oxford: Basil Blackwell.

Malinvaud, E. (1980) "Macroeconomic rationing of employment," in *Unemployment in Western Countries*, Malinvaud, E. and J.-P. Fitoussi (eds), Macmillan.

Malinvaud, E. (1981) "Econometric implications of macro-disequilibrium theory," INSEE working paper no. 8114.

Malinvaud, E. (1982) "An econometric model for macro-disequilibrium analysis," in *Current Developments in the Interface: economics, econometrics, mathematics*, Hazewinkel, M. and A.H.G. Rinnooy Kan (eds), Reidel: Dordrecht.

Manski, C.F. and S.R. Lerman (1981) "On the use of simulated frequencies to approximate choice probabilities," in *Structural Analysis of Discrete Data* (*with Econometric Applications*), Manski, C.F. and D. McFadden (eds), Cambridge, MA: MIT Press.

Marsaglia, G. (1963) "Expressing the normal distribution with covariance matrix $A + B$ in terms of one with covariance matrix A," *Biometrika*, 50, 535–8.

McFadden, D. (1973) "Conditional logit analysis of qualitative choice behavior," in

Frontiers in Econometrics, Zarembka, P. (ed), New York: Academic Press.

Meade, E.E. (1985) "An open economy disequilibrium model with anticipatory pricing," Princeton University, mimeo.

Missiakoulis, S. (1983) "Sargan densities: which one?," *Journal of Econometrics*, 23, 223–34.

Moffitt, R. (1980) "Disequilibrium econometrics and non-linear budget constraints," *Economics Letters*, 5, 49–52.

Moffitt, R. (1982) "The tobit model, hours of work and institutional constraints," *Review of Economics and Statistics*, 64, 510–15.

Mouchart, M. and R. Orsi (1986) "A note on price adjustment models in disequilibrium econometrics," *Journal of Econometrics*, 31, 209–18.

Muellbauer, J. (1977) "Macromodels with regime changes: discrete vs. continuous formulations of non-clearing markets," Birkbeck College, mimeo.

Muellbauer, J. (1978) "Macrotheory vs. macroeconometrics: the treatment of disequilibrium in macromodels," discussion paper no. 29, Birkbeck College, April.

Muellbauer, J. and R. Portes (1978) "Macroeconomic models with quantity rationing," *Economic Journal*, 88, 788–821.

Muellbauer, J. and D. Winter (1980) "Unemployment, employment and exports in British manufacturing: a non-clearing markets approach," *European Economic Review*, 13, 383–409.

Nasim, A. and S. Satchell (1982) "A nonlinear least squares method for estimating markets in disequilibrium," Essex economic papers no. 208.

Nasim, A. and S. Satchell (1984) "Limited information methods for estimating disequilibrium models with a stochastic price adjustment equation," Essex economic papers no. 248.

Nishimizu, M., R.E. Quandt and H.S. Rosen (1982) "The demand and supply of investment goods: does the market clear?," *Journal of Macroeconomics*, 4, 1–21.

Olsen, R.J. (1978) "Note on the uniqueness of the maximum likelihood estimator for the tobit model," *Econometrica*, 46, 1211–15.

Orsi, R. (1982a) "A simultaneous disequilibrium model for Italian export goods," *Empirical Economics*, 7, 139–54.

Orsi, R. (1982b) "On the dynamic specification of disequilibrium econometrics: an analysis of Italian male and female labor markets," discussion paper no. 8228, CORE, Louvain-la-Neuve.

Orsi, R. (1983) "A spillover model of male and female labour markets," paper presented at the Econometric Society Meetings, Pisa, August 28 to September 3.

Orsi, R. (1984) "A dynamic disequilibrium analysis of the labour market in the Italian manufacturing industry," discussion paper no. 8443, CORE, Louvain-la-Neuve.

Owen, D.B. (1956) "Tables for computing bivariate normal probabilities," *Annals of Mathematical Statistics*, 27, 1075–90.

Peel, D.A. and I. Walker (1978) "Short-run employment functions, excess supply and the speed of adjustment: a note," *Economica*, 45, 195–202.

Plant, M. (1984) "An empirical analysis of welfare dependence," *American Economic Review*, 74, 673–84.

Podkaminer, L. (1982) "Estimates of the disequilibrium in Poland's consumer markets, 1965–1978," *Review of Economics and Statistics*, 64, 423–31.

Podkaminer, L. (1983) "Estimates of the disequilibrium in Poland's consumer markets (1965–1978)," in *Modelling Growing Economies in Equilibrium and Disequilibrium*, Kelley, Williamson and Sanders (eds), Duke University Press.

Poirier, D.J. and P.A. Ruud (1981) "On the appropriateness of endogenous switching," *Journal of Econometrics*, 16, 249–56.

Portes, R. (1977) "Effective demand and spillovers in empirical two-market disequilibrium models," discussion paper no. 595, Harvard Institute of Economic Research, Harvard University, December.

Portes, R. (1981) "Macroeconomic equilibrium and disequilibrium in centrally planned economies," *Economic Inquiry*, XIX, 559–78.

Portes, R., R.E. Quandt, D. Winter and S. Yeo (1984) "Planning the consumption goods market: preliminary estimates for Poland, 1955–1980," in *Contemporary Macroeconomic Modelling*, Malgrange, P. and R.A. Muet (eds), Oxford: Basil Blackwell.

Portes, R., R.E. Quandt, D. Winter and S. Yeo (1985) "Estimation de la taille des erreurs de planification," *Annales de l'INSEE*, 55–6, 245–55.

Portes, R., R.E. Quandt, D. Winter and S. Yeo (1987) "Macroeconomic planning and disequilibrium: estimates for Poland, 1955–1980." *Econometrica*, 55, 19–42.

Portes, R., R.E. Quandt and S. Yeo (1985) "Testing the 'all-excess-demand' hypothesis," research memo. no. 59, Financial Research Center, Princeton University.

Portes, R. and D. Winter (1977) "The supply of consumption goods in centrally planned economies," *Journal of Comparative Economics*, 1, 351–65.

Portes, R. and D. Winter (1978) "Disequilibrium estimates for consumption goods markets in centrally planned economies," discussion paper no. 612, Harvard Institute of Economic Research, Harvard University, March.

Portes, R. and D. Winter (1980) "Disequilibrium estimates for consumption goods markets in centrally planned economies," *Review of Economic Studies*, XLVII, 137–59.

Quandt, R.E. (1976) "Testing hypotheses in disequilibrium models," Research memo. no. 197, Econometric Research Program, Princeton University.

Quandt, R.E. (1978a) "Maximum likelihood estimation of disequilibrium models," in *Pioneering Economics*, Bagiotti, T. and G. Franco (eds), Padova: Edizioni Cedam.

Quandt, R.E. (1978b) "Tests of the equilibrium vs. disequilibrium hypothesis," *International Economic Review*, 19, 435–52.

Quandt, R.E. (1979) "A note on the tobit likelihood function," *Economics Letters*, 4, 361–2.

Quandt, R.E. (1980) "Equilibrium and disequilibrium: transitional models," research memo. no. 269, Econometric Research Program, Princeton University.

Quandt, R.E. (1981) "Autocorrelated errors in simple disequilibrium models," *Economics Letters*, 7, 55–62.

Quandt, R.E. (1982a) "Econometric disequilibrium models," *Econometric Reviews*, 1, 1–63.

Quandt, R.E. (1982b) "The structure of disequilibrium models," research memo. no. 295, Econometric Research Program, Princeton University.

Quandt, R.E. (1983a) "Switching between equilibrium and disequilibrium," *Review of Economics and Statistics*, LXV, 684–7.

Quandt, R.E. (1983b) "Computational problems and methods," *Handbook of Econometrics*, vol. I, Amsterdam: North Holland.

Quandt, R.E. (1985a) "Concepts and structures in disequilibrium models," *Rivista Internazionale de Scienze Economiche e Commerciali*, XXXII, 207–32.

Quandt, R.E. (1985b) "On the identification of structural parameters in 'all-excess-demand' disequilibrium models," research memo. no. 56, Financial Research Center, Princeton University.

Quandt, R.E. (1986a) "Estimation in disequilibrium models with aggregation," research memo no. 68, Financial Research Center, Princeton University.

Quandt, R.E. (1986b) "A note on estimating disequilibrium models with aggregation," *Empirical Economics*, 11, 223–42.

Quandt, R.E. and J.B. Ramsey (1978) "Estimating mixtures of normal distributions and switching regressions," *Journal of the American Statistical Association*, 73, 730–73.

Quandt, R.E. and H.S. Rosen (1985) "Is there a chronic excess supply of labor?," *Economics Letters*, 19, 193–8.

Quandt, R.E. and H.S. Rosen (1986a) "Unemployment, disequilibrium, and the short run Phillips curve: an econometric approach," *Journal of Applied Econometrics*, 1, 235–54.

Quandt, R.E. and H.S. Rosen (1986b) "Some further results on Rosen and Quandt's labor market model: queries and disagreements," *European Economic Review*, 30, 457–9.

Quandt, R.E. and H.S. Rosen (1988) *The Conflict Between Equilibrium and Disequilibrium Theories: the Case of the U.S. Labor Market*, Kalamazoo MI: Upjohn.

Rao, C.R. (1973) *Linear Statistical Inference and Its Applications*, 2nd edn, New York: Wiley.

Reece, W.S. (1976) "Aggregate excess labor demand and the rate of change of nominal wages," *The Manchester School*, 44, 356–72.

Ritschard, G. and D. Roger (1983) "A geometric approach to disequilibrium exchange rate fluctuations: the case of Switzerland," *European Economic Review*, 22, 373–404.

Robinson, P. (1982) "On the asymptotic properties of estimates of models containing limited dependent variables," *Econometrica*, 50, 27–41.

Rockafellar, R.T. (1970) *Convex Analysis*, Princeton, NJ: Princeton University Press.

Rogers, A.J. (1984) "Tests of some hypotheses in latent variable models with stochastic exogenous variables," research memo. no. 49, Financial Research Center, Princeton University.

Romer, D. (1981) "Rosen and Quandt's disequilibrium model of the labor market: a revision," *Review of Economics and Statistics*, LXIII, 145–6.

Rosen, H.S. and R.E. Quandt (1978) "Estimation of a disequilibrium aggregate labor market," *Review of Economics and Statistics*, LX, 371–9.

Rubinstein, R.Y. (1981) *Simulation and the Monte Carlo Method*, New York: Wiley.

Rudebusch, G. (1985) "A disequilibrium model of the labor market with exact excess demand indicators," Dept of Economics, University of Pennsylvania, mimeo.

Rudebusch, G. (1986) "Testing for labor market equilibrium with an exact excess demand disequilibrium model," *Review of Economics and Statistics*, LXVIII, 468–76.

Salop, S.C. (1979) "A model of the natural rate of unemployment," *American Economic Review*, 69, 117–25.

Samelson, H., R.M. Thrall and O. Wesler (1958) "A partition theorem for euclidean n-space," *Proceedings of the American Mathematical Society*, 9, 805–7.

Sarantis, N. (1980) "A disequilibrium model of investment, working capital and borrowing for the UK company sector," *Applied Economics*, 12, 377-98.

Sarantis, N. (1981) "Employment, labor supply and real wages in market disequilibrium," *Journal of Macroeconomics*, 3, 335-54.

Schmidt, P. (1978) "Constraints on the parameters in simultaneous tobit and probit models,' Michigan State University.

Schmidt, P. (1982) "An improved version of the Quandt-Ramsey MGD estimator for mixtures of normal distributions and switching regressions," *Econometrica*, 50, 501-16.

Sealey, Jr, C.W. (1979) "Credit rationing in the commercial loan market: estimates of a structural model under conditions of disequilibrium," *Journal of Finance*, 34, 689-702.

Siebrand, J.C. (1979) *Towards Operational Disequilibrium Macro Models*, The Hague: Martinus Nijhoff.

Smith, G. and W. Brainard (1982) "A disequilibrium model of savings and loan associations," *The Journal of Finance*, 37, 1277-93.

Smyth, D. (1982) "The British labor market in disequilibrium: did the dole reduce employment in interwar Britain?," working paper no. 165, Wayne State University.

Smyth, D. (1984) "Unemployment insurance and labor supply and demand: a time series analysis for the United States," Wayne State University.

Sneessens, H. (1979) "On the econometrics of quantity rationing models," research memo. no. 250, Econometric Research Program, Princeton University.

Sneessens, H. (1981a) *Theory and Estimation of Macroeconomic Rationing Models*, New York: Springer Verlag.

Sneessens, H. (1981b) "Alternative stochastic specifications and estimation methods for quantity rationing models: a Monte Carlo study," London School of Economics, mimeo.

Sneessens, H. (1982) "Keynesian and classical unemployment in Western economies," Faculté Libre des Sciences Economiques, Lille.

Sneessens, H. (1983) "A macroeconomic rationing model of the Belgian economy," *European Economic Review*, 20, 193-215.

Sneessens, H. (1985) "Two alternative stochastic specifications and estimation methods for quantity rationing models," *European Economic Review*, 29, 111-36.

Spencer, P.D. (1975) "A disequilibrium model of personal sector bank advances 1964-1974: some preliminary results," working paper, HM Treasury.

Stalder, P. (1984) "Schaetzung von Ungleichgewichtsmodellen auf der Basis eines Adaptierten 'nonlinear least squares' – Verfahrens," paper no. 11 Konjunkturforschungsstelle, ETH, Zurich.

Stalder, P. (1985) "Schaetzung eines kleines Ungleichgewichtsmodelles fuer den Schweizerischen Arbeitsmarkt," paper no. 13, Konjunkturforschungsstelle, ETH, Zurich.

Stenius, M. and M. Viren (1984) "Some further results on Rosen and Quandt's labor market model," *European Economic Review*, 26, 369-77.

Stroud, A.H. (1974) *Numerical Quadrature and Solution of Ordinary Differential Equations*, New York: Springer Verlag.

Stroud, A.H. and D. Secrest (1966) *Gaussian Quadrature Formulas*, Englewood Cliffs, NJ: Prentice-Hall.

Suits, D. (1955) "An econometric model of the watermelon market," *Journal of Farm Economics*, 37, 237–51.

Svensson, L.E.O. (1980) "Effective demand and stochastic rationing," *Review of Economic Studies*, XLVII, 339–56.

Theil, H. (1971) *Principles of Econometrics*, Wiley.

Timmer, G.T. (1984) *Global Optimization: a stochastic approach*, Amsterdam: Centrum voor Wiskunde en Informatica.

Tishler, A. and I. Zang (1977) "Maximum likelihood methods for switching regression models without *a priori* conditions," Israel Institute of Business Research, Tel Aviv University.

Tishler, A. and I. Zang (1979) "A switching regression method using inequality conditions," *Journal of Econometrics*, 11, 259–74.

Train, K. (1986) *Qualitative Choice Analysis*, Cambridge, MA: MIT Press.

Tse, Y.K. (1987) "A note on the Sargan densities," *Journal of Econometrics*, 34, 349–54.

Upcher, M.R. (1982) "A note on estimation and testing of equilibrium econometric models," working paper no. 6/82, Department of Econometrics and Operations Research, Monash University.

Upcher, M.R. (1984) "The problem of aggregation over time in disequilibrium models," working paper no. 11/84, Department of Econometrics and Operations Research, Monash University.

Vilares, M.J. (1982) "Macroeconometric model with structural change and disequilibrium," paper prepared for the IXth International Conference of Applied Econometrics, Budapest.

Wald, A. (1943) "A note on the consistency of the maximum likelihood estimator," *Annals of Mathematical Statistics*, 20, 595–601.

White, H. (1980) "A heteroscedasticity-consistent covariance estimator and a direct test for heteroscedasticity," *Econometrica*, 48, 817–38.

Winiecki, J. (1985) "*Portes ante portas*: a critique of the revisionist interpretation of inflation under central planning," *Comparative Economic Studies*, XXVII, 25–51.

Yatchew, A.J. (1982) "Further evidence on estimation of a disequilibrium labor market," *Review of Economics and Statistics*, 63, 142–4.

Yellen, J.L. (1984) "Efficiency wage models of unemployment," *American Economic Review, Papers and Proceedings*, 74, 200–5.

Zellner, A. (1971) *An Introduction to Bayesian Inference in Econometrics*, New York: Wiley.

Subject Index

Author Index